The Laws of Emotion

The Laws of Emotion

Nico H. Frijda

2007
LAWRENCE ERLBAUM ASSOCIATES, PUBLISHERS
Mahwah, New Jersey   London

Copyright © 2007 by Lawrence Erlbaum Associates, Inc.

Lawrence Erlbaum Associates, Inc., Publishers
10 Industrial Avenue
Mahwah, New Jersey 07430
www.erlbaum.com

Cover design by Jan Bons & Tomai Maridou

CIP information for this book can be obtained by contacting the Library of Congress

ISBN 0-8058-2597-5 (cloth : alk. paper)
ISBN 0-8058-2598-3 (pbk. : alk. paper)

Books published by Lawrence Erlbaum Associates are printed on acid-free paper, and their bindings are chosen for strength and durability.

Printed in the United States of America
10 9 8 7 6 5 4 3 2

For David and for Roos

Contents

Preface

This book resulted from pondering emotions, after I wrote my 1986 book *The Emotions*. It reflects several papers that I wrote since, one of which inspired the title of this volume, and of chapter 1. What made me ponder, and motivated me to write this book, is the desire to understand emotions at the level of underlying mechanisms. Most of the work on the psychology of emotions moves at what Dennett called the intentional or phenomenological level of analysis. One talks about feelings, appraisals, motives or concerns, without too much analytical reflection on the processes that might underlie those phenomena.

That left me unsatisfied. Small wonder. Not all basic emotion processes are well explored; the issues are difficult. So I tried to conceive how to fill the gaps that analysis at the intentional level leaves. Seeking to fill the gaps may be useful for additional reasons than probing into the processes underlying emotional phenomena. It tries to construct an alternative for two current ways of explaining emotions. Going below the intentional level is mostly being undertaken in one of two ways. The first consists of evoking evolution. Emotional phenomena are there because evolution made them be there, for supposed reasons of variable plausibility. Evolutionary explanations can rather easily be found, and they only probe into these distal evolutionary processes. They do not examine how these distal processes may have translated into proximal processes, how the system now does it. The other way consists of neuroscience research, that enormously fascinating field that produces such a wealth of novel insights. But that research also mostly leaves the gaps that I am talking about. Neuroscience by itself does not yield analysis at the functional level, and it often seeks to invent such analysis on its own, without detailed analysis of the findings from the psychological viewpoint.

The book begins by stating a number of principles governing emotional phenomena, that I consider to be the laws of emotion. Then it posits that emotions are passions; that is, it posits that we have to assume motivational processes in order to understand emotional behavior, it examines why we have to do that, and how one may conceive of such motivational processes at the functional level of analysis.

It then seeks to understand the nature of pleasure (and by implication of pain), arguing that neither pleasure nor pain are unanalyzable qualia. They have content beyond their (often) being feelings. I examine what causes them, and what their functional role might be.

I further examine the processes that lead to emotion arousal, and often are being called *appraisal*. They usually are in some way cognitive in nature; they do not just use simple stimulus information. Information, moreover, functions as appraisal only when it has turned into embodied information, and when it rests on what animals and people appear to care for—their concerns. The book then goes on to explore the nature of concerns: why one cares for what one cares for.

The next chapters take emotional intensity apart, and that much neglected aspect of emotions: their course over time. I then analyze the nature of conscious emotional experience, usually denoted by the word *feeling*.

The last chapters seek to apply the obtained insights to complex emotion domains like those of sex, revenge, and the desire to commemorate past people and events.

The book will be of interest mainly to a professional audience: social, cognitive, and developmental psychologists; social scientists; philosophers; neuroscientists. It will serve as a text for advanced courses in the psychology of emotions or the neuroscience of emotions. I used a nontechnical, occasionally relaxed style, with the hope that it would be readable to a sophisticated layperson interested in the subject. It does not assume familiarity with the emotion literature in general.

The present volume reflects the research done over the past 10 years, and many of the chapters are based on papers that came out of it. It thus owes much to those whom I had the fortune of being able to collaborate with: Andrew Ortony, Gerald Clore, and Joep Sonnemans, with whom I worked on the papers that underlie chapter 6; Batja Mesquita, Stephanie van Goozen, and Joep Sonnemans, with whom I wrote the paper that developed the ideas at the root of chapter 7; Batja Mesquita, with whom I wrote on emotions and beliefs, and on emotions and culture, and from which collaboration came much friendship, and many insights on appraisal in chapter 3 and on feelings in chapter 8; and Walter Everaerd and Ellen Laan, thanks to whom I came to chapter 9, on sexual emotions. Chapter 3 grew out of the paper I could contribute to the book of friends for Bob Zajonc.

Other chapters are also based on earlier papers. Chapter 1, with some changes, reproduces a paper in the *American Psychologist* with the same name. Chapter 2 stems from many earlier things, among which a paper at a 1999 meeting on emotion and action and my paper in the 2001 Feelings and Emotions symposium. Chapter 4 grew out of a paper written for *Cognition and Emotion*'s special issue (1993) on appraisal; chapter 5 out of a paper at the 1998 meeting of the European Society for Philosophical Psychology in Lisbon. The bulk of chapter 8 reproduces a paper in *Cognition and Emotion*, 2005. Chapter 10 is a reworking of my paper at the 1992 Amsterdam Symposium on Feelings and Emotions. Chapter 11 came out of a presentation I was asked to give by the Dutch Organization for Scientific Research and the Organization for Arts and Sciences (OKW) to commemorate the 50th anniversary of our liberation from occupation, and corrects some ambiguities in its earlier English translation.

Much inspiration, and more, came from my fellow members of the Consortium for European Research on Emotion: the group of friends who are or were also colleagues, or colleagues who are or were also friends: the late Matty Chiva, Heiner Ellgring, Tony Manstead, Pio Ricci-Bitti, Bernard Rimé, and Klaus Scherer. For years, we regularly met at the Maison des Sciences de l'Homme in Paris or elsewhere, and where we chatted and ate and drank—quantities of each of them.

And I am very much indebted to those with whom I had lengthy discussions or e-mail exchanges, or who read parts of the book and whose comments were invaluable. I list those who were not already mentioned: Erika Apfelbaum, Kent Berridge, Phoebe Ellsworth, Jon Elster, Itziar Extebarria, Michael Frijda, Stevan Harnad, Michael Kubovy, Marc Lewis, Tony Marcel, David Moffat, Keith Oatley, Jaak Panksepp, Linlan Phan, Rainer Reisenzein, Hetty Rombouts, Ira Roseman, Aaron Sloman, Bob Solomon, Louise Sundararajan, Ed Tan, Vanda Zammuner, and Louis Tas, who also served as my older brother. But, being who I am, I no doubt forgot to mention several others.

I thank Jan Bons, my so dear friend, who again designed a cover for me, Daniel Bouw, who helped me to the traditional melody that serves as motto for chapter 11, and my dear friend Liesbeth Hoppen, who selected the passage and wrote it out for me. I thank Jetteke Frijda, my sister. Who so often critically responded to what I said or wrote, and who helped me by reading the proofs.

Merlin, Michael, and Miranda: it is a grace of nature to have them. It also is a grace to recognize something of one's thinking and feeling in others. Even when criticism pervades it, or because of that.

I would have done the work with much less pleasure, happiness, and opportunity without Roos. I give it to our David and to her. One learns about emotions outside experiments and the literature.

Amsterdam. September 2005.

Permissions

Major parts of chapter 1 are reprinted from The Laws of Emotion, *American Psychologist*, 1988, 43, 349–358, copyright © 1988 by the American Psychological Association. Adapted with permission.

Chapter 3 is for the most part adapted from pages 71–94 from *Unraveling the Complexities of Social Life: A Festschrift in Honor of Robert B. Zajonc*. Copyright 2001 by the American Psychological Association. Adapted with permission.

Chapter 6 reproduces major portions from M. Clark (Ed.), *Emotion: Review of Personality and Social Psychology*, Vol. 13, pages 60–89, copyright 1992 by Sage Publications. Reprinted by permission of Sage Publications Inc.

Chapter 7 reproduces Tables 2.2.1, 2.2.11, and 3.13 (extract) from J. Sonnemans, *Structure and Determinants of Emotional Intensity*, unpublished PhD thesis. Reproduced by permission from Dr. J. Sonnemans. It also reproduces Table 6 from Sonnemans, J., & Frijda, N. H. The determinants of subjective emotional intensity. *Cognition and Emotion*, Vol. 9, 1995, by kind permission of Psychology Press Ltd, http://www.psypress.co.uk/journals.asp, 2005.

Chapter 8 contains an adapted reproduction of pages 473–498 from N. H. Frijda, "Emotion Experience," *Cognition and Emotion*, Vol.19, 2005, by kind permission of Psychology Press Ltd, http://www.psypress.co.uk/journals.asp, 2005.

1

Laws

Emotions are probably the most individual and often idiosyncratic of human phenomena. They express what the world means to the individual, as a particular person at a particular crossroads in the world, and they compose his or her individual reaction to that crossroads. Yet, at the same time, emotions are lawful. They emerge and develop according to definite laws that can, at last in principle, be specified. In this first chapter I sketch these laws. The laws summarize the major regularities in the emotional phenomena.

These laws of emotion were first written down in 1987, after interest in emotions had exploded over the preceding 10 or 20 years, and made emotions reenter psychology as one of its major areas of concern.[1] The article's title was a proud one. I felt that our insight in emotions had advanced enough to venture laws. We were obtaining a grip that would allow siding emotions with other natural phenomena, without sacrificing that which makes them the most idiosyncratic of human phenomena and which reflects the meaning the individual assigns to his or her life. The aim of this book is to seek to understand those regularities. This book is driven by the pathos to, one day, understand the regularities without sacrificing the individualities and personal meanings.

The laws of emotion summarize the main points of how one can view emotions as natural, fully determined phenomena. I did not change them much. Over the past 20 years, considerable advances in knowledge and insight regarding emotions have been achieved. Much more is known both about emotional phenomena, through evolution and over cultures, and much more is also known about emotional differences between species, cultures, and individuals. Considerable advances have been made in understanding the processes of emotion arousal and their development over time; the advances allowed making several of my laws more precise (notably those of Situational Meaning and Apparent Reality). Affective neuroscience has emerged as an almost novel discipline.[2] So far, however, they gave me no inspiration or grounds for further generalizations at the level of these laws.

Also, the considerable progress notwithstanding, basic puzzles in understanding emotions stand out almost equally as they did 20 years ago. These puzzles are conceptual as well as empirical. They concern the nature of elementary processes involved. They include the following: What is the structure of emotional action, and how do actions like self-protection, flight, and intimate interaction come about? What are the mechanisms involved, and how are they related to the subjective experiences of urge or impulse, and the behavioral manifestations that give rise to the notions of impulse or urge? What is the nature of pleasure and of pain (in the wide sense of unpleasantness), and what is the functional nature of the processes involved? How do emotions interact with cognition; that is, how do the dispositions for emotional reaction interact with impinging as well as earlier and expected information? What is the nature of feeling, and its role in the totality of emotional processes? These are the main topics to which I seek to return in the coming chapters.

The laws of emotions recapitulate the main points of how one can view emotions as natural, fully determined phenomena. Formulating a set of laws of emotion implies not only that the study of emotion has developed sufficiently to do so but also that emotional phenomena are indeed lawful. They emerge, develop, and wax and wane according to rules in strictly determined fashion. When experiencing emotions, people are subject to laws. They are manifesting the workings of laws.

There is a place for obvious reservations here. Can lawfulness be expected, given individual idiosyncrasies? Yes, it can. Lawfulness can be hidden behind the chance encounters of multiple unconnected lawful sequences. One should recall Simon's parable of the ant: The simple mind of an ant makes it follow an erratic path that nevertheless ends at a water edge, because the straight path for which its mind is set meets the local laws of encountering pebbles and gusts of wind.[3]

More important is the reservation that laws imply invariable validity, but little is invariable in the domain of emotion. Sure, most emotions can be easily predicted. Loudly cry wolf and most people will become afraid. Still, not all people will. Some shrug their shoulders. Other become angry, blaming you for stirring trouble. In the domain of emotion, the regular causal connections are perhaps better captured by more modest terms. They may indicate "mechanisms" that operate over an indistinct range under indistinct, unpredictable conditions. This proposal comes from Elster.[4] He stresses that different mechanisms may make opposite predictions that both apply under circumstances that can be specified only *post hoc*, and perhaps not exhaustively. Mechanism 1: Oppression promotes conformity. Mechanism 2: Oppression breeds revolt. The laws of emotion described here are midway between mechanisms in Elster's sense and fully specific laws, if only because no forms of quantitative relationships are specified. The laws are observed or suggested empirical regularities that merely allude to the underlying causal laws in a stricter sense.

The mechanisms hide the underlying laws behind the operation of their joint effects of multiple simultaneous influences and the nonlinearity of many of them. Of this, the progress of Simon's ant is but a poor representative. Progress in each process is strongly determined by immediate feedback from its own results, as well as from overall effects of co-occurring processes and the shifting balances and imbalances between them. The cadre for appropriate viewing the true laws is that of dynamic systems theory, ably sketched for emotions by Lewis.[5]

It has been objected that what I propose in this chapter are not even laws at all but tautological statements that can be derived from a conceptual analysis of "emotion".[6] The risk of tautology is not illusionary, because most or all of definitions of emotion contain interpretative statements that refer not to observables but to relations among them. But the risk can be escaped from. One can arrive at criteria for "emotion" that are logically independent of the other phenomena that the laws relate to them, and that has been done here.[7] One can arrive at such criteria empirically, in bootstrapping fashion. One can begin with noting that what we loosely call "emotions" are responses to emotional events: to events that are important to the individual and that modify the continuity of its behavior or feeling. That definition is obviously circular. But one can then proceed to ask what the responses to such events consist of, observe what other kinds of events elicit such responses, and what further responses co-occur with them, in such a way building up noncircular descriptions both of emotional events and of the emotional responses themselves. The latter are what the laws are about.

Among the responses, one class of phenomena stands out, because its occurrence so much overlaps with the intuitive designations of "emotions." That class consists of states of action readiness: readiness to achieve a particular aim, such as protecting oneself, opposing someone, or obtaining intimate proximity. States of action readiness are felt phenomena, often present in verbal self-reports of experienced emotions. People report impulses to approach or avoid, desires to shout and sing or move, urges to re-taliate. They report feelings of loss of control as well as, on occasion, loss of readiness, absence of desire to do anything, or lack of interest.[8] Such felt states of action readiness correspond to behavioral signs of states of readiness. One sees others ready to flee or embrace or, while fleeing or embracing, to be set to somehow complete the actions involved. There is readiness to execute or complete them.

State of action readiness is a central notion in emotion. Its extension roughly corresponds with the extension of the emotion notion. If an event has no repercussion on an individual's inclinations to act, one will hesitate to call it an emotion, except perhaps in the case of emotions evoked by art.[9] This applies in particular when action readiness and action have particular features: those of involving striving and interference with ongoing actions or goal pursuits. They were among the features leading to the concepts of *affection* and *passion*, which were the predecessors of the emotion concept. Discussion of the laws of emotion is therefore best preceded by stating a *principle of passion*.

THE PRINCIPLE OF PASSION

Many human and animal processes and phenomena manifest the principle of passion: *to manifest states of action readiness, and feelings of readiness that bear on the aim of achieving or maintaining, or terminating or decreasing one's relationship to a particular object or event; and to have the characteristics of emerging involuntarily, of appearing to be set towards completing the aim in the face of delays and difficulties, and to seek precedence over ongoing behavior or interference from other sources.*

Such states occur in response to emotional events. They are discussed in detail in chapter 2 and are what is meant by *emotions* in the laws that follow.

THE LAWS

The Law of Situational Meaning

Emotions arise in response to patterns of information that represent the meaning of eliciting situations. In principle, different emotions arise in response to different meanings.

The Law of Situational Meaning is phrased slightly differently from its earlier version. Emotions are determined by the meaning structures of events in principle precisely determined fashion. "Meanings" and "meaning structures" refer to the full spatial and temporal context of events, including their evoked associated information. The "in principle" refers to the fact that emotion may in addition be modulated by prevailing state of action readiness, and by availability or unavailability of relevant information. Information may be scant—for instance, when an event happens fast and unexpectedly. The information picked up or evoked may apply to different emotions simultaneously, and that emotion in fact appears to which the individual is at that moment inclined. Pain may elicit anger more readily when the individual is already angry, or recently was. It otherwise might have elicited sadness, disgust, or fear.[10]

On a global plane, this law refers to obvious and almost trivial regularities. Emotions tend to be elicited by particular types of event. Grief is usually elicited by personal loss, anger by insults or frustrations, joy by success, etcetera. This obviousness should not obscure the fact that regularity and mechanism are involved. Emotions, quite generally, arise in response to events that are important to the individual; he or she has to grasp that importance in some way. Particular types of event tend to evoke particular emotions. Events that appear to satisfy an individual's concerns, or promise to do so, yield positive emotions or are felt to be pleasant; events that harm or threaten concerns are felt to be unpleasant or lead to negative emotions. Input some event linked to a particular kind of meaning, out comes an emotion of a particular kind. That is the law of situational meaning in its simplest form. In goes loss, and out comes grief. In goes frustration or offense, and out comes anger. In comes concern satisfaction, and out comes joy or happiness.

But the law is not properly phrased in this crude manner. It is meanings and the individual's appraisals that count; not stimuli or events per se. Events are not pleasant or unpleasant by themselves; they are appraised, apprehended that way. "Loss" is not a stimulus event but absence of a previous valued state of affairs. Loss, as an emotional event, moreover, implies an absence felt to be irremediable. Only when an event with those aspects goes in, out comes grief, with a high degree of probability. In goes pain, or a frustration or an offense, and out comes anger—but with some certainty only when someone to blame is around or has actually caused the pain or frustration. And even then, the outputs are only highly probable, and not certain. Inputs can still be appraised in different fashions. Serious, irremediable personal loss can be viewed as being in the nature of things; there then will be resignation. Frustration or offense can be seen as caused by someone who is dangerous, and fear rather than anger will come out. These subtleties do not undermine the Law of Situational Meaning. On the contrary, they underscore it. Emotions change when meanings change. Emotions are changed when events are appraised differently. Input is changed, whether because of changed external input or because of changed appraisal, and output changes accordingly.

Situational meaning structures thus are lawfully connected to forms of action readiness. Events play on the piano of the available modes of action readiness, and other emotional response components. Events as appraised—the processes set in motion by events—are the emotional piano player's finger strokes; available modes of action readiness are the keys that are tapped, plus the strings; changes in action readiness are the tones brought forth.

The keys, the available modes of action readiness, correspond to the behavior systems and general response modes with which humans are endowed: motivations for changing person–object relationships and programs for behavioral patterns to achieve that, which programs include elementary defensive and aggressive behaviors, laughter, crying, and facial expressions. They also include the various autonomic and hormonal responses and response patterns, such as orienting and active and passive coping.[11] The response modes finally include the action control changes that are manifest in behavioral interference and that are experienced as preoccupation and urgency; sometimes, these are the only aspect of change in action readiness felt or shown.

Situational meaning structure itself is a hypothetical construct. It is inferred in part from how people consciously experience emotional situations and in part from the observed effects of earlier experiences, current context, and current subject conditions (fatigue, alertness) on emotions. How emotional events are consciously experienced is not isomorphic to what elicits emotion, though, because it has also other determinants, including emotional response itself.[12] Meaning structures such as play the action readiness piano may operate fully out of awareness.[13] They emerge automatically, and some of them innately do so, such as looming objects, familiar stimuli, sexual stimuli in the mature organism.

The Law of Situational Meaning contains the gist of what has often been called *cognitive emotion theory* or *appraisal theory*, initiated by Arnold, Lazarus, and Solomon.[14] It provides the overarching framework to organize findings on the cognitive variables that account for the various emotions and their intensity.[15] Self-reports and analyses of the semantics of emotion terms have offered converging suggestions on the major variables involved;[16] experimental studies corroborate the importance of many of them.[17]

The workings of the Law of Situational Meaning are not always transparent, because they can be overridden by conscious control or by less conscious counterforces that will be discussed later. The law is most evident when resources for control and counterforces fail, such as in illness or exhaustion. Posttraumatic syndromes show that, under these conditions, almost every obstruction is a stimulus for angry irritation, every loss or failure one for sorrow, every uncertainty one for insecurity or anxiety, and almost every kindness one for tears.

Under more normal circumstances, the automatic workings of the Law of Situational Meaning are commonly evident. One example is that of *senti-*

mentality, the almost compulsive emergence of tearful emotions when one of a small set of themes is touched on, in films or stories about miracle workers,[18] brides marrying in white, and the like. The themes include separation-reunion, justice in jeopardy, and inspiration of awe. Tears are drawn by a precise kind of sequence. Expectations are evoked regarding a bad outcome of the theme, but they are carefully held in abeyance, and then one is brusquely confronted with their successful outcome. The sequence is emotionally more potent than the observer's intellectual or emotional sophistication.[19]

Another example is falling in love. Data from questionnaire studies suggest that it, too, is triggered by a specific sequence of events. In that sequence, the qualities of the love object are of minor importance. One is ready to fall in love, for any of one of a number of reasons: loneliness, sexual need, desire for intimacy, or need of variety. An object then incites interest, again for one of a number of reasons, such as novelty, attractiveness, or mere proximity. And then: give the person a moment of promise, a brief response from the object that suggests interest. It may be a confidence; it may be a single glance, such as a young girl may think she received from a pop star. Then give him or her a brief lapse of time—anywhere between half an hour or half a day, the self-reports suggest—during which fantasies can develop. After that sequence, no more than one single confirmation, real or imagined, is needed to precipitate having fallen in love,[20] even if one does not want to.

The Law of Concern

The Law of Situational Meaning has a necessary complement. *Emotions arise in response to events that are important to the individual's concerns.* Every emotion hides a concern, that is, a motive or need, a major goal or value, a more or less enduring disposition to prefer particular states of the world. A concern is what gives a particular event its emotional meaning. You suffer when ills befall someone because, and as long as, you love him or her. You glow with pride upon success and are dejected on failure when and because you strive for achievement, in general or in that particular trade. Emotions point to the presence of some concern. The concern may be different from one occurrence of an emotion to another. We fear the things we fear for many different reasons. Note that the Law of Concern joins different and even opposite emotions. One suffers when a cherished person is gravely ill; one feels joy at his or her fortune or recovery; one is angry at those who harm him or her. Emotions arise from the interaction of situational meanings and concerns.

One may question whether a concern can be found behind every single instance of emotion. It would not be meaningful to posit a "concern for the unexpected" behind startle (but, also, it may not be meaningful to regard startle as an emotion).[21] It may not be meaningful to posit a "concern for survival" behind dislike of pain or fear of death; it may even obscure analysis. Concerns blend over into sensitivities—for body damage, for inability to move or act, for certain smells and tastes—that form the basis for emotions when they cannot be escaped from, or when one is unable to achieve their pleasures. I will subsume sensitivities under concerns, even if they are not motives or goals. But even apart from sensitivities, the Law of Concern is the basis for understanding emotions. Why does he gets upset on the news of this person's illness? Because he appears to love her. Why does he feel that terrible jealousy? Because, perhaps, he yearns for continuous possession and symbiotic proximity. Emotions form the prime material in the exploration of an individual's concerns, and concerns represent the ultimate explanation of emotions.

Concerns also form the root of much of emotional complexity and conflict. People want contradictory things. They want personal autonomy and belongingness; they want freedom and they want restraint in the freedom of others. One and the same event can touch on incompatible concerns. One wants to have one's cake and eat it; when one's partner leaves, that gives freedom as well as having been abandoned. Emotions can result from one concern and clash with another: triumph for one, shame for another. The incompatibility of simultaneous satisfaction of all one's concerns is one of the most prominent features of human nature, with tremendous political implications, as Berlin cogently showed.[22] It underlies intra- as well as interpersonal conflict with, in the event, the powerful emotions of anger, guilt, remorse, regret, and spite.

The Law of Apparent Reality

According to the Law of Situational Meaning, emotions are dictated by the way a person perceives the situation. One aspect of this perception involves an appraisal that is particularly important for emotion elicitation. I will call it the situation's *apparent reality*. Emotions are subject to the Law of Apparent Reality. *Emotions are elicited by events with meanings appraised as real, and their intensity corresponds to the degree to which this is the case.*

Events that are taken to be real elicit emotions. Threats deploying in front of one's eyes, opportunities that are for the taking with smells, gestures, or glances that caress and evoke terror or tenderness or mellowness within. What does not impress as true and unavoidable elicits no emotion, or a weaker one. Warnings and promises often are just words and stories. The law applies to events taken to be real when in fact they are not. Rumors may trigger revolts when they are untrue but believed. It also applies to events that are real but of which the implications are still far away. Whatever is present, to the hands and the senses, counts; whatever lies merely in the future can be taken lightly or be disregarded, however grim or attractive the prospects. People prefer immediate rewards over larger rewards at a later time—the phenomenon of *time discounting*[23] They discount possible later punishments over the pains of current abstention or efforts.[24] Examples are found in the responses to nuclear energy dangers that tended to evoke emotions only when consequences are felt; unrest arose in Europe when restrictions on milk consumption were imposed after the Chernobyl disaster and not after the news from Chernobyl itself. Symbolic information generally has weak impact, compared with the impact of pictures and of events actually seen—the "vividness effect" discussed in social psychology.[25] A photograph of one distressed child in Vietnam had more effect than reports about thousands killed. Full knowledge of the dangers of nuclear war left most people cool, until emotions rose for a few weeks after the showing the film "The Day After".[26] Full knowledge of the risks of unsafe sex or of smoking often fail to restrain.

Examples abound from less dramatic contexts. Telling a phobic person that spiders are harmless is powerless when he or she sees the crawling animal. Knowing means less than seeing. When someone tells you in a sweet and friendly fashion that she does not appreciate your attentions, you tend not to heed her. Words mean less than tone of voice. When someone steps on your toes, you get angry even when you know that he or she is not to blame. Feeling means more than knowing.

I call this the Law of Apparent Reality. The word *reality* is chosen to characterize the stimulus properties at hand; Ortony, Clore & Collins extensively discussed the issue under the same heading;[27] so did Ben-Ze'ev.[28] The anecdotal examples given are paralleled by experimental results. Bridger and Mandel showed that a conditioned fear response, established by the warning that shock will follow a signal light, extinguished at once when shock electrodes were removed. It did not, however, when one single strong shock reinforcement had actually been delivered.[29] Conditioned Electrodermal Response (EDR) persisted indefinitely after shock. Many similar experimental findings are reviewed by Öhman & Mineka.[30] The powerlessness of verbal reassurance to diminish phobic anxiety contrasts with the abatement of phobia sometimes obtained by "live modeling plus participation," that is, by making the patient actually touch the snake or spider after a model has been seen to do it.[31]

The Law of Apparent Reality applies to numerous instances of strong emotion in everyday life and explains important phenomena, such as absence of strong emotions where one might have expected them. Grief dawns only gradually and slowly after personal loss. It often does not arise when being told of loss and the loss is merely known. One may just not believe it, or it remains an abstract fact. It may break through only when the lost person is truly missed, when the arm reaches out in vain or the desire to communicate finds its target to be absent.[32] The Law also accounts for the weakness of Reason as opposed to the strength of Passion, in the traditional sense of that word. *Passion* involves the effects of what is actually here to entice or repel, or of ideas that act in similar fashion; *Reason* refers to considering satisfactions and pains that are far away and only symbolically mediated.

What is the source of the Law of Apparent Reality? What do actual stimuli, such as shock, fires, live encounters, truly missing someone, and actions such as touching a snake, have in common? I call it their "reality," because visual presence, temporal imminence, earlier bodily encounters and pain, and actual, acute impacts on movement and action appear important for emotional impact. But the term *reality* begs the question. Meanings are felt as real and indubitable when one's society firmly believes them; for many people, God, His punishments and His promises of paradise are or were more real than current injustices. Also, objects of art—drama, novels, paintings—may have strong emotional impact while one is perfectly aware of their fictive nature.[33] What makes information emotionally "real" forms one of the major questions in emotion psychology. There is a good hypothesis. Events are "real" in the emotional sense when they affect one's affective and bodily existence—when they involve embodiment. I will return to this in chapters 4 and 6.

The Laws of Change, Habituation, and Comparative Feeling

What elicits emotions must be still further specified, because emotions obey the Law of Change: *Emotions are elicited not so much by the presence of favorable or unfavorable conditions but by actual or expected changes in favorable or unfavorable conditions.* The law is not new: Hume already mentioned it.[34] It is change that does it—change with respect to expectations or current adaptation level.[35] General well-being does not change much over the long run when economic conditions improve, at least above a threshold of adequate per capita income.[36] Major positive and negative events have major emotional impacts. Lottery winners experience considerable joy and elation, and traffic accidents that render the victims paraplegic elicit sorrow and despair, but both do so only for a limited time.[37] The inverse also occurs. In intimate relationships, partners are often taken for granted after awhile, and even felt as sources of irritation, to be gravely missed after they die or leave. One never stops to wonder, until a person's gone.

The Law of Change is, to an important extent, based on the Law of Habituation: *Continued pleasures wear off; continued hardships lose their poignancy.* Habituation is known experimentally over a large range of phenomena: from the orienting response that wanes when novelty wanes, to decreasing response to repeated exposure to phobic objects or electric shocks,[38] to the waning of excitement in initially interesting activities,[39] to the grave misfortunes mentioned, and to the moral blunting by continued exposure to inhumanities. The adaptation to welfare and favorable circumstances has given rise to the notions of the "hedonic treadmill"[40] and of the "joyless economy",[41] although there are limits to adaptation and habituation, to be discussed shortly.

As to the Law of Change itself: The greater the change, the stronger the subsequent emotion. Pleasure after suspense is considerably stronger than what the same event produces without prior uncertainty. Laughter generally follows what has been called the *suspense–mastery* or *arousal–safety* sequence.[42] Rough-and-tumble play evokes laughter in an infant only at the stage of development when such an event is just on the verge between being under control and being beyond control.[43] A similar sequence underlies the enjoyment of suspense in crime and adventure tales. It underlies even those of mountain climbing and stunt riding. After conquering a climb or mastering a stunt, one searches for a novel challenge, where success may result in a peak experience.[44]

The Law of Change has many variants. One is the Law of Affective Contrast. Loss of satisfaction yields not a neutral condition but positive misery. Loss of misery yields not a sense of normality but positive happiness. The Law of Affective Contrast was formulated by Beebe-Center as a result of adaptation level shifts, and by Solomon as due to "opponent processes" that seek to restabilize previous pleasure or pain.[45] Whatever its source, it is a law of considerable practical consequence. It is the basis of the play of take-and-give that proves so effective in, for instance, brainwashing. You take privileges away, and subsequently give them back in part, with the emotions of gratitude and attachment as results.

The Law of Change can take treacherous forms, as adaptation level is not its only frame of reference. Hopes, perspectives on the future, contribute. Goal-gradient phenomena seem to find herein their root: rats run faster when close to the goal, prisoners more frequently seek to escape when the end of their term comes near, and revolutions tend to break out when oppression starts to show lenience.[46] The Law of Change itself expresses a more encompassing generality that we can name the *Law of Comparative Feeling: The nature and intensity of emotion depend on the relationship between an event and some frame of reference with which the event is compared.* It is not the magnitude of the event that decides the emotion, but its magnitude relative to that frame of reference. If one's salary raise is less than expected, or than what others get, or what one feels one is entitled to, that raise makes one sad rather than happy. The frame of reference is often the prevailing state of affairs,[47] but it can also be an expectation, as it is in the conditions for relief, disappointment, or the enhancement of joy by previous suspense. It can be provided by the fate and condition of other people. Ratings of subjective well-being have been shown to vary with prior exposure to descriptions of the past as times of poverty or as times of personal closeness. One tends to feel less well off when others fare better. Envy and *Schadenfreude* are names for emotions rooted in comparisons of this kind.[48] Comparisons can be chosen: One can make upward or downward comparisons, and contexts differ in which one or the other is preferred.[49]

Generally speaking, the frame of reference that determines what counts as an emotional event, and how, consists of readily conceivable counterfactual alternatives.[50] This holds with considerable generality. Those who wring their hands in despair still entertain hopes; they have not really abandoned desiring. Those who grieve and mourn have not really taken their leave from the departed person; they still expect her or him at the other end of their arms, bed, or table. Those who feel that they should be able to cope suffer when they cannot cope. The point needs to be stressed and elaborated, because internal locus of control, achievement motivation, being in control, are generally held to be factors that contribute to coping with stress. They are, and do, as long as there exist ways to cope. They bring extra burdens when there are no such ways. Anecdotal evidence from concentration camps and trauma research, as well as experimental studies with animals and humans, supports this conclusion.[51]

The Law of Hedonic Asymmetry

The Laws of Comparative Feeling and of Habituation operate within certain limits. Many joys, sorrows, and frustrations carry intrinsic pleasures and pains that are independent of whether others do better or worse, or whatever are the norms or prospects. Also, likings increase rather than decrease with familiarity;[52] irritations may likewise grow rather than diminish when noises or interpersonal aggravations continue.[53]

Irritations form an instance of true emotions—likings and dislikes with changes in action readiness—to which one does not habituate. They form a modest instance. There exist miseries to which one does not get used; there is deprivation to which one does not adapt. Across cultures, subjective well-being does strongly correlate with human rights maintenance, and it does correlate negatively with true poverty, that is, with per capita income, at the lowest income levels.[54] Chronic intractable pain does not abate with time, which renders euthanasia, when requested by the patient, a matter of charity and humanity, and withholding it a matter of cruel imposition of one's standards on others.

The fact of emotional nonhabituation to continuing events has, it appears, no counterpart for positive emotions. Joy, bliss, relief, and fascination almost invariably tend to fade toward neutrality or some pale contentment. One must posit a Law of Hedonic Asymmetry, with its corollary, the Law of Asymmetrical Adaptation to Pleasure or Pain: *Pleasure is always contingent on change and disappears with continuous satisfaction. Pain may persist under persisting adverse conditions.* One gets used to the events that, earlier, delighted and caused joy; one does not get used to continuous harassment or humiliation, or shame, for that matter.[55] Fear can go on forever; hopes have limited duration, except in religious matters. The hedonic treadmill does not operate equally extensively for pleasures and for pains. Recall that the joys of freedom, for those who have suffered oppression, do not last as long as the sorrows of oppression did. True enough, the situations underlying these examples are not altogether transparent. It is difficult to disentangle the effects of repetition, accumulation, and sheer persistence of a given state of affairs. Oppression and institutional humiliation make themselves known each day; liberty, as an event, occurs only at the day of liberation. Be that as it may, at a gross level the Law appears to hold and to manifest itself in many ways, dramatic as well as commonplace. The grief on one's partner being gone is much, much more poignant and enduring than the joy caused by her or his presence a month before or the joy after her or his return one month later.

The Law of Hedonic Asymmetry is a stern and bitter law. It shows in many aspects of processing, not only in adaptation. Cacioppo and colleagues[56] pointed out a number of "affective asymmetries" that indicate that pleasure and pain result from different mechanisms with different functions. It is an almost necessary law, considering its roots that, theoretically, are so obvious. Emotions exist for the sake of signaling states of the world that have to be responded to or that no longer need response and action. Once the "no more action needed" signal has sounded, the signaling system can be switched off; there is no further need for it.[57] It shows the human mind to have been made not for happiness but for instantiating the biological laws of survival.

But it is not only that. I mentioned the very considerable adaptations that appear possible to adverse circumstances, like the almost average subjective well-being of hemiplegic individuals, confined to their wheelchairs.[58] The possibility of such adjustment says nothing about its mechanism. Reorientation toward a new restricted way of life that itself does not continue to present continuous aversive events is certainly different from the fading of the emotional impact of improved circumstances. It says nothing about the costs involved in this or other adjustments to adversity, such as emotional blunting under prolonged fear, alienation under prolonged humiliation and curtailing of initiatives, or deprivation of major concerns such as that of the need for intimacy and belongingness. Adjustment to adaptation levels occurs automatically, one would guess; adjustment to truly adverse circumstances does not. There is true asymmetry.

On the other hand, the hedonic treadmill is not unavoidable. In fact, by far the majority of people interviewed in most parts of the world indicate their state of well-being as better than neutral.[59] The significance of well-being ratings is not very clear, but it contradicts the predicted effects of the hedonic treadmill. Perhaps the explanation is that emotional adaptation does not necessarily entail affective blandness but just the disappearance of the emotional amplification connected to novelty.[60] Habit is comforting and comfortable, when emotion chasing emotion has not itself become the adaptation level. Well functioning in other than routine actions is always accompanied by positive affect.[61]

In addition, adaptation to satisfaction can be counteracted by constantly being aware of how fortunate one's condition is, and how it could have been otherwise, or actually was otherwise before—by rekindling impact through recollection and imagination. One can, at each Easter, recall one's Exodus, and leave the door open to strangers. Carless Sundays might be instituted as a measure for mental health. Enduring happiness is possible, it would seem, and it can be understood theoretically through the distinction between affect (liking and dislike) and emotion. However, note that such happiness does not come naturally, by itself. It requires attention to what might be or could have been.

The Law of Conservation of Emotional Momentum

The Law of Change or, at least, the Law of Habituation, shows a further restriction. One of its consequences seems to be that emotions diminish with time. This supposition, or one of its forms, is expressed in the common adage that "time heals all wounds." That adage, however, is untrue. Time heals no wounds. On the contrary, what accounts for habituation is repeated exposure to the emotional event within the bounds of asymmetry of adaptation. It is repetition that does it, when it does, not time. Time does not really soften emotions. We may phrase the Law of Conservation of Emotional Momentum thus: *Emotional events retain their power to elicit emotions indefinitely, unless counteracted by repetitive exposures that permit extinction or habituation, to the extent that these latter are possible.*

The law will be difficult to prove, because it asserts resistance against change when nothing happens. Yet it is of value to propose it, and there is evidence to support it. As regards its value, behavior therapy and trauma theory both appear to hold the silent supposition that enduring trauma effects need explanation in terms of avoidance, denial, secondary gain, or whatever. Yet traditional extinction theory, as well as the interference theory of forgetting, make it more reasonable to assume that the emotional impact of traumatic events never really wanes; it can only be overwritten. As regards the evidence, it is ample, although mostly clinical or anecdotal.

Loss of a child never appears to become a neutral event.[62] The persistence or recurrence of other trauma effects is, of course, well known. Emotions surge up when stimuli resembling the original stimuli are encountered, or when aroused by "unbidden" images (the term is Horowitz's),[63] in nightmares or even while awake. The sudden fear—shivering, palpitations, a sense of panic—on the smell of burning in former fire victims is a more common occurrence. Equally common is the unexpected outburst of tears when, many years later, a letter, a toy, a piece of clothing of a child who died is stumbled on; or the blood that rushes to one's face when recalling an embarrassing act committed years ago. The emotional experiences tend to be fresh, as poignant and as articulate as they were at the original occasion, or perhaps even more so. Certain old pains just do not grow old; they only refer to old events.

The Law of Closure

The preceding laws discussed the lawful determination of emotional reactions: situational meaning, concerns, apparent reality, change, and momentum. Emotional reaction itself also has its lawful properties. The most prominent and characteristic of those can be subsumed under the Law of Closure: *Emotions tend to be closed to considerations that its aims may be of relative and passing importance. They are closed to the requirements of interests other than those of their own aims. They claim top priority and are absolute with regard to appraisals of urgency and necessity of action, and to control over action.*

It may well be that the causes of emotion are relative ones—relative to one's current frame of reference, that is, as the Law of Comparative Feeling affirms. Emotional response does not know this and does not recognize this. For someone who is truly angry, the thing that happened is absolutely bad. It is disgraceful. It is not merely disgraceful, but it flows from its actor's very disgraceful nature and disposition. Somebody who has acted so disgracefully *is* disgraceful and will always be. The offense and the misery it causes will cling forever. In strong grief, life is felt as devoid of meaning; one cannot go on without her or him. Each time one falls in love, one feels that one never felt like that before. One dies a thousand deaths without the other. Every feature or action of the love object has an untarnishable gloss, for as long as the infatuation lasts. Cravings—think of when you tried to lose weight, stop smoking, or get off drugs—feel as if you will die when they are not satisfied. The pain is insupportable, even while one knows that the pang of desire will be over in a minute or two. Verbal expressions of emotions tend to reflect this absoluteness in quality and time: "I could kill him"; "I cannot live without her"; "I *must* have my cigarette, and I must have it *now*."

The closure of emotion is manifest not only in the absoluteness of feeling but also in the fact that emotions know no probabilities. They do not weigh likelihoods. What they know, they know for sure. Could it be that your friend is meeting someone else? Your jealousy is certain. Could it be that your partner is an inattentive person? Your anger is certain. Does she love me? Love now is certain that she does and then is certain that she does not. When jealous, thoughts of scenes of unfaithfulness crop up, and one suffers from images self-created. The same is true for the delights and the anxieties of love. Love is consummated 10 times before it actually is; and, when uncertain whether he or she will be at the rendezvous, one already prepares the reproachful speech over the telephone.

This closure of emotions is mirrored by what people do. They tend to act on their urges to act. The primary phenomenon of emotion is the control precedence of its action readiness.[64] The action readiness of emotion tends to occupy center stage. It tends to override other concerns, other goals, and other actions. It tends to override considerations of appropriateness or long-term consequence. Control precedence applies to action as well as to inaction, to the impulse to flee of fear as well as to the lethargy of grief or despair. It applies to single actions, such as shouting or crying, as well as to the execution of long-term plans, as when passionate love makes a person neglect his obligations. It applies to attentional control.[65] It also applies to the information processing involved in action preparation and execution, where it shows in the effects of emotion on performance—activating under some conditions and interfering under others.

Closure, or control precedence, may well be considered the essential feature of emotion, its distinguishing mark, much more so than autonomic arousal or the occurrence of innate responses such as crying or facial expressions. It is in fact the distinguishing mark of passion, because it tries to capture the involuntary nature of emotional impulse, or even apathy, its characteristic of being an urge, both as experienced and in behavior. It also seeks to capture that emotions appear to operate like cognitive impenetrable modules. Emotions are closed, not because they are impenetrable to information (after all, even when blindly in love, one seeks out the loved one, wherever she or he is) but because they are impenetrable to information that is irrelevant for, or incompatible with, their aims. And that is, I think, not because the connections of emotional stimuli with their responses are prewired, as in reflexes, but because this closure forms their mode of operation. The states of action readiness seek to marshal all resources to accomplish their aims. It defines them as passionate. Moreover, they not only seek to do so, but they actually do so when readiness is so high as to have reached a "point of no return," as after giving in to an urge to cry, or when overcome by blind anger, panicky flight, or blind desire. These may occur, for instance, by the proximity of their aim. The law of closure is under the dictate of the law of apparent reality. More about this in chapter 2.

The Law of Care for Consequence

Emotions are not always as absolute as just sketched. Emotions do manifest deliberation, calculation, or consideration. Infatuation can be stingy, and anger can be prudent. Although closure reflects the basic shape of emotions, that basic shape may run into opposite tendencies, usually caught under the heading of emotion regulation or emotion control. These manifest the Law of Care for Consequence. *Every emotional impulse elicits a secondary impulse that tends to modify it in view of its possible consequences.* The major effect is response moderation. Its major mechanism is response inhibition.

Presence of a tendency toward moderation or inhibition of response—that is, presence of emotion control—is a ubiquitous fact of emotion. Its ubiquity, and thus the validity of the law, is paradoxically evident from those instances when it fails, as happens in the blind reactions mentioned—the rare instances of uncontrolled, violent emotion; their occurrence with neurological disturbances like temporal epilepsy[66] or experimental decortication,[67] and under toxic influences like alcohol. Normally, even fury or passion, however violent, is in some measure controlled. In anger, one rarely smashes one's truly precious objects. When madly in love, one still waits to get home before consummating. Something snaps when going from there to blind frenzy.

The Law of Care for Consequence, too, is largely a law of emotion. Control is not only, or perhaps not mainly, a consequence of the dictates of reason. One cannot shed restraint at will, as little as one can at will shed anxiety or timidity. As Spinoza argued, emotion control is effective only when it follows from emotional motives.[68] Anxiety—rigid anxiety, freezing—is in fact its most complete expression. Control is often elicited or maintained by signals for possible adverse consequences of uninhibited response such as retaliation or reprobation[69] or, as potently, by the mere presence of critical onlookers. But the signals for care of consequences are often the signs or thoughts of consequences that are remote in time and thus have to do without calling the Law of Apparent Reality.

Conversely, the Law of Apparent Reality does apply in maintaining as well as lifting control. Restraint and spontaneity are a function of how the social environment is appraised. How much the environment can induce inhibition is illustrated by the mentioned audience effects of critical onlookers, familiar from examinations and auditions. Disinhibitory effects appear in the surprising emotional responsiveness triggered in therapy and sensitivity training groups, in meetings of sects, and in religious and political mass meetings. Tears stream widely and easily, embarrassments drop, sexual restraint may vanish.

Care for consequence is part of the mechanisms of emotion. It is always an option, as long as resources for restraint and the use of remote information are not exhausted and as long as the seductions from apparent reality and the gains of lack of restraint do not outweigh them.

The Laws of Lightest Load and Greatest Gain

Emotion control is not dictated only by external cues. More precisely, to the extent that it is dominated by external cues, those cues themselves are, within limits, at the person's discretion. One can focus now on this, then on that aspect of reality. One can complement reality with imagination or detract from it by not thinking of particular implications. The construction of situational meaning structures, in other words, offers leeway for emotional control that has its origins within the object him- or herself. Situational meaning structures can be chosen in ways that decrease emotional intensity, prevent occurrence of emotion, or make events appear more tolerable or more pleasing. The situational meaning structure that dictates emotion, in accordance with our first law, is in part shaped and transformed by its own expected outcomes and consequences. Transformation follows various principles. One of these can be phrased as the Law of the Lightest Load: *Whenever a situation can be viewed in alternative ways, a tendency exists to view it in a way that minimizes negative emotional load.* "Negative emotional load" refers to the degree to which a situation is painful and hard to endure.

Defensive denial is commonplace and widely described.[70] The many ways to minimize emotional load, however, merit emphasis; mechanisms exist to ensure it at different levels of the process by which meaning structures are constructed. Denial, avoidant thinking, and the entertaining of illusionary hopes operate at almost the conscious, voluntary, level.[71] People often claim that they had always known that their illness was fatal, the loss they suffered permanent, the malfunctioning in the nuclear plant dangerous, their denials at the time notwithstanding. Note that such knowledge does not prevent the denials to be resistant to correction, presumably because the load reduction they effect is so considerable.

Other mechanisms of load lightening operate at a much more elementary level. They include the mechanisms that affect the appraisal of apparent reality. They are the mechanisms of depersonalization and derealization that put a veil over emotional feeling. Depersonalization and derealization both occur under all conditions of shock, severe trauma, severe threat, and severe pain. They have been described as contingent upon accidents, serious personal loss or social failure, torture, and sexual abuse.[72]

Denial and derealization are by no means the only ways of lightening emotional load. The interplay of emotion and cognition takes many shapes that often are as difficult to recognize for the subject, as they are difficult to bear. There occur painful emotions that appear to replace still more devastating ones. For instance, people may entertain a "worst-case hypothesis," preferring the apparent certainty of a disastrous prospect over the uncertainty of a future unknown. They may be convinced of suffering from a fatal illness, which shields them from possible shock when being told while unprepared. Or, one may view oneself as a blameworthy responsible agent, when in fact one is a victim of arbitrary maltreatment. The guilt feelings that, paradoxically, are so common in victims of sexual or other child abuse appear to serve the purpose of retaining the view that adults are dependable and right in what they do. The guilt feelings and contingent parentification are the lesser price to pay than the despair and disorientation that would follow when admitting the truth. They let one see sense in a fate that contains none.[73]

Load lightening also occurs strategically. Care for consequence may prevent emotionally risky actions; an agoraphobic may just stay home and be free from worry. One may also forgo possible future gains to prevent regret and disappointment.[74]

The Law of the Lightest Load blends into the Law of the Greatest Gain: *Whenever a situation can be viewed in alternative ways, a tendency exists to view it in a way that maximizes positive emotional gain.* Emotions produce gains that differ from one emotion to another. Anger intimidates and instills docility. Fear saves the efforts of trying to overcome risks. Guilt feelings for misdeeds done confer high moral standing. Grief provides excuses, confers the right to be treated with consideration, and gives off calls for help. Often, when crying in distress or anger, you cast half an eye for signs of sympathy or mollification. Anticipation of such consequences, it can be argued, belongs to the factors that generate one particular situational meaning structure rather than another and thus brings one particular emotion rather than another into existence. The mechanism involved is transparent. One focuses, for instance, on the idea that an other is to blame, in order to permit emergence of an anger that makes the other refrain from what he or she is doing. The mechanism operates in jealousy, and the coercive effects perpetuate much marital quarreling. Even if the pain of jealousy may not originate in the wish to prevent the partner from being unfaithful, that wish strongly sustains jealousy; it does so particularly when the partner yields and gives up part of her or his freedom of action. Who would wish to make you suffer so? Here, too, certain painful emotions appear to result from something resembling choice—choice of a painful emotion over a still more painful one. That process in fact is rather general. Grief on loss, for instance, tends to be willfully prolonged, not only because it provides excuses but also because it keeps the lost person nearby, so to speak. When grief is over, true loneliness sets in. Both lightening emotional load and pursuing greatest gain may be driven emotionally and without intent, as well as strategically, with foresight of what they may yield.[75]

LAWS: SO WHAT?

The account of emotions that is implied in the laws described largely corresponds to that elaborated in my 1986 book. It is best summarized in Fig. 1.1, which resembles a figure in that book. The processes are presented in a sort of logical order, in that one or more processes earlier in the sequence are necessary for the emergence of later processes. Each box, though, hides puzzles, which in the present book I seek to explore further than the older one did. Also, the actual sequence of processes involved in emotions is not as presented in the figure. Emotion, with its appraisal and action readiness, may already be present when an emotional event arrives. Generation of a new emotion (action readiness, affect, arousal) begins right when a first element of a new event is appraised and while appraisal of the event is still going on. Feedback loops abound; appraisal is influenced by ongoing action readiness and resulting behavior; behavior influences uptake of event information. The boxes are not true boxes. They indicate sets of subprocesses that are influenced by the outcomes of other processes, including the subprocess set as a whole. As indicated earlier, the actual organization of emotion processes is best conceived in terms of dynamic systems theory.[76] Nevertheless, the elementary processes of generating appraisal, affect, action readiness, and behavior are distinct ones.

The purpose of the paper from which this chapter grew was to show that emotions are governed by laws. The contents of this chapter still seek to make that point. Emotions emerge and manifest themselves the way they do because lawfully operating mechanisms dictate them. We are subjected to these mechanisms and obey the laws.

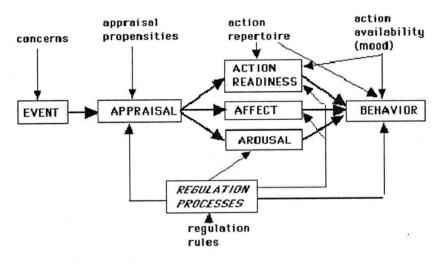

Figure 1.1   The emotion process.

True enough, humans are not entirely and blindly subjected to them. Emotions are passions; but we are not passion's slaves.[77] There is the Law of Care for Consequence, which opposes the operation of other laws, given certain resources. One can seek to willfully supplant or complement a given situational meaning structure with prospects of the future that represent the Voice of Reason. One can exert voluntary emotion control and substitute deliberate action for impulsive emotional response. It is not very clear, though, how the relationship and difference between the two modes of action control—control by situational meaning structure and impulse and control by deliberate intent—are to be viewed. There is the current distinction between *automatic* and *controlled processing*. It is not evident, however, that this distinction helps more to understand the difference between the two action control modes more than did the old distinction between Emotions and the Will,[78] because automatic responses include unlearned or field-driven impulsive ones and not only overlearned ones. But, as Ainslie[79] argued, time discounting, which results from the Law of Apparent Reality, may go some way to illuminating it. One can turn one's back to *that* reality, or tie oneself to the mast like Ulysses did when approaching the Sirens.

But even if we are not subjected blindly to the laws of emotion, still we are subjected to them. When falling in love, when suffering grief for a lost dear one, when tortured by jealousy, when blaming others or fate for our misfortunes, when saying "never" when we mean "now," when unable to refrain from making that one remark that will spoil one's evening together, when driven by addiction, one is propelled by the big hand of emotion mechanism. Does this take away from our sense that emotions are ours, that they reflect whom we are, and our freedom to feel as we do? Does not the view that emotions are fully determined phenomena throw us into fatalistic passivity?

I think not. First, it may, on the contrary, make us happy. Viewing and phrasing the laws of emotion did make me happy. It gives delight to feel the winds of Nature breathe through what one is, feels, and does. There is comfort in the notion of the lawfulness of emotion and in one's participation in the laws of nature implied by that notion. It is the comfort that resides in the recognition of necessity generally. Mention was made of the Law of Comparative Feeling. Emotions are proportional to the difference between what is and what is deemed possible. Recognizing necessity where there is necessity, where nature limits one's control, where many things are not possible and can only wrongly be considered possible, can considerably decrease emotional load. More important, there is, I think, no true opposition between lawfulness and freedom. Freedom, wrote Spinoza, consists in acting according to one's own laws rather than to those imposed by someone else.

Second, neither is there a fundamental opposition between Emotion and Reason. Reason consists of basing choices upon the perspectives of emotions at some later time. Reason dictates that one not give in to one's impulses because doing so may cause the greater suffering or less pleasure later. Reason dictates environmental protection because we expect more sorrow from pollution than pleasure from unlimited use of gasoline, if not for ourselves then for our children, whose fate fills us with emotion, at least when the time of dramatic climate changes has become all too nonapparent reality. The true opposition is that between the dictates of the Law of Apparent Reality, which tend to attach to the here and now, and the weakness of remote information to penetrate the walls of Closure, and that thereby lacks emotional force.

It is here that the laws of emotion and Reason may meet. Both emotion and Reason can be extended so as to make them coincide more fully with one's own laws. Following Reason does not necessarily imply exertion of the voluntary capacities to suppress emotion or turning one's back to the here and now. It does not necessarily involve depriving apparent reality of its emotive powers. On the contrary: Our voluntary capacities allow us to draw more of reality into the sphere of emotion and its laws. They allow turning the Law of Apparent Reality into a Law of Reality. Voluntary control of cognitive capacities allows letting reality—full reality, including long-term consequences—to be what determines emotion. They allow emotions to be elicited not merely by the proximal, or the perceptual, or that which directly interferes with one's actions, but by all that which in fact touches on one's concerns, whether proximal or distal, whether occurring now or in the future, whether interfering with one's own life or that of others. It is accomplished with the help of imagination and deeper processing. These procedures can confer emotive power on stimuli that do not by their nature have it. They can extend the driving forces of emotion to the spheres of moral responsibility, for instance. The laws of emotion can extend to the calls of reason as much as to those of immediate interests. The problems obviously lie in that the same capabilities can be marshaled by the Voices of Unreason.

NOTES

[1]Frijda, 1987a, 1988.
[2]Panksepp, 1998.
[3]Simon, 1973.
[4]Elster, 1999a.
[5]Lewis, 2005.
[6]Smedslund, 1992.
[7]Eilan, 1992; Frijda, 1992.
[8]Davitz, 1969; Frijda, 1986, 1987.
[9]Elster,1999a.
[10]See chapter 2 for more detail.
[11]e.g., Obrist, 1981.

[12]See chapter 4 for further treatment.

[13]Bargh, 1997.

[14]Arnold, 1960; Lazarus, 1966; Solomon, 1993.

[15]For up-to-date overviews, see Ellsworth & Scherer 2003, and Scherer, Schorr, & Johnstone, 2001.

[16]e.g., Ortony, Clore, & Collins, 1988.

[17]e.g., Dalgleish & Power, 1999.

[18]Efran & Spangler, 1979.

[19]Tan & Frijda, 1999.

[20]Rombouts, 1992.

[21]cf. Ekman, Friesen & Simons, 1985.

[22]Berlin, 1969.

[23]Ainslie, 2001.

[24]Frank, 1988.

[25]Fiske & Taylor, 1984.

[26]Fiske 1987.

[27]Ortony et al. 1988.

[28]Ben-Ze'ev, 2000.

[29]Bridger and Mandel, 1964; also Hugdahl & Öhman 1977.

[30]Öhman & Mineka, 2001.

[31]Bandura, 1969.

[32]Parkes, 1972.

[33]Frijda, 1989.

[34]Hume, 1739/1740/1969.

[35]Kahneman & Miller, 1986; Parducci, 1995.

[36]Diener & Suh, 1999.

[37]Brickman, Coates, & Janoff-Bulman, 1978.

[38]e.g., S. Epstein, 1973.

[39]McSweeney & Swindell, 1999.

[40]Brickman & Campbell, 1971.

[41]Scitovsky, 1976.

[42]Rothbart, 1973.

[43]Sroufe & Waters, 1976.

[44]Csikszentmihalyi, 1990; Piët, 1987.

[45]Beebe-Center, 1932: Solomon, 1980.

[46]Gurr, 1970.

[47]as in Kahneman & Tversky's prospect theory; Kahneman & Tversky, 1984.

[48]Ben-Ze'ev, 2000.

[49]Taylor & Lobel, 1989.

[50]"Norm theory"; Kahneman & Miller, 1986.

[51]Rothbaum, Weisz, & Snyder, 1982; Weiss, 1971; Wortman & Brehm, 1975.

[52]Zajonc, 2004.

[53]Frederick & Loewenstein, 1999.
[54]Diener, Diener, & Diener, 1995.
[55]For some consequences, see Chapters 10, and 11.
[56]Cacioppo et al., 2004.
[57]Taylor, 1991.
[58]Brickman et al. 1978.
[59]Diener & Suh, 1999.
[60]Kahneman, 1999.
[61]see chapter 3.
[62]Lehman, Wortman, & Williams, 1987.
[63]Horowitz, 1992.
[64]Frijda, 1986.
[65]Mandler, 1984.
[66]Mark & Ervin, 1970.
[67]Bard, 1934.
[68]Spinoza, 1677/1989.
[69]Gray, 1982.
[70]For instance, Lazarus & Folkman, 1984.
[71]See Weisman's (1972) concept of "middle knowledge."
[72]e.g., Cappon & Banks, 1961.
[73]Kroon, 1988.
[74]Van Dijk, 1999; Zeelenberg, Van Dijk, Manstead, & Van der Pligt, 1998.
[75]Frijda, 1986.
[76]Lewis, 2005.
[77]Solomon, 2004b.
[78]Bain, 1865.
[79]Ainslie, 2001.

2

Passion

In chapter 1, emotions were characterized by the principle of passion. Their passionate nature is their most distinctive feature. Yet, in psychological literature they have been mostly described as feelings, as states of bodily arousal, as behavior patterns, or as judgments. These ways of describing them all miss the point of what the notion of emotion emerged for in the first place: the phenomena of passion.

Love certainly is not just a state of arousal. "Love and fire are similar"; in love "you don't know where you are going." So it is for other emotions. Joy transports. Anger may rage like a tempest. Grief for a lost child tears one's heart apart. Shame may make one want to die, and often did make people seek death. Infatuation may make one disregard obstacles and moral scruples. Desire for revenge can make one harm oneself.

True enough, most everyday emotions are not very passionate. They hardly make one interrupt one's work; they just are inner stirrings. But the truly passionate ones are paradigmatic for emotions. Everyday emotions can be viewed as the thin trail of smoke arising above a volcano. They betray the stirrings below. Truly passionate emotions show those stirrings in full—the motive states from which behavior, feeling, bodily upset, and the coloring of judgment flow. In everyday emotions, these motive states can be recognized, but they often are weak or have not passed the checkpoints that exert control, inhibition, and consideration. In his book on love, Stendhal[1] complained about the pettiness of love in France in the early 19th century, contrasted with *l'amour à l'Italienne*. But even French love was about wanting to be close to a cherished person.

Passion: it is the core characteristic of emotions. Emotions are geared to actions. They want something or relish in something. They harbor powder stores. As Tomkins (1962) wrote, emotions amplify whatever reasons for acting there are.[2] What goes out tends to have more power than what went in. Watch grief: Someone merely left you, and you are flattened for weeks. Watch sex. Watch sexual pursuit. Watch cocks and male ducks in springtime: the females' feathers fly around but, miraculously, do not seek escape. Or watch fights between male animals. When threat displays in dogs flip over into angry assault, more force comes out than is needed to hurt the opponent and may continue when the latter is down.

All this shows one of the core aspects of every emotion: The individual is engaged in what is going on and is interested by it. Emotions—all emotions—involve engagement as the most general form of action readiness.[3] They are variants of interest, as the most fundamental emotion. It may well be *the* basic emotion: engaging with the event, and engaging with it wholesale, not merely with one's viscera. Emotions result from events that affect one's state and that one has to *do* something with or about.

This chapter examines the passionate nature of emotions: their nature as involving motive states that I call *states of action readiness*. States of action readiness, I argue, form the core of most emotions. This holds in particular for that subset of such states that I call *action tendencies*, which generate striving and feelings of urge and desire.

Motive states and action tendencies pose a fundamental problem. Action tendencies lead to unpremeditated, impulsive behaviors. These behaviors are not fixed and stereotyped; they appear regulated by an aim. How can that be? What is the structure of such motive states, to make that possible?

WHY ASSUME MOTIVE STATES IN EMOTIONS?

Why not just describe emotions in terms of movements, physiological reactions, and feelings contingent on that? Because the phenomena of passion ask for it. They show two sorts of features that do so: the phenomena of direction and vigor,[4] or of intent and energizing.[5] Phenomena of intent are those suggesting that behavior is oriented toward some future state. Phenomena of energizing include the quantitative and dynamic variations of behaviors and of feelings.

Motive states as meant here are occurrent states. *Action readiness* does not refer to dispositional states (in this book to be called *concerns*) that cause the individual to be interested in a particular type of event or actions, like sex or eating. Also, the terms *action readiness* and *action tendency* emphasize that the motive states involved are not mere wishes. They are actual, embodied states, or states on the verge of embodiment in action, to be released when circumstances permit.

Occurrent motivational concepts are in general introduced in the psychological analysis of behavior to account for the two features of *intent* and *energizing*. The features can be described more tangibly. With regard to emotions, I think a somewhat different distinction is useful: object relatedness, finality, control precedence, and behavioral prosody. The first two suggest intent; the other two, energizing. I briefly elaborate on them.

Object Relatedness

Most emotional behavior is intentional, in the sense that it is about on an object or event, sometimes about the world as a whole. Feelings, too, are about an object or event. Emotional behaviors are not movements but actions. More specifically, they involve actions that each establish or modify a particular relationship with an object, event, or the world as a whole, largely to strengthen or weaken a relation.

Finality

Emotional behavior, by and large, appears to be shaped by aims. "Action readiness," as meant in this book, does not refer to readiness for particular actions. It refers to readiness for achieving a particular aim (or, in the event, to unreadiness). Indeed, Roseman[6] refers to them as "emotivational goals." The aims are mostly relational aims: to attain, regain, reject, remove particular objects from interaction. Emotional behaviors, although essentially unpremeditated and impulsive, possess intentionality also in the more common sense of being oriented toward a future state.

Intentional direction of course appears from feelings about urges and desires. They want changes in relationships, such as proximity, safety, possession. But it is also suggested by functional analysis of the emotional behavior. Emotional behavior largely consists of approach and withdrawal; opening up or exposing oneself; shielding off, entertaining, enhancing, or weakening interactions; efforts to influence other individuals; or suspending interaction. Analyses of expressive behavior have been undertaken along these lines. The form of expressive behaviors can meaningfully and consistently be linked to functions like these.[7] Expressive behaviors in embarrassment, for instance, consist of gaze aversion, smiling with smile suppression, head bending, and reducing one's apparent height, that all four can be understood as actions that make the subject appear as nonaggressive or submissive, apt to appease an individual with superior status, and all four appear in humans and in other animals.[8]

The most forceful basis for inferring finality of behaviors is the equifinality of different behaviors that occur in a given emotional situation. Equifinality of emotional behaviors shows that the general formulation that emotional stimuli elicit reactions or behaviors is unsatisfactory. They elicit strivings for a particular end-state. The smell of food or of a sexual partner elicits not just elicit locomotion but an inclination to approach a particular object; such approach varies topographically from one occasion to the next and may vary from walking to swimming. Avoidance in fearful flight is similar. Motivation indeed is usually inferred, in animal research, when a large and rather arbitrary range of behaviors can be learned, if only they produce a given outcome.[9] Equifinality also appears from the quite different naturally occurring behaviors that a given type of stimulus may evoke. A signal of forthcoming electric shock makes a rat to show one of a set of "species specific defense reactions"[10]: The animal may run, jump, freeze, or hide. The four SSDRs share the outcome of lessening object–subject contact. In human anger, the actions of hitting, shouting, stabbing, and insulting all serve to hurt or intimidate their target. Joy leads to laughter, saying and doing unnecessary things, slapping people on the shoulders, increased movement amplitude. These all are exuberant behaviors that make sense as fleeting, nonserious, playful interactions that enhance gratuitously relating to the environment.[11] They, in turn, share elements with social and cognitive behaviors that are enhanced in positive moods and emotions: openness to novel exploits, to novel interpersonal contacts, to the plights of others, and to divergent thought.[12] Together, they suggest an action tendency that Fredrickson (2001) characterized as that of "broadening and building," notably of the scope of attention and thought–action repertoires;[13] experiment confirms that under positive emotions, such outcomes indeed appear.[14]

Equifinality within sets of emotional behaviors is usually caught in the notion of *behavioral systems*, which presumably are shaped by evolution to serve the purposes here called *aims*. They can readily be conceived as motivational systems[15] containing a direction that binds the behaviors together and allows prewired innate as well as reinforcement-guided acquired behaviors to enter the same system.

Control Precedence

Control precedence is the hallmark of passion. The notion refers to the fact that emotions tend to interfere with other pursuits.[16] Long-term passions, like love relationships, hatreds, and dominant interests, usurp time, attention, and resources. Emotions in general tend to assume precedence in the control of action and attention. Work is interrupted when an alarm sounds or when the boss makes a remark that hurts. Perceptual salience is increased; such salience is blocked when emotional appraisal is blocked.[17] Control precedence is most vividly illustrated by the effects of bodily pain. Pain almost irresistibly draws attention and takes it away from other pursuits.[18] Anxiety and fear also distinctly channel it toward sources of threat, and so do threatening stimuli[19]. Control precedence extends to positive emotions. When faced with positively valued events, attention tends to be narrowed to those.[20]

Persistence in the face of obstacles is another manifestation of control precedence. Thorndike locked cats in a cage. The cats persisted in trying to escape by means of every possible action, until they hit upon whatever bolt there was that happened to open the door. I once captured a small wild turtle and put it in a terrarium. It kept me awake for the whole night by the incessant clatter of it nails against the glass. Strength of desire generally is defined by persistence in spending effort to overcome obstacles.[21] Duncan (2003) measured such persistence by varying the weight of a movable fence a hen on the point of laying was willing to displace to return to her nest.[22] Control precedence also shows in resumption of action after interruption and in speed of running or other relevant action. It is subjectively manifest in feelings of urge that are frequently mentioned in emotion self-reports.[23]

In passionate behavior, the tendency toward precedence changes over from precedence into actually assuming control for the striving concerned. As my examples of the ducks in spring and the hen on the point of laying her egg indicated, passion is not uniquely human. But I add some examples. I once owned a she-dog. When she was in heat, I kept her home. A big Dalmatian wailed at my window for hours. When I left for my office, he followed me, waited for me, followed me back home. When at my doorstep, he decided he had better me than nothing, and stood up with his paws on my shoulder, giving me a love bite in the neck. Animals also know grief as a passion. Goodall[24] described a chimpanzee youngster whose mother died. He sat motionless beside her corpse until he himself died from exhaustion.

Control precedence extends from control over action to the control of cognition. There is an extensive literature on the influence of emotions on beliefs.[25] Momentary action readiness exerts such control not only by way of attention distribution but also by differentially sensitizing perception for certain events[26] and by differentially facilitating certain interpretations and recollections.

All this has a striking consequence: The reasons for action are rendered cognitively impenetrable. Action is not readily abandoned when there is good reason to do so. In anger, one often says things while realizing that one will regret them afterward. One hits someone considerably stronger and well trained. One seeks revenge even if it costs one's life, and one knows it in advance. Falling in love not rarely destroys one's family, including oneself; Anna Karenina is the classical illustration. Impenetrability is due to the desires rather than, say, to the innateness of relevant behavior patterns. In anger, people use daggers, firearms, and insults as readily as they use fists.

Behavioral Prosody

I borrow the term *behavioral prosody* in the present sense from Lambie and Marcel.[27] *Behavioral prosody* refers to the temporal properties of behavior, such as speed, flow of amplitude and force; to temporal coordination of aspects; and to the fullness of behavior. *Fullness* of behavior refers to the extent to which the body participates in a given behavior: One can grasp a teacup with two fingers, one's full hand, or by in addition bending over. Fullness and temporal aspects are linked, because a finger can move differently in time from what an arm or shoulder can.

Prosodic aspects of behavior suggest momentary strength of motivation and how it varies over time and changes in balance between motivation and restraint. Prosody is what can render behavior manifestly passionate. A passionate kiss endures. It neglects passers-by. The bodies intertwine, and not the mouths only. The kisses have full amplitude, or tremble from restraint. And when the kissing ends, it lingers. The bodies come apart slowly, with eyes and hands remaining behind, so to speak. I return to prosody in chapter 7.

EMOTIONS AND ACTION READINESS

Not all states of action readiness in emotion involve relational aims or give rise to striving. They do not all manifest the four features just discussed. Each of the four features can vary, down to outright absence or null states. Still, those variations are informative. They represent emotions, in that they embody the individual's current relational stance and motivational propensity with regard to ongoing events. For example, object relatedness on occasion gets lost. This happens in exhaustion and in deep despair or despondency. Explicitly abandoning to relate is the limiting instance of relatedness, the relationship of no relationship, of living apart together. Closely similar is disinclination to act, as in apathy. Apathy, too, has relational and motivational meaning, be it in the negative sense of motive loss or motivational disorganization. Sheer undirected excitement is again not dissimilar. The individual runs aimlessly here and there. There is evident action readiness, there also is reason for action—threat, uncertainty, waiting for a reward to come—but the conditions are such that no aim can be formed. All this is the reason for distinguishing the notions of action readiness and action tendency, introduced earlier. But one feature of passion does remain: control precedence. Apathy is as difficult to shake off as is angry frenzy, and they may share that the emotional reasons for clinging to them.

Even so, not all emotions as defined earlier (responses to emotional events) call for the assumption of states of action readiness. There exist emotional responses that consist of stereotyped patterns without flexibility. They are found in invertebrates: A mussel closes its shell when tapped or perhaps when the water gets unruly. They still occur in mammals, including humans. The startle response to sudden loud noises or light flashes is an example: interruption of ongoing behavior; reflexlike forceful eye closure; drawing in the head or hunching the shoulders.[28] Freezing, generalized inhibition, is another.

Perhaps such reactions compose all of "emotion" in invertebrates and insects. "Emotion" is put in quotation marks here because the term can be reserved for responses with flexibility, as several authors[29] do. Apart from that, flexibility increases with complexity of brain architecture. MacLean[30] distinguished three such levels: those of the reptilian brain, paleomammalian brain or limbic system, and the neomammalian brain. Nonvertebrates, insects, and fish have only the first (to the extent that nonvertebrates have brains at all), and reptiles hardly more.

However, at least in mammals even simple stimuli do not just trigger simple responses. They tend to engage entire behavioral systems, including both autonomic responses and a more or less extensive action repertoire. The four SSDR's in the fear system, mentioned earlier[31], form an example. Moreover, the systems respond not just to the stimuli but also to their context and their temporal aspects, which control selection of a particular system, or of a particular action, such as a particular SSDR, within a system.[32] The separate actions are geared to that context; they manifest flexibility.

Somewhere along the road enter positive and negative affect. I discuss what that means in the next chapter. For the moment, they are defined by motivations for enhancing or decreasing interaction with their object, combined with generalized behavioral effects such as arousal changes; motor excitement; and, on occasion, behavioral disorganization. Indeed, according to the descriptions, even the rats in LeDoux's experiments of which amygdala–cortex connections were severed not only froze but also showed signs of panic: extreme autonomic upset and attentional alertness. The sound stimulus acted as an aversive stimulus; it evoked distress. Like intact rats, they show hypervigilance and, presumably, enhanced behavioral response to fearful stimuli.[33]

It may be that positive and negative affect, in fact, intervene in eliciting or facilitating the more elementary responses and transform the behavioral systems into motivational dispositions. Lang and Bradley and their collaborators[34] indeed conceptualize the effects of pleasant pictures as activating an appetitive motivational system, and unpleasant pictures as activating a defensive one, that in turn attenuate or potentiate the startle response and freezing, just as both pleasant and unpleasant pictures increase general arousal and activation.[35] When linked to the additional information from stimulus content or context, the motivations to enhance or decrease interaction call specific behavior systems or fail in doing so and thus turn into action tendencies or other forms of action readiness.

The scope and complexity of how and what actions action tendencies call are increased by expectancies of rewards and punishments. They thus are increased by evolutionary gains in the cognitive capabilities to entertain such expectancies. Action tendencies not merely are for going along with what an evoked action program happens to lead one to, but also to call actions known to enable satisfying a particular expectancy. Hostile or sexual approaches are no longer triggered only by the attractive or threatening appearance or smell of an object; the range of triggers and possible actions is expanded by expectations of what they may entail.

Finally, such expectancies can turn into explicit expectations, that is, by representations of states of the world or oneself to be achieved. They turn action tendencies into true intentions to achieve emotional goals.

The above suggests five steps in the phylogenetic development of emotional (and "emotional") response: a reactive level, a systems-activation level, an affect-driven level, an action tendency driven level, and a level driven by goals. Where, in phylogeny, do motivation, action readiness, and action tendency emerge? The question does not, I think, allow of a simple answer. It would be worth the effort to systematically explore phylogenetic data on the emergence of motive states. Pending the outcomes of such study, I can only make some guesses.

Aim must be present in phylogeny at a very early stage. The complex instinctual action sequences of insects, notably in reproduction, are well known. They are sequential in a fixed, stereotyped fashion. After interruption, the sequence is usually not resumed at the point of interruption but starts right over again.[36] The female digger wasp, when ready to lay her eggs, digs a hole, seeks a caterpillar, paralyzes it by a sting, drags it to the hole, lays her eggs in the caterpillar, seeks a stone, and closes the hole with it. When the researchers took away the stone, the wasp did not go seek a new stone, but started to dig a new hole.[37] After having been interfered with repeatedly, however, she did become flexible and seek a new stone.[38] A nice instance of how behavioral stereotypy and flexibility interact, much higher in phylogeny, is the way a breeding gray goose recovers an egg that has fallen out of her nest. She stretches her neck, places her beak over the egg, and by small jerks brings it towards the nest. The ground being uneven, the path is irregular; lateral movements by the beak maintain the general direction. When the egg is removed during the process, the jerky movements follow a straight line till the beak is near the nest.[39] Evidently, there is an organizing principle "going toward the nest" that adjusts to circumstance.

Some flexibility is also present, at least from fishes onward, in the parameters of behavior. "Urgency," for instance, is a category that Shizgal (1999) deemed necessary to understand variations in rate and delay of behavior as a function of magnitude of reinforcement in goldfish.[40]

Reptiles, which have little more than a "reptilian brain," indeed mainly show standard routines of rather stereotyped actions,[41] yet not all their actions are stereotyped. When something unexpected happens, a blue lizard seeks to hide, an action that obviously depends on the location of a possible hiding place. Nor is all behavior stimulus induced. A healthy male lizard begins each morning with displaying his daily routine: warming up in the sun; then going for food; then, perhaps, performing a sexually inviting display. However, the routine is spontaneously initiated, and in some sense organized, by the homologue of what in mammals are the basal ganglia. If they are damaged, the animal stops initiating its daily routine, exactly like a human Parkinson patient.[42]

Insects as well as reptiles (and perhaps fish) also manifest prolonged motivation. Dragonflies may spend minutes in sexual pursuit and courting. Reptiles may continue for hours trying to escape when caught; recall my recollection of the captured turtle. In higher animals, emotional interactions also are often extended in time. A familiar sight is that of a cat stalking and chasing a butterfly. Dogs have extended fights. Chimpanzees are capable of diffuse, aimless excitement under fear conditions. When Kortlandt (1962) exposed wild chimpanzees to a stuffed but moving leopard, they excitedly huddled together, shrieking excitedly and swinging their arms, until one of the older females took courage, broke a branch and hit the intruder—itself a flexible emotional action.[43] Such variation in behavior, its duration, and flexibility appear to be a function of increased neural complexity.[44]

Control precedence is obvious in much of animal behavior. Experimentally, it has been investigated by means of the CER, the *conditioned emotional response:* the disruption of ongoing instrumental activity by conditioned signals for, for instance, electrical shock.

Goal-directedness, with its attendant behavior equifinality, is also evident in animals, at least in mammals. A newborn kitten by reflexes hisses, unsheathes its nails, and bares its teeth on appearance of something unfamiliar. Very soon, however, the stereotyped reactions begin to be directed at intrusions, which may appear in different places. Likewise, a hungry rat puppy roots, that is, moves about until it meets a nipple, but very soon it stops doing so if milk is not forthcoming[45].

MODES OF ACTION READINESS

Focused states of action readiness—that is, action tendencies—involve readiness to establish, maintain, or modify relationships. Each mode of action tendency seeks to do so in a particular fashion. That is, each aims at a particular kind of relationship; these aims in fact define different action tendencies. The major modes of action readiness are given in Table 2.1.[46] They

TABLE 2.1
Action Readiness Factors

Moving toward
Moving away
Moving against
Helpless
Submission
Rest
In command
Excited
Apathy, disinterest
Undo

are derived from correlations between the responses to questionnaire items that, in turn, were inferred from patterns of emotional behavior and from respondents' descriptions of their emotions[47.] Each item represents some possible mode of action readiness. The items are given in Table 2.2. The first 20 pertain to action tendencies; the other 8 pertain to variants of action readiness as such.

Modes of action readiness establish or modify relationships; even apathy does by abandoning them. Action tendencies generally do so in the service of concerns. Moving away, moving against, and moving toward all three may safeguard any concern, depending on whether the event threatens or promotes it; other action tendencies, such as attending, are instrumental to achieving such aims.

Major mode tend to map on major emotion categories. "Fear" corresponds with a tendency to move away, "anger" with the tendency to move against (or "oppose" as well as "hurt"), "sadness" to being helpless, and so forth. The modes are not truly linked to particular emotion categories, though. Different emotions may share the same action tendency, as do timidity and fear, and humility and shame. Different instances of one emotion class may differ in action tendency; so, for instance, "anger out" and "anger in."

The mentioned modes of action readiness may be universal. At least several, and perhaps the majority, are. There is solid evidence for the near-universality of at least six, and probably more, linguistic emotion categories that tend to correspond with modes of action readiness. Each language of which Russell examined the lexicon contained a word for all but one or two of the six basic emotion categories: anger, disgust, fear, joy, sadness, and surprise. Hupka found that some language from each of 60 language groups contained at least one word for a member of each of 15 major emotion categories.[48]

That does not mean, however, that all modes of action readiness play equal roles everywhere. Mesquita[49] pointed out that large discrepancies may exist between emotion potential and emotion practice. Emotions may

TABLE 2.2
Action Readiness Modes

Attend	Paying attention to what is happening.
Interest, savor	Desiring to take in and experience the situation or person.
Shut off	Seeking to shut off stimulation or interaction.
Approach	Desiring to be close by.
Withdraw	Desiring to avoid, to be out of reach, or to protect oneself.
Reject	Desiring to put or keep object at a distance.
Oppose	Desiring to resist or oppose.
Disappear from view	Desiring to disappear, not to be seen.
Be with	Desiring to closely interact.
Fuse with	Desiring to fuse, to lose distance or identity.
Dominate	Desiring to control the behavior of others.
Submit	Desiring to submit to others or to someone else.
Possess	Desiring to possess or get hold of.
Care for	Desiring to be tender, help, comfort, care for.
Amend	Desiring to make up for what has happened.
Undo	Desiring to undo what had happened, to erase the event.
Hurt	Desiring to hurt.
Reactant	Desiring to undertake action to overcome an obstacle.
Broaden and build	Desiring to enlarge range of interactions.
Depend	Desiring to hand the initiative to someone else, to obtain help.
Action suspension	Interruption of striving.
Helpless	inability to construct meaningful striving.
Relaxed	Desiring to be or remain relaxed.
Tense	Readiness to act without cues to act.
Inhibited	Inhibition of striving or feeling.
Apathetic	Desiring not to do anything, not desiring to interact.
Disinterest	Being disinterested.
Rest	Desiring to return to, or stay in, a state of rest.

Note. Derived from Frijda et al. (1995).

be universal while not being universally experienced or shown. For instance, comparison of about 40 Dutch, Indonesian, and Japanese emotions by means of self-report questionnaires showed rather similar structures of action readiness components. However, very large differences were found in the amount of variance that each of those components explained. Among the Dutch student respondents, antagonist tendency explained 6.8% of the variance over emotions; in the other two groups it explained about 3.5%. "Moving towards," among the Dutch, explained 11.6%, and in the other two groups it explained more than double that: 30.9 and 27.2%, respectively. Dependency ("Want help") explained 13.4% in the Indonesians and about 5% in the others.[50]

Some emotions are nearly absent in some cultures while playing a huge role in others. Anger is, or was, infrequent among the Utku Inuit[51]. Shame is a dominant theme in Muslim cultures,[52] as it was in many 19th-century Christian ones. These differences are best explained by differences in dominant modes of appraisal. Individuals may, for instance, blame themselves rather than the perpetrator when being the target of offense[53]. Modes of action readiness may also be subject to social encouragement or disapproval. Anger is rejected as childish among the Utku, as harming social harmony among the Japanese, and as proving one's independence and social aptitude in modern North America. At the same time, it is likely that all action tendencies, and the emotions that embody them, may emerge everywhere when circumstances are conducive to it. The Utku on occasion did manifest anger: toward their dogs, or toward the anthropologist who studied their anger.[54] Everyone may display fear and anger under extreme hardship, unless exhaustion has used up their resources.

VARIANTS OF ACTION READINESS

Modes of action readiness do not all have the same structure. For one thing, they can be tonic or phasic. Exhausted despair is a tonic emotion: It can go on indefinitely. Desire and craving also are tonic. So are the emotions that strive to maintain a particular relationship; love is one; the emotion of interest is another. As Tan[55] has argued, interest is the key emotion evoked by art. Its action tendency has control precedence; it can be quite passionate. It is what drives watching a film for 2 hours, wanting to know what happens next, keeping the eyes fixed on the screen while absent-mindedly grabbing for chips, and getting very angry when the show is cut short or someone tries to draw away your attention.

States of action readiness also vary in focus. Apathy, excitement, and disinterest have none, or so it appears. Others are diffuse. General readiness to maintain a current situation is called *contentment*. Happiness and feeling on top of the world, when going out in the sunshine on an early morning, may induce opening up for everything around, being receptive for shinings on the leaves and caressings by the breeze. Craving may be intense but still be diffuse, undirected readiness to obtain a given satisfaction, escape from longing, without a known location to turn it into readiness for approach. Some suffering involves only a passive longing that a change may occur; such an emotion is often called *distress*. Readiness that has shrunk to nothing but being prepared to accept any change in one's condition characterizes exhausted despair. Major action tendencies, such as those in fear, anger, and desire, are articulate and aim at a definite end-state: decreased vulnerability, having hurt or controlled someone, attainment of a desired end. But the aims of others again are open. They involve readiness to notice any opportunity for interaction and use it in the way the opportunity suggests. Such it is with interest, that takes what it can get, for various purposes. The action readiness of joy, described earlier, is similar. It does not seek to fill a deficit but to spill a plenitude. "Broadening and building"[56] is its apt characterization, bolstered by the behaviors shown under positive moods in many experiments,[57] as well as by the actions observed in rough-and-tumble play. An intriguing diffuse state of action readiness is doing nothing, often a variant of apathy. It may represent waiting how things develop, it may be enduring and waiting for harm to come to an end; it represents meaningful, passive coping.[58]

Such openness of aim has rather interesting consequences. The interactions that result challenge anew the modes of action readiness that brought them about. Negative feedback cycles of point attractors make place for positive feedback trajectories. In curiosity the known world expands and offers new unknown areas at its frontiers. The novel contacts from joy invite probing for intimacy. And so forth. DeSousa (1998) impressively described these outcomes as the "serendipity of emotions."[59] When striving, one may find more or other than one came for. This is not even confined to humans. Dogs and cats that are not locked up in fourth-floor apartments are saliently curious. Even rats are, when in richer environments than cages with activity wheels. Bindra described how they roam around, sniffing and looking.[60]

In fact, it is appropriate to say that emotions are modulations of a near-incessant endeavor to interact, as a basic property of animated organisms beyond a certain stage of phylogenetic development. Emotions are variants of interest, both in the affective and cognitive senses of that word. Interest is a fundamental emotion in at least one major emotion theory.[61] As already indicated it may well be *the* basic emotion. Emotions, for the larger part, result from being interested in what may harm or satisfy one's concerns, or they explicitly manifest loss of such interest. People and animals also are interested in exercising their capabilities. The young of the species start to get upright on their legs, or to extend their arms, almost as soon as they are born; a little later, they follow the urge to engage in gratuitous rough-and-tumble play. Perhaps the simplest as well as clearest instantiations of spontaneous interest are found in the motivation to know about the world and the meanings of what can be discerned in it and to interact with it: curiosity.

The phenomena of emotional amplification, desire, interest, curiosity, playing, and joy carry a lesson. Emotions should not be primarily understood as reactions. They are best viewed as modulations of a prevailing background of continuous engagement with the environment. Fear evoked by a sudden stimulus is not the paradigm of emotion—not in humans, and not in mammals that explore and run around. Interest and desire are better paradigms, and so are lust and love. Positive emotions in general are paradigmatic of what the emotion system is capable of and geared for. Strivings to broaden and build are not odd exceptions but consequences of release from the necessities to fend for one's concerns. Or, to shift perspective: Emotions are not guided solely or primarily by seeking to adapt to some environmental niche. Their aim and function are often to expand that niche without necessity, by using spare behavioral and emotional capacities. Action readiness is not merely geared to adaptation but equally to exaptation, the expansion of niches, of potential for adaptation, and of scope of interaction. That point, of course, has been advanced by Varela, Thompson, and Rosch; by Gould; by Piaget before them; and, recently, by Gottlieb.[62] That expansion is an evolutionary force, by presenting new adaptational pressures.

I thus give action readiness a central place in the analysis of emotions. One has objected to this, because supposedly there are no action tendencies in aesthetic emotions.[63] Is that so? I certainly disagree.

AESTHETIC EMOTIONS

"Aesthetic emotions" are real emotions that do usurp interest and that can grip the body. They grip the body not merely by speeding up breathing or heartbeat. When there indeed is real emotion, and not just appreciation, the action tendency of interest is intense. It has full control precedence. One is engrossed, fascinated, or spellbound, at the exclusion of everything else. One seeks exposure. One may stand outside in the rain listening to that violin playing inside; one hangs a reproduction of Botticelli's Flora on one's wall, and inwardly (or overtly) nods at it every time one passes by. "Seeking exposure," moreover, does not do justice to the action readiness. One enters the attitude of being a witness and may extend it to that of contemplation. In that attitude, one willingly enters a different world and mentally moves inside it.

Then there are the emotions of being moved. Being moved too has control precedence. It intrudes on whatever one is doing. One falls silent. One is knocked over—*bouleversé,* as they say in French. Tears are welling up. One may indeed weep silently; that is best understood, I think, as deference behavior, a variant of submissive behavior.[64] One recognizes something greater than oneself; gives oneself over to it; and adopts the corresponding humble, deferential position, just as when, with tears, touching the hem of the dress of the great spiritual guide.

No action tendency? Beauty may also engender enthusiasm. In my first effort to touch on the present issues,[65] I described how, when 18 years old, I for the first time heard Stravinsky's *Sacre du Printemps*, applauded until my fingers hurt, and left the Concertgebouw carried by the decision to become a good person (it did not stay long).

But enthusiasm can also take a reflective form, mindfulness in the Buddhist sense, remaining in inner contemplation of what is encountered. It may take the form of the action tendency of rest, of peace, the sense of having arrived or of being there, the fulfillment of motivation, recognizing novel possibilities of existence that the work of art reveals.

There is much more action tendency in aesthetic emotions than this; only it does not come to action. Aesthetic emotions are filled with virtual action tendencies, in *Einfühlung*[66]—empathy. One mentally moves with musical flow and a dancer's movements, probably through involuntary covert imitation through engaging the mirror neurons,[67] sometimes resulting in the actual muscle contractions of motor mimicry. Such virtual action tendencies may be taken over by the subject and expanded into true empathic feeling, and action readiness to participate in or fuse with movements, people, or spectacles seen and music heard.

WHAT IS THE READINESS IN ACTION READINESS?

The motive states in emotions are states of action readiness. Action tendencies are states of readiness to achieve some aim, not for performing some particular action. States of action readiness other than action tendencies are variants in having aims as such, including a decrease in readiness and motivational decay or disorganization.

At the same time, all these motive states are states of *action* readiness, or unreadiness. Action tendencies are not mere representations of desirable states; they are not mere wishes. They are states of preparation to achieve their aims; the preparation may be merely central, or extend to the muscles, the thoughts, and the glands. States of action readiness that are not action tendencies are states of absent, diffuse, partial, or disorganized preparation.

That preparation constitutes readiness in two ways. It represents some stage in the development of some action that serves an action tendency's aim, and thus constitutes readiness for that development, or else reflects the failure in such development. It also constitutes readiness for that aim itself: for obtaining a given relationship. It embodies readiness to establish contact, to ward off, to oppose, to dominate or submit, or whatever is the case; or, again, it reflects the absence, disorganization, or decay of relational readiness.

Action readiness means preparation, which means potentiating wide and diverse ranges of action dispositions. Potentiation, as just alluded to, may involve preliminary or complete muscular activity. It may also, however, merely involve central nervous system activation that can occur with absence of any muscle activation, or precede the latter by up to one third of a second.[68]

More important, such central nervous system activation has been shown to occur with great frequency without muscular activity, namely, when watching others move. Neurons in the parietal premotor area are called *mirror neurons* because they respond to observed intentional movements of conspecifics (macaque monkeys, in much of the research).[69] Neural activity is similar to, or the same as, that which occurs when actually oneself executing the movements; but it thus also occurs without movement. It can be there as neural state of action readiness. The neural representation represents the intentional relationships with environmental movement context, such as objects the animal reaches for or sees another animal reach for. The neural pattern reoccurs when the final stage of grasping an object is hidden from the subject animal's view: the representation thus appears to include the movement's aim; it properly represents action.[70]

The action dispositions relevant to emotions include those for approach and withdrawal; acquired and hostile, self-protective, and social actions, both unlearned and unlearned; facial expressions; and postures.[71] These dispositions, like those for intentional movements, are best understood as programs. The word *program* should not be taken too literally. It designates dispositions for action that have "open slots," where the situation at the moment of execution determines action's precise further course. The dispositions further include those for regulating sensory intake—both for maximizing and for minimizing it—and for the various forms of attention, such as focused and diffusely receptive attention. These dispositions, in turn, command dispositions for specific actions, which include facial expressions, postures, and whole-body movements.

Facial expressions are interesting in this connection. They are not primarily communication signals. They are best viewed as relational actions that are part of the mentioned action programs for approach and withdrawal, stimulus intake, attention and attention regulation, or that signal other individuals to modify the relationship from their side;[72] they are part of dispositions that include postures and whole-body actions. Also, they are best regarded not as prewired patterns corresponding to particular emotions, as is the currently dominant view[73] but as composites of components or "action units"[74] that each have their particular relational or effort-regulating functions, and that are assembled ad hoc by current action readiness and situational requirements.[75] One example is how the smile of enjoyment, the so-called *Duchenne smile*, can be understood. It consists of two components: lifting the mouth corners and lifting the lower eyelids. Lifting the corners of the mouth may well be a general social signal for nonhostile approach. Lifting the lower eyelid then enhances this by attenuating the confrontational aspects of gazing. Postures, too, are best understood along these lines.[76]

In actions that are more complex than facial expressions, execution of the programs instigated by action readiness involves progressive specification of that action readiness. The hierarchical structure of action guidance, the hierarchical generation of subgoals by goals, in traditional programming terminology, implies progressive specification of action readiness. In fear, the desire to-get-rid-of changes into the desire to-get-away-from into to-run-away into to-run-that-way into to-run-that-way-fast, by the reciprocal interaction of action readiness with information from the event as appraised and often also as changing during action.

The dispositions alerted by action readiness not only include dispositions for motor action but also extend to cognitive processes. These include modulating attention, setting sensory sensitivities and expectancies, setting sensitivity for more cognitive information, and influencing estimates of event and outcome probabilities.[77] Fear—that is, the self-protective tendency—enhances sensitivity to threatening stimuli in general, and for particular stimuli, such as spiders, and increases estimates of how likely they are.[78] It enhances detection of ways of escape,. Anger generates search for culprits[79] and modifies beliefs, in part by modifying information acceptance thresholds.[80] Such cognitive processes can operate at quite simple levels. For instance, when given electric foot-shocks, rats may attack other nearby rats.[81] The cognitive processes also can be complex: Fear and anger motivate rumination about the nature of the event and its implications and possible ways to cope or deal with it.[82] There is another side to this: In all these ways, action readiness contributes to neglect of information that is not relevant to it or that may be incompatible with its arousal. The components of action readiness implement emotions as passions. Action readiness not only motivates but also gives that motivation its dominance, its control precedence, and its persistence, as it affects the individual's entire functioning.

Action readiness thus also forms the basis for what Scherer called *synchronization of response components*.[83] It binds these components together, in interaction with on-line incoming information and on-line raised expectancies. In addition, the components themselves facilitate and inhibit one another, thus providing for internal organization. Muscle activities form coordinated structures (e.g., looking upward facilitates brow raising,[84] preparation for muscular activity enhances heart rate, most smiles require only moderate innervation of all three muscle groups involved, and so forth.

Motive states in emotions are organizers. They are high-level processes in a hierarchical process architecture.[85] They potentiate sets of action programs that in turn potentiate higher level action programs that potentiate lower level motor programs that potentiate muscle activity, increasingly specifying action readiness in the process. The organization is also heterarchical: Each lower order disposition can be potentiated by different kinds of motive state.

Action potentiation itself occurs at manifold levels. Between enhanced activity of central nervous system circuits and overt behavior, preparation can pass all possible levels: preparatory motor adjustment (e.g., bodily orientation toward the motivational object); increase in muscle tone; autonomic energy mobilization and intention movements; clenching fists; rapid eyeblinks or fleeting frowns; cognitive actions, such as angrily muttering by oneself as a trial run for actual action in an encounter. Action readiness may in fact remain at the stage of central activity, and felt urge in emotion awareness may reflect just that.

At low levels of motor readiness, action readiness is often present as continuous flow. Such flow may proceed along with other activities; it may just influence the behavioral prosody of these activities, as when talking more hurriedly when feeling excited. On occasion, however, it breaks out in actual action and assumes full control precedence. The emotion gains center stage. Emotions in this full sense, what Scherer called *affect bursts*[86], are climactic crystallizations of such continuously modulated nonovert action readiness. They represent some sort of phase transition from the latter. In affect bursts, synchronization by the interactions between components reaches its full status. The transition also activates regulatory control processes and taxes them. Those transitions tend to occur suddenly. Felt apprehension, for instance, flips over into fear, fear into panic. Alertness and watchfulness may flip over into rage and felt sadness into full grief or despondency. The transitions often involve a point of no return.[87] When fear, anger, or crying explode, it is very difficult to bring them under control again. The transitions also may distinctly show hysteresis.[88] I suspect that at the moment that affect bursts emerge, they show much higher underlying intensity of action readiness than at the point at which they subsequently disappear.

PASSION AND ACTION

Passion does not necessarily entail action, although it is difficult to conceive of instances of passion, as defined here, that do not translate into action. It is possible, though: a love that remains hidden, only felt, only manifest in frequent distraction.

The issue, however, is more general. Action readiness is not action and it does not always lead to action. It may remain a central state manifest in feeling or leading only to passing motor or autonomic concomitants—the small signs of flow of action readiness.

There are several reasons for the split between action readiness and action. Action readiness may be too weak and the emotional event not very important. But vigorous and powerful emotions also may not involve powerful action tendencies. It can be that no relevant action disposition is available in one's repertoire, or that no action appears feasible. The emotional event may be overwhelming; actions may have been considered or tried and have shown to be useless. One witnesses the constellation every day on the newsreels: victims of war, deportation, or natural disasters that drag their remaining possessions over the roads with bland faces and without tears. Action tendencies of fear, anger, or grief, if ever they were there, have been transformed into other modes of action readiness such as apathy or disinterest.

Action also may not arise because of regulatory control and inhibition,[89] themselves instigated by the costs entailed by obeying action tendency: retaliation, distraction, loss of friends, and so forth. Regulatory control occurs at widely different levels, ranging from automatic hypothalamic influences (e.g., attenuation of anger during play) to conscious suppression.

By contrast, action may also be facilitated beyond what action tendency and elements in the specific situation call forth. Passions as such may be subject of social approval and conform to cultural ideology and an individual's self-image. The legends of Achilles's anger and of Tristan's love for Isolde illustrate cultural models that help shaping behavior as well as rendering less passionate individuals unhappy for falling so short of what passionate love should look like. Although passion is at the very heart of emotions, as I tried to convincingly argue in this chapter's first sections, the extent to which emotions are passionate is not a natural function of, say, the importance of their instigation but is determined by normative influences. This is so in humans, but it is not entirely restricted to them. Recall the quoted incident of a male chimpanzee transgressing the borders of chimpanzee anger control with respect to infants and the evoked social disturbance.

Splits between action readiness and action also occur in a quite different manner than that due to weakness of impulse, restraint, or unavailability of actions. They are prominent in emotional responses to events in which one is not, at that moment, personally engaged: events that befall others, imagined events, or events from which one detaches oneself. Under those conditions, emotions can emerge that, together, I will call *inner emotions*. In a sense, they are subthreshold emotions—that is, subthreshold for overt action at the moment of their occurrence. They fill much of an individual's daily emotional life. They are interesting here in that they show that the place of action readiness in emotions can be much larger than might appear from behavior and from manifestations of control precedence.

What I call inner emotions are emotional feelings that are accompanied by no noticeable trace of motor tenseness or even of autonomic change, but that yet allow the individual to notice and name them: I briefly felt sad, I feel attracted, I feel a passing anger. One can feel joy or happiness that is merely manifest in deep and slow breathing,[90] without any motor expansiveness. One can feel love without moving either body or lips, or sadness that just involves a sad thought and staring out of the window for a second. All these feelings, it would seem, involve action readiness, but merely felt or glimpsed, as a sinking, gladdening, or pungent feeling. The feelings reflect mere action sketches or sketches of action preparation that nevertheless allow the person to call them feelings of fear or love or being attracted. These may well stem from activation of the neural bases of the relevant action programs, similar or identical to the activation of the mirror neurons when watching actions by others or when watching objects offering affordance.[91]

I call these emotions *small emotions*. They are small with regard to motor engagement and, perhaps, autonomic reaction. They are not without impact or consequence, however—at least, that is what reports on such experience suggest. They modulate attention, either to those feelings or to the events eliciting them. They drive cognition further than making the person stop and notice events. They may make him or her notice aspects of events, such as the horrid nature of what was said on the newsreel. They modify appraisal, by modifying the angle from which an event or person is viewed. One comes to view the target person with respect, for instance, that is, from a modest and submissive perspective, or with contempt, that is, from a condescending position. One may be led to take the target person as a model and seek to assimilate or emulate his or her views or capacities. There effectively is action readiness even without overt action, in the adoption of relational stances that in a physically real situation would lead to respectful, affectionate, or hostile body posture.

These small emotions are not necessarily weak emotions. They can be powerful in their effects. Small emotions may form the basis of highly consequential decisions, such as subscribing to a particular political party; deciding to donate money to a cause; or to hide a persecuted person, with risk for one's own life. Bertrand Russell (1968), in his autobiography, describes how one day, on coming home, he realizes that he does not love his wife any more. He does not describe a violent emotion, but he gets on his bicycle, never to return. Decisions to hide a persecuted person tend to be related with similar tones: as no more than emotionally toned convictions that such is the proper thing to do.[92]

Another variant of inner emotions are what I call *virtual emotions*. They mostly consist of emotion images: images of appraised events, together with imagined sketches of tendencies or actions that could occur. The sketches contain incipient readiness, for instance for drawing back or for bursting out, if this or that would happen. The image may obtain physical, motor support as when, while in thought, one makes a small withdrawing jerk or frowns. Emotion images form the substance of empathy. They form the substance of one's *mimesis*[93] when immersed in the fate of other individuals in film or fiction. One does not really share in their emotions. The emotions are obviously those of the displayed persons and not one's own. But the images have a degree of reality that is best understood as virtual readiness, an image of striving with motor underpinnings, for which the neural evidence was just mentioned. Virtual emotions also are what an actor experiences. When playing Othello, he is not jealous; that is, his jealousy is gone when meeting Desdemona in the dressing room.

Virtual emotions also exist as emotion anticipations: representations of the emotion one would have under certain circumstances, including virtual readiness for particular types of action and posture. One views oneself acting angrily, or weeping, or shrinking when confronting someone with power and prestige. Emotion anticipations have considerable action-instigating power. Much of our life is dictated by virtual emotions. We act with modesty not (or not only) because we are ashamed but to forestall anticipated shame. We act in prudent and conscientious ways not because we feel guilty but to forestall future feelings of guilt. We help others in need not because we suffer with them but because pity precisely is compassion: imagery of what their suffering is like, imagery of their emotional tendencies. All those anticipated emotions are not cognitions in propositional format, but images—images with sometimes motor support—of actions and strivings.

Then, finally, there is an entire domain of emotions with little connection to overt action but that, I suggest, include virtual action readiness as their main substance. They can occur in true emotional encounters, to gain time and weigh options before emotionally acting, or instead of doing so. They occur more often in the contemplative attitude that in Chinese psychology is called "savoring"[94] and that generates the special class of emotions that in Indian psychology are referred to as *rasa*[95] They form the main body of aesthetic emotions, which merit closer study under this virtual-emotions perspective, by someone who is up to that task.

Note that virtual action readiness is not an outlandish notion. Purely central action readiness exists. For instance, central readiness for a simple grasping movement demonstrably exists, at least three-tenths of a second before any muscle innervation.[96] That emotions are body states is therefore pure currently popular myth that can only be proven true, but not assumed to be, except of course insofar as brain states also are body states.

THE PROCESSES OF ACTION READINESS

What are those motivational states? In what form do they carry their aims? Note the basic problem involved. Wishes and the aims of deliberate actions are often articulate. They exist as goals: "I want him to go away"; "I want to hit him on the nose!"; "I want to hold her in my arms." But the aims of action tendencies are not always of that sort. Emotional behaviors paradigmatically are impulsive actions and always are in nonhuman organisms. That is, they are pushed by readiness rather than pulled by foresight of their outcomes. They are in some sense goal directed, and yet there is no prior aim. Very often it cannot be other than that. Take a male butterfly in search of—well, not in search of anything, but he follows a female's scent, and he gets there, without knowing what he was on his way for. And he could not know. He has not learned to follow the scent because of prior reinforcement by what a female offers; he may follow such a scent only once in his lifetime. And yet there is an aim. Following up a scent is an action defined by "following up," and not by a set of movements. It implements an aim, a desire, that dictates its own path, which in this case depends on where he and where she is.

Control precedence forms a second great puzzle of action readiness. Although action tendencies involve some aim, they are, or they tend to be, what Elster calls *reward insensitive*.[97] Foresight of bad outcomes tends not to deflect from their purpose. In panic, you press among the crowd in a too-narrow way out; in urge for revenge, you risk sacrificing your life; in addiction, as well as in sexual desire, you shrug your shoulders at unsafe actions.

Aims. Let us first consider the problem of how these aims are represented. Are they thoughts? No. The issue is not specific to aims in emotional motive states. It is shared by all purposive behaviors that are not preceded by explicit thoughts of setting goals, which includes most everyday actions. When in conversation at a dinner, you do not really plan to pick up the salt cellar, neither do you truly intend to do it; you just do it. Your action possesses what Searle called *intention in action,* which is implicit in the action but defines where that action ends, its "satisfaction condition."[98] The aims of motive states are represented as the satisfaction conditions for the actions that motive states call, and thus as states of being set to achieve these satisfaction conditions. Action readiness consists of being set to select and, in the event execute, actions that can achieve those conditions.

A framework to conceptualize what happens is given by so-called *efferent copy theory* of action.[99] All purposive action (including impulsive action) begins by, and is guided by, setting its course and to-be-achieved end-state.

Put in a sophisticated form: "When we act, we also imagine what the sensory consequences of action will be".[100] But it also works without images. Efferent copy theory was originated by Von Holst and Mittelsteadt to account for head adjustments made by flies in response to moving stimuli, such as vertical stripes in a turning cylindrical cage.[101] Normally, the fly sits motionless when its cage is turning. However, when feedback is disturbed by interchanging the muscles that ensure horizontal head movements, the animal gets into continuous turning with the stripes' movement. Efferent copy no longer matches *reafference* from the fly's own movement. The efferent copy mechanism is invoked to explain that normally, an animal, including a human, experiences a motionless world when she herself shifts her eyes but experiences a moving world when someone else pushes them. Efferent copy mechanisms thus involve implicit foresight—foresight not in the form of an explicit representation.

Preafference is the name for setting the efferent copy. It may involve setting muscle spindles to match expected muscle tension at action completion, or setting the location of the target of eye fixation or a grasping movement, and of the direction of those movements, before tensing any muscle, as single neuron recordings demonstrate.[102] Sensory settings are also made for exteroceptive sensations expected to come. If you take a sip of hot chocolate when you expect coffee, you spit it out even if you like hot chocolate; you get confused when stepping onto a stationary escalator, even if you had seen that it is standing still.

Efferent copy theory gives substance to the notion of a satisfaction condition. It explains how actions can vary topographically from instance to instance—the simplest instance of behavior equifinality. Learning to grasp means not acquiring a movement pattern but learning to translate hand–object disparities into efferent copies for action[103] and simultaneously setting the muscle-innervation parameters that roughly correspond to correcting the disparity.[104] Learning to grasp means acquiring an action program with aims and open slots.[105] In general, action skills, from those for eye focusing upward, include provisions for shaping efferent copies and feedback from match or mismatch with current sensory input.

This helps to specify what states of action readiness are and, in particular, what action tendencies are. They are states of readiness for particular sets of actions that share the satisfaction conditions defining them as a particular kind of action. Grasping sets out for closing fingers around an object; approach sets out for being near an object, and stopping there; hostile behavior sets out to hurt or block interference. States of action readiness also include the set's readiness in a strict sense: control precedence, maintaining readiness to transform one of the set's members into actual action when circumstances permit or call, and sensory or cognitive orientation toward detecting their satisfaction condition—the actual motivational state.

Calling action dispositions. How can a state of action readiness find the action dispositions that may fulfill it? It can because action dispositions are action skills that harbor their satisfaction states, and which satisfaction states match the action readiness' aim. The aim stems from how the emotional event is perceived, and why it is perceived as "emotional" in the first place. It is "appraised" in a particular way, a topic we will turn to in chapter 4. Roughly, when not emotionally neutral, events are perceived in one of three ways. We may say that appraisal always results in one of three kinds of contingency: congruence with what is desired, discongruence with what is desired, and possible but not actual congruence. The three contingencies correspond to action readiness that aims at retaining the current subject-object relationship, at modifying it, or at obtaining one, paralleling affective states of pleasure, displeasure, and desire.

But further information from the situation of the moment—aspects from the entire spatio-temporal context of the event, including memories and other knowledge—also influences selection from among the various action readiness modes and action systems. Action readiness conforms to the dual potentiation theory of motivation. Morgan and Stellar[106] propose that motivated action is the outcome of simultaneous potentiation of action dispositions by motive state and by the moment's situational information. That action disposition is in fact activated which is potentiated by both sources. The process is recursive: the particular action, its spatio-temporal course, for instance, come about in similar dual fashion.[107]

Which action readiness, and which actions, are called thus depends on that appraisal. The process of calling depends on the poverty or richness of available information which, in turn, depends on the individual's capacity to pick up and use that information. The process of calling varies accordingly.

The simplest process occurs when input information is scant, as with appearance of a single unpleasant stimulus and no time to take in its context,– sounding of an aversively conditioned sound, for instance. It can incite a simple form of striving, since unpleasantness is inherently unstable and incites motivation for change. It may as such stir locomotion.[108] If the sound's is heard to come from a particular direction that provides direction for striving: there is action tendency to move away. If it can come from anywhere in space, no options remain than the aimless action readiness of mere upset, freezing, or decay of readiness in apathetic despair. A pleasant stimulus guides in a similar way. Pleasantness may represent stability, and then shapes the aim for having it continue or execute potentiated consummatory actions. It may also represent instability when consummatory actions cannot be executed: desire. Following up an intensity gradient, or finding it by zigzagging flight increases the pleasantness or action enablement, and decreases the instability. That is what happens to the male butterfly smelling a female, without even knowing that there is a she-butterfly at the end. In all three contingencies, action tendency follows the "lines of force in the field", to take a metaphor from Lewin.[109] The aims are self-organized. They are not given by foresight, but by "insight," as that term was used in Gestalt psychology. Point attractor stabilization is the appropriate model.

Attractor-guided strivings need not terminate at points of rest. Action may terminate when reaching situations that enable further action, and such enablement may precisely be their aim. For instance, familiar surroundings are surroundings that the subject knows how to deal with,[110] and approaching them is to in fact deal with them. The aims of social, affinitive emotional action tendencies are similar. Their satisfaction conditions consist of enablement of interaction with others,– all instances of open action tendency aims discussed previously.

Action selection. Thus, action readiness and action are driven by processes of appraisal.[111] But this poses a problem of how appraisal information, action readiness, and appropriate action dispositions are connected. When seeing a coveted object out there, how come the baby hits upon the idea to reach for it, and how to move?

Only the study of motor development can throw light on this; I can only speculate. Aims, actions, and the latter's satisfaction conditions are obviously connected, sometimes in a way that is accessible to awareness. Wertham[112] described what he called "catathymic crises": gradually mounting urges to commit acts of violence, without a precipitating event; the urge seeks a target. Mark and Ervin[113] described similar experiences in epileptic subjects given temporal electrical stimulation. "Doctor, please don't do it, I do not want to harm you!". Searching for a culprit is of course common in ordinary rage when elicited by impersonal frustration or pain. But action readiness may also construct relevant actions on the spot. You are threatened, you find a stone and you throw it; you are threatened in a wood and you break off a branch and hit with it (recall the chimpanzee anecdote); or you are linguistically fluent, and invent novel insults. There of course are a large number of hard-wired primitive responses with each having their hard-wired input sensitivities. In many instances, these responses are organized into systems, meaning that they are activated by overlapping sets of input information, and each by distinct, differentiating context appraisals, that they may share specific neuromodulator facilitation, and perhaps mutual recruitments.[114] Examples are found in the systems for fear, hunger, and sex.[115] In other instances, the satisfaction conditions of actions are built up by experience. Again, learning to grasp presumably consists of building up cues for constructing efferent copies, with the satisfaction condition of object in hand.

Interestingly, the relationship between action readiness and action dispositions appears to be bidirectional. Action readiness calls actions, and actions can call action readiness. Retroaction of expressive movements on felt emotion, on physiological components, and on action readiness as such, has been amply demonstrated in the experimental literature.[116] One should not exaggerate the importance of such retroaction, nor the size of its effects, nor their nature: expressive movements have no invariable effects on judgment or affect.[117] Also, it only occurs under particular circumstances, and the circumstances determine the nature of the retroactive affect. That such retroaction can emerge is by itself not too much of a puzzle. Willfully executing expressive behaviors tends to facilitate aims and action readiness, because making these movements is facilitated by adopting a corresponding inner attitude, that is, by adopting a particular aim. Smoothly making a smile or an angry face is almost impossible without: how otherwise to get and keep all the components in place, and in the proper prosodic fashion? The best way to manage a warm and friendly smile is to bend over towards the person with a warm and friendly intent, even if faked. Even holding a pencil in your mouth may necessitate such an integrative effort. Action readiness is the organizing principle for action components. This also explains how, on occasion, true emotion can be facilitated by executing relational actions with conviction. Violent action tends to elicit anger, as anecdotes of cool police brutality turning into indignation toward its victim suggest. Facilitation also occurs because action readiness carries expectancies about properties of its target, being set toward perceiving them, which gear readiness towards the properties of its target. In these retroactions—as in normal emotional action—dynamic self-organization may well play. It may be that action dispositions are addressable by their satisfaction condition as well as by their entry point, their sensitivity. After all, the two closely match.

ENERGIZING AND CONTROL PRECEDENCE

Most emotional action readiness has a double potentiating effect. The information contained in the eliciting event-as-appraised potentiates particular action dispositions. The appraisals of "apparent reality" and concern relevance also potentiate the individual's propensity to actually act, evoking urges to strive toward the action readiness's aim. I will further discuss those appraisals in chapter 4. The appraisals facilitate the event's incentive value and implement control precedence. Control precedence constitutes the passionate nature of emotions, and so does full and ample prosody.

The event as appraised according to the laws of apparent reality and concern sets off the widespread components of action readiness. These components involve the multiple systems discussed in a previous section, of which attention focus and changes in accessing consequences, or weighing their probabilities, instigating "time discounting"[118] probably are the most general. All this is effected, in all likelihood, by these appraisals triggering the neural system that is variously labeled the Seeking System, Wanting System, Incentive Facilitation System, or Behavioral Approach System.[119] I will refer to it as the System Named Desire. Neurophysiologically, this amounts to activation of the mesolimbic dopamine system that stretches from the hindbrain's substantia nigra to the midbrain's nucleus accumbens, and to the basic ganglia. Its role in its nucleus accumbens branch is to induce acquisition of incentive properties in stimuli.[120] Its influence on the motor circuits of the basal ganglia is to control activity. If dopamine antagonists block it, even liked objects fail to induce approach; they also potentiate antagonistic withdrawal behavior, or energy-conserving apathy.[121] Whether energizing and priorities also result from engaging the desire system in negative emotions is a matter of debate.

Energizing thus means prioritization of emotional aims and their actions, and the persistence of that prioritization over time. Tapping energy resources is a consequence of that precedence; resources are allocated corresponding to precedence. Control precedence thus is not only an energetic issue, but also one of evaluative priorities, that is, of the appraised importance of the emotional events that will be discussed in chapters 4 through 6. In fact, control precedence is the essential processing aspect that allows emotions to fulfill their control function, and any multi-concern agent to respond to vital contingencies. Sloman,[122] for that purpose, gave "insistence" and "attention filtering" a central place in his analysis of autonomous agents. Presumably, that variable influences the enhancement of motor responses that comes from the diffuse activity of the medial branch of the so-called emotional motor system.[123] Energizing is also manifest in balances between simultaneous enhancement and inhibition, giving rise to prosodic features like those in responses of impotent anger as well as in well-aimed aggressive actions.

Propensities for given modes of action readiness are influenced by mood; in fact, mood is best interpreted as low ongoing readiness, or decreased arousal threshold. Bad mood renders generally pessimistic and murky, more easily thrown into sad emotion, and the like.[124] They are also influenced by previous priming of the given emotion. One gets more easily angry when irritated before, or suffering pain.[125] Neurohumoral influences also have their share: for instance, hormonal influences such as in the premenstrual syndrome increase anger proneness.[126] Primings may even go from one type of arousal to another, as from aggression to sex.[127] One may conclude with Buck[128] that different modes of action readiness possess different resting states of activation that vary from moment to moment and from person to person. Indeed, there are important individual differences in emotion propensities. Major personality dimensions are best understood in that way: extraversion as propensity for positive affect, neuroticism for negative affect, trait anger for hostility or moving against, as Depue, Gray,

Spielberger, Tellegen, and Watson demonstrated.[129] A major aspect influencing emotional energizing may be overall capacity for it, something like mental energy. Self-ratings of mental energy correlate substantially between monozygotic twins, and thus have a genetic basis; the variable appears related to interest, joy, and effectance motivation.[130]

Not all modes of action readiness involve the desire system, though, nor does all emotion energize. Some appraisals do not incite wanting or achieving: one has achieved what one wants. Contentment and enjoyment of contemplating beauty are examples. There, action readiness is for relaxation, rest, and being receptive. It still has control precedence, though. One resents interruption, and one may forget duty.

THE ORGANIZATION OF EMOTIONS

Emotions arise by the interaction of events with dispositions of the individual of a particular species. The dispositions enable motivational, behavioral, physiological and consciously felt response components. Each of these dispositions has at least three elements: a set of response dispositions proper, a sensitivity that renders it responsive to a particular kind of input; and a transfer function that maps variations of the inputs to variations in potentiation of the response dispositions. One task for emotion theory is to make good guesses on the content and structure of these dispositions.

The guesses strongly depend on how one thinks that the dispositions are organized. There are two major types of conception of such organizations: the basic emotion, and the multi-componential views. The basic emotions view is known from the work by its major representatives Buck, Ekman, Izard, Oatley and Johnson-Laird, Plutchik, and Tomkins.[131] In this view, each emotion disposition consists of a tight package of dispositions for particular neural, behavioral, physiological, and subjective experience components; the behavioral components include particular facial expressions, that thus characterize the different basic emotions. The packages are thought to be potentiated wholesale when the emotion is aroused. Each basic emotion is supposedly evoked by a particular set of stimuli,[132] or by a particular complex appraisal,[133] such as what Lazarus named "core relational themes,"[134] with threat to physical welfare (which elicits fear) and personal loss (which elicits sadness) as examples. All nonbasic emotions instantiate one of these packages, specified by its object (e.g., indignation, as a variant of anger), or represent blends of a few of them.

Basic emotions theory has been criticized because so far no agreement has been reached on which emotions belong to the basic set.[135] More problematic for the theory is the finding that instances of each supposedly basic emotion only show moderate correlation between response components, which does not suggest a true package.[136] For instance, feelings of fear, facial expressions of fear, and autonomic arousal do not always go together; facial expressions for any kind of emotion tend to vary widely. The objection has no great force, however. Transfer functions may well differ for activation of different response components, and activation of each component may well be influenced by situational context, as dual potentiation theory of motivation would predict.

These moderate inter-component correlations nevertheless form the starting point for the multiple-componential view, of which Scherer is the most explicit proponent.[137] In this view, each emotion consists of a large number of components that vary more or less independently, and result from activation of independent dispositions for the separate components—for facial expression aspects, for voice intonation, for motivational state, and so forth. Each component disposition independently responds to particular inputs; for Scherer, these are appraisal variables, to be discussed in chapter 4.[138] The view fits better than the basic emotions view to the variations of emotion phenomena with interaction types and emotional development.[139]

The domain of emotion component dispositions is without preset organization. Their independence allows in principle for as many different emotions as there exist combinations of appraisal components. However, organization of the emotion domain still is produced in two ways. Response components exert reciprocal facilitation and inhibition; activation of one entrains or blocks another. They include coordinative structures. Producing facial expressions, for instance, forces changes in respiration.[140] And appraisal components happen to occur in clusters due to the vicissitudes of ecology. They produce regularly occurring emotional response patterns. What others consider as basic emotions may thus be understood as "modal emotions".[141] Fear and anger occur as universal emotion categories because threats and obstructive competition are recurring facts of life everywhere. The two conceptions, although in principle drastically different, in practice do not lead to very different predictions.

Recognizing the central role of action readiness leads to a third conception, midway between the basic emotions and multicomponential views. The emotion dispositions are viewed as centered on the motive state provisions. They form the core of emotions, except in the latter's most primitive form. When evoked by events as appraised, they potentiate the required action dispositions that call required autonomic and attentional mechanisms, and so forth. They also provide access to, and integration of divergent information, such as anticipations and information on context. Organization within emotions, and synchronization of components, is provided by the common potentiation of components by state of action readiness, plus all the reciprocal interactions that ensue.

Emotion dispositions—and under the present perspective that means motivational, action readiness dispositions—consist of sensitivities for particular kinds of information, linked to a motivational disposition, and to relevant action dispositions. Sensitivities form the entry points of the dispositions, and transform input information into aims to correct discrepancies or retain concordance. They provide access to relevant action dispositions, and to call control precedence and energizing. This sketch of the emotion dispositions, of course, just completes what was said before about the nature of action readiness.

When a relevant event occurs, that disposition is evoked that obtains the highest activation, as a joint product of its resting activation and activation increase due to the event. Activation by the events is presumably influenced by degree of match between the event as picked up and appraised, and what the action readiness disposition is optimally sensitive for. Particular emotions thus are allowed to arise following only minimal input. Any unexpected stimulus may elicit anger when anger propensity is high and low cognitive readiness precludes full information scanning, or when unexpectedness multiplied by propensity gives anger the highest activation value.

On occasion, several dispositions are simultaneously potentiated because their sensitivities overlap. One carries the day, but without necessarily obliterating potentiation of the other. Fear may dominate over anger, which then may surface as soon as threat becomes less urgent or offensiveness more salient. Also, subthreshold potentiation may inhibit or weaken activation of the dominant disposition, in the way that considerateness and concurrent sympathy may do with anger. Motivational dispositions appears to operate in continuous interplay between circuits seeking at each moment to settle into a momentary stable state, much as described by Freeman at the neural level.[142]

Which different dispositions are there? The question relates to the discussion about basic emotions. Do they exist, or don't they? The issue is a confused one. Many different principles are invoked to support assuming or denying them. Some look for elementary, unlearned, universal motivational or behavioral systems, and some for elementary, unlearned, emotionally potent contingencies or event types. Anger is easiest defined by the former terms, envy by the latter; so does shame. The two are not the same, the categories that can be distinguished overlap but only partly so. For instance, submission forms a basic behavioral and motivational system; but it occurs in shame as well as in humility and admiration, and shame, response to shameful events, may show in hiding away as well as in submission. Emotions underlie a "dual principle of categorization".[143]

Then the notion of basic emotions contains the idea of a restricted set of emotions that compose all existing emotions, either in pure form, as atoms, or as mixtures, as molecules.[144] The evidence does not support the hypothesis.[145] One of the problems is that forms of action readiness, that are among the major aspects to distinguish emotions, exist in more and in less definite forms. As set forth in a preceding section, there are action tendencies with specific aims, and other states of readiness or unreadiness that do not have those. They are at a higher, less specified level of description, so to speak. Apathy, excitement, distress, upset, are action readiness modes at that level. They each occur with a wide range of eliciting events that, each, underlie a particular appraisal pattern and an emotion name such as envy, regret, hope. The atom-molecule idea of basic emotions is misleading and inappropriate. In any case, polemics between proponents starting from different points of view should be abandoned as pointless. Emotions may be basic from either point of view in the dual principle of categorization.

In this book, I choose for states of action readiness as a meaningful starting point for understanding and differentiating emotions. It led to the meaningful expectation of a restricted set of motivational or action readiness dispositions. The set of dispositions does not necessarily fully match the set of distinct modes of action readiness. Some forms of readiness or unreadiness may result from malfunction of dispositions. Diffuse excitement may be a side-tracked form of readiness, because no focus or action program can be found. Apathy (or some apathy) may be a form of unreadiness when energetic or cognitive conditions for readiness fail. The discussion just points to the option that modes of action readiness and dispositions may diverge.

Again: which dispositions may be there? Cues have come from types of relational actions (approach, close interpersonal interaction, self-protection etc.) and from major contingencies that call them (loss, proximity of selected individuals, threats etc.). The final word, I think, will have to come from neuroscience: from finding dedicated neural circuits, and from finding neuropeptides that differentially affect them. Evidence for such circuits and neurohumoral controls is extensive. Buck, Panksepp, and others reviewed these findings.[146] LeDoux and Fanselow advanced evidence for a fear or defensive circuit. Gray and Davis proposed an additional circuit for inhibitory anxiety. Panksepp presented convincing evidence for systems for joy and play, for separation distress, for affinitive motivation. All these cited evidence for a disposition mediating hostility or anger. Many investigators identified a system that has to do with approach motivation, that is often called the Reward System, called by Panksepp[147] the Seeking System, and that I call the Desire System. There further is some evidence for a disposition for submission,[148] and thus underlying all emotions that involve this aim, such as shame and humbleness. There may be an additional system for commanding apathy, for passive coping, for doing nothing in order to cope with stress, or to recuperate from deep body pain,[149] suggesting that apathy is not always a failure response. The neural circuits involved all are best understood as motivational circuits, and the neurohumors as controlling their sensitivity and activation.

The motivational dispositions themselves may possess an internally differentiated structure. At least, the fear or defensive system controls reflex-type emotional response patterns as well as the various forms of flexible action readiness.[150] The lower the response type, the simpler the information needed to set it off, and the lower down in the neural circuits the location of the response disposition; the more complex the dispositions, the more information they need, or the more time for processing,[151] and the stronger electrical brain stimulation,[152] the higher up the neural involvement extends. The simpler forms may still involve substantial organization and information integration occurring autonomously out of reach of motivational mechanisms.[153]

The motivational dispositions exert their influence on actual behavior by way of efferent connections to activating, organizing, and effectuate dispositions further down. Together, these are called the Emotional Motor System, that has been shown to be involved in laughter and crying, freezing, lordosis, and other responses connected with basic biological functions such as micturition.[154] Part of this system (the medial part) diffusely regulates thresholds and intensity of each of those mechanisms, including that of locomotion.

However, as yet there is no agreement among neuroscience researchers about which motivational dispositions to distinguish. The various negative emotions like fear, anger, and disgust might be manifestations of one common defensive motivational system, and feeding, sex, and care-giving of one common appetitive system.[155] Apparently distinct systems might merely indicate the intervention of pleasure and pain dispositions that activate separate response modules, together with available stimulus information and the outcomes of learning.[156] Also, it is not sure that all behavior systems are commanded by dedicated neural circuits. The universal tendency for ego-loss and fusion, for instance, may be a by-product of loss of self-awareness. The very evidence for motivation-specific circuits is also being contested.[157] They may in fact function at some other level. For instance, the "anger" circuit may bear primarily on forceful approach or "reactance",[158] (angerproneness and actual anger also enhance left-frontal activation)[159] the basis for joy lies in a play system,[160] and affiliation and separation panic may both derive from an affiliation system, or even from a still more basic comfort system.[161] But all these are empirical matters. The lack of agreement does not form a good argument against hypotheses of basic emotion circuits or mechanisms, contrary to what Ortony and Turner and Russell argued.[162]

Extending this alternative possibility is the existence of plausible alternative options to the hypothesis that the specific action readiness dispositions each are represented by specific neural structures. It still is possible that what is universal are not emotional dispositions, but human and animal concerns plus the contingencies in subject-environment interaction that emotions respond to: threat, need and opportunity for bonding, and the like. One may also argue that what is finite and restricted are the limited sets of possible or conceivable relational changes, such as self-protection and forceful opposition. Primacy may come to the action dispositions appropriate to these aims, and laid down in body structures like claws, teeth, arms for embracing and skins for sensing, with self-organization shaping those into coherent dispositions when the time for having them arrives—a possible basis for Scherer's modal emotions.[163] A blowfish may have one different type of emotion from all of us. Some dispositions may even have nothing to do with bodily mechanisms as such. Turning around and turning your back is an anger action only when "anger" is defined by event appraisal, and not by hostile action tendency.

Whatever their foundation: emotion arousal may well be seen as the activation of one or a few of these dispositions, except when deactivation of such dispositions or disorganization of the system is involved. More than one may in fact be involved in every truly passionate emotion, since in all those attentional deployment and the desire system are engaged, in addition to the more specific dispositions.[164]

NOTES

[1]The first quote is from a poem by the ancient Persian poet Bulleh Shah; the second quote is from Stendhal, 1820, 1949.
[2]Tomkins, 1962.
[3]Solomon, 2004a.
[4]Hebb, 1949.
[5]Morgan, 1943.
[6]Roseman, Wiest, & Swartz, 1994.
[7]see Frijda, 1986; Frijda & Tcherkassof, 1997, for recent efforts that extend those of earlier writers, including Darwin.
[8]Keltner & Buswell, 1997.
[9]Mook, 1996.
[10]Bolles, 1970.
[11]Owren & Bachorowski, 2000.
[12]Isen, 2004.
[13]Fredrickson, 2001.
[14]Fredrickson & Branigan, 2005.
[15]Toates, 1986.
[16]Frijda, 1986.
[17]Anderson & Phelps, 2001.
[18]Eccleston & Crombez, 1999.

[19]Eysenck, 1997; Koster, Crombez, Van Damme, Verschuere, & De Houwer, 2004; Niedenthal & Kitayama, 1994; Öhman, Flykt, & Esteves, 2001; see Williams, Watts, MacLeod, & Mathews, 1997 for an overview.
[20]Meinhardt & Pekrun, 2003.
[21]Bolles & Fanselow, 1980.
[22]Duncan, K.
[23]Davitz, 1969; Frijda, 1986.
[24]See also De Waal (1996) for more on animal grief.
[25]See Frijda, Manstead, & Bem, 2000.
[26]e.g., Niedenthal, Halberstadt, & Setterlund, 1997.
[27]Lambie & Marcel, 2002.
[28]Landis & Hunt, 1939.
[29]e.g., Ekman, Friesen, & Simons, 1985.
[30]MacLean 1990.
[31]Bolles & Fanselow, 1980.
[32]Bouton, 2005; Timberlake, 2001; Tucker, Deryberry, & Luu, 2000.
[33]Rosen & Schulkin, 1998.
[34]Bradley et al., 2001; Lang, 1994.
[35]Bradley et al., 2001; Lang et al., 1990.
[36]Tinbergen, 1951.
[37]Tinbergen, 1951.
[38]I have not been able to retrace my source.
[39]Lorenz & Tinbergen, 1938.
[40]Shizgal, 1999.
[41]MacLean 1990.
[42]Maclean, 1990.
[43]Kortlandt, 1962. The scene was present in a film taken during the experiment with the stuffed leopard in the Congo forest.
[44]Tucker et al. 2000.
[45]Teitelbaum, 1971.
[46]Davitz, 1969; Frijda et al., 1995.
[47]Frijda, 1987b; Frijda, Kuipers, & Terschure, 1989; Frijda et al., 1995; Roseman et al., 1994.
[48]Hupka, Lenton, & Hutchison, 1999; Russell, 1991.
[49]Mesquita & Markus, 2004.
[50]Frijda, Marka, Sato, & Wiers, 1995.
[51]Briggs, 1970.
[52]e.g., Abu-Lughod, 1986.
[53]Mesquita, 2001b.
[54]Briggs, 1970.
[55]Tan, 1996, 2000.
[56]Fredrickson & Branigan, 2001.
[57]Isen, 2004.

[58]Rothbaum, Weisz, & Snyder ,1982.
[59]De Sousa, 1998.
[60]Bindra, 1961.
[61]Izard, 1977.
[62]Gottlieb, 2002; Gould, 1991; Piaget, 1976/1978; Varela, Thompson, & Rosch, 1991.
[63]e.g., De Sousa, 1987; Elster, 1999a; Reisenzein, 1996.
[64]Frijda, 2001.
[65]Frijda, 2004.
[66]Lipps, 1907.
[67]Meltzoff, 2002; Niedenthal et al., 2005; Rizzolatti et al, 1999.
[68]Georgopoulos, 1995.
[69]Gallese, 2005; Gallese & Metzinger, 2003; Rizzolatti et al., 1999.
[70]Gallese & Metzinger, 2003.
[71]De Gelder, Snyder, Greve, Gerard, & Hadjikhani, 2004; De Meijer, 1991; Frijda & Tcherkassof, 1997; Grammer et al., 2004; Mehrabian, 1968.
[72]Frijda, 1953, 1986.
[73]Ekman, 1984; Ekman, Friesen, Ellsworth, 1982.
[74]Ekman & Friesen, 1978.
[75]For support for this view, see Camras 2000, Ortony & Turner 1990, and Scherer, 1992.
[76]Grammer et al., 2004.
[77]Derryberry & Tucker, 1994; Eysenck, 1997; Phelps, 2005.
[78]Arntz, Rauner, & Van den Hout, 1995.
[79]Keltner, Ellsworth, & Edwards, K. 1993.
[80]See also the other contributions in Frijda et al., 2000.
[81]Laborit, 1979.
[82]Rimé, 2005, Rime et al., 1992.
[83]Scherer, 2000.
[84]Camras, 2000.
[85]Gallistel, 1980; Jeannerod, 1997; Mook, 1996.
[86]Scherer, 1994a.
[87]Frijda, 1986, ch. 4, for this notion.
[88]Scherer, 2000.
[89]Frijda, 1986; Gross, 1999; Tucker et al., 2000.
[90]Boiten, Frijda, & Wientjes, 1994.
[91]Meltzoff, 2002; Rizzolatti et al, 1999.
[92]in Block & Drucker, 1992.
[93]Oatley, 1992.
[94]Sundararajan, 2005.
[95]Shweder & Haidt, 2000.
[96]Georgopoulos, 1995.
[97]Elster, 1999b.

[98]Searle, 1983.
[99]See Gallistel, 1980.
[100]Mook, 1996, p. 328.
[101]Von Holst & Mittelsteadt, 1950.
[102]Keele, 1982; Georgopoulos, 1995.
[103]Thelen, 1995.
[104]Erlhagen & Schöner, 2002.
[105]Keele, 1982.
[106]Morgan, 1943; Stellar, 1977. See also Gallistel, 1980; Mook, 1996.
[107]e.g., in the examples of fear response described by Tucker, Derryberry, & Luu, 2000.
[108]Bandler & Keay, 1996; Nieuwenhuys, 1996.
[109]Lewin, 1937.
[110]Zajonc, 2004.
[111]Scherer, 2000.
[112]Wertham, 1978.
[113]Mark & Ervin, 1970.
[114]Panksepp, 1998.
[115]Bandler & Keay, 1996; Bouton, 2005; Tucker et al., 2000.
[116]Niedenthal, Barsalou, & Winkielman, 2005, for a review.
[117]see Clore et al., 2005, for these conditions; in particular, the experiments by Tamir and colleagues, quoted there.
[118]Ainslie, 2001.
[119]Panksepp, 1999; Berridge, 1999; Depue & Collins, 1997; Gray, 1987, in that order.
[120]Ikemoto & Panksepp, 1999.
[121]Berridge, 1999; Shizgal, 1999.
[122]Sloman, 1987.
[123]Nieuwenhuys, 1996.
[124]Frijda, 1993b.
[125]Berkowitz & Harmon-Jones, 2004.
[126]Van Goozen, Frijda, & Van de Poll, 1992.
[127]Zillmann, 1998.
[128]Buck 1999.
[129]e.g., Depue & Morrone-Strupinsky, 2004; Gray, 1994; Spielberger et al., 1983; Tellegen & Waller, 1997; Watson, 2000.
[130]Lykken, 1999.
[131]Buck, 1999; Ekman et al.1982; Izard, 1977, Oatley & Johnson-Laid, 1987; Plutchik, 2002, Tomkins, 1962.
[132]e.g., Öhman & Mineka, 2001.
[133]e.g., Lazarus, 1991; Oatley, 1992.
[134]Lazarus, 1991.
[135]Ortony & Turner, 1990; Russell, 1991.

[136]e.g., Scherer, 1984. For recent illustration, see Reisenzein, 2000.

[137]Scherer, 1984, 1994a.

[138]Scherer, 2000.

[139]See also Camras, 2000; the various contributions in Mascolo & Griffin, 1998.

[140]Boiten, 1996.

[141]Scherer, 1994b.

[142]Freeman, 1999.

[143]Frijda, 1986

[144]Johnson-Laird & Oatley, 1989.

[145]Reisenzein, 1995.

[146]Buck, 1999; Davis & Shi, 1999; Fanselow, 1994; Gray, 1990; LeDoux, 1996; Öhman & Mineka, 2001; Panksepp, 1998.

[147]Panksepp, 1998

[148]Adams, 1979.

[149]Bandler & Keay, 1996; Bohus, 1993; Brehm, 1966; Stuss, Van Reekum, & Murphy, 2000.

[150]Fanselow, 1994.

[151]Gray & McNaughton, 1996.

[152]Panksepp, 1998, p. 213.

[153]Tucker et al., 2000.

[154]Holstege, 1997; Nieuwenhuys, 1996.

[155]Bradley et al., 2001.

[156]Bradley et al., 2001; Öhman & Mineka, 2001; Russell, 2003.

[157]F. C. Murphy et al., 2003; Phan et al., 2002.

[158]Brehm, 1966.

[159]Harmon-Jones & Sigelman, 2001.

[160]Panksepp, 1998.

[161]Depue & Morrone, 2004; Panksepp, Nelson, & Bekkedal, 1997.

[162]Ortony & Turner, 1990; Russell, 1991.

[163]Scherer, 1994b.

[164]as argued by, for instance, Buck, 1999, and Panksepp, 1998.

3

Pleasure

Emotions, by and large, are passionate; they involve motive states. These motive states center around pleasure and pain. They urge to get rid of pain, to follow what appears pleasant, or to remain in pleasant quiescence. Pleasure and pain are pivotal in emotions, and for many investigators they form the criterion for a state being an emotion or not.[1] But what are pleasure and pain themselves? I will focus on pleasure. Pain, taken in the extended sense of displeasure, I will discuss only in passing. As a shorthand, I will refer to pleasure and pain together as *affects*.[2]

What is pleasure? The word *pleasure* has a multitude of meanings, and so have the words that fulfill roughly equivalent functions in other languages. The French *plaisir,* for instance, implies a certain richness and fullness. The German *Lust* has a cruder connotation. But they have something in common. They all point to a common domain of experience.

THE EXPERIENCE OF PLEASURE

What is that common domain? The first answer coming to mind is that pleasure is a feeling. But what is a feeling, in the emotional sense of the word? It certainly differs from other experiences that are denoted by *feeling* in English, such as feelings of warmth or the feel of velvet.

For old introspective psychology, feelings were a kind of conscious mental content that differs from the other kinds: sensory sensations, mental images, and thoughts.[3] Feelings of pleasure and pain were seen as irreducible *qualia*, the only affective qualia that could not be reduced to the other kinds of mental content. Experiences such as feelings of joy and anger were conceived as states of feeling of pleasure or pain with admixtures of sensations, images, and thoughts. Pleasure and pain themselves were thought to vary along three dimensions: pleasant–unpleasant, excited–quiet, and tense–relaxed. Feelings differ from the other kinds of mental content in several characteristics. They are "evanescent": they evaporate whenever attention is focused upon them; they are subjective: they reside "in" or "with" oneself, their subject, and do not pertain to external objects; they are evaluative; they cannot be localized in space or in some sense organ; and they do not exist by themselves but are "comments" to sensations, images or thoughts.[4] These characteristics of feelings seem valid, but they also are problematic.

Evanescent?

Take evanescence. Pleasure indeed tends to evaporate when attention is directed at it. When focusing attention on the pleasure produced by a sweet substance, all that remains is the experience of a sweet substance. When focusing what is so nice about a familiar object, all that remains is the object; it may not even appear familiar any longer. The same appears to apply to pain. Buddhist meditation recommends mindfulness of pain as the way to conquer it, and experimental research supports this recommendation.[5] However, there is little evanescence when attention does not focus the feeling but the felt event. Pleasure can make people act with control precedence. The events can fill one's mind and usurp attention, and this can continue indefinitely. No evanescence there, in interpersonal contact, in sex, in gluttony, in listening to music, in play. Obviously not: Who would focus the feeling rather than the event, under normal emotional circumstances? It would interrupt the interaction; it would drastically alter the very experience.

Feelings Not Sensations?

True, experiences of pleasure (and of pain) cannot be reduced to other kinds of awareness: not to images, not to judgments or thought; not to body sensations. That at least is Arnold's conclusion of careful analysis of the evidence from the introspective experimentation of that long time ago.[6] Body experience does occur in emotional feelings, as James, and many others before and after him, argued. It may be prominent in such experience. Yet feelings of pleasure do not reduce to it. For one thing, body experiences themselves may (and may not) be pleasant or unpleasant. For another thing: even if irreducible qualia, they are structured experiences. They are not closed in themselves, as sensations of red, and even of "light pressure," are.[7] They have some sort of meaning; they point beyond themselves.[8]

Are Feelings Subjective?

Pleasure is not subjective. At least, the experience of pleasure is not, or not necessarily. Theoretically, of course, pleasure depends on the subject, because the same event may give pleasure to one person and not to another. But that fact does not usually form part of the feeling. The feeling often has nothing subjective. On the contrary, the pleasantness usually is out there. It is experienced as a property of the object perceived. As far as the feeling itself is concerned, it is objective fact. The newborn baby is indubitably charming, to its mother and father. Its charm appears as an intrinsic quality; aren't they lucky to have been graced with such a charming baby? Of course, reflection may spoil the innocence of such pleasure; but in the innocence it was there.

Evaluative Nature

The evaluative nature of feelings is its core aspect. Affect introduces value in a world of fact,[9] of factual perceptions and sensations. It creates preferences and behavioral priorities other than those based on habit strength. Pleasure is good and pain is bad, and so are their objects. But the problem is to get explicit about what that means. What are "good" and "bad" in this connection? They do not involve cognitive anticipation of what the objects may lead to. That is psychologically implausible: What might the good consequences of Italian ice cream or a Picasso painting be? Moreover, seeking the "good" of pleasure in its consequences would lead to infinite regress: What is good or bad about these consequence? Why care about death, if not because one does not like it? One could invoke evolutionary criteria—survival is good for the individual or the species; an ice cream's sugar is good for your energy—but that does not explain the experience.

Feelings Not Localized in Space?

Wundt said so, and Titchener agreed. One need not agree with either, though. As pointed out above, the good or the bad of many objects or events is often experienced as one of their properties. The loveliness of a face is in the face, or in part of it. In Wundt's terms, pleasure and pain are carried by sensations. In phenomenological terms, pleasure and pain are intentional. They have an object. They are about something, at least most of the time. Something is liked or disliked, something appears attractive or repulsive. It is the face that is lovely, or the event out there that is repulsive; one turns one's eyes away from it. Even physical pain is about something, namely, about one's body. Feelings are evanescent precisely because directing attention on them cuts the tie with the intentional object. Being about something other than itself is precisely feeling's most relevant aspect. "Feeling" that is focused on is therefore paradoxical, it is like the sound of one hand clapping.

The nature of the object of pleasure can vary. Objects of pleasure (and of pain) include objects in the normal sense: persons (among which oneself), or material objects. They include events: what someone does, or what befalls him or her, or oneself. They include activities: dancing can be wonderful, and so can solving a puzzle. They include momentary states. One can like the state one is in, one's body state, one's mood, or the outcome of one's actions. In fact, the object of pleasure may vary within one and the same encounter. As Duncker subtly made clear: When drinking wine, the pleasure may pertain to the wine, to the act of drinking, or to the sensations produced by that drinking the wine.[10]

Pointing beyond itself applies even to objectless moods. Moods may have no object,[11] but still are about one's momentary relationship with the world as a whole, or with oneself. Feeling light in the morning is not like feeling weight loss in a zero-gravity machine. It is like being free from gravity.

Are Pleasure and Pain "Feelings"?

The intentionality of feeling, its adherence to some object—a true object, a state of oneself, a state of the world, performance of an action—highlights a major question about pleasure and pain. *Are* they feelings? Are pleasure and pain felt as "inner" experiences that float around in the consciousness bowl? It may just be a myth to talk about feelings in this way. One may wonder: *Are* there experiences of pleasure or of pleasantness? Do they exist? Does one find such an experience when looking inward? When hearing music, or seeing a beautiful person, is there pleasure in the air, hovering about the sound or the face? Is there a little experiential gem that one cherishes in one's experience purse?

PHENOMENOLOGY OF PLEASURE EXPERIENCE

Pleasure usually is not a feeling, not "an experience of pleasure," not some felt inner state. Such experience only emerges in a self-directed mental attitude, in which attention is directed toward one's experience rather than to the emotional object.[12] When, as is more usual, attention is toward objects, experience is of a liked or pleasant object. It is a niceness gloss to whatever the pleasure is about. Even if the object gives rise to bodily reactions, the pleasure does not dissolve in the body feeling. Even there, added to the body feeling, is a niceness gloss. A similar description applies to unpleasantness: It first of all occurs as an experienced badness gloss.

I will restrict my analysis to pleasure. I also restrict it to pleasure as such, abstracted from the emotion that pleasure may be part of and its particular state of action readiness. The niceness gloss indeed in some sense is an unanalyzable *quale:* It is "like something" but cannot be reduced to a sensory property. Yet it does a number of things. First of all, it makes the object hold attention. It obtains a sort of glow. Recall the cartoons of new parents, looking through the glass of the hospital's nursery at the plastic boxes with twenty babies. Among those, one stands out. In the cartoons, it is drawn with one's nametag in front and with little sparkles all around. The baby in it shines. Then, in holding attention, it guides action. One might argue that it incites approach. Psychological theory indeed often does focus that connection.[13] But it cannot be essential in feeling pleasure. For one thing, there exists pleasure without approach, namely, when one is already there. There is pleasure during orgasm, and after; there is pleasure during a concert. For another thing, one approaches in uncertainty, curiosity and anger. Third, pleasure and approach can be decoupled, as Berridge showed.[14]

What the niceness gloss incites is to accept the object, activity, or state that carries the gloss. It is intrinsic in the kind of attention. It makes one treat the object as an object for having commerce with. The commerce may be just perceptual watching, feeling, or it may go beyond, toward interaction, in chatting, holding hands, pursuing a thought's implications, or repeating the act again and again. Acceptance and commerce form the core phenomena of pleasure. Likewise, unpleasantness does not accept its object, and signals its object as one not to have commerce with. These characterizations are found widely.[15] The content of these glosses indeed is accessible to introspection. In an experiment on pleasantness of fragrances, one of P. T. Young's subjects reported: "When I say 'pleasant,' it does not stand for anything more than 'I would smell it more if I could.'"[16] Pleasantness is the demand character of things-to-be-dwelt-with or interactions-to-be-continued-with. A liked number, one that is rated as "nice"—say, 3 or 7—is one that one attends to a fraction longer than the other numbers between 1 and 10, and with indulgence. It is selected more frequently when asked for a number under 10.[17] A pleasant event is one that one welcomes, approves of, and in the event, seeks to encounter again.

Experiencing pleasure or encountering pleasant objects has more implications. It represents a more or less stable state, unless it is adulterated by, for instance, the uncertainty about whether a wonderful promise will be fulfilled. In pleasure as such, one is and remains in a basin of attraction, moving about so as to enhance that stability, or awareness of it. Unpleasantness, by contrast, is inherently unstable. It calls out for change and alerts readiness to effect this. This, it would seem, is the major asymmetry between pleasure and pain that several investigators focus on.[18] Whether pleasure is a fully stable state, or includes striving for enhancement depends on what the pleasure is about: acceptability found and acceptance achieved, or promises of extensions. That, in turn, depends on the grounds for acceptance: satisfaction of some desire, intrinsic pleasantness, relief from unpleasantness, or whatever the kind of pleasure involved, and to which I will come.

Pleasure can also, and perhaps better, be described as a state of harmony. There is agreement between what one gets and what one does and between the various things that one can do, get, and want. Depending on the components, harmony can be calm or filled with tension; pleasures can be serene and they can be highly excited. But a main thing, in pleasure, is that there are several things that go together and fit together, and keep a dynamic balance: attention for the pleasant thing, and obedient receding to the background of the other things; or the acceptance of the thing as such and the expected acceptability of its implications.

The experience of pleasure fits the actions of accepting that it may induce. It fits them snugly and smoothly. Acceptance means taking in whatever comes from the object, sensation, or activity involved, and enhancing one's commerce with it. They belong to what are commonly called consummatory behaviors. I will call them *acceptance wriggles*, borrowing from Humphrey's treatment of consciousness and qualia.[19] They all unite the individual with its objects. All pleasure, I think, involves some sort of unification. There is unity between the object and oneself, unity between one's willingness for interaction and proximity, and one's actions to achieve and enhance it, and unity between the quality of that which is so pleasant, the nature of the object as perceived and the action as performed. Verbal expressions show traces of this. One relishes a smell, or the music, or one's fabulous achievement. One delights in it. Some languages, among which English, French and Dutch, indeed use the same word for one's attitude toward preferred foods and drinks, and for one's attitude toward the person whom one prefers to share bed, bread, and prayers with. One loves them all. Equivalently, displeasure tends to show in rejection wriggles and to separate, and one hates one's enemies and mildewed bread.

The unification in pleasure happens almost literally, because of the role of the acceptance wriggles. One feels, looks, smells, absorbs. But the most central aspect of accepting is that the object—the object proper, the experience, the knowledge, the action—is made part of oneself. It is assimilated. The experience of pleasure, as feeling in the strict sense or as pleasant perception, is an expansive one. One stretches out. This has another side. In doing so, one expands what is within one's domain of accepted things, just as in general assimilation and expansion go hand in hand.[20] The expansion is sometimes present in bodily action, when pleasure goes together with deep breathing and enhanced activation.

These various aspects combine in the essential aspect of pleasure experience: one's sense of unimpeded functioning. It is what served Aristotle for his definition of pleasure. Things go as they should go; things have come together. One may object to Aristotle's definition because it defines pleasure by way of what it is not: not impeded. Spinoza's definitions improve on this: "Pleasure is man's transition from a less state of perfection to a greater" and "Pain is man's transition from a greater state of perfection to a lesser."[21] *Perfection*, here, has a fairly down-to-earth meaning. It refers to the completeness with which the person manages to realize his or her desires and thus, according to Spinoza, manages to persist in his (or her) being. The expansion in pleasure is part of it.

The evaluative nature of experiences of pleasure consists of those four things together: the glow, the salience of the object; perceived acceptability, and one's sense of communion with the object; readiness to continue interaction; and sense of stability, of unimpeded functioning, of expansion and increase in "perfection." They come together in the sense that interacting with the object or doing the activity is worth it. In view of these multiple facets, one may doubt that the feeling of pleasure indeed can be considered a *quale*. It has more of a pointer or gateway to further elucidations as just sketched, or to the actions these elucidations elucidate.

In full human experience of pleasure and pain, these elucidations are actually retrieved. But in most pleasure experiences one is given over to relish the object or event. One just treats it as acceptable, as to be interacted with, being interacted with, and seeking it out for interaction. The converse holds for pain experience. Experience is merely perceptual, without awareness topping it.[22] It serves as a signal for acceptance and rejection wriggles. In this sense, and for these reasons, experience of pleasure and pain may and must be supposed to exist in animals.

But pleasure is not only niceness or pleasantness of objects, acts, and so forth. It is also a state of oneself; that is, it can be, when attention switches from the world to oneself. One's state is accepted as one to stay in. It has its own stability and harmony; they are the carriers of the unimpeded functioning.

ACCEPTANCE WRIGGLES

Acceptance wriggles deserve a few sentences; they have to be discussed separately because they do not form part of the phenomenology of pleasure experience but of the actions of enjoyment. They importantly contribute to the experience, however, because they generate the experience. As Bradley and colleagues[23] put it, pleasure "facilitates perceptual processing," and it does so in varied ways. Devoting attention is one, which corresponds with perceptual salience, and which pleasure shares with unpleasantness.[24] But prolonging interaction is another. More interesting is the large variety of more specific wriggles. In tasting with delight, your tongue curves around the morsel and lets the drink caress it. Berridge extensively describes the gustatory reactions to pleasant tastes in mice that allow one to investigate liking in those animals, separate from their desire to obtain the food: eyes sparkle and whiskers tremble. Babies also show distinct gusto-facial actions; even anencephalic infants show them.[25] A large portion of erotic interaction consists of wriggles that aim at enhancing visual, tactual, proprioceptive, and cognitive stimulus intake. In fact, acts of acceptance are highly specific for the kind of pleasurable thing. The way one accepts, by sniffing, looking, embracing, investigating eagerly and lovingly, doing it repeatedly, turning it over and over in one's mind, match the corresponding sensory, cognitive, motor, and emotional feels. And these acts of acceptance range widely in scope, duration, and kind. They are sometimes of an investigating, focusing kind, as when following music note by note and phrase by phrase. Sometimes they are not "wriggles" at all but consist of motionless receptiveness that is as open as possible for holistic impressions, or for letting the presences stream in, or shutting distracting presences out, as when closing one's eyes while listening. *Savoring* has already been mentioned as a collective term for what those wriggles aim at: enhancing, deepening pleasurable awareness.[26]

Each acceptance wriggle brings its own information that carries its niceness gloss. It renders each pleasure different from each other one. It does so in particular because the various wriggles differ in interpersonal, relational implications: in fullness of engagement, in proximity, in responses other than those of pleasure only that they evoke. Nibbling, eating, kissing, glancing, glancing into eyes, all fit in different program contexts and enable different further feelings and actions. They make pleasure develop into different pleasurable emotions: different relation-establishing forms of action readiness and action. And they change pleasure experience profoundly. They transform pleasure experience into a pleasant state when the wriggles blend with the skilled action in which one is immersed in performing.

PLEASURE WITHOUT PLEASANT FEELING

As I said, in perceiving the glow of one's baby, pleasure is not properly speaking a conscious experience. When interacting rather than observing with pleasure, the pleasure dissolves into the perceived valence of sensations, objects, activities, and states. But even that valence is quite often not an object of awareness. Often, one has other things to do than notice one's likings. One has to interact, and just willingly, and with engagement, enters

the interaction. One willingly continues in it. Pleasure is only *felt* as pleasure after having withdrawn from full engagement. Hence the old paradox:
One can never be truly happy and know it until afterwards. Still, one was
truly happy: One would have prolonged the interaction if one could have
done so, and one would gladly do it again.

Pleasure without a distinct experience of pleasure is not a rare occurrence. It is usual when engaged with eagerness in interactions and with eagerness prolonging them. I am referring to what Csikszentmihalyi called
"optimal experiences" and experiences of *flow*.[27] A scientist may work tire-
lessly through the night trying to solve a problem and return to it after a
brief sleep. Mountain climbers may climb under grave risks and do so under feelings of effort, fatigue, and full awareness of the dangers. Pleasure
usually is not experienced until the work is finished, and one looks back on
it, and sees that it is good; or after some difficulty has been resolved. The
work itself does not appear to be undertaken and pursued for the sake of
that pleasure.[28] When asked why it is performed and why one returns to it,
the answer is that one likes it; not that one does it for the final gains. Interestingly, final success and public acclaim function more as confirmation of the
value of what one has done, than as the reward for which it all was done.

Such work indeed answers most of the criteria for "pleasure." The
chores are accepted. One remains at it, and one returns to it. It involved unimpeded functioning, for which *flow* indeed is the best summary term. *Optimal experience* means that one is immersed in the work and that one uses
one's resources to the full. It also means that doing what one does generates
the sense of being at, or of going towards, one's destination.

Similar constellations are present in other contexts. Take the satisfactions
of friendship under harsh circumstances, such as under conditions of war
or political resistance. Retrospectively, such episodes of intense collaboration and mutual attunements fill one with pleasure. At the time, they did
not; but they filled the participants with purpose, and they filled their lives.
And that fullness, too, was lived rather than experienced, and only became
salient post hoc, in the emptiness that befell so many soldiers and resistance
fighters after the fighting was over.

Sometimes, such events are deemed pleasurable—one calls them that after the fact, one returns to them, one dwells on them while conscious feeling, at the time, was that of pain. It may happen during highly valued
events of different sorts. A piece of music or a painting may be felt as un-
bearably beautiful; it hurts. Being in love often has the same structure. It is
an agony, it cuts one's breath. Yet, one would not want to miss it for anything, and yearns for the experience when it is over. In all these events, there
is full engagement, of the stability and harmony described earlier, but at
high levels of tension, and that possess the core elements of pleasure: acceptance, remaining there, and willingness to return to the constellation.

THE PLEASURE PROCESS

The previous examples suggest that there exists nonconscious pleasure. Said more precisely: that there exist nonconscious pleasure states and processes that are the same as the processes leading to conscious pleasure: engagement with objects or events, acceptance of them, continued commerce with them, returning to them if occasions are found, and acceptance wriggles if events are conducive to them. I call it a pleasure process; Murphy[29] calls it feeling without thinking; Berridge[30] calls it *core liking*.

The pleasure process is demonstrated in experiments in which stimuli that usually, when of sufficient strength, are evaluated positively are shown outside awareness and then still produce positive effects.

The experiments used a backward masking procedure. In that procedure, a visual stimulus is presented for a very brief time, and is followed by another, meaningless stimulus, such as an abstract drawing or a Chinese ideograph, that blocks awareness of the first stimulus. In the experiments concerned, the first stimulus is one that is generally liked: a drawing rendered familiar by repeated exposure,[31] or the picture of a smiling face. Experimental subjects generally report not to have perceived anything. However, if asked to rate the pleasantness of the masking stimulus, it is rated as more pleasant than when a neutral or unpleasant stimulus had been exposed as the first stimulus.[32] Such an effect is obtained after exposure times as short as 20 msec. In an experiment by Berridge and Winkielman, the effect was behavioral.[33] After the stimulus exposure, experimental participants could drink fruit juice from a pitcher standing nearby. Thirsty participants drank more when the masked, unseen stimulus had been a smiling face than when it had been an angry face, and while neither had been consciously perceived. Evidently, the pleasantness of the masked stimulus has been recorded unconsciously; and evidently, a resulting pleasure-related state or process had been capable of influencing a subsequent conscious hedonic impression or activity of acceptance. Interestingly, the process may "bind" to any relevant input that comes on rapidly. When exposure duration of the first stimulus is longer so that it gets to awareness, no such binding occurs; the process binds to its proper stimulus.[34]

The pleasure process thus involves much more than acceptance and continued interaction. It extends to a global attunement of the organism to facilitate actions and propensities that suit situational demand characteristics. First, it invests the eliciting stimulus or activity with incentive power to obtain further interaction.[35] It does so with distant pleasant stimuli like smells and sights; they induce approach. Pain likewise stirs actions that weaken interaction.[36] Second, and notably when pleasure occurs unexpectedly, it activates learning mechanisms that produce learning of place preferences—preference for locations where pleasure had emerged in the past—and other forms of evaluative conditioning.[37] This learning effect has been emphasized by Schroeder[38] in his analysis of what makes rewards to be reinforcements. Third, the process attenuates discomfort, as when a baby stops crying when stroked or given a few drops of sweetened water.[39] Rate of respiration tends to decrease and its time curves tend to assume a less angular form.[40] The pleasure process appears to entail a generally more relaxed form of functioning control.

Research by Isen[41] shows that pleasant mood has extensive cognitive and social effects. It enhances openness to social as well as nonsocial information, augments responsiveness and flexibility of response to such information, and augments prosocial feeling and behavior. Pleasure also tends to facilitate a receptive and holistic, rather than active, analytical mode of attention, although the evidence is mixed.[42] There is evidence for threshold decrease for all sensory, bodily, and mental actions geared to maintaining or extending interactions, which includes the mentioned increase in attention[43] and greater access to pleasant memories. Positive emotions like joy entail expanding one's dealings with the environment.[44]

Of course, pleasure also instigates approach, even if it is not to be identified with approach readiness. It often holds for pleasant smells and sights; it holds in particular for pleasure anticipations that smelling, seeing, and hearing particular objects may evoke.

Presumably, aroused pleasure processes decay over time, unless maintained by information processing or instigated striving. Conscious experience of pleasure may well slow down decay; it is a form of rehearsal. Spontaneous decay is reflected in the decay of automatic affective priming, that is, of suboptimal pleasant primes rendering subsequent neutral stimuli more pleasant. Such effects peak at 150 msec after stimulus termination, and have faded after some 300 to 400 msec.[45]

Pleasure and pain processes arise largely automatically and ubiquitously when the relevant events are perceived.[46] Almost any stimulus is rated as pleasant or unpleasant, as Osgood, Suci, and Tannenbaum (1957) showed, and Russell (2003) confirmed in the field of the emotion lexicon.[47] Affective effects emerge before the stimulus is consciously identified, although nonconscious cognitive identification processes do precede them.[48] Stimulus processing differentiates between pleasant and unpleasant stimuli at a very early stage; evoked brain response potentials at 120 msec after stimulus presentation tend to be larger for unpleasant than for pleasant stimuli.[49]

Evidence for a pleasure process suggests dedicated neural and neurohumoral processes. The major elements of these latter are known; Berridge[50] provided a full account. The nucleus accumbens shell, at the base of the frontal lobe, appears to play a core role. Microinjections of morphine enhanced liking for pleasant taste, and a bittersweet taste was treated by the experimental animals like a sweet one; microinjections of dopamine there enhanced bar-pressing for self-stimulation.[51] The ventral pallidum in the basal ganglia, and the parabrachial nucleus in the pons, appear also involved. Microinjections of benzodiazepine there also enhance taste liking reactions. Elements of the pleasure circuit thus extend from fore- to hindbrain. Opiates—endorphins—and, surprisingly, benzodiazepines ensure their operation. Blocking opioids causes at least some sensory pleasures to disappear. Both opioids and benzodiazepines potently enhance liking-reactions to tastes in rats. Dopamine may be involved[52] but may have more to do with enhancing incentive motivation than with enhancing pleasure processes as such.[53]

Feeling pleasure can be considered the conscious read-out of the nonconscious pleasure process. It engages neural circuits that differ from those of the pleasure process. Most frequently mentioned is the perigenual anterior cingulate cortex, which appears relevant also for other kinds of conscious emotional experience.[54]

Interestingly, the spatial extent of circuits causally involved in pleasure, shows that even lowest hindbrain parts can influence liking. Parts (or layers) of that circuit appear sufficient to respond with part of the liking responses. This suggests that pleasure responses can occur without information about what initiated it. Neurally, free-floating pleasure is plausible.[55]

Whether these circuits and neurohumors play a role in sensory pleasures only, or in all kinds of pleasure, remains to be investigated. Scattered evidence suggests that the circuits indicated may well form a final common pathway.

KINDS OF PLEASURE

Why does pleasure exist? Examining the kinds of things that evoke pleasure can shed light on its functional role. It may also shed light on the processes whereby it is aroused: different pleasures may come about in different ways.

One can distinguish pleasures of several kinds. Tiger[56] enumerates *physiopleasures* (sensory pleasures), *sociopleasures* (social pleasures), *psychopleasures* (pleasures in benefiting others) and *ideopleasures* (pleasures of thought). Rozin[57] distinguishes pleasures of sense, aesthetic pleasures, and pleasures of mastery, and Kubovy[58] between pleasures of the body and pleasures of the mind. I find the following distinction useful (see Table 3.1).

Sensory Pleasures

Certain sensory stimuli are intrinsically pleasant, at least at moderate intensities; that is, they are pleasant without indicating other favorable events to

TABLE 3.1
Kinds of Pleasure

Sensory pleasures

Nonsensory likings

Pleasures of gain and relief

Achievement and mastery pleasures

Activity pleasures

Social pleasures

Aesthetic pleasures

---

come, and while their pleasantness does not stem from association with other pleasant things. Sweet substances are innately liked in a number of animal species, from birth onwards, and not only when alleviating hunger. Drops of sucrose solution quiet a crying newborn baby.[59] Gentle caresses also quiet babies, lead to obtaining more of them, and make them smile. Many smells, and tastes other than sweet ones, are intrinsically liked, and several of them innately so, although many others are learned, witness the considerable cultural differences in preferences.[60] There also are likings for smells (and perhaps tastes) that have no obvious relationship to feeding, such as the smell of roses and other flowers. The sensory pleasures of course include sexual stimuli: smells, touches, visual stimuli like feathers in birds, body shapes, and perceived motor displays such as courting displays.

Not only simple sensory stimuli are intrinsically liked. Courting displays are complex patterns in time; animals can be quite fickle about which patterns attract or excite them, and which do not.[61] Familiar stimuli, too, tend to be intrinsically liked, whereas familiarity is not properly a stimulus attribute.

Most sensory pleasures come from objects that can be considered good for reproduction or survival. Sweetness comes from sugar, which provides energy; pleasantly bright colors include those coming from ripe fruits; potential sexual partners smell and look nice probably because that helps reproduction. Harmless familiar stimuli are at the same time safety signals;[62] and so on. Thus, long lists of "primary reinforcers" can be established, as did Rolls with a list that ranges from "salt taste" over "colorful flowers" to nonsensory reinforcers like "solving an intellectual problem."[63]

One may assume that, for the innately pleasant (and unpleasant) stimuli there are built-in sensitivities, some sort of templates, say, that recognize them and link them to the hedonic processes. Likes and dislikes built by conditioning presumably also have created such sensitivities. Evidently, the 20-msec presentation times in the backward masking experiments indicate that the sensitivities can respond to very brief and, by necessity, fragmentary information.

However, the structure and operation of these assumed sensitivities is not always simple, and perhaps never. First, and as already mentioned, the various stimuli lead to pleasure only at medium stimulus intensity ranges. Their pleasantness/intensity relationship shows the well-known Wundt curve: Stimuli of moderate intensity are liked, and those too weak and too intense are not.[64] Then, sensory pleasures adapt upon continuous stimulation and upon repetition, in correspondence with the Law of Change. The stimuli may obtain neutral valence, and may even become aversive; as far as I know, this applies to all sensory pleasures.

Further, pleasantness of many intrinsically pleasant stimuli depends on the individual's state of deprivation or satisfaction with respect to the stimulus object concerned.[65] Cabanac called this *alliesthesia*.[66] Foods that are liked when the animal is hungry become neutral when it is satiated; this is mirrored by the responsiveness of certain neurons in the ventromedial frontal cortex of a hungry animal, but not when it is satiated.[67] Ambient warmth is pleasant when skin temperature is low, and unpleasant when it is high. Specific deprivations, such as sodium shortage, may lead to specific appetites. Liking for slightly salted food might always reflect some degree of need for salt. Whether sexual stimuli elicit interest, and thus presumably are liked varies with momentary sexual responsiveness. Female animals outside their receptive periods are indifferent to them; so are males that were castrated before puberty; so are most young animals and human children. Interestingly, the stimuli that manifest alliesthesia appear to be those that also call complex action programs—eating, sexual pursuit and interaction, temperature regulation—that also terminate in pleasure: the satisfaction of a full stomach, stretching before the fireplace, orgasm. Alliesthesia thus leads to the consideration: Do we act upon those stimuli because we like them, or do we like them because they instigate action? There is no evidence that this holds generally, but the line of thought merits following up.

Nonsensory Likings

Stimuli providing sensory pleasures form only a fraction of pleasant events. Not all pleasures come from intrinsically pleasurable stimuli, nor do they all come from stimuli. Stimuli can be pleasant by association with pleasures from other sources: by evaluative conditioning, for instance, or because they satisfied desires in the past, or earlier took part in pleasant interactions or hold promise to do so in the future. Think of attractive faces, of people one likes, the sound of the bell that announces dinner, or receiving an invitation to a party. The categories includes books one liked, and activities that give joy or gave joy. One likes places that one felt well before—place preferences were already mentioned, but this includes liking one's home and friends. All those likings (as well as parallel dislikes) reflect some joint effect of the encounters in which they originated or of the out-comes they were connected to by several intervening steps; the many steps are illustrated by the fact that one can like or dislike certain words. The lik-ings thus represent what Kahneman (1999) called *remembered utility*.[68] But they of course shift the problem of understanding them to understanding the sources of that "utility," the unconditioned stimuli, the sources of why the interactions were pleasant, or the invitation, or the book. That is, in un-derstanding nonsensory likings one is referred to other kinds of pleasure.

Pleasures of Gain and Relief

Playing a preferred game often partakes in the pleasures of gain. There are pleasures caused by increase in pleasantness or decrease in pain. They ex-emplify the Law of Change, or the Law of Comparative Feeling, from chap-ter 1. They include relief pleasures.[69] Relief can be a true source for pleasure, and not merely a decrease in pain. When unexpected, or previously uncer-tain about it, it can lead to positive emotions like joy.

The intriguing thing, of course, again is that these changes are not stim-uli. Understanding their affective impact calls for different explanations than sensory pleasures; drive reduction was one such explanatory attempt. Decrease of discomfort has a deep and general significance. It was, one will remember, the basic mechanism for aesthetic pleasure in Berlyne's theory of the arousal jag,[70] and perhaps it explains the pleasures derived from aversive experiences, as in roller coasters and parachute jumping, and per-haps even those gained from eating Mexican peppers. They may all, as Rozin (1999) suggests, result from the gain over threat or threat of loss.[71]

The affective impact of gain and relief, as well as loss, differs from that of the value of what is gained, regained, and lost as such. Degree of pleasure does not as a rule correspond to that value, but to the degree of surpassing one's standard of comparison—that what one had before in this case. There also is asymmetry between the pleasures of gain and the pains of loss. Peo-ple are loss aversive: the function relating pain of loss to magnitude of loss is steeper than the one relating pleasure of gain and amount gained.[72]

Pleasures of comparison include the pleasures of being or having more than someone else, and of *Schadenfreude* or *malign joy*.[73] They have their painful counterparts in the pains of loss, particularly sadness and grief, as well as in disappointment, regret and envy, that all are based on reference to what could have been.[74] How to account for all this? I return to it later.

Achievement and Mastery Pleasures

Progress toward a major goal is widely recognized as one of the major sources of pleasure: acquiring a longed-for possession, being united with one's lover, passing one's degree, solving a puzzle. In several emotion theories, it is pleasure's main source.[75] More generally (since the notion of *goal* suggests prior striving), a main source of pleasure is progress toward satisfaction of a concern, obtaining such satisfaction, or returning to it. Pleasures of achievement again underline that not all pleasure comes from meeting or attaining pleasant stimuli. Progress and achievements are to be described in terms of matches between events and concerns.

Achievement includes mastery pleasures, the pleasures of obtaining and exerting a skill. The pleasures of mastery do not fully depend on the value of the skill. Amateur sport yields achievement pleasures, even when the goals set for the level of skill and exertion are private, and trivial by external standards. Rough-and-tumble play forms an exquisite instance. It is almost universal among young mammals, at least among the young males of the species.[76] What is so nice about engaging in it? It may be evolutionarily useful, but that is not what drives the children. What is so nice to them, I think, is the game of challenges and meeting challenges. Its pleasure comes from a continuous game with small achievements, as Oatley and Jenkins[77] so nicely describe it: kicking well, tricking well, getting the better of the other, being able to fail gracefully, and believing that your turn will come. Performing actions when one cannot take successful performance for granted represents a challenge, responding to a challenge with chance of success is a pleasure, and successful completion a further one. This applies to all mastery pleasures, including self-set mastery goals. A boring job such as constructing a fence can be turned into fun when one sets the goal to have all nails straight and neat and to have the job completed before sunset.

Mastery is often less tangible. There are cognitive challenges and their satisfaction. "Novelty" can be a challenge rather than a threat and a challenge that can be mastered in cognitive assimilation. It is a threat when one feels it cannot be mastered, a pleasure when one expects one can, and a pleasure when one has.

Activity Pleasures

Pleasure from progress toward a goal depends on the importance of that goal, but only to some degree. The activity of goal pursuit and of exerting one's skills as such appear to produce some satisfaction, in particular if in the activity some obstacle had to be overcome. Pleasures of goal pursuit as such, and of exerting skills, are exemplars of what Charlotte Bühler[78] has labeled *Funktionslust*, function pleasure, pleasure in just doing. Infants move their fingers, and they do it attentively, over and over again. They put blocks on blocks, throw them over, and repeat this. Much adult action, too, gives pleasure for its own sake, irrespective of further benefits like increase in self-esteem. Its epitome, of course, is the satisfaction of work in which one is immersed; it leads to optimal experience. The pleasure is primarily in the doing, notably when the doing goes superbly smoothly: when the thoughts come by themselves while writing, fingers by themselves go about their skilled ways, in pianists and surgeons, one's foot goes exactly at the place where the soccer ball comes down and effortlessly sends it off in the right direction with the right speed. They are instances of experiences of flow; the examples all are from the work of Csikszentmihalyi, referred to earlier.[79]

Unencumbered activity does not invariably produce pleasure. One walks, eats, and breathes with no affect. One does so, though, when there is or was some uncertainty about smooth progress. Pleasure results when reaching the goal or completing one's actions is not entirely to be taken for granted. Unhampered breathing does yield pleasure when nose or throat have cleared after a cold. Walking does become a pleasure when illness had prevented one's walking for some time. But just walking, too, can become a pleasure when one has set one's mind to it. Mindfulness can render any action not entirely self-evident. In the actions that produce flow this cannot be otherwise: One works at the limit of one's abilities.

A simple instance of this constellation is offered by dancing. You dance, you dance well, you have a wonderful evening. Dancing well here means performing well and with precision the movements that you wanted to perform. It requires constant control and, at its best, constant control that manages itself, that flows. The same goes for singing, when it succeeds, if only a little. You come home happy from your choir's exercise. You did it with concentration and abandonment, at the fringe of your ability. To remain pleasurable, the activities must remain at that fringe. One arranges little contests with oneself, one seeks for a difficult note to be sung purely. True enough, all these pleasures no doubt also feed on the erotic, social, and narcissistic aspects of the dancing and the singing. But they do not live by it. Doing them with reasonable success in the first place represents *Funktionslust*.

Any activity, then, appears a source of pleasure if exercising it is not self-evident. Strongest evidence that this is so comes from Premack's work for his theory of reinforcement.[80] Premack has shown that exerting a capability for any action is reinforcing when such exertion is not a matter of course. When, in an experiment, opportunity for drinking is made to depend on prior running, drinking reinforces running. When opportunity to run is made to depend on prior drinking, running reinforces drinking.

Spontaneous actions also appear to be undertaken for the sake of the pleasure they give. Rats, mice, and hamsters periodically engage in activity bouts, as evident in their running in activity wheels. Such spontaneous activity is modulated by factors such as hunger and, in female animals, the estrous cycle.[81] Independently of that, however, it shows its own circadian cycle. The final explanation appears to be that the animals do it for fun.[82] It does not strike as different from what makes a few-weeks-old baby to extend its arms and move about in its crib.

Activity pleasures make the activities intrinsically motivating. One need not be sentimental about these pleasures, though. They also include exerting violence. Boys' Saturday Night Fever, in the Middle Ages, consisted in going out with a gang of friends to a neighboring village, fight with the boys there, and rape the girls.[83]

Social Pleasures

Quite diverse forms of social interaction produce pleasure, and, again, not primarily for the secondary profits they may yield. The pleasures of being together with people one loves or is familiar with, and that one receives warmth or affection from, appear as basic and elementary as those of the senses.[84] They include the pleasures of emotional exchange, emotional proximity, grooming, mentally or physically huddling together as sparrows on a telephone wire. Animals of various species seek each others' company, and indulge in interacting; so do humans. The pleasures extend to those deriving from close attachment, from intimacy with a particular individual. Being dependent on that individual, being the target of its nurturance, forms a further pleasure; it is singled out in the Japanese notion of *amae*.[85] The elementary social pleasures include those at the other extreme end of relationships: exerting power over others and seeing them at one's feet. That pleasure, too, appears elementary, not only due to material or other gains. Finally, there are the pervasive pleasure of just watching others, and the satisfactions that generate the willingness to view the fates and adventures of indifferent people in television serials, for hours at a stretch, as well as the eagerness to listen to accounts of the emotions of others in social emotion sharing.[86]

This is a whole list of pleasures. They are not sensory pleasures, nor precisely pleasures of achievement or action. They are pleasures of interaction: of complex plays of give and take, do and receive, of efforts to relate or modify relationships.

Aesthetic Pleasures

Aesthetic pleasures are distinguished from other pleasures by both Kubovy[87] and Rozin.[88] In Indian philosophy, they form the emotion category of *rasa*,[89] that is treated as fully separate from the emotions of normal interaction. The distinction is made for good reason. Aesthetic pleasures have been defined as "disinterested pleasures." They result from perceiving objects or events in which one has no personal stake, that provide no further gain, and that may involve few pleasant sensory sensations.

They have further puzzling aspects. Some aesthetic pleasures do stand in close relation to biologically based preferences. Certain female forms impress as beautiful and give great pleasure, to many men and to many women.[90] Female beauty has sufficiently general appeal to have our parks, monuments, and advertisements filled with it, and to lead to producing curved objects such as iMac computers. But the scope of biological factors remains unclear. Liking for bright colors related to that for ripe fruits? Music to mating and warning calls? Who knows. But of course aesthetic emotions mainly come from much more complex patterns, and their appeal from other sources.[91]

Another puzzling aspect is the decisive role of the perceiver's attitude towards the objects for the emergence of aesthetic pleasure. On one side, all aesthetic objects may fail to evoke pleasure, in different subjects as well as in any individual subjects. What moves you on Monday may leave you cold on Tuesday, even when you know that the object "is" beautiful, and that it may delight you on Wednesday. On another side, every object can become an object of aesthetic pleasure under the appropriate perceptual attitude. La Vecchia in Giorgone's painting is beautiful, and so is Mad Babbe, the old hag in a Jeroen Bosch painting. The role of attitude is clear by aesthetic pleasure being favored by conditions that block engaging in interaction. Footlights are interposed between spectators and spectacles, paintings are put in frames, and books are labeled "fiction." Aesthetic objects are presented within rather clearly defined "aesthetic" frames.[92] "Aesthetic distance" is a major concept from aesthetic theory, and a necessary presupposition for experiencing the "sublime," to which I will come. So is "detachment".[93] Few people would experience pleasure when meeting La Vecchia on the street. In film and the theater, aesthetic emotions are witness emotions, not participant emotions.[94] Conversely, a detached attitude that creates aesthetic distance can turn any object into a spender of pleasure. The frame around La Vecchia contributes to the picture's beauty and, in fact, a frame around any ordinary object turns it into an object of beauty. Ordinary objects obtain aesthetic appeal in still life paintings; in photography; in pop art; and, if you have an eye for it, in objects found on the beach. Ordinary objects, but most notably human beings, can move to tears when suddenly viewed as individual things revealing a mode of existence.[95] Analysis of aesthetic distance and detachment may bring understanding the puzzles of aesthetic pleasure closer.

EXPLAINING PLEASURES

The pleasures of achievement and mastery arise when what is being undertaken is, or has been, going well. Progress and outcomes correspond to goals set, or surpass them, and to obtaining or regaining concern satisfaction. A similar formulation applies to the activity pleasures. Exerting skill goes smoothly, and perhaps a trifle better than before. Pleasures of gain and relief are close: things go better and correspond to wishes, or threat was overcome. One can generalize: These pleasures result when a competence functions well. *Competence* will be my term for a behavior system or skill for which there is a criterion for functioning well: the goal, the mastery, the proper or perfect execution and completion of the action, achieved match between one's concerns and the state of the world, between gains and standards of comparison. It is in full accordance with Aristotle's interpretation: All these pleasures results from unimpeded functioning.

The mentioned pleasures can thus be subsumed under one common conception. They are responses that signal that an individual's competences are functioning well. Such signals go off when functioning well has not been routine, or was not expected. This can itself be generalized. Pleasure is the positive outcome of constantly monitoring one's functioning, and competences are doing what they are for. It results from such monitoring when there is or was good reason for not taking that functioning for granted. Pain of course fits this generalization: Pain is such monitoring's failure signal. This conception is hardly novel. Carver and Scheier[97] proposed that pleasure results when progress towards a goal is faster than expected, and pain when it is slower. Pribram[98] proposed that feelings are monitors, monitors of adequate functioning. Scherer gave a similar formulation for feelings generally.[99] Schroeder recently brought out that pleasure thus is a representation. It represents a net increase, in his formulation a net increase in desire satisfaction.[100] I think its representational scope is larger: a net increase in functioning well.

Monitoring functioning can be expected to extend beyond monitoring progress, and to extend to detecting occasions for exerting one's competences. And indeed it does. As noticed before, sensory pleasures tend to come from objects that are the proper triggers of appetitive competences. Approaching and consuming food, noticing and assimilating novel stimuli, all start operating upon when recognizing fit objects. They start operating when there is reason to do so. There is a dynamic interplay between propensity for exerting the competences and sensitivity for their triggers. Recall the phenomenon of alliesthesia. Food looks and smells pleasant when one is hungry; strange things look interesting when one is not afraid of them. In addition, there is pleasure in completing competences. Food also tastes good, at least when one is hungry; recognizing a puzzling novel object is a pleasure; meeting one's beloved is a joy. Pleasure occurs at the front end as well at the rear end of competences.

This two-ended nature of what gives pleasure is very clear in the domain of sex. Human males take pleasure in watching women, particularly those experienced as pretty. In animals, sexual pheromones presumably smell nice, and attract. And sexual climax is also pleasant; it presumably also is in animals, since they seek to repeat the experience. One may well assume that the sight of women and the smell of pheromones were pleasant before a first sexual climax and thus were not learned from the terminal pleasures. The pleasures may well come from what the sensory experiences at the front and rear ends of the competences are for: starting and terminating them. One may not be attracted by what one likes, but like that what attracts; one may not like satisfactions, but like that what satisfies. These dynamics of liking may go beyond alliesthesia. They may one day be found to result from the interplay between the components of any competence.

Interestingly, in sex, not only starting and terminal conditions give pleasure. All intervening stimuli or activities on the path from start to terminus do. Flirting is pleasant; necking is pleasant; caresses are pleasant. Eyeplay is fun and foreplay is fun. All this suggests that what enables a function to operate generates pleasure, its smooth functioning itself generates pleasure, and reaching its terminal state generates pleasure. Monitoring functioning, one might say, operates as if foresight was involved. The anatomy of competences takes care of what foresight may not always be capable of ensuring.

Monitoring functioning is also easily applied to social pleasures. They arise from the many social competences that humans develop but that are solidly rooted in the human endowments. Humans like to talk, be together, seek one another, live together, because they have the abilities to do so, abilities for sensing and for doing. The abilities include skills to understand the actions and intentions of others. Tomasello convincingly argued that such ability, or its basis, is innate in humans and in other primates.[101] The pleasures accompany the starting points for these competences, as well as the outcomes of the performance they were meant for.

The affective value of novelty can be understood from the same perspective. Perceived stimuli engage processes of cognitive assimilation. They are (or are not) recognized, involving what old-time psychology called the *Höffding-step*: recognition results from matching an input to some memory trace.[102] It thus involves integration of information into one's knowledge reservoir. Feelings of familiarity result from successful assimilation, feelings of unfamiliarity from its failure, and novel stimuli offer a challenge to the process. In moderate novelty, the challenge can be met, and gives pleasure. More extreme novelty—no foothold for assimilation—results in failure and is disliked.[103]

Of course, the proposed conception also fits the pleasures of the mind. Pleasures of the mind, as defined by Kubovy,[104] are the epitome of functioning well. They are pleasures that result from a sequences of emotions, of which the overall hedonic outcome is pleasant. Kubovy gives the example of dining and drinking with good friends in a good restaurant; other examples include looking back at the friendships and interactions from difficult times, with their anxieties withstood and withstood together.

Pleasure and pain both also exist as moods. Morris[105] considered moods to be an index of one's current store of resources. They thus fit smoothly in the notion of monitoring the quality of overall functioning.

But not all sensory pleasures fit the interpretation of signaling functioning well. They cannot all in an obvious way be seen as indicating that. They cannot all be seen as satisfactions of desires or concerns. Schroeder[106] tries to show that they can. I do not think he is successful; his reasoning appears circular.[107] But to the extent that sensory pleasures form the entry points of competences of which other sensory pleasures are the termination points, and to the extent that both are controlled by alliesthesia, the distinction between sensory and other pleasures may be more apparent than real.

Aesthetic Pleasures Again.   Aesthetic pleasure forms a problem and a challenge for any theory of pleasure. I do not feel competent to approach the problem in general. But at least some aesthetic pleasures may fit the present explanatory viewpoint. Indeed, some extant theories of aesthetic appreciation come close to it.

Gaver and Mandler, and Meyer,[108] relate the pleasure taken in music to first challenging and then satisfying expectations, by a deviation from musical schemas: the expectancy-confirmation, or discrepancy-arousal-and-solution approach. Such a mechanism is probably involved. It cannot, however, be the whole thing, since it predicts boredom when the music becomes familiar. According to Kubovy,[109] Narmour's[110] analysis of melodic structures opens perspectives that may meet this objection. Arousal and tension may spring from effort needed in integrating deviations from universal (perhaps innate) schemas into the implications that those schemas evoke. Pleasure is aroused when those efforts succeed and deviation is resolved. One succeeds in finding unity-in-complexity.[111] Of course, music often requires integrative effort, even if it is familiar. Attention must remain focused upon a number of features simultaneously, as it would have to be to grasp the coherence in a Bach fugue.

This brings at least some aesthetic pleasures in the neighborhood of the pleasures of familiarity and curiosity. They result from cognitive operations that are challenged and then succeed. But the success is not only that of cognitive operations. The integrations in music are not just cognitive. They probably are more relational, in the subject–object relation sense. They may have more to do with assimilation of the music heard to one's motor schemas or motor imagination, which themselves are connected to emotional schemas, whereby music heard becomes a part of oneself.

To what extent this perspective is valid, and to what extent it may apply to other domains than music, I am unable to gauge. But perhaps it is and does. Most aesthetic pleasure derives from grasping meanings, from grasping the nature, scope, and existence of possible or actual life forms, and from one's actual or potential coherence with, or assimilation of, those life forms.

KINDS OF PLEASURES?

Functional considerations apart: do the different kinds of pleasure described all embody one and the same kind of pleasure? Is it justified to use the same word for all, or is this linguistic convention?

The question is an ancient one. Psychology has considered it at length; Dumas,[112] for instance, gave a full discussion. It also is a relevant question, because it really asks whether or not it is meaningful to compare pleasures, or to sum or average them over time, to determine someone's "happiness," and to compare the happiness of people or policies. What is there in common between smelling a rose and satisfying one's goals or concerns? There thus may be essentially different sorts of pleasure, and many authors indeed have held this view. Hutcheson,[113] an early economist, held that "intensity was the measure for lower affections, to be distinguished from dignity differentiating the higher ones."

Thus: can pleasure be regarded as a "common currency," as Cabanac and others argued,[114] by which the benefits from different sources can be compared? No, it cannot, said Hutcheson, among others. Yes, said Bentham,[115] when arguing that morality and the law should aim for the greatest pleasure in the greatest number of people. To an important extent, the discussion on the unity of all pleasure is as meaningful as that about whether a glass is half-full or half-empty. The outcome depends on what is being focused on. Each experience of pleasure is different because, as all conscious experience, is synthetic. It blends and integrates information sources. Pleasures always are pleasures about something or of something, and because of something—because of a concern or sensitivity, and wider implications. Solomon and Stone vigorously stressed this point.[116] They always point to acceptance wriggles that are particular to the nature of the thing involved: sniffing, cognitive integration, physical intimacy, to name a few, that each have extensive relational implications, as mentioned earlier.

But at the same time, all pleasures do have something in common, something functional: acceptance. The phenomenology of pleasure reflects this. However, phenomenology is not the only possible criterion. A different answer about the unity of pleasure can come from underlying process. Do all pleasure processes involve the same information processing and neuro-humoral provisions? The answer is not yet there, although Berridge[117] points to evidence that a positive answer is not unlikely.

Still, sensory pleasures and pleasures of functioning well, although similar and related, are different in some respect. Sensory pleasures can be conceptualized as due to fitting templates; pleasures of functioning well in general cannot. Intuitively, sensory pleasures impress as being the phylogenetically oldest ones; pleasures from monitoring functioning appear more complex. Rozin[118] indeed suggests that sensory pleasures could be "preadaptations" for the other pleasures: facilities that other useful outcomes came to make use of, just as development of speaking made use of the mouth that happened already to be there for eating. The pleasure mechanisms may have gained increased accessibility in phylogenetic evolution, and have developed from an input-selection provision into a monitor of proper functioning.

PLEASURE AND PAIN

Are pleasure and pain opposite poles of one bipolar continuum? Or are they different kinds? The first position was that of Wundt and Beebe-Center[119] and is now being elaborated by Russell.[120] The second was held by McDougall and by Ruckmick and currently by Cacioppo[122] and by Watson and Tellegen.[123] Pleasure and pain, in their view, each represent a unipolar dimension from hedonic neutrality to respectively maximal pleasure or pain.

One's position is in part a matter of focus: on the phenomenology of experience, or on the underlying process. Phenomenally, pleasure and pain are opposites: One cannot feel both at the same time with respect to the same object attribute, and the words are treated as opposites. Also, the actions they manifestly tend to incite are incompatible: acceptance and non-acceptance, approach and rejection or avoidance.

Yet, both can be experienced at the same time, even with regard to the same object. Use of unipolar rating scales provides convincing evidence. One can feel both pleasure and unpleasantness; some measure of pleasure does not necessarily entail zero unpleasantness. By consequence, the midpoint on a bipolar pleasantness–unpleasantness scale is ambiguous. It may mean no affect, and it may mean ambivalence. On unipolar scales, ambivalence is notable when specific emotion experiences are rated, rather than general feelings about some issue or object: nonzero scores are obtained on both the pleasure and the pain scales.[124] Behavior, too, can evidence simultaneous pleasure and pain: an infant monkey and a baby, when confronted with a novel object, look and then look away, and then look rapidly again, meanwhile clinging more solidly at their mother. Evidence favors the view that pleasure and pain can interact in various fashions: by reciprocal activation (activating one weakens the other), and by coactivation (both occur independently, as in ambivalence).[125] Reciprocal activation may be due primarily to the incompatibility of approach and avoidance just mentioned. Coactivation is probably most prominent at moderate ranges of both pleasure and pain; when one of them becomes extreme, their interplay tends to shift to reciprocal activation.[126]

Ambivalence may not be the most general designation of the result of coactivity. *Mixed feelings* is much better.[127] Pleasure and pain can interpenetrate deeply and generally. The *opponent process* theory of affect offers a rationale: Every pleasure enhances one's propensity for pain, and vice versa.[128] Their incompatibility is a cultural presupposition. Pain has often been considered the reverse side of pleasure, rather than its opposite. Some cultures and thinkers indeed see it differently. This was so in Plato's analyses,[129] it is in that of Solomon and Stone[130] and in Indian and Chinese philosophy. Experience of pleasure carries a sense of its fragility and limits. This is due to the many-sidedness of emotions. Emotions usually are not just good or bad, positive or negative. Solomon and Stone recently extensively discussed this issue.[131] It is meaningless to call anger a negative emotion and *Schadenfreude* a positive one. The distinction is often made in psychology and has even led to its weird branch called "positive psychology." It is confusing and untenable. Pleasure arises in emotions at many different points, as should have transpired in the preceding pages. It arises in appraisal of instigating events, in appraisal of the outcome of one's emotional action, in evaluating the significance of that emotion for one's moral standards and one's self-image. Arjuna, in the *Bhagavad Gita*, mourns the suffering that his victory will inflict.[132] In anger, someone's insult hurts, his arrogance hurts, one's anger disturbs one's balance, but at the same time it represents a delight and proud liberation, throwing an insult back is a triumph, and the opponent's hurt look yields peace of mind, although morality may mix it with disquiet. Is anger a negative emotion, near the negative pole of a bidimensional plot? Artifact!

Interpenetration of pleasure and pain is most prominent in emotions that derive their pleasure from concurrent pains. Ambivalence is not their proper designation at all. Those pleasures include those from pungent foods like chili peppers.[133] They also include the pleasures of suspense, of what Burke called *the sublime,* [134] and of the less sublime fascinations evoked by tales of murder and torture, and even by watching real horrid wholesale destruction.[135] The pleasures are enhanced by the shudders; they not just coexist with them. The same for the pleasures of self-sacrifice and other suffering induced by devotion, extreme effort, and outstanding performance. There, too, the pains do not diminish the pleasures but contribute to them. They move functioning to a higher plane, or engage higher order concerns, such as deference to divine authority or viewing oneself as fearless, the grandiose pride of humility. Difficulties faced are part of what constitutes certain pleasures of the mind, such as the finest hours of having been in great danger together. Where do the pleasures come from? Broadening and building one's competence in sharing and supporting them, I think. A similar thing applies to masochism. Masochistic pleasure does not mean that pain can on occasion be pleasant. It precisely means that the painfulness of pain can add to pleasure of achieving some other aim, such as that of submission or blind obedience, or of being accepted by the supreme loving agent. This interpenetration of pleasure and pain implies that their coactivation changes their experience. Nostalgia shows this perhaps most clearly. It is a true bittersweet emotion: pain because of pleasures past, or pleasure because of pleasures that have gone. The pleasure is not full; the pain not pungent.

These various phenomena indicate that two separate processes are involved. Reward and punishment appear to involve different pathways.[136] Separateness of processes is supported by the asymmetries between them, such as stability versus motivational imbalance, and the "positivity offset" and "negativity bias," described by Cacioppo and collaborators.[137] Weakly activating pleasant stimuli appear to be more pleasant than that equally weakly activating unpleasant stimuli are unpleasant (positivity offset); and with increasing activation, felt pain increases more steeply than does felt pleasure (negativity bias). Unpleasant stimuli and events generally incite stronger responses than pleasant ones;[138] for instance, losses are disliked more than equivalent gains are liked.[139]

NOTES

[1]e.g., Cacioppo, Larsen, Smith, & Berntson, 2004; Ortony, Clore, & Collins, 1988.
[2]The word is, of course, also used with entirely different meanings elsewhere in the literature. Here, it resembles the notion of "core affect" in the work of Russell (2003) but does not include their independent dimension of arousal.
[3]Titchener, 1908, Wundt, 1902; imageless thoughts were introduced by Bühler, 1908.
[4]Titchener, 1908.
[5]Ahles, Blanchard, & Leventhal, 1983.
[6]Arnold, 1960.
[7]"Light pressure" is how Nafe (1924) described pleasant feeling, in an effort to reduce it to body sensation.
[8]Wundt, 1902.
[9]The phrase forms the title of Köhler, 1948.
[10]Duncker, 1941.
[11]Frijda, 1993b.
[12]More about this in chapter 8.
[13]For instance, Cacioppo et al., 2004.
[14]Berridge, 1999.
[15]Kahneman, 1999, p. 4; Rozin, 1999, p. 112.
[16]P. T. Young 1927, quoted from Arnold, 1960.
[17]Milikowski & Elshout, 1995.
[18]e.g., Cacioppo et al., 2004.
[19]Humphrey, 1993.
[20]Piaget, 1936; Varela, Thompson, & Rosch, 1991.
[21]Spinoza (1677/1989, III, Definitions of the Emotions, 2 and 3). This follows Parkinson's translation, in the cited Spinoza edition p. 128. It should

be said that, to Spinoza, "pleasure" and "pain" are not experiences, or emotion components, but basic emotions. Parkinson used "pleasure" and "pain" to translate *laetitia* and *tristitia*, which others translate as *gladness* and *sadness*. In interpreting "perfection," I take Spinoza's *conatus* to refer not to biological survival but to retaining identity (see Frijda, 2000).

[22]Lambie & Marcel, 2002; Chapter 8.

[23]Bradley, Codispoti, Cuthbert, and Lang, 2001.

[24]Anderson & Phelps, 2001.

[25]Berridge, 2003; Steiner, Glaser, Hawilo, & Berridge, 2001.

[26]Frijda, 2005; Sundararajan, 2005.

[27]Csikszentmihalyi, 1990.

[28]see Piët, 1987, for accounts by mountain climbers and stuntmen.

[29]S. T. Murphy, 2000.

[30]Berridge, 2003.

[31]Zajonc, 1968.

[32]Murphy & Zajonc, 1993; Zajonc, 2004.

[33]Berridge & Winkielman, 2003.

[34]Clore, Storbeck, Robinson, & Centerbar, 2005; S. T. Murphy & Zajonc, 1993.

[35]Berridge, 1999, 2003.

[36]Bargh, 1997.

[37]Bayens, Eelen, & Van den Bergh, 1990; De Houwer, Baeyens, & Field, 2005; Levey & Martin, 1990; Shizgal, 1999.

[38]Schroeder, 2004.

[39]Blass & Shah, 1995.

[40]Boiten, Frijda, & Wientjes, 1994.

[41]Isen, 2004.

[42]Isen, 2004; Schwarz & Bless, 1991.

[43]e.g., Anderson & Phelps, 2001; Smith et al., 2006.

[44]Fredrickson & Branigan, 2005.

[45]affective priming: Fazio, 2001. Decay time: Hermans, De Houwer, & Eelen, 2001.

[46]Bargh, 1997.

[47]Osgood, Suci, & Tannenbaum, 1957; Russell, 2003.

[48]Storbeck, Robinson, & McCourt 2006.

[49]Smith et al., in press.

[50]Berridge, 2003.

[51]Hoebel et al., 1999.

[52]Hoebel et al., 1999; Shizgal, 1999.

[53]Berridge, 2003.

[54]Schroeder, 2004.

[55]Berridge, 2003.

[56]Tiger, L., 1992.

[57]Rozin, 1999.
[58]Kubovy, 1999.
[59]Blass & Shah, 1995.
[60]Rozin, Haidt, & McCauley, 2000.
[61]Goldschmidt, 1996.
[62]Zajonc, 2004.
[63]Rolls, 1999.
[64]Beebe-Center, 1932; Pfaffman, 1960; Wundt, 1902.
[65]Pfaffman, 1960; Rolls, 1999; Rozin, 1999.
[66]Cabanac, 1992.
[67]Rolls, 1999.
[68]Kahneman, 1999.
[69]Kubovy, 1999.
[70]Berlyne, 1960.
[71]Rozin, 1999.
[72]Kahneman, 1999; Kahneman & Tversky, 1979.
[73]See Ben-Ze'ev, 2000; Van Dijk et al., 2005.
[74]Kahneman & Tversky, 1982; Landman, 1993; Zeelenberg, van Dijk, Manstead, & van der Pligt, J., 1998.
[75]e.g., Carver & Scheier, 1990; Oatley, 1992; Stein & Trabasso, 1992.
[76]Panksepp, 1998.
[77]Oatley & Jenkins, 1996.
[78]C. Bühler,1931.
[79]Csikszentmihalyi, 1990.
[80]Premack, 1962.
[81]Bolles, 1975; Richter, 1927.
[82]I vaguely recall that Premack, too, finally came to that conclusion.
[83]Muchembled, 1989; Rossiaud, 1988.
[84]Harlow, 1958.
[85]Markus & Kitayama, 1991.
[86]Rimé, 2005.
[87]Kubovy, 1999.
[88]Rozin 1999.
[89]Shweder & Haidt, 2000.
[90]Etcoff, 1999.
[91]e.g. Kreitler & Kreitler, 1972.
[92]Goffman, E., 1974.
[93]Frijda, 2005; Sundararajan, 2005.
[94]Tan, 2000.
[95]Frijda, 2001.
[96]Spinoza, 1677/1989, III, "Definitions of the emotions".
[97]Carver & Scheier,1990.
[98]Pribram, 1970.

[99]Scherer, 2004.
[100]Schroeder, 2004.
[101]Tomasello, Carpenter, Call, Behne, & Moll, 2004.
[102]Höffding, 1893.
[103]Bornstein, 1989; Zajonc, 1968.
[104]Kubovy, 1999.
[105]W. N. Morris, 1999.
[106]Schroeder, 2004.
[107]I think the effort by Schroeder to view them as satisfied desires for precisely those pleasures appears to me unsuccessful.
[108]Gaver & Mandler, 1987; L. B. Meyer, 1956.
[109]Kubovy, 1999.
[110]Narmour, 1990.
[111]Kreitler & Kreitler, 1972.
[112]Dumas, 1933.
[113]Hutcheson, 1728/1972.
[114]Cabanac, 1992; Kahneman, 1999; Shizgal, 1999.
[115]Bentham, 1823/1970.
[116]Solomon & Stone, 2002.
[117]Berridge, 1999.
[118]Rozin 1999.
[119]Beebe-Center, 1932; Wundt, 1896.
[120]Russell, 2003.
[121]McDougall, 1908; Ruckmick, 1925.
[122]Cacioppo et al., 2004.
[123]D. Watson et al., 1999.
[124]J. T. Larsen, McGraw & Cacioppo, 2001; Schimmack, 2001.
[125]Cacioppo et al., 2004.
[126]Schimmack, 2001.
[127]Schimmack, 2001.
[128]Solomon, 1988.
[129]Numenmaa, 1997.
[130]Solomon & Stone, 2002.
[131]Solomon & Stone, 2002.
[132]Bhagavad Gita, (book 1).
[133]Rozin, 1999.
[134]Burke, 1757/1990.
[135]Rimé, Delfosse, & Corsini, 2005.
[136]Gray, 1994.
[137]Cacioppo et al., 2004.
[138]Taylor, 1991.
[139]Kahneman & Tversky, 1979.

4

Appraisal

APPRAISAL AS AN EMOTION COMPONENT

Emotions are aroused when some object is being appraised. Some event, action, or object is experienced as pleasant or unpleasant, or is treated as such. It is liked or disliked, accepted or rejected, and treated as carrying further meanings. It is for this reason that emotions have sometimes been described as judgments,[1] even the emotions of a mouse or cat. A mouse, in some sense, appraises a cat as dangerous, as it seeks to keep away from it.

This use of the term *appraisal* is uncontroversial (apart, perhaps, from the judgment comparison). Objects and events affect behavior and experience in ways that go beyond what hits the senses. Their appraisal forms part of emotion experience, and of what the words mean by which such experience is described, words like *dangerous, nasty,* and *lovely.* Appraisal, in this sense of the notion, does not have a causal relation to emotions as a whole, but a meaning relation.

Emotions can be distinct by how the events that elicit them are appraised. They may be seen as representing different "core relational themes"[2] or different "goal juncture contingencies".[3] Sadness typically consists of experiencing a personal loss, anger of experiencing offense or frustration, and fear of perceived serious threat.

These appraisals can also be described more flexibly: as a pattern formed from a small set of appraisal components. Each event theme or contingency can be dissolved into such a pattern. "Offense" is in fact an event appraised as unpleasant and as due to an agent who is to blame; "personal loss" is an event in which an object was appraised as valuable but now perceived as forever gone. Description by component patterns allows an indefinitely large number of different patterns. It is better able to pinpoint why a particular event has aroused that particular emotion: that the personal loss is personal, for instance, and that the loss is felt to be final. Both kinds of description differentiate emotions, though, and both provide insight in the structure of various emotions.[4]

Various component sets have been proposed, that show a high degree of overlap.[5] Table 4.1 gives an example. It shows the sort of components (dimensions, actually) that have indeed been shown to differentiate one emotion from another. Respondents' ratings of recollected emotion incidents, in terms of such components, corresponded to the emotion labels that they used for these recollections to a substantial degree. Discriminant analysis from appraisal ratings produced 45% correct predictions from among 8 emotions,[6] and 39% from among 29 emotions by Dutch subjects, 39% by Indonesian subjects, and 41% by Japanese subjects.[7]

The componential analysis of appraisals offers promise of a "structural emotion theory." Emotions might be represented by patterns of entries in a table in which emotion labels form the rows, and the appraisal components the columns; a sort of periodic table of emotions. Such tables are indeed presented in several studies.[8] Even Spinoza's analyses can be formalized in this

TABLE 4.1
Appraisal Dimensions

Intrinsic pleasantness/painfulness

Novelty, unexpectedness

Concern congruence/incongruence

Outcome probability/certainty

Coping ability

    Control potential

    Power potential

    Adjustment potential

Agency: other/self/circumstances

Compatibility with values, standards

Note. Based on Ellsworth & Scherer (2003).

manner.[9] The approach offers a tool for developing a standard representation of emotion experiences. It provides a basis for specifying the experiences that various emotion words refer to. It permits comparing different emotions: how they are similar and different. It allows systematic examination of individual and cultural differences[10] and shows substantial cross-cultural validity and usefulness.[11] It has also enabled showing that emotions that are distinguished in a given language (in this case, shame and guilt) are also distinguished in a culture that does not have distinct names for them.[12] Some interesting research seeks to examine the relative merits of particular schemes or component sets;[13] however, settling on a definitive set is not in sight.

This is in part due to a serious problem. When trying to account for additional emotion concepts or kinds of experiences, more components and finer distinctions appear needed. Added emotions ask for added components. For instance, awe involves appraisal of vastness of the object and one's felt inability to fully grasp that vastness.[14] Disappointment hinges on appraisal of thwarted expectation, which is a variant of the often-identified component of goal obstructiveness, but a rather specific one.[15] Pity implies appraising the fate and emotions of someone else, and pleasure in others' misfortunes appraisal of deservedness of such misfortune.[16] Understanding disgust in certain cultures requires notions of purity and impurity.[17] When examining emotions of African participants, one has to distinguish suprapersonal agency (by gods or magic), from agency by others, self, or circumstances,[18] and so forth. Ben-Ze'ev (2000) indeed talks about "the subtlety of emotions."[19] It is as yet uncertain whether appraisal patterns indeed in a satisfactory and parsimonious fashion can grasp the full domain of emotion distinctions over a wide range of languages.

Descriptive appraisal research, as it stands, shows other problems. Its empirical studies are largely based on recollected emotions. One does not know the extent to which the self-reports reflect actual experiences, or memory schemas and cultural scripts. They also suffer from scarcity of atypical or unreasonable instances: when asked to describe an instance of anger, few people will recall an anger that they considered foolish.[20] Also, analyses usually result in average response patterns for each emotion in a group of participants that do not allow to distinguish between necessary, contributory, or sufficient components or patterns.[21] Most of these problems recur in studies of emotion antecedents, and I will return to them later in this chapter.

The goal of a structural emotion theory may in fact be impossible to attain. For one thing, it is bound to remain open and unfinished, because the dependent variable in most of this enterprise, emotion words, is imprecise. Emotion words do not represent deterministic concepts. For another thing, within and across major emotion classes different languages may make very different distinctions, and continuously create novel ones. Dutch, over the last decades, has developed a concept similar to the famous Ifaluk *nguch*:[22] *balen*. On the other hand, instead of seeking a structural theory in which appraisal patterns are linked to emotions, one may do better to look not for emotion names as the dependents but for logically independent other emotion components.[23] Multicomponential emotion theory views this as a more appropriate approach. It evidently is the only meaningful approach when appraisals are viewed not as emotion components but as emotion antecedents.

APPRAISAL AS AN EMOTION ANTECEDENT

Distinguishing one emotion from another was the rationale for Scherer, for Smith and Ellsworth, and for Frijda, in their analyses of appraisal patterns.[24] However, these patterns were often interpreted also as reflecting what caused the emotions—the emotion antecedents.[25] Emotions can be seen as caused by events appraised in particular ways, and different emotions as caused by different appraisals. The confusion is understandable. Reported appraisal may well reflect appraisal that caused the emotions. It certainly often does, insofar as emotion reports include the eliciting event. But it certainly unreliably reflects causality: it unreliably reflects event appraisal prior to emotional response.

The reasons for this doubt have been extensively discussed by Parkinson.[26] People are generally bad at accounting for why they feel what they do feel. Nisbett and Wilson[27] gave overwhelming evidence of discrepancies between how people explained their preferences for objects in a shop window, and experimental manipulations that had caused these preferences (such as objects at the left in a shop window being preferred). Often, reported appraisals could only have been made after the emotion had been aroused. In a study of severe guilt feelings, all subjects appraised themselves as highly responsible for harm suffered by someone else, even when they knew they had not actually been responsible.[28] Such appraisals stem from cognitive elaborations that are motivated by the emotions of guilt themselves; they post hoc serve to explain or justify the emotion.[29] The most important doubt on the meaning of appraisal–emotion correlations based on self-report studies comes from confounding the two. In those studies, emotions are usually defined by emotion names, that often imply antecedent events and their appraisal. "Sadness," first of all, means pain about personal loss.[30]

Nonetheless, the real promise of the appraisal notion was and is that it may provide that causal explanation of emotions: why they occur, and why which emotion occurs when. Arnold and Lazarus[31] introduced the notion largely for this purpose.

Roseman and Smith[32] carefully detailed the facts that appraisal processes are invoked to explain. First: Facts that hit the senses are transformed into facts with value. Second: Given events lead to different emotions in different individuals, in different cultures, and in the same individual at different times. Third: Emotions are usually elicited by complex events occurring within a spatiotemporal context and not by single stimuli—by an unexpected stimulus, a stimulus that signals something to come, or an event that implies someone past. Sadness is elicited not by a friend but by loss of a friend. Fourth: Each major kind of emotion is elicited by a large variety of stimulus events. Sadness comes from loss of a friend and from an unhappy marriage. Fifth: emotional impact of events usually depends on these events' meanings. Loss of a friend is not the same as loss of a foe. Recall the Law of Concern.

Explanation of all five points calls for processes internal to the subject: processes of appraisal. *Appraisal*, in the causal sense, refers to processes in or by the individual that intervene between events as such, and emotional experiences and other emotional responses. The two meanings of *appraisal*, the descriptive and the causal one, must be sharply kept apart.

The appraisal explanation of the five points just mentioned embody two general hypotheses. The differential antecedent hypothesis assumes that identical events can produce different emotions because the events are differentially appraised. Personal achievements are major causes of joy in American students; they are not in Japanese students. Achieving and maintaining social harmony are major reasons for joy in Japanese students, and not in American ones. The explanation: The cultures appraise events by way of different models of agency that are linked to different prominent concerns, for achievement and social harmony, respectively.[33] The universal contingency hypothesis holds: "If people from different cultures appraise a situation in the same way, they will experience the same emotion".[34]

The assumption of a causal role of appraisal processes in emotion arousal forms the common ground of theorists stressing the role of emotional appraisal. This causal notion of appraisal is more controversial than the descriptive one. It has often been rejected because taken to imply conscious evaluation. That may have been due to the voluntaristic language that appraisal theorists so frequently used. The appraisal processes themselves are essentially thought to be nonconscious, though. It cannot be otherwise, since they determine conscious emotion experience—appraisal in the descriptive sense—as well as the other emotional response components. They sometimes originate in conscious thoughts; one may become conscious of them; they also may have never entered awareness. Appraisal theory also has been often rejected because emotions supposedly occur fast, not allowing time for much information processing. Both objections are mistaken. Cognitive processes can be nonconscious as well as very fast, as shown by the processes of syntactic analysis involved in speaking and hearing sentences, as well as by visual perception.[35]

But the true problems concern the nature of the appraisal processes. If not deliberate and conscious, how do they operate? Are they plausible in the animals low in phylogeny that produce similar contact-seeking, avoidant and hostile actions that we consider emotional in humans? I will approach these problems after considering one further role of appraisal.

APPRAISAL AS AN EMOTION CONSEQUENT

Appraisals are not only emotion antecedents and components, but also consequents. Emotions change appraisal itself, the way events appear, and the meanings assigned to them. Emotions change beliefs. That fact has long been central in treatments of emotion, from Aristotle and Spinoza onward; the contributions in a volume on Emotions and Beliefs review current relevant research.[36] There indeed is no contradiction or vagueness in the conclusion by several appraisal theorists that appraisals occur as antecedents, constituents, as well as consequents of emotions.[37] All three occur.

There are many ways in which emotions can change appraisal. One is by way of the actions induced by emotions. They may cause changes in the subject-environment relationship that are in turn appraised. Emotions also involve changes in attention. Novel event aspects are detected, and those already in focus may become more salient.[38] Guilt emotion caused by harm to others expands to sense of responsibility, which includes appraisal of self-agency. Fear induces appraisals of danger: "If I feel anxious, there must be danger"[39] Anger searches a reason, a justification, and a culprit. Feeling depressed is a lead to search for cues that might be responsible. One's emotion itself thus serves as information that acts on event appraisal.[40]

An important consequent appraisal is appraisal of the emotion itself, and of its likely or actual effects on others. For the latter, Parkinson, Fischer, and Manstead[41] coined the notion of "social appraisal": Overt response is suppressed if appraised as harmful or hurtful. Appraisal of emotions themselves—as immoral, soft, subtle or distinguished—are part of emotion regulation and emotion significance.[42]

ELEMENTARY APPRAISALS

I return to appraisal as an emotion antecedent. The processes that turn stimuli that hit the senses into events-as-appraised, and on to affective or other responses, vary from very simple to complex ones. Their simplest I call *elementary appraisals*; Ellsworth and Scherer refer to them as providing "appraisal of intrinsic pleasantness or unpleasantness," and Leventhal and Scherer described them as the sensory-motor level of appraisal.[43] Simple

stimuli directly evoke affect and, in certain instances, changes in physiological arousal, without the intervention of further information. The appraisal
process consists of no more than that some sensitivity exists that, when
touched upon, activates pleasure or pain processes, and perhaps additional
ones. Pain sensors and connected nerves and central circuits form a clear
and rather simple example. If they do not operate properly, as in congenital
analgesia, pinpricks, cuts, and burns may be felt but do not cause pain.[44] In
more complex instances, the sensitivities are not simple sensors, but one
must assume dispositions more like internal representations or templates.
That which allows a bird or rodent to get frightened by its species' alarm
calls must be of this sort.

Such elementary appraisal is involved in affect arousal by the innately liked
and disliked stimuli briefly discussed in the preceding chapter. It is the same
with so-called "prepared" aversive stimuli: stimuli that may not innately be
aversive but can very rapidly become so by learning. The sight of spiders and
snakes are of this sort. A chimpanzee learns to fear a snake (by the fright of
other chimpanzees) more readily than it does other objects; once acquired, the
fear does not as easily extinguish as happens to arbitrary conditioned stimuli.
Prepared and innate affective stimuli show that elementary appraisals have
various effects. Öhman and Mineka gave an extensive overview of them.[45]
They draw attention when among neutral stimuli: An angry face stands out in
the crowd. When used as conditioned stimuli preceding electric shock in a
conditioning experiment, they enhance heart rate and prolong resistance to extinction, compared to neutral stimuli like flowers and mushrooms, and they
produce illusionary correlations. Even crude aspects of snake or spider displays can elicit these reactions, as appears from the affective influence of the
scant information that can come through in backward masking of 40-msec
presentations of such stimuli.[46]

One may still consider "intrinsically pleasant or unpleasant" stimuli
that have obtained their valence by conditioning. Evaluative conditioning
was touched upon in chapter 3, and that notion can be held to apply to signals for shock and food, including Pavlov's bell. Human participants not
always recall what gave the stimulus its affective value, nor have they always been aware of it when it happened. With intense stimuli, the cortex is
not needed for the appraisal to occur: Conditioned stimuli may evoke affective response when limbic–cortical connections are cut.[47]

The notion of appraisal is applied to explain these various immediate
stimulus effects because some sensitivity is involved, which is subject
bound and subject dependent. The effects drop out when central evaluation processes are disturbed by brain malfunctions. Congenital analgesia
(not due to peripheral nerve disease) was just mentioned. LeDoux also assumes as much: "Perhaps neurons in the amygdala that process prepared
stimuli have some prewired ... connections to other cells that control emo-

tional responses."[48] These neurons can only be understood as functioning as specific sensitivities or templates. Such templates are different, but not too deeply different, from memory traces representing learned connections.[49] In addition, more general evaluating processes appear critical, notably for appreciating negative emotion signals.[50] There are more such mechanisms. Orbitofrontal lesions cause indifference towards acquired response consequences; interference with opioid processes in the nucleus accumbens interferes with appetitive responses to formerly preferred stimuli.[51]

Many intrinsically valent stimuli, including innate ones, are not just appraised as pleasant or unpleasant; the appraisal process appears slightly more complex. They are experienced as frightening, disgusting, attractive , exciting, or cute. Examples are angry faces, mutilated bodies, beautiful faces, nudes, and babies, or pictures of them, the sort of pictures used in a nice research tool, the International Affective Picture Set or IAPS.[52] Pictures of the mentioned kind appear to automatically potentiate particular action readiness dispositions, even without prior experience with mutilated bodies, nudes, or babies. Babies are cute: They touch on an infant-care system. Angry faces are seen as frightening: they appear to directly activate the fear system; they indeed readily cause freezing.[53] Disgusting pictures, tastes and smells directly activate specific rejection wriggles.[54] Sex stimuli such as visual intercourse displays can directly activate autonomic arousal, motor activation (spinal T-reflex enhancement), and genital responses;[55] they may even do so when the displays are deemed disgusting. Some of the relevant stimuli are quite complex. Sexual intercourse displays are; so are courtship displays.

However, it is not always clear how elementary the appraisal process really is. It is not always clear whether and when stimuli like those mentioned just are pleasant or unpleasant, or indeed by themselves also instigate more specific emotional reactions such as fear, disgust, or sexual interest. Genital reactions to sexual stimuli obviously are specific. The fear-relevant stimuli that Öhman and Mineka discuss may just be intrinsically aversive. They may, in first instance, only activate a non-specific defensive negative affect system, as Lang and colleagues suggest.[56] All aversive stimuli in the International Affective Picture Show activate the unspecific defensive mechanisms of startle enhancement and freezing that may be part of that system.[57] The critical factor that causes such stimuli to trigger anger, excitement, disgust, or submissiveness[58] may well be context information, added by association or memory, or other instigated responses. The defensive response system indeed conforms to a "defense cascade model"[59] that implies added information: freezing occurs when the aversive stimulus is remote or in indistinct location, to be replaced by flight or fight, and heart rate acceleration, when it becomes "proximal" or "imminent",[60] which points to the role of more than elementary appraisal.

Indeed, the processes involved in intrinsic valence may frequently well be more complex than just touching on some template. It can and has been argued that spiders and snakes derive their fearfulness from being unpredictable and slippery (itself perhaps intrinsically aversive), or from covert expectancies.[61] The aversiveness of schematic renderings of angry faces may just be a variant of the aversiveness of being looked at generally, or just of eyes, as every peacock-butterfly knows, so to speak; their attentional prominence may just be due to staring eyes being aversive and inciting avoidance.[62] The aversiveness of mutilated bodies may stem not from body damage being evolutionarily aversive[63] but from the fact that others' bodies are perceived in terms of one's own body, as is evident from motor mimicry.[64] Seeing someone else cut his or her finger causes an awkward feeling in one's own finger. Frowning when seeing a frown may not come from an innate aversiveness of a perceived frown, but directly from "motor categorization" of what is seen.[65]

Moreover, intrinsically pleasant or unpleasant stimuli may well, by themselves and without further information, elicit positive or negative affects, but not emotions. One may safely assume that they sensitize the affect systems[66] but not that they necessarily evoke any more specific, motivational emotion system. Sexual stimuli may by themselves increase genital blood volume, while not eliciting sexual desire or motivation, like this happens in hypogonadal men,[67] as well as in women who dislike the witnessed scenes.[68] Disgusting stimuli may well evoke true disgust only when ingestion or touching are actual or imminent, or when witnessing humiliation of others makes one's body cringe. Pain may facilitate anger,[69] but truly generate anger only when an appropriate target is around. Indeed, the immediate effects of intrinsically valenced stimuli in backward masking studies are weakened by longer exposure durations that allow context cues to come through that signal nonrelevance of the stimuli by conscious prime recognition,[70] only (presumably) to regain strength when context does signal relevance.[71] Only then, according to present evidence, do intrinsically valent stimuli cause emergence of action readiness that extends in time for more than two seconds or so beyond stimulus presentation.

"COGNITIVE APPRAISAL"

Context is essential in practically all emotion. Emotions are responses to constellations of objects or situations in a spatiotemporal context, except when context is abolished by very brief exposure and backward masking. It is confusing to designate what elicits emotions as "emotionally competent stimuli".[72] Surprise comes from something unexpected, curiosity from something not seen before, and sadness from loss of what previously was there. What elicits emotions involves "cognitions," at the least by picking up context.

Constellations belong to the major determinants of emotions. Remote threat tends to elicit freezing; proximal threat tends to induce flight; inescapable threat tends to induce fight—I already cited Fanselow;[73] in humans, threat that cannot be localized elicits anxiety: the threat can be anywhere. It may be impossible to enumerate the stimuli or events that elicit a given emotion. It may well be possible by enumerating constellations. That indeed is what appraisal theory seeks to do. Constellations, besides spatiotemporal context, contain the numerous aspects that real-life situations present: previous experiences, memories, meanings dug from the present or the past. Hebb,[74] at the time, described how one and the same stimulus—perceiving a skull, by chimpanzees—elicited now interest, then fear, then anger, then distress, perhaps the animals now focused novelty, then strangeness, then possible hostile implications, then that they did not know how to cope with it, some of the appraisal components in Table 4.1. In the present discussion, replace "emotions" by "states of action readiness," to prevent ambiguity. Constellations, rather than stimuli, are what elicit particular states of action readiness.

This will not always have been so, in phylogeny. It implies considerable change from the elementary appraisals as about the only processing that lower organisms like shellfish or insects are capable of, to the sensitivity for context, memories, expectations and so forth that higher animals can command. How this change from only elementary appraisals to constellation-sensitive ones has proceeded, I can only guess. One may plausibly assume that evolutionary development made use of "preadaptations," to again borrow from Rozin.[75] The preadaptations were present in various stimulus-driven defensive, aggressive, rejecting, appetitive, and affinitive response repertoires in the lower organisms. They were available when cognitive development allowed broader sensitivities.

Stimuli, then, are augmented by other information. I call their use in emotion arousal *cognitive appraisal*. True enough, the term *cognitive* may cause confusion. It suggests declarative as well as conscious representations, neither of which is implied when appraisal theorists use the word. I will nonetheless continue to use the *cognitive* designation, as a shorthand for the distinction from *elementary*.

Emotion arousal is shot through by cognition. Many events owe their emotional impact—their primary appraisal—by its meaning for future actions and future satisfaction of concerns. Take a very basic example: movement restraint. It induces stress in animals; for Selye it was the paradigmatic manipulation to do so. It has impact, not because the stimulus of being held is so unpleasant, but because what the animal can do clashes with what it intends or wants to do.

"Cognitive appraisal"—information use—is frequently denied or not recognized, whereas it even operates in the elicitation of nonconscious affective priming. Clore and colleagues have extensively argued and shown this.[76] In backward masking experiments, the stimuli of course *are* identified, even if not consciously. Priming in lexical decision tasks in which semantic and affective decisions are pitted against each other, shows precedence of semantic decisions. Contrary to what Zajonc[77] argued, affect does not precede cognition. Reaction time data show memory decisions to be faster than affective decisions.[78] As Storbeck and Robinson conclude from an extensive review of neuroscience data: an elaborate cascade of cognitive processes occurs prior to differential amygdala activation; the cascade includes categorization of the visual information.[79] What does occur is that awareness of affect may precede awareness of cognitive outcomes. Such an inversion of the sequence of generation in what comes to awareness is in fact common in the genesis of awareness.[80]

Information beyond elementary appraisal is very general. It is evident in the almost ubiquitous contextual control of emotions such as anxiety, fear, and panic in rats, witness the research by Bouton.[81] Context cues (in the strict sense of spatiotemporal context) like the chamber in which shocks are delivered influence reinstatement and renewal of extinguished responses, and the relapse of abstaining addicts; occurrence of fear, anxiety, or panic depend on the proximity of the expected aversive event in time. Events signaling likelihood of rewards, called *occasion setters* in behavior theory,[82] facilitate striving; they instigate what appraisal theorists call appraisals of goal conduciveness.

Comparison of current stimulus events with expectations, actions one is set for, actions by and rewards obtained by others is widespread. The Law of Comparative Feeling is demonstrated not only in human but also in animal research. It creeps in stealthily and gradually, even when responding to single, isolated stimuli. Even the effect of familiarity on liking illustrates this. It occurs even if the stimuli are not consciously recognized as familiar,[83] but obviously, the stimuli must have been compared nonconsciously to a memory trace. Movement restraint likewise involves some comparison: its emotional effect comes from mismatch between movement and movement intent. Hens that are satisfied after eating resume eating when seeing other hens begin;[84] rats distribute their choices according to Herrnstein's "matching law" in proportion to the probability of reinforcement from the various choices.[85]

Appreciable experimental evidence has been obtained, in humans as well as animals, for causal effects of predictability and of controllability of shock and loud noise on felt upset and autonomic arousal.[86] Similar findings were on effects of stimulus novelty, controllability, and unexpectedness on curiosity, surprise, fear, disappointment, and joy.[87] Effects of instructions on resulting distress where demonstrated in the old experiments by Lazarus, in which participants watched gruesome films. Subjective and physiological emotion indices varied according to having been told to emotionally engage or to disengage, or that the films were either authentic or fake.[88] At a more complex level, reported causes for joy cohered with event's relevance to culturally dominant concerns. Among Americans, the major joy antecedents had to do with personal achievement; among Japanese, they mainly had to do with having maintained interpersonal engagement.[89]

A major appraisal component, according to appraisal theory, is indicated by terms like difficulty, appraised coping potential, action outcome uncertainty, and anticipated effort. Dogs well trained in conditioned escape upon shock signals show no signs of emotion.[90] In humans, subjective estimates of task difficulty have been found to correlate with sympathetic arousal, heart rate increase, and frowning, and with readiness to spend effort in goal achievement.[91] Considerable evidence consists with respect to "social appraisal," appraisal of the possible consequences of one's emotional expression. It strongly modulates strength of that expression and, on the whole, the experience of the corresponding emotion.[92]

Systematic influence of cognitive variables on emergence of different emotions is strongly suggested by self-reports of the events that led to the various emotions. Reports of antecedent events can be held to suffer less from self-report biases than appraisal ratings. Strong links appear between event types and different emotions; they tend to hold up in cross-cultural comparisons.[93] As hinted at earlier in this chapter, event types are readily (though somewhat grossly) translated into appraisal patterns. As an example, sadness is reported as due to personal loss, but also prolonged adverse circumstances (hunger, poverty, hardships, prolonged aversive treatment by spouse, child, or boss), and to drastic changes in circumstances to which adjustment takes time and effort, such as moving house and even professional promotion.[94] These event types can all be plausibly seen as involving appraisal of unpleasantness, difficulty to control or inability to undo the unpleasantness, and thus low appraisal of coping potential that, indeed, all tend to correlate with sadness ratings in the studies by Scherer and others. At the same time, the evidence is weak in that the links of event types are with emotion names; event types may well enter the common meanings of these names. For "sadness," personal loss is the first feature to come to mind. Yet analysis of reported antecedents also yields important insights.

How valid is appraisal theory? How much does it explain? Does the evidence support a structural theory of emotions?

Experimental studies show correlations of cognitive variables with emotions, though mainly with emotion strength. Reports on antecedent events show correlations with different emotions, as identified by name, which is problematic evidence. Hardly any systematic evidence exists that seeks to link appraisal variables or patterns to modes of action readiness. This thus is an almost virginal field of research.

However, when such research is undertaken, some caveats are in order. As mentioned earlier, observed appraisal–emotion correlations can mean very different things. Observed or inferred appraisal variables may be necessary or sufficient for arousal of particular state of action readiness, or they may be unique for that mode, facilitate its occurrence or strength, or weaken inhibition of its occurrence. An elegantly designed study by Kuppens and colleagues[95] shows few of the context appraisals to be necessary for a particular emotion names to apply. They asked participants for recollections of three recent unpleasant incidents in which a given one of a set of appraisal components was either present or absent. Questionnaires assessed presence and strength of the appraisals of agency by someone else, high appraised coping potential, and blameworthiness of action, as well as of particular emotions, among which anger. They conclude that "none of the selected components can be considered as a truly singly necessary or singly sufficient condition for anger"[96]—not even that someone else was to blame. Use of the word "anger" is not a criterion for a mode of action readiness, but Kuppens' findings are corroborated by the extensive survey of anger antecedents by Stanley Hall.[97] Some antecedents indeed lacked agency by someone else (e.g., having stumbled over a stone). Interestingly, in many instances in Kuppens' study, frustrated coping effort rather than high appraised coping potential appeared at stake, whereas coping or control potential usually comes out in self-report studies as an important anger appraisal component.[98] Coping potential is clearly weak in impotent anger, where the rage seems fed by the awareness that one's anger has no effect on the antagonist. The only thing that all anger antecedents appear to have in common is highly unspecific: unpleasantness, whatever its agent, kind, or source.[99]

Similar findings may show up on clear scrutiny of the antecedents of specified states of action readiness. For instance, the variety of antecedents of guilt emotions has already been alluded to. Guilt, in the study involved, almost invariably implied pain, and desire to undo the harm. But appraisals varied. Blaming oneself, usually considered vital, appeared not essential, and indeed, guilt emotions are weak after intentionally inflicted harm.[100] Feeling responsible was an invariably mentioned constituent rather than a causal antecedent of feeling guilty. What did appear very general was that harm had occurred to someone one cared for—a child, intimate kin or friend, or God;[101] guilt emotion may just be caused by harm to someone loved, and concomitant fear of loss of love. Emotions or modes of action readiness appear to respond probabilistically to restricted sets of appraisal components, in which now this, then that subset suffices for arousal, the conclusion indeed advanced by Kuppens and colleagues.[102]

Taking the evidence together, one can conclude that appraisal processes are crucial in emotion generation. Different patterns of appraisal tend to lead to different emotions, as defined by states of action readiness. At that level, a universal connection between antecedents and consequents may hold, be it not in determinate but probabilistic fashion.

THE NATURE OF APPRAISALS

Appraisal processes may be crucial, but what are they? How do they operate? Appraisals are sometimes designated as "mental representations" and emotions as "being elicited by appraisals." These designations are misleading. Appraisals do not occur in the form of representations, separate from perception of the events-as-appraised; at least, most usually they do not. Also, appraisal processes are, in principle, nonconscious. Their outcomes may become conscious, in how one sees and experiences emotional events; but if they do, it generally is after the fact of having elicited changes in action readiness and other responses. This does not only apply to the appraisal of affective valence, which was extensively documented by Murphy and Zajonc, Bargh, and many others (see notes 70, 139). In clever experiments, it has also been demonstrated for appraisals of motivational valence, congruence and discongruence, and of target status.[102a]

Appraisal also poses the effectiveness problem. Some events elicit emotions, and others do not, even when both carry information that is in principle emotion-relevant. Recall the Law of Apparent Reality from chapter 1. Recall that smokers know that smoking may give lung-cancer, and still smoke happily; impassioned people well know the risks of unsafe sex; and many or most phobics know that spiders are harmless. So: when and why is information emotionally effective or "apparently real," and when and why is it not when it logically should be?

This question has been discussed frequently. Lazarus[103] distinguished knowledge and appraisal; that, however, merely restated the problem. Proposals have been made for distinguishing different cognitive processing systems or types of representation. Some of these systems or types supposedly are emotionally inert, notably "propositional representations"; others—"analogic" and "associative" representations, that come directly from stimuli with intrinsic valence—do have emotional power.[104] "Schematic" or "implicational" representations, which integrate the other types of representation with information from the body and actions, also are emotionally effective. They can be illustrated by the experiences that poems call up. The distinctions are suggestive and helpful, but do not really clarify what is involved. It may help to look more closely at the process of appraising, and the contexts in which it occurs.

Emotions in their most direct form occur "on-line." They emerge in actual interactions. They are elicited by events that are being appraised while actually dealing with them. You bump into them, and they bump into you.

One is facing events that deploy within their spatiotemporal context and its changes. Appraisal there is an aspect of "situated cognition".[105]

Moreover, emotions are rooted in the appraisal of events that affect or affected body and action in direct ways. They stop, interrupt, or enable actions, and imply or prevent interactions. They also affect ongoing expectancies. One rarely is without expectancies and without being set for action to meet those. Being insulted in company clashes with expectations of polite discourse; someone not answering with a smile when greeted behaves oddly, and one's greeting falls flat. Emotions occur in embodied contexts. Appraisal is an instance, not only of situated, but also of embodied cognition.[106] One is bodily and actively present in the same space as one's emotions' causes and effects. There are no appraisal representations. There is appraised information coming in from different sources: from a valued object, from its present context, from within oneself, one's body and one's memory store. They interact, and together they shape situational meaning as well as motivational and behavioral response.

The effectiveness problem is solved, I think, by considering this context. There and then, appraisal variables are real in some direct, often physical way. They are presentations rather than representations, bumpings-into and actings-upon, and signals that these will happen. When going beyond what is present on-line, in thought or fantasy, they consist of schematic or implicational representations: the stored embodied representations as discussed by Barsalou and Wiener-Hastings[107] and that evoke expectations or images of direct affection. On-line appraisal processes consist of the same things that enter situated and embodied knowledge representations, but then in the flesh.

Appraisal is embodied. But note: "embodied appraisal," as approached here, differs from how it is conceived by, for instance, Damasio and Prinz.[108] The embodiment does not primarily involve "gut reactions." Nor is it due to appraisals causing bodily reactions. It often involves affection of the body by external events: one is bumped into or stroked. This includes the elementary appraisals that make one tremble and shrink anyway. Interestingly, after Lazarus showed the effects of instructions on emotional response, Horowitz and Becker[109] showed these effects to be short-lived. Regardless of what they were told, participants tended to wake up during the following night, after restless sleep and dreams, and subject to unbidden images.

But first and foremost, embodiment involves affection of the operation of basic cognitive processes, of action planning, and of action. Descriptions of emotion experiences are filled with statements to that effect.[110] In surprise, you cannot place what happens. In joy the world appears open, can be conquered without constraint; it enables action. In frustration, ongoing action is blocked, or being set for particular sensations does not find them.

It is argued here that such embodiment constitutes the core of many or most appraisal variables. Several appraisal variables are the output of perceptual processes that interaction calls upon. Novelty appraisal is the output of recognition processes that fail; perceiving something as familiar mirrors fluency of those processes. Experimental data support this inference.[111] Unexpectedness appraisal of simple stimuli is the immediate result of mismatch with a neuronal model, and carries the orienting reflex with it.[112]

Intrinsic pleasantness and unpleasantness operate at the same direct level. Their immediate effects are the induction of acceptance and non-acceptance tuning, as argued in the preceding chapter. Pain hurts, stink stinks, and sexual stimuli excite. Skin contracts in anticipation when seeing big sharp teeth approaching; pain is felt in your finger when seeing someone else cut his or hers. It all affects, and may result in further action readiness for continuation or change, approach or avoidance. When cognitive mediation is involved, the affective valence is just an aspect of the embodied representations that the triggers call up.[113]

Major appraisal variables are on-line; they are part of the perception of events. Escape routes are seen or searched for, as animal observation shows. Causality and the intentions of others, that is, agency appraisal, are equally perceptual, or can be.[114] In actual confrontations these are not matters of interpretation but of information pickup.[115] Still, they are "appraisals," since the pickup is not automatic but involves circular self-organization, when attention detects features that direct attention that detect features.[116] Event pickup indeed may not take place when attention is restricted or information intake is blocked; backward masking precisely does that. Longer prime exposure times allow context to be picked up, that may contribute to, or interfere with, the affect information coming through during the first few milliseconds.[117] Context influences may remain when cortex is blocked, but disappear when hippocampus is, for instance by stress[118] and otherwise influence appraisal even without the subject being aware of it.[119]

Many context appraisals are similar to perceptual affordances that provide action guidance. Affordances consist of perceived fitness for particular actions:[120] places to put things in, depths to fall into, obstacles to be jumped over, objects that allow handling, biting in, pecking at or, as with fellow humans, that intend and call for interacting. Affordances emerge because visual appearance fits requirements or suitability for particular actions; the peckability of a grain must do so for a newly hatched chick. Affordance often is the outcome of previous actions. Cats view objects as obstacles to avoid or to be reached because they did actively move about in their environment; no active moving about, no avoidance of obstacles.[121] Visual cliff avoidance in infants likewise results from having acquired ability to crawl and the needed control knowledge, rather than from experiences of having fallen. Aversion to heights stems from appraising discrepancies between vestibular and visual information on self-motion.[122] Generally, previous appraisals become part of the situated knowledge representations in memory, that are reinstated when corresponding events are met anew, since, as Barsalou (1993) showed, fittingness to actions is part of those representations.[123]

The various context appraisals emerge because what cues them is met in a context of action. A visual cliff instigates fear in an infant who crawls. A gutter is a barrier for a cat that preys. Action and appraisal are intimately intertwined. Goal conduciveness and obstructiveness appraisals result from sensed impact on prepared or ongoing action, or action that one is set for. They are not representations of an event helping or hindering in attaining one's goals, but outcomes of finding a prepared action to be or not to be feasible, success of execution to be or not to be likely, expectations implied in the efferent copies of one's actions to be thwarted. Appraisal of personal loss is not so much an image of perpetual absence, as noticing that initiated action planning will be vain. Action monitoring procedures automatically take care of all that. One sees access to be open, and progress to be free; one sees one's progress to be obstructed, and actions rendered futile. And if it is not seen, it is readily foreseen. A dog eating a bone gets nervous when another dog comes near.

I mentioned instigation of anger by movement restraint, when activity is halted before the motivation is, when somebody stops you while hurrying on, or when the point of your pencil breaks while writing with passion. These are the prototypes of interference with goal achievement. The processes are not essentially different when your thoughts proceed fluently but suddenly halt because they do not solve what one had set out for.[124] All this involves non-propositional information inherent in action monitoring and affecting the matching of preafference that one is being set for. The processes impinge on the automatic planning and shaping of actions, as when a cat "decides" whether to jump the gutter to catch a butterfly, or let go of it, and before the jump makes preparatory trial movements. The appraisals are written on the monitoring of action planning and execution.

This is, I think, what that major appraisal component of "coping potential" or "task difficulty" consists of. Appraisal of coping potential sounds sophisticated, but usually is not. A victorious mouse enters fights with other mice more easily than one with a history of defeat.[125] Appraisals do not typically occur in individuals who sit back and make computations. They occur in the heat of action preparation. One of the possible outputs of such preparation is that no feasible action comes to mind, as in submission under hostility, in appraising the finality of loss in full grief, and in the hopelessness of despair.

Appraisal by action control processes extends to novelty and unexpectedness: both leave the subject without direct cues for which action to take. Surprise does not merely consist in finding out that an event does not match expectations, but also that available action options do not fit the moment's requirements. Action preparation is closely linked to expectancies. The example was given earlier of the painful blow to self esteem when ignored at a cocktail party. It was not what one was being set for. Similarly, sublime and awe-inspiring objects are objects that are beyond comparison to one's coping potential. One falls back on watching in humility.

The above analysis is modeled on on-line interactions. Pencil points break under your hands; people do not respond to your greetings. Of course, many emotions do not arise in actual interactions. They emerge when pondering, foreseeing, told about incidents, recollecting. But the elements discussed—affects, processing outcomes, affordances, action impacts—are equally part of the representations that drive or fill those thoughts and recollections. One may predict that emotions arise in as far as such elements indeed are present in the representations, or prominent in the actual thoughts derived from them. This is the point of the notions of implicational or schematic representations, and of their embodiment. Along these lines one may come to understand the Law of Apparent Reality. As real appears what is present to the senses, present in affect, or engages action and action planning.

Apparent reality does not come only from sensory impact or impact on action. It also comes from "social reality"—beliefs and expectations embedded in beliefs and expectations of those around you. The godhead is everywhere, everybody says so, acts accordingly, and expects you to do likewise. The same for magical influences such as the effects of spells and curses. They indeed form one of the main appraisal variables in non-European cultures.[126]

"Non-real" information can be made implicational, schematic, or embodied by adding interactional and bodily information through imagination. It can give the thoughts reality. It is what I hinted at at the end of chapter 1. One can emotionalize reason. It happens spontaneously when meaning dawns on a person after the fact of an event. It also happens by the influence of potent experiences such as visions, or by the impact of a charismatic person. Conversions sometimes operate in this fashion.[127]

All this solves the efficiency problem. Information becomes emotional appraisal when it consists of affect- and action-relevant embodied cognition. Only if it does so, it forms appraisal that differs from knowledge.

Along these lines one can understand the Law of Closure.[128] Closure has been described as "informational encapsulation".[129] Conditioned fear responses are very difficult to extinguish, if at all, when the unconditioned stimulus was traumatic (like the severe shocks in LeDoux's [1996] experiments with rats),[130] or when the conditioned stimulus (CS) was a prepared stimulus such as the a snake or spider picture. Hugdahl & Öhman[131] found that warning subjects that shock would follow blinking of a light immediately established conditioned EDR to the light. They also found that such conditioned EDR immediately disappeared when the shock electrode was removed. However, it did not disappear when the CS had been a snake or spider picture. Informational encapsulation has been ascribed to the structure of evolutionarily shaped emotion modules, such as a fear module.[132] But, as mentioned in chapter 1, Bridger and Mandel (1964) a long time ago found that the same happens when, in a conditioning experiment, some CS had been followed just once by a painful electric shock: detaching the shock electrodes did not abolish conditioned fear response, as mentioned before.[133] "Encapsulation" widely occurs when affective learning was early and socially embedded, as with culturally acquired food preferences and aversions;[134] they are notoriously hard to modify. Encapsulation also occurs for the effects of positive stimuli. Infatuation, of course, is paradigmatic for the law of closure, where "no!" is taken to mean "yes," in particular if said in a friendly voice by a nice face. Closure is the inverse of apparent reality, and a general law of emotion, not only of evolutionarily shaped modules.

In a similar way one can come to understand time discounting. The further away in time are expected outcomes, the weaker their reality—the weaker the cues for acting, the less direct and palpable the interferences or action facilitations, and the less urgent to act.[135] This likewise explains the indifference, when under the sway of emotion, to information that contradict the harmfulness of threat or the benefit of emotional pursuit, as in infatuation. Such information has more the character of knowledge. It has little body, and thus cannot compete with the seduction by what is vivid and close.

In a similar way again, one can understand detachment and disengagement. They involve adopting a mental attitude in which one is set for not acting, and for treating events as spectacles. They unroll as if in a different space of one's own, as they do when separated from the scene by a footlight. Direct impact on one's body and action are blocked. Embodiment yields its place to transformation of action impacts and impulses into images of such impacts and of action tendencies; meanings are doubled by their reflexive awareness. Appraisals still occur, but not in the way as sketched above. They are not encapsulated, and are abandoned as soon as detachment is given up.[136]

Appraisals being rooted in elementary and embodied cognitive processes does not contradict that propensity for particular appraisals varies between individuals and cultures. Trait-anger predisposes to appraising offense; cultural belief in magic predisposes to viewing agency in misfortunes; individually and culturally dominant concerns predispose to appraisals in particular content areas.[137]

APPRAISING PROCESSES

Appraisals thus emerge on-line, in engaged actual interaction with events, or when such interaction plays in thought and imagination. But this is by no means always the case. Many appraisals come ready made. Clore and Ortony made the important distinction between computed and reinstated appraisals, and Fiske introduced the notions of "affect schemas" and "schema-triggered affect" that shape reactions to familiar entities.[138] Appraisals are part of stored knowledge that is replete with evaluations, recalled actions, and calls to action. The stored appraisals come from previous emotional encounters, or from their having been explicit or implicit in behavior by others and their verbal messages. Affective evaluation often is just one of the features of the memory schema linked to an event or object, a person's name, a social group's name, or a word denoting a personality trait such as "generous" or "stingy." Bargh[139] reviewed the experimental data that showed how readily these valences attached to words operate in priming tasks.

Event appraisal is thus shaped by information from widely divergent sources: from the stimulus, if there is one; from its context, including the current social background; from ongoing events; from one's previous experiences and other contents of long-term memory. One may say, by way of metaphor, that it is all entered on a "blackboard," continuously supplanting, supplementing, and modifying what is already there.

How does all the information with its various sources combine into an appraisal pattern? This is a wrong question. Such a thing usually does not exist. The blackboard is just a metaphor. An "appraisal pattern" is a fiction. We do not experience appraisals; we experience events as appraised. Appraisal patterns are descriptions, abstracted from the properties of perceived events that activate emotions, develop in interactions, and sometimes are constructed after the fact.

In some sense, it even is inappropriate to talk about an "appraisal process." Appraisal has been conceptualized by a searchlight model: as a process that searches incoming information for relevance and subjects it to a number of appraisal checks.[140] But this, too, is a metaphor. Event appraisal is not specific to emotions, and not made in view of them. Appraisals are continuously made, and appraisal is around anyway, because animals and humans are set to make sense of the environment and what happens there. Their eyes—their minds—are set to notice causes, agents, intentions, and emotional relevance. This renders moving barking furry self-propelling creatures to be perceived as bite-ready but avoidable dogs. Such making sense goes on continuously, employing assimilation to familiar categories as well as making novel inferences. It uses not only what is there, but also what is expected or hoped to be there, and against the background of what went before.

Parallel to making sense, and in interaction with it, goes the continuous responsiveness of action dispositions to the events as appraised that they are responsive to. While appraising and having appraised, action readinesses are aroused, and actions prepared and executed. While the fingers play, the keyboard moves, the strings tremble.

All that appraising is relevant for emotion arousal, but the processes themselves have little to do with emotions. The information forming appraisal mostly is there, on the blackboard, along with other information (where you are, the color of the sky, that the cat purrs—all those useless things that are found in flashback memories of traumatic events). For that reason, the blackboard is not well designated as "appraisal register".[141] When emotions are at stake, appraisal largely comes for free. The emotion dispositions that are responsive to reward, threat, offense, or loss find reward, threat, offense, and loss for the taking. As Clore and Ketelaar[142] argued, they often find affective valence as part of the schemas in terms of which events are recognized. The same holds for perception of oneself. One does not, in general, appraise one's coping potential. Such appraisal arises on the spot when called to prepare action. Quite generally there is appraisal, yes, simply because that is how the cognitive system works. It plays the action readiness keyboard. And some of that appraisal enters emotion experience, as what Lambie and Marcel called an *ED*, an evaluative description.[143]

EMOTION ELICITATION

The information on the blackboard—the activated set of component representations—elicits emotion, following the conception developed in chapter 2. It elicits an action tendency that may lead to action or, in the event, merely one of the more general dispositions. such as those for positive and negative affect, and more general modes of action readiness such as increase and decrease in activation. Each of those dispositions possesses its own sensitivity for a particular appraisal pattern. This model applies not only to action readiness arousal but, equally, to other response components such as physiological responses, along the lines proposed by Scherer[144] and others.

But appraisal is not a one-shot process. The process goes on very much as described by Lewis in his dynamic systems analysis.[145] Formation of an appraisal pattern capable of evoking a state of action readiness that leads to action is a process that stretches out over time. Information pickup, extension from stored knowledge, and integration are not instantaneous. Affect arousal may occur within 10 or 20 msec; context, which needs the hippocampus, needs longer; recall the results of the experiments by Murphy and Zajonc, those of Stapel and others, in which increasing exposure times leads to outcome changes due to integration of more information.[146] Feedback from attention and changes in its focus modify the available information. Circular causality may come in, when conceptual representations change the impact of lower order information. These interactions recruit aspects of appraisal and potentiation of action tendency, that amplify until felt and observable emotion peaks; they cover onset latency. Appraisal stabilizes when it has developed so that a given action readiness has emerged and settles in preparation and execution of action. Feedback from action readiness and action further stabilizes the appraisal. They may also change it when they bring changes in thoughts or the interpersonal interaction; antecedent appraisals, appraisals as response components, and consequent appraisals all enter the process. All this may take between 40 and 120 msec in a startle response, with its elementary appraisal, and several minutes, or more, in the growth of anger.

Presumably, action readiness dispositions are potentiated at any moment during the process: those that the process has touched upon so far. They may be reinforced or annulled by subsequent information, as happens when longer exposure times diminish the diffuse affect generated in the mentioned backward masking experiments. But urgency or intensity may cut the process short, and an emotion will emerge in response to an event that could easily have been appraised in a different manner, since fuller information was available: excitement instead of anger, for instance. The process may also continue, and the excitement as yet transform into anger.

Activation of action readiness dispositions results from a resonance-like or recognition-like process. When activated information matches the sensitivity of some disposition, that disposition is activated. Said otherwise: The sensitivities filter the available information. At this point, an appraisal is formed.

Appraisals result when information meets action readiness disposition. In this meeting, appraisal may match several emotion dispositions. Presumably, in principle that emotion is aroused that shows the highest match, as in distributed network activation models. Complete match may not be needed for activation; some minimal match may suffice. Such minimal match need not involve particular necessary or sufficient components, but correspond to some disjunctive function of components reaching a critical value.[147]

Appraisal information may simultaneously match several dispositions to an equal degree, because their sensitivity patterns overlap. Being threatened by someone may evoke fear because there is threat, and anger because there is agency. Current residual activation level of the action readiness dispositions may well play a complementary role. It may even bias activation toward an emotion with lower match but higher residual activation state. That emotion is probably aroused that shows the highest match/activation product or other combination. About residual activation more will be said presently.

Minimally sufficient match—response threshold, in fact—may depend on urgency. When impact is strong and urgency high, match criteria may be more lenient. If the available information is insufficient for response disposition, a disposition of lesser specificity may be aroused: mere discomfort, or "upset," mere excitement, or mere "desire for change,"-any of these.

Residual activation of motivational dispositions is a plausible concept. It may be due to previous activation, to mood, and to personality dispositions like trait anger, trait anxiety, or extraversion. Evidence for each of those exists. One may get angry about a trifle when angered a minute ago, as in so many anger experiments.[148] Irritable mood also makes trifles precipitate anger, as it may do in premenstrual states.[149] Correlations have been found between trait anger and state anger after stress or offense.[150]

Residual activation may also result from activation of other previous emotional tendencies. As mentioned, anger is generally facilitated by any unpleasant condition (pain, heat, bad smells, smoke, fatigue).[151] Sexual excitement can subsequently facilitate anger evoked by provocation, and anger as well as strenuous physical activity, fear of shock, and pain can facilitate sexual excitability.[152] Some of these transfers, however, may go by way of appraisals (the effects of sexual arousal on aggressive impulse appear mediated by "callousness" toward women). The precise mechanisms for these various forms of facilitation are not fully clear. Zillmann's excitation transfer theory supposes that sympathetic arousal left over from the previous engagements adds to the motivation evoked by subsequent stimuli.[153] More central theories may trace the transfer to shared involvement of the Seeking or Desire system.[154] Transfer can also be described as due to influences on appraisal propensities,[155] which is equivalent to greater sensitivity of the emotion dispositions.

It may well be that not only the emotion disposition with highest match is activated. Several emotions may well be simultaneously aroused by a given event, to the degree each emotion's sensitivity is matched by information on the blackboard. Winner takes all, perhaps, in inhibiting the losers, but latent, subthreshold activation may still exist and exert later facilitation.

The preceding tried to construct a plausible sketch of what elicits emotions. I argued that in some sense appraisals are not antecedents of emotions, as defined by action readiness and other response components. Appraisal and response develop in mutual interaction. But still, emotions result from events and the subject's own actions, as appraised. Events and actions come first. Also, appraised events and actions still are the causes of action readiness change at the micro-level of the mechanisms in dynamic system processes.

I conclude that "appraisal" in a wide definition is essential to arousal of emotion. Emotions emerge when events are appraised as pleasant or unpleasant, as satisfying or threatening concerns, or as fitting particular action programs. In this, "cognitive appraisal" plays an important part. It is always involved in arousal of emotions if "emotions" are defined by states of action readiness that flexibly motivate flexible actions.

The remaining tasks are huge. They include research into which, in fact, are the sensitivities for each emotion, and what is the logic of their operation. It is doubtful that each emotion disposition responds only to one specific appraisal pattern. Emotions appear to respond more flexibly, on occasion to a minimal subset of appraisal elements, which in combination with residual activation outweighs the minimal subset for any other disposition. The tasks of course include finding empirical bases for formulating the various interaction and transition rules.

An important qualification needs to be added, with respect to the treatment of what elicits emotions. All the previous in this chapter starts from the assumption that emotions are elicited by events that are in some way appraised. However, this does not appear true for all emotions.

Certain events may induce emotions directly. They directly activate states of action readiness that may transform into action under certain circumstances.

What I have in mind are emotions induced by self-produced "expressive" movements, by perceiving such movements in others, and by music. The "expressive" in quotation marks refers to movements with the prosodic properties that come from being generated by states of action readiness and their regulation. Induction of emotions by making such movements has been alluded at in chapter 2, when discussing retroaction of expressive movements on emotion and action readiness. Viewing the movements in others activates central action dispositions, presumably by activating mirror neurons.[156] Hearing imitable temporal patterns may in some way do likewise; in any case, experiencing movement impulse when hearing music is common occurrence, and acting upon it can be observed in young people in any streetcar. Probably, imitative impulse comes from the mirror neuron system functioning as a nonverbal coding mechanism: observed behavior is coded in terms of one's own action repertoire,[157] as also happens when observing instrumental behavior when verbal coding is difficult.[158]

Under which circumstances such activated action disposition turns into action readiness, with its intentional content, and under which circumstances it leads to overt action, is as yet unclear. Filling out corresponding appraisal may be one way— the way of emotion contagion perhaps. The wish or need to understand others, or predict their behavior, may be another. Motor mimicry is most noticeable (and perhaps restricted to) watching others under non-engaged conditions of being a witness,[159] as when looking at a tightrope walker or participating in an expression recognition experiment. A third may be the wish to participate in actions of others, as in dancing or communal chanting. In response to music, the evoked states of action readiness probable tend to be of the "open" kind discerned in chapter 2.

I do not know whether more can be said about these emotions that are not triggered by events as appraised. At this point, their mention serves to round off the discussion of emotion elicitation.

NOTES

[1]Nussbaum, 2001; Solomon, 1993.
[2]Lazarus, 1991.
[3]Oatley, 1992; Oatley & Johnson-Laird, 1987.
[4]Power & Dalgleish, 1997.
[5]e.g., Frijda, 1986; Roseman, 1991; C. A. Smith & Ellsworth, 1985.
[6]Scherer, 1993.
[7]Frijda, Markam, Sato, & Wiers, 1995.
[8]Frijda, Kuipers, & Terschure, 1989; Roseman, 1984, 1991; Scherer, 1997; C. A. Smith & Ellsworth, 1985.
[9]Frijda, 2000.
[10]e.g., Scherer, Walbott, & Summerfield, 1986; Scherer, 1997.
[11]e.g., Frijda, et al. 1995; Mauro, Sato, & Tucker, 1992; Roseman, Dhawan, Rettek, Naidu, & Thapa, 1995; Scherer, 1997.
[12]Breugelmans, 2004.
[13]e.g., Chwelos & Oatley, 1994; Roseman, 1991; Scherer, 1993.
[14]Keltner & Haidt, 2003.
[15]Zeelenberg, Van Dijk, Manstead, & Vander Pligt, 1998.
[16]Ben-Ze'ev, 2000; Van Dijk et al., 2005.
[17]Rozin, Haidt, & McCauley, 2000; Shweder, 1991.
[18]Mesquita, 2001a; Scherer, 1997.
[19]Ben-Ze'ev, 2000.
[20]Parkinson, 1999; Robinson & Clore, 2002.
[21]Kuppens, Van Mechelen, Smits, & De Boeck, 2003.
[22]Lutz, 1988. The Dutch word, the verb *balen*, means feeling strong discomfort due to any sort of external event.
[23]Frijda & Zeelenberg, 2001.
[24]Frijda, 1986; Scherer,1984; C. A. Smith and Ellsworth; 1985.
[25]e.g., Lazarus, 1991; Scherer, 1997.
[26]Parkinson, 1995.
[27]Nisbett and Wilson 1977.
[28]Frijda, 1993b; Kroon, 1988.
[29]e.g., Keltner, Ellsworth, & Edwards, 1993.
[30]Frijda & Zeelenberg, 2001.
[31]Arnold 1960; Lazarus 1966.
[32]Roseman and Smith 2001.
[33]Mesquita, 2001a; Mesquita & Markus, 2004.
[34]Mesquita & Ellsworth, 2001, p. 233. Scherer, 1997, for the same hypothesis.
[35]Storbeck & Robinson, 2004.
[36]Frijda, Manstead, & Bem, 2000.
[37]e.g., Lazarus, 1991; Scherer, 2000.
[38]Eysenck, 1997; Kahneman, 1999.

[39]Arntz, Rauner, & Van den Hout, 1995.

[40]Schwarz & Clore, 1988.

[41]Parkinson, Fischer, & Manstead, 2005.

[42]Frijda, 1986.

[43]Ellsworth & Scherer, 2003; Leventhal & Scherer, 1987; Scherer, 1984

[44]Ervin & Sternbach, 1960.

[45]Öhman & Mineka, 2001.

[46]S. T. Murphy & Zajonc, 1993.

[47]LeDoux, 1996.

[48]LeDoux, 1996, p. 254.

[49]Clore & Ketelaar, 1997; Clore & Ortony, 2000.

[50]LeDoux, 1996; J. S. Morris, Öhman, & Dolan, 1998; Panksepp, 1998.

[51]Berridge, 2003; Damasio, 1994; Rolls, 1999.

[52]Lang, Bradley, & Cuthbert, 1990.

[53]Bradley, Codispoti, Cuthbert, & Lang, 2001; Flykt, 2006; Öhman, Lundqvist, & Esteves, 2001.

[54]Rozin, et al. 2000; Steiner et al., 2001.

[55]Both, Everaerd, & Laan, 2003

[56]Bradley et al, 2001.

[57]Lang, et al.1990.

[58]For anger: Berkowitz and Harmon-Jones, 2004, and Hebb, 1946; for excitement: Hebb, 1946; for submissiveness: Öhman and Mineka, 2001.

[59]Bradley et al. 2001.

[60]Fanselow, 1994.

[61]For the slippery: see Rozin et al., 2000; for the unpredictable: see Merkelbach, de Jong, Muris, and van denHout, 1996; for covert expectancies: Davey, 1995.

[62]Dijksterhuis & Aarts, 2003; Ellsworth, Carlsmith, & Henson, 1972.

[63]Bradley et al., 2001.

[64]Meltzoff, 2002.

[65]Barsalou, 1999; Frijda, 1953.

[66]Gray, 1987.

[67]Bancroft, 1995.

[68]Laan, Everaerd, Van Bellen, & Hanewald, 1994.

[69]Berkowitz & Harmon-Jones, 2004.

[70]e.g. Murphy & Zajonc, 1993; Rotteveel, de Groot, Geutskens, & Phaf, 2001.

[71]Stapel & Koomen, 2000.

[72]Damasio, 2003.

[73]Fanselow, 1994.

[74]Hebb, 1946.

[75]Rozin, 1999.

[76]Clore, Storbeck, Robinson, & Centerbar, 2005.

[77]Zajonc 1980.

[78]Mandler & Shebo, 1983.
[79]Storbeck, Robinson & McCourt, 2006.
[80]Marcel, 1983.
[81]Bouton, 2005.
[82]Holland, 1992.
[83]Zajonc, 1968, 2004.
[84]Katz, 1944.
[85]cf. Ainslie, 2001.
[86]See Glass and Singer, 1972, for predictability; G. Mineka, Cook, and Miller, 1984, for coping options; S. Mineka and Hendersen, 1985, for controllability and predictability.
[87]See, for example, Ortony, Clore, and Collins, 1988, for joy; W. V. Meyer, Reisenzein, and Schützwohl, 1997, and Reisenzein, 2000, for surprise; Suomi and Harlow, 1976, for fear and curiosity in rhesus infants.
[88]Lazarus 1966.
[89]Kitayama, Markus, & Kurokawa, 2000; Mesquita & Markus, 2004.
[90]Solomon & Wynne, 1953.
[91]Kaiser & Wehrle, 2001; Pecchinenda, 2001; Pope & Smith, 1994; Wright, 1996.
[92]Parkinson et al. 2005; Zaalberg, 2005.
[93]Scherer & Walbott, 1994; Scherer, et al., 1986.
[94]Marris, 1974.
[95]Kuppens et al., 2003.
[96]Kuppens et al., 2003, p. 266.
[97]Hall, 1899.
[98]e.g., Roseman, 2001; Scherer, 1993.
[99]Berkowitz & Harmon-Jones, 2004.
[100]McGraw, 1987
[101]Frijda, 1993b Parkinson, 1999.
[102]Kuppens et al. 2003.
[102a]Moors & De Houwer, 2005; Moors et al., 2004
[103]Lazarus 1991.
[104]e.g., Power and Dalgleish, 1997; Teasdale and Barnard, 1993.
[105]Barsalou, 1999.
[106]Merleau-Ponty, 1945; Varela, Thompson, & Rosch, 1991.
[107]Barsalou & Wiemer-Hastings, 2004; Niedenthal, Barsalou, Ric, & Krauth-Gruber, 2005.
[108]Damasio, 2003; Prinz, 2004.
[109]Horowitz and Becker 1973.
[110]Davitz, 1969.
[111]Reber, Winkielman, & Schwarz, 1998; Winkielman & Cacioppo, 2001.
[112]Sokolov, 1963.
[113]Clore & Ketelaar, 1997.

[114]Michotte, 1946/1954; Spelke, Philips, & Woodword, 1995.
[115]Gibson, 1979; Parkinson, 1995.
[116]Lewis, 2005.
[117]S. T. Murphy & Zajonc, 1993; Stapel & Koomen, 2000.
[118]Jacobs & Nadel, 1985.
[119]Nisbett and Wilson, 1977; Clore & Ortony, 2000.
[120]Gibson, 1979.
[121]Held & Heir, 1958.
[122]Bertenthal, Campos, and Kermoian, 1994.
[123]Barsalou, 1999.
[124](see Chapter 2)
[125]Mineka & Zimbarg, 1996.
[126]Scherer & Wallsott, 1994.
[127]James, 1902/1982.
[128]This analysis borrows from Elster, 1999b.
[129]e.g., Öhman & Mineka, 2001.
[130]LeDoux, 1996.
[131]Hugdahl & Öhman 1977.
[132]Öhman & Mineka, 2001.
[133]Bridger and Mandel 1964.
[134]Rozin, et al., 2000.
[135]Ainslie, 2001; Elster, 1999b.
[136]Sundararajan, 2005.
[137]Mesquita, 2001b.
[138]Fiske 1982; Clore and Ortony 2000; see also Parkinson, 2001.
[139]Bargh 1997.
[140]Scherer, 1984.
[141]Scherer, 2001; C. A. Smith & Kirby, 2000.
[142]Clore and Ketelaar 1997.
[143]Lambie & Marcel, 2002.
[144]Scherer 2001.
[145]Lewis, 1996, 2005.
[146]S. T. Murphy & Zajonc, 1993; Rotteveel et al., 2001; Stapel & Koomen, 2000; Clore, et al. (2005) for comments.
[147]Kuppens et al. 2003.
[148]e.g., Berkowitz& Harmon-Jones, 2004.
[149]Van Goozen, Frijda, & Van de Poll, 1992.
[150]e.g., Spielberger, Jacobs, Russell, & Crane, 1983.
[151]Berkowitz & Harmon-Jones, 2004.
[152]Zillmann, 1998.
[153]Zillmann, 1998.
[154]see Chapter 2.
[155]Scherer, 2001.

[156]Rizzolatti, Fadiga, Fogassi, & Gallese, 1999.
[157]Frijda, 1953, 1956.
[158]Berger & Hadley, 1975.
[159]Tan, 2000.

5

Concerns

Emotions arise when some event is appraised as relevant to the individual's concerns. That is what the Law of Concern proposed. Concerns are what give events their emotional meaning: The events are appraised as satisfying or harming one's concerns, and the function of emotions is to safeguard those concerns.

This is a main tenet of many emotion theories.[1] For what I call *concern*, they use notions like motives, needs, strivings, desires, and major goals. I prefer *concern*, because it refers to the disposition that underlies motives, goals, and so on, as well as to why people care, while not itself carrying connotations of striving or having a goal. People care about many things that they at that moment do not strive for. They may care about events that just happen to them. Also, many activities are purposive without being guided by a goal, as Solomon[2] pointed out. Many activities just converge towards certain states, and come to rest there. Friendship has been discussed under this light[3]. One interacts, and friendship emerges as if one was always ready for it.

Individuals and cultures differ in nature and strength of their concerns; they thus differ in what elicits emotions.[4] Concerns are inferred from what elicits emotions as well as from what forms the end-point of striving: particular states of the world or oneself, or relationships between the two. The individual evidently considers them desirable or aversive, and worth attaining. They are also inferred from what people say they strive for, and why they think they care about a particular event. Concerns thus provide the final explanation for emotions and for striving.

Such explanation can be given at various levels. One dislikes an insult because one dislikes being slighted because one likes being considered someone to be treated with respect because one cares for social regard and self-esteem. Perhaps concerns entertain hierarchical relationships; in any case, some appear more basic than others; that is, they are more general over populations, explain a larger array of motion-eliciting events, and may explain more ill effects when thwarted or not satisfied.[5] Some others are clearly instrumental for satisfying more basic ones, such as feeding being instrumental to retaining health and survival.

There exists no consensus on which concerns it is meaningful to distinguish, nor on which concerns are the basic ones. An illustrative set, coming from Murray,[6] consists of biological needs such as hunger and thirst, and "psychogenic needs." The psychogenic needs are given in Table 5.1. A different set, at a quite different level of analysis, is Schwartz's[7] list of 11 motivational types, presented in Table 5.2. They come from the correlations between questionnaire ratings ("how important as a guiding principle in my life is …") by respondents from 20 cultures. They thus are recognized fairly generally, although considerable variation between cultures exists in how important they are held to be. Each motivational type assembles several values that tend to occur together; some of them are included in the table.

It is useful to distinguish concerns like those listed, as *source concerns*, from *surface concerns*.[8] Source concerns are defined in terms of general kinds of goals and satisfactions. Surface concerns are defined by such goals and satisfactions with regard to a particular person or object or state of affairs. Surface concerns are about persons, objects, and so forth, appraised as instrumental in satisfying or threatening one or several source concerns. Examples include attachments to and hatreds of particular individuals—one's mother, one's beloved, one's erotic rival—hobbies, interests, and life goals.

In this chapter I seek to understand the nature of concerns. What is their modus operandi? How can they be understood in functional terms, as mental processes and their conditions? These are relevant questions, for several issues. The first is, since concerns underlie both striving and emotion: what is the relationship between those two? The second: Since concerns are central in the explanation of emotions: How, then, might such appraisal of relevance proceed? Seeking an answer for this issue means descending from the personal and phenomenological to the subpersonal and functional level of description. I begin with the first.

TABLE 5.1
Psychogenic Needs

n Abasement	To accept punishment
n Achievement	To overcome obstacles and succeed
n Acquisition	To obtain possessions
n Affiliation	To associate and make friends
n Aggression	To injure others
n Autonomy	To resist others and stand strong
n Blameavoidance	To avoid blame and obey the rules
n Construction	To build or create
n Contrariance	To be unique
n Counteraction	To defend honor
n Defendance	To justify actions
n Deference	To follow a superior, to serve
n Dominance	Or power: to control and lead others
n Exhibition	To attract attention
n Exposition	To provide information, educate
n Harmavoidance	To avoid pain
n Infavoidance	To avoid failure, shame, or to conceal a weakness
n Nurturance	To protect the helpless
n Order	To arrange, organize, and be precise
n Play	To relieve tension, have fun, or relax
n Recognition	To gain approval and social status
n Rejection	To exclude another
n Sentience	To enjoy sensuous impressions
n Sex	To form and enjoy an erotic relationship
n Similance	To empathize
n Succorance	To seek protection or sympathy
n Understanding	To analyze and experience, to seek knowledge

Note. Based on Murray (1938).

EMOTIONS AND STRIVING

Shand[9] argued that emotions reflect the fate of strivings: their being blocked, proceeding smoothly, or having attained their end. But what makes certain states of the world, of oneself, and of one's relationships satisfactions or things to strive after? Why would we want to do that? Is not a concern just the representation of something that elicits pleasure or pain? Is not the explanation of emotions by concerns an instance of circular reason-

TABLE 5.2
Motivational Types and Some Included Values

Types	Examples
Self-direction	Self-respect, choosing one's goals, freedom
Stimulation	Daring; variety
Hedonism	Pleasure; enjoying life
Achievement	Being ambitious; successful
Power	Social power; authority; preserving one's social image
Security	Family security; sense of belonging; national security
Conformity	Obedience; politeness; self-discipline
Tradition	Respect for tradition; devout; humble
Spirituality	A spiritual life; inner harmony
Benevolence	Helpful; true friendship; a world at peace
Universalism	Social justice; equality; wisdom

Note. Based on Schwartz (1992).

ing: We like it when we get what we like, and we don't like it when we can't get it? Big surprise!

The state of affairs is not as bad as that. Emotions are not just states of pleasure or pain, of affect, but involve changes in action readiness. The relationship between affect and striving then still is problematic, however. Do we strive because what we strive for gives us pleasure, or do we get pleasure when we obtain what we strive for? Do we strive to get rid of pain, or does it give pain not to get what we strive for, or to lose what we had?

The problem is evident. Two different answers have traditionally been proposed; Duncker[10] has labeled them *hormism* and *hedonism,* borrowing from MacDougall.[11] "Hormism" is the view that gives concerns the primary place in explaining both striving and emotion. Humans have a number of major desires; striving seeks to fulfill those; emotions arise from the prospects of fulfillment. The view is indeed ancient. It dominated Plato's treatment of the emotions;[12] it was one of the bases of McDougall's purposive psychology;[13] it is the tenet of the many emotion theories referred to above. Emotions are results not causes. They result from the fate of strivings towards fulfillment of desires. They come from the beliefs that certain types of event and actions satisfy or hamper our desires.[14]

Hedonism is as ancient, though. We act in search of pleasure. Our strivings are motivated by promotion of pleasure and prevention of pain. Hedonic theory is present in Aristotle,[15] finds explicit espousal in Hume,[16] and elaboration in Bentham.[17] It has found its expression in the American constitution. It finds a modern variant in the reinforcement theory of emotions (e.g., Rolls),[18] in which "pleasure" is replaced by "reinforcement" or "reward."

Both views coexist, and they continue to coexist, because each can marshal impressive evidence in its favor. Each also runs into equally impressive difficulties.

Hormism provides a coherent explanation of emotions. Emotions monitor and regulate progress toward concern satisfaction. They signal when goal shifts are needed or urgent. Hormic theory also provides a coherent account of different types of emotion: the concern-satisfaction contingencies that appraisal theory describes. Some emotions that are not easily seen as reflecting the fate of concerns represent being in, and moving about in the satisfaction states of concerns. Love, admiration, and respect embody relationships of safe intimacy, of looking up to an admirable person or object, of deference toward a respected individual, that directly or indirectly satisfy desires for intimacy, protection and guidance, having a safe place, and the like.

Its problems come from the pleasures that are difficult to trace to the success of some form of striving; we saw the issue in the sensory pleasures, discussed in chapter 3. Plato already admitted this. In the *Philebus* he wonders what striving might possibly underlie the pleasure from the smell of his roses when he enters his garden in the early morning.[19] Action pleasures, too, appear to resist a concern-based account. Dancing is fun; so is loudly singing in the bathroom. The difficulties in putting aesthetic pleasures into a hormic context have also been touched on.

The most direct arguments for hedonic theory thus are precisely those emotions or affects that offer difficulties for hormic theory. Bodily pain forms their clearest instance. One strives to prevent pain, and to get rid of it once it is there, period. True enough, hormic theory often tends to posit concerns, such as a "need for physical health," an "instinct for safety," or a "survival instinct," to explain why threat or pain evoke emotions. Assuming such concerns does no more than doubling up the observed phenomena, though, just as supposing a *vis dormativa* did not explain sleep. The procedure indeed brought the downfall of McDougall's hormic theory: postulating an instinct of pugnacity, for instance, adds nothing to explaining anger. Similarly, Plato's explanation of the emotion of desiring unity in love by a desire for restoring original unity does not really help understanding love.

There is massive support for hedonic motivation. People do spend effort and money in seeking fun, amusement, pleasures of all kinds, and in doing what they can to prevent pain and other discomfort. The issue is not to doubt the pursuit of pleasure or happiness as an important motive. The issue is whether or not it is *the* motive (or *the* major motive), and not one concern among many others.

HEDONISM

To evaluate hedonism as a general theory of motivation, two readings of the notion of hedonism must be distinguished. In the first, hedonism is the idea that whatever people do, they always strive to increase their personal benefit, or to improve their personal pleasure-pain ratio. This is the notion of *universal egoism,* as Batson[20] names it, or unsophisticated hedonism. In this reading, a hedonistic view of human motivation is manifestly false. Batson[21] and Miller[22] have extensively reviewed the abundant evidence that humans often forego actual or forthcoming pleasure for the benefit of others or for the sake of some higher goal, and that they are willing to take risks in doing so. An illustration comes from the so-called ultimatum game.[23] In that game, played by two participants, one is free to divide a sum of money between him- or herself and the other. Whatever the proposed division, he or she will obtain the money when the partner accepts it. In by far the majority of cases, participants divide the money in close to equal parts. Fairness wins over greediness.

In the second, more subtle and sophisticated reading, hedonism affirms that whenever we can, what we strive to do indeed is in the end to increase pleasure and to decrease pain. But pleasures not only include directly personal benefits, and the pains not only direct personal pains. The pangs of conscience and the pains of emphatic distress from witnessing the distress of others enter the pleasure–pain balance. When acting for the benefit of others, so does the glowing pride of having done good things. In addition, future pleasures and pains enter into the pleasure-pain balance. One gladly makes sacrifices for the future happiness of one's children; one abstains from actions that yield later regrets. Still, what we strive for is to obtain as favorable a balance of pleasure and suffering as we can. This is the General Hedonistic Motivation Theory, neatly detailed by Reisenzein.[24] It becomes a theory of universal hedonism if all other strivings also strive what they strive for because the outcome is pleasure or decrease of pain. That is the form of hedonism that is meaningfully put in opposition to hormism by Duncker.

Under that more subtle reading, is it still appropriate to say that all that people strive for is to obtain pleasure or diminished pain? Let us examine the relations between pleasure and striving more closely.

RELATIONSHIPS BETWEEN PLEASURE AND STRIVING

Those relations indeed are strong and intimate, and it is in fact difficult to separate them. I will fairly closely follow Duncker's exposition here.

Pleasure has a central place in human striving, whether it is the latter's prime mover or not. The tie between positive affect and striving is solid and strong. Lack of striving and lack of pleasure go hand in hand. Lack of striving is equivalent to anhedonia. Conversely, positive mood and mania are often accompanied by a restless emergence of initiatives. Mr. Toad in *The Wind in the Willows* illustrates the combination. Mania and anhedonia both suggests that the relationship between affect and striving may well be bidirectional.

The centrality of pleasure also appears from the fact, discussed in chapter 3, that it is, to some extent, the common currency in decision making. To some extent, one pleasure can be substituted for another. Pleasures share a certain "utility." No love? Then devotion to a cause or a dog, or eating chocolates.

Utility has distinct limits, however, as was also discussed in chapter 3. Different pleasures differ. A dog is not really a loved one. There is quite a bit of fun that a dog is unable to provide; you cannot converse with it, and it does not come with you to the movies. The same for pains. Each pain bites with different teeth and leaves different scars. Also, pleasures and pains hardly compensate. Loss of a loved one is not truly counterbalanced by pleasures from professional success. The loss still bites at night and leaves one longing. It can hardly be otherwise. Objects of concern satisfy different concerns, and often more than one concern; hedonic outcomes from different objects thus are inequivalent. A spouse not only satisfies sex and warmth; he or she also satisfies intimacy, and one is intertwined by years of shared habits.

If one pleasure cannot always compensate for another, then striving is not towards pleasure alone. It can still be argued that, even then, we still may always strive for something pleasant. If the object of desire suddenly turned neutral or aversive, would we keep desiring it? This argument for hedonism has been advanced by Duncker, who took it from Hume.[25] The solidity of this argument can be questioned, though. There is solid evidence that cravings occur or persist in the face of outcomes that have lost their pleasantness, or even are only painful. Drug cravings after long-lasting abuse form one example;[26] infatuations in the face of consistent rejection are another.

Moreover, the strong ties between pleasure and striving do not imply the causal relationship posited by hedonism. Even if successful striving is always pleasant, this does not imply that that is what we *strove* for. It may just be that striving, whatever its motive, tends to come to rest at pleasure, and chapter 3 argued just that. Moreover, successful outcomes of striving can be defined otherwise than by pleasure. They are often defined by arrival at a setpoint, a settling point (a point where opposing forces are in balance), or a standard.

The issue is most clearly illustrated by the striving instigated by sentiments and values. Sentiments are dispositions for positive or negative appraisals of persons, objects or issues when these are met or just thought of. They also are dispositions for emergence of states of readiness to act to enhance or weaken the existence of the target objects or persons, or to promote or obstruct the target issues. Duncker emphasized their role for the present discussion. Sentiments are surface concerns, in which availability or integrity of the object is at stake. One strives for the well-being of one's children and gets emotional when they fall ill. But does one strive for their well-being, or for one's pleasure when they fare well and to end one's discomfort when they do not? Does one defend freedom for oneself or for others, or justice and equality for the law, because it produces pleasure or prevents distress?

The question is: What comes first, hormics or hedonics, striving to safeguard concerns, or to obtain pleasure and the reduction of pain? It can only be clearly answered by examining the nature of concerns.

THE STRUCTURE OF CONCERNS

How to understand concerns from a functional perspective, so that we can understand their connections with strivings, with pleasure, and with emotions. Why do we strive and why do we care?

The problem that theory must resolve is that both striving and caring are defined by future states: the end-points of striving, or the alternatives that are preferred to those that obtain. Theories of motivation traditionally have sought to resolve that problem in various ways. One is by using homeostatic models, in which deviation from a setpoint or settling point creates a "need" to which the system seeks to return; food deprivation creates such deviation. The setpoint or settling point implicitly represents the future state. "Drive" is another proposed solution: accumulation of some resource that creates imbalance that the system seeks to restore by action. Neither of these is generally satisfactory.[27] For instance, although homeostasis is certainly involved in the regulation of food intake, it usually is not what directly determines eating and its termination; palatability, seeing and smelling food, the clock, and sensations of stomach tension are more immediately involved than the organismic need being met. Resource accumulation cannot be demonstrated in motivations such as sex and curiosity. A third model introduces foresight based on former experience or reasoning. It applies to much human and animal striving, but cannot be what operates in motivated action in primitive and in naïve animals. Naïve organisms may strive towards satisfactions that they never experienced before, as does the butterfly invoked in chapter 2. In that butterfly, sexual activity presumably was initiated by an attractive smell. But how can that lead to finding and mating with a she-butterfly?

Concerns: The dispositions that allow us to strive and care, and make us do so. Motivation research has shown that concerns come in various shapes.[28] They largely correspond to different architectures of the animal's minds, that is, the kinds of information processing and control processes that they are capable of.[29] One of the major shapes is again suggested by that butterfly. It is the smell that does it. That role of smell as initiator and guide for striving suggests the model of incentive motivation: Striving and action are elicited by incentive stimuli.[30] Some stimuli can do so because a disposition allows it, and makes the individual do so: This kind of disposition has been described in the last chapter, when seeking to account for elementary appraisal. It consists of two parts: a sensitivity that responds when a particular certain stimulus event in some way matches with it and impinges on it and a connected response disposition that is activated when the sensitivity responds.

The simplest forms have been specified there a little further. Sensitivities respond to simple stimuli or stimulus patterns, and they are linked to the dispositions for pleasure that drive stimulus acceptance and further action. The sensitivities can have various forms: that of rather specific neural receptor subtypes, or of representations of external information. They may extend to responding to information that signals advent of the simple stimuli or patterns: contexts, persons, expected event outcomes.

However simple, concerns of this elementary kind are still concerns. They still give rise to the whole gamut of emotions that the various appraisal contingencies explain. Unexpected advent of a pleasant stimulus elicits enjoyment that energizes acceptance wriggles; preventing or interrupting those wriggles generates anger or excitement; decrease in stimulus intensity causes disappointment or sadness; and so forth. They also may lead to simple forms of striving, to enhance pleasure or decrease discomfort, when following the gradients of forces of the field, and thus happening to move towards or away from the sources of smell or sound, or whatever pleasure and pain came from. No further pleasantness increase, and absence of pain, function as set-points. There can be no search, though. The concerns are awakened when the animal bumps into the objects that represent, carry, or emit the stimuli. For this reason, I call them "mini-concerns."

More complex are concerns in which sensitivities access competences: complex response dispositions, and systems composed by interlocking sequences of such dispositions. The competences include sensitivities that, when triggered, induce their potentiation. Separate segments interlock in part because all are, or can be, potentiated by the initiating stimulus. In part, they interlock because outcomes of a segment touch upon the sensitivity of the next one.

This, I think, is the structure of major biologically-based motivational systems. Their action dispositions within the competences are largely, at some level, given by evolution, though the precise actions in the various segments may be shaped by interaction with the environment and by learning. To illustrate what is meant by competences: think of the nurturance motive, triggered by perceived cuteness and helpless behavior, with the action repertoire of feeding, protecting, and providing warmth. Think of the infant–mother affiliative system, with ability to recognize one's offspring or parent, sensitivity for being handled and being stroked in the baby, and the sensations from handling and stroking in the mother; for facial cuteness[31] smiles, cooing sounds and distress calls, and perhaps for manifest helplessness in mothers; with the competences of smiling, clinging, following, uttering following-inducing calls, and so forth.[32] Or think of the feeding system with sensitivities that include palatability discrimination, and the competences of preparatory handling—pecking, biting, chewing—and of ingestion. Think of curiosity, with its sensitivity to information gaps, and its competence that includes exploration and the cognitive processes of information assimilation.[33] Its role as a motor of evolution has been stressed in chapter 2.

The competences include provisions to set their sensitivities and to potentiate the action repertoires. These provisions largely consist of neurohumoral mechanisms. Sex is enabled by adequate ontogenetic preparation by, and perhaps actual levels of, hormones like testosterone and androsterone. Affiliation is enabled by oxytocin and vasopressin, the first dominant in the social propensities of females, the latter of males.[34] Sensitivities include neural receptor distributions that differ between individuals and species, and can vary under the influence of stimulation or activity. For instance, particular oxytocin and vasopressin receptors in certain brain regions are more frequent in monogamous than in nonmonogamous voles.[35]

Major concerns are composed of various more or less distinct sets of competences. For instance, concern for parent–infant affiliation can be considered a subset of a more general "need to belong." Baumeister and Leary defined the latter by two aims: having frequent, affectively pleasant interactions with one or a few other people; and a stable and enduring affective concern for each other's welfare—bonding[36] and caring. In its developed, human form, the competence includes sensitivities and action dispositions for effortless and non-demanding interpersonal exchange, skills for gauging others' intentions,[37] for huddling together, for being together without too much conflict, for empathic concern, capacity for reciprocity of expression of emotions and interests, and for undertaking nurturing and protective actions. "Warmth," "closeness," and intimacy then cover not only bodily warmth and physical proximity, but also the experiences of effortlessness interactions, without much reason to restrain them. Without those skills (or the trust that enables them), acquired in part by peer interactions, no bonds develop after that of mother–infant attachment.[38]

The entire "Need to Belong" is instructive, in that its contingent satisfactions cannot be subsumed under the heading of obtaining pleasant stimuli. The terminal situations consists of tight intertwined social skills of both (or more) participants, each showing and reciprocating the effects of those skills in the other(s). One's approach is accepted. One's smiles elicit smiles, and those smiles one can respond to. Also instructive is that the sensitivities touched upon by search for warm interaction are largely the same as those involved in body warmth and physical proximity: predictable and affinitive actions by the target; reciprocity in the action repertoires, which implies understandable target actions, that is, actions that fit one's empathic abilities;[39] and, most of all, familiarity and the resulting trust,[40] be it by some sort of imprinting (as in mother–child interaction and in infatuation), or continued experience, as in most pair bonding.

Affiliation or need to belong includes a number of aspects, or involves a number of related concerns: caring for offspring, for partners, for a smaller or wider social group, and for institutions such as one's country or one's community of the faithful. To what extent this entire group indeed represents a coherent system remains to be examined. It may equally represent a set of distinct but overlapping systems. They all may depend on intactness and level of oxytocin and vasopressin. These neuropeptides appear essential for activating defense against intruders, for care giving, and, together with dopamine, for partner bonding; but species and genders do not always do so in parallel. In any case, the whole set of affiliative concerns illustrates the convergence of potentiating neurohumoral motivational antecedents, competence-linked sensitivities, and differentiated action repertoires.

How about striving? Concerns with this structure allow desire, but it is blind desire. Striving proceeds without guidance by information on what the outcomes of this striving should be, and without anticipation of possible resulting pleasures. Desire only urges completion of competence segments that happen to terminate when action outcomes happen to match with the sensitivity that set off the segment, and finally the competence as a whole, and thus annul its activation. Such match, in turn, is guided by the efference copies inherent in each segment, as set forth in chapter 2. But execution of the competence is initiated merely by events impinging on the initial sensitivity. Information that contains a gap (or is appraised so) leads to exploration and inspection leads to novel information leads to cognitive assimilation that fills the gap. Proximity of a familiar person who smiles leads to interest leads to smiling in return leads to settling in the other's arms leads to warmth and quietening or continued reciprocal interaction. The male butterfly gets at the female butterfly that turns into his mate, and he does there what her presence triggers him to do there. Annulment of the triggering event as appraised, and/or termination of the last segment function as setpoints, but as local setpoints only. The male butterfly that sets out does so "towards" increase of the pleasant smell (or so); he stops acting upon ejaculation that, presumably, blocks smell attractiveness and because no further segment is provided for; he can only fly away.

In these concerns, the sensitivities respond to unlearned incentive stimuli. The smell, song, or call of distant sex partners presumably evokes the sexual concern without learning. So may the sight of males or females of the species do, or the patterns of their courtship movements.[41] The histories of the isolated children Victor and Genie suggest this to apply to humans, too, as do the fairly universal aspects in dominant mate preferences.[42] In the affiliative concern, the sensitivities for smiles, cooing, and perceived affordance of the mother's fur are presumably unlearned.[43] Sensitivities for distal cues thus may well form integral parts of the various biological competences. They in some way trigger what is called the appetitive phase of motivated behavior: "wanting," desire, the nonspecific motivation to bring the individual in contact with stimulus events that enable and elicit consummatory actions such as acceptance wriggles, ingestion, stroking, feeding, or copulation. The process by which that happens is unclear. It may consist on the one hand of potentiation by sensitivity's output of the entire competence, including preparatory responses and potentiation of consummatory response dispositions. Attractive food smells elicit salivation; attractive sexual smells may well ready the sexual system in advance of proximity to a partner. On the other hand, the nonspecific desire system, is probably also sensitive to discrepancies between the situation that includes the distal stimuli, and what is needed to enable the consummatory responses. What else initiates locomotion towards the object? It is likely: the function of the Desire System, according to Berridge, is to enhance incentive salience, in order, as Panksepp phrases it, to go seeking.[44] In addition, it is to fix the seeking to particular targets: the mother, the infant, a particular sexual partner.

Striving truly loses its blindness, and desire obtains focus, aim, and remote setpoint, when concerns then have become shaped by experience and cognitive capacity.[45] These latter may add to prewired competences, or be built up on the basis of pleasure and pain processes only. They finally instantiate the belief–desire module cherished by philosophers.[46]

Such concerns include provisions for the operation of context and of cues that identify the objects carrying the satisfying or harmful proximal stimuli. The provisions are stored appraisal schemas. As conditioned information, these form additional sensitivities that provide access to the consummatory responses dispositions. They also allow activation of the nonspecific appetitive and defensive, or approach and escape motivational systems, presumably by a mechanism like that suggested before. This is the model of incentive learning, as detailed by Dickinson and Balleine.[47] With regard to approach, this means that the sensitivities provide access to the desire system, presumably originally by way of the pleasure process, and later by the sensitivities for the conditioned stimuli directly.[48] Learning thus can turn mini-concerns into full-blown concerns that allow striving. They allow formation of concerns like fondness for sweets or alcohol in general, or for ice cream or tequila in particular, and strivings for going in search of them when the thought happens to come up.

Competences develop or expand by learning. They come to include instrumental actions in the appetitive phase of concerns and perhaps—why not—consummatory actions that happen to elicit rewarding response in interaction partners. This is possible only, as Dickinson and Balleine argue,[49] if cognitive capacities of the species concerned allow formation of representations of such outcomes, as well as of causal action–outcome links.

Both elements, learning additional instrumental action and emergence of expectations of outcomes as caused by these actions, in fact underlie the transition to a further form of concerns: those in which action is guided by outcome expectations that were generated by perception of incentive objects. Sensitivities then have come to include responsiveness to those actions, stimuli that enable them (the occasion setters), and the goal objects concerned. Together, these constitute the basis for true striving towards an expected or aimed-for end. They constitute goals in the true sense of that word. Action termination then can occur not merely when a competence has come to the end of its last action segment, but also when the representation of the terminal state is among the elements the sensitivity was receptive for to begin with.

At the same time, such emergence of goals and of anticipations of reaching them generates needs for those goals and pleasures: needs as felt deficits. In other than truly homeostatic concerns, felt needs result from implicit expectations, as in activated competences underway to completion, or when such expectations are thwarted. Such unfulfilled expectations underlie the appraisal contingency of absence of concern satisfaction.

CONCERN STRENGTH: INTERNAL ACTIVATION AND SETTING SENSITIVITIES

In all variants of concerns, activation depends on internal conditions as well as incentive stimuli (or recollections and thoughts that represent them). They thus operate according to the dual potentiation model of motivation, sketched in chapter 2. A need state of hunger activates the food-intake concern; so do palatable stimuli. However, the internal need state of hunger, or the drive state caused by seasonal increase of hormone secretion alone may lead to actions that do not fit the incentive motivation model. On such occasions, internal conditions lead to diffuse activation or undirected action. Hungry infants become restless and fussy, and manifest rooting.[50] Hormonal changes in spring or when in heat, too, cause restlessness, urges to roam about outside the house, and make sexual calls or start singing. They also render the individual responsive to sight and smells of potential sexual partners when these are encountered. Humans supplement such diffuse activations by actions that generate stimulus events: fantasies and thoughts. Sure enough, fantasies and thoughts function as incentive stimuli; but they may be generated spontaneously by the inner determinants, in daydreaming and dreaming.[51]

One may perhaps include the example of the foal that endeavors to stand within minutes from being born. What activates it, I do not know. It may be internally determined, or by its beginning to breathe, or by the cold outside the womb. Another concern that may make itself known without being elicited is curiosity or interest. As argued in chapter 2, it may seek for incentives by having the eyes wide open and looking or feeling around.

The internal conditions are modified, and sometimes brought about, by stimulus events. Hormonal changes are influenced by external stimuli and the individual's own responses. Female prairie voles are brought into oestrus by chemosignals from males, as well as by sustained mating, that both induce oxytocin release.[52] So do feeding and giving birth, where the resulting hormonal releases activate further responses.

Internal conditions not only lead to potentiating responses. They also set sensitivities for stimuli, giving them incentive value. In fact, concern strength can be defined by both response propensity and response magnitudes, and by sensitivity thresholds. Sensitivities can vary both qualitatively and quantitatively. A smaller or larger range of events can obtain incentive value. Under high internal activation, irrelevant stimuli may obtain it, as when a cat in heat shows lordosis when a human holds her flanks between his or her fingers. Weak incentive stimuli can be expected to activate concerns that are potentiated by internal conditions; choosiness does decrease, responsiveness increase. The world is full of spiders to the spider phobic, just as the world is full of insects to the passionate entomologist, and as everything reminds the adolescent of sex. As priming experiments have shown, concerns can be activated by nonconscious stimuli, but the more readily so when the concern is important to the individual.[53]

In fact, the incentive motivation model proposes that internal conditions—organic deficits, hormonal changes, deviations from setpoints—only rarely affect behavior directly. Most of their activation they do by enhancing relevant sensitivities. Alliesthesia has been mentioned as one of the outcomes of need states and other inner motivational states. Incentive value of foods and drinks increases with deprivation and decreases with being satisfied.[54] Sexual sensitivities increase with onset of hormonal maturity. Similarly for affiliative concern. Sensitivity for baby crying and feelings of tenderness is enhanced in the mother by increased oxytocin metabolism after birth.[55] Interpersonal trust (best conceived as decreased neophobia and decreased sensitivity for threat signs) increases with increased oxytocin. Even nasal oxytocin sprays can have that effect, and to be specific for acceptance of social risks, not to any sort of risk.[56] Interest, that basic concern, goes up and down with general energy and health.[57] Other influences on setting sensitivities, and thereby incentive values, include sensitization and habituation,[58] and individual propensities such as phobic fears, and particular appraisal orientations. Examples of the latter are self-confidence and propensity to distrust; others come from self-regulatory principles. A prominent bias comes from concern either for the prevention of harm, or to the promotion of satisfaction. Higgins[59] has amply demonstrated its impact on generating different emotions with regard to similar events.

Needs, in the sense of organic deficits, are among the internal states that set sensitivities. Other than organic needs can equally do so. I just mentioned such a type of need: as yet unfulfilled expectations. A major constellation under which that happens is being engaged in active goal pursuit. Goal gradient phenomena—response enhancement when nearing a goal—fall under this heading. So are concerns that are instrumental to other concerns, such as desire for interpersonal warmth. Desire for warmth can become a manifest need when under threat or insecurity; at the time, Schachter demonstrated this.[60] Lack of interpersonal warmth may well render young animals and infants depressed or insecure, even if warmth had never been experienced, because refuge and safety signals are lacking, as well as opportunities to exert the skills for social cohesion. It may also set sensitivities so that other individuals with friendly gestures are eagerly accepted and trusted, even on insufficient grounds. In other words: the "need" concept may not be silly, even for other than organismic needs, not because they would reflect unfulfilled desires, but because absence of certain satisfactions may have negative effects for other concerns.

SURFACE CONCERNS AND HEDONIC CONCERNS

Experience creates perceived objects or event types to function as conditioned concern elicitors. They allow the formation of what I earlier called surface concerns. The content of surface concerns consists of "affective schemas,"[61] -more or less coherent collections of information representations linked, as a whole, to representation of positive or negative appraisal. They function as sensitivities to any input in which an element of the collection figures. They owe their incentive value to the source concerns upon which they are based, and for which the object is felt to be instrumental. Objects of surface concerns are or were instrumental in satisfying one or more source concerns because they carried or produced the latter's unconditioned elicitors. Attachment persons may become attachment persons in this way.[62] Other objects or issues obtain such value by sociocultural or verbal transmission.

Surface concerns share two important properties. The first has been mentioned earlier in this chapter. Most of their objects obtained incentive value for more than one source concern. Love for a particular individual has to do with actual or expected satisfaction of sexual desires, of desires for warmth and intimacy, for effortless diversions, for familiarity, and for cognitive and emotional exchange.

The second property is that the objects of surface concerns have acquired their own incentive value. Mother is good; the topic of one's interest is interesting. Surface concerns also have acquired their own sensitivity: for availability and integrity of their target object. That is why these incentive values do not vary much with degrees of deprivation or satisfaction of the source concerns that fed the surface concern. Surface concerns possess what Allport referred to as "functional autonomy."[63] They are not invariably weakened when one of their constituents drop out; they may survive absence of any satisfaction. Love may survive decrease of sexual passion and, indeed, of any satisfaction, and attachment to one's country or religion may survive its offending one's major convictions.

Surface concerns are not the only concerns created by learning. So are *hedonic concerns:* concerns elicited by the incentive stimuli or thoughts that produce prospects of pleasure (and of pain, for that matter). As detailed above, those foresights may constitute goals, as well as the competences that bring them about. On occasion, such foresight may turn into a general concern for preventing, avoiding or diminishing pain, and for obtaining and increasing pleasure. Sensitivity for such concerns responds to the anticipated outcomes of the stimuli for all kinds of concerns enumerated.

CONCERNS FOR FUNCTIONING WELL

Concerns discussed so far derive from positively valenced incentive stimuli or competence outcomes. One may, however, distinguish concerns about what you get and concerns about what you do. Many concerns are about the latter: about one's competences functioning well. In fact, many competence outcomes are appraised as pleasant or unpleasant on that ground; I gave examples in chapter 3. Recall the example of frustration when one's pencil point breaks during writing. It angers. Evidently, smooth continuation of an ongoing act represents a concern. The issue is not that one's writing will be finished half a minute later, but that pursuing one's active intent was halted before its time. Examples of a similar kind are when reaching for the salt cellar, say, and someone snatches it away when you're on the point of grasping. Even when he snatches it to hand it over to you, you feel bad. Your hand floats idly in space, stupidly. Or when you are angrily voicing a reproach, but the other person apologizing before you have finished. Or when, in the dark, your foot moves for the next step on the stairs but you are already at the top.

Is writing a competence? Is grasping? No doubt. But what in any case is a major and fundamental competence is completing goal directed activities, once efferent copies are established and the motor system is engaged. This includes reaching one's aim in simple acts, which means fulfilling expectancies when the organism is set for encountering and recognizing an expected event. It represents a fundamental building block of the ability for goal-directed action. The competence may go down even to just making movements. As we know, restraining an infant by holding it evokes violent protests.[64]

Concern for functioning well was illustrated at another level when, after having been confined to one's bed by illness for a week or so, one is taking one's first simple walk, unaided. Or: "Having my hand out of a cast after 6 weeks makes it a wonderful experience to be able to write at all".[65] Walking and writing are skills that demand no effort, and evoke no pleasure—unless exerting the skill smoothly is not self-evident. But the extreme illustrations come from halting desires and strivings evoked by powerful incentive stimuli, or when unavailability of their targets prevents their fulfillment: the conditions for cravings in addictions and being in love.

Several concerns are rooted in requirements of functioning well under particular conditions. Familiarity is a concern: animals and humans tend to seek familiar surroundings, the company of familiar conspecifics, and prefer familiar objects over novel ones—the effect of mere exposure.[66] Why? One explanation is that harmless familiar objects are known to be harmless; their familiarity functions as a safety signal.[67] A more general explanation is that familiar objects carry information on what to expect from them, and how to deal with them. They represent cues on how to act or not to act. Concern for spatial orientation is similar. Lack of orientation is a source of anxiety—recall the panic in a building when you don't know where are its frontside and where its backside. Disorientation prevents action planning; orientation allows it. One of the most serious threats to competence indeed is when situations are so unfamiliar or unstable that no inkling on how to grasp or handle them can be obtained.

Concerns of exploration and curiosity are not very different. Curiosity, as argued above and in chapter 3, means exercising one's competence for cognitive assimilation. That competence is satisfied when assimilation is achieved. When it is going smoothly, it gives pleasure.[68] When it succeeds after effort it gives joy or even exhilaration, and negative affect when it fails. It even tends to give joy when occasion for exerting it comes up, and variety provides challenges. Curiosity is not by itself an aversive state, as for instance Loewenstein posits,[69] as long as its resolution—completion of its competence—is not delayed for too long. Closely related is the "need for cognitive closure".[70]

One could continue. Conservatism, cherishing habit and continuation of the state of the world as it is, saves enormous amounts of effort for readjustment and acquiring novel competences. Concerns for autonomy and freedom utilize elaborate appraisal schemas of what might touch them but, I think, are ultimately based on concerns for unencumbered execution of intentions and competences, as well as on that for the absence of pain—freedom to and freedom from.[71] Autonomy and freedom thus can be expected to represent concerns without corresponding cultural norms and labels. How prominent they are as values, though, will depend on such norms, and the range and value of self-initiated actions they define, and how much curtailment of autonomous exertion of competences is habitual and approved of or, by contrast, is encouraged.

Concern for self-esteem may be added. Self-esteem comes partly from interpersonal evaluations: how you think that others view you. But a separate source consists of appraisals of confidence in success of coming social and physical actions. Self-esteem indeed improves competence accordingly.[72] This may hold even for mice, which win fights more often after a history of victories than of defeat.[73] Such confidence is vital for planning adequate instrumental and social behavior.[74] When generalized as self-esteem, confidence protects against existential anxieties such as fear of death. Fear of death itself may primarily mean fear from the prospect of total loss of competence that dying implies, and that one cannot imagine not experiencing after death. Confidence in social action outcomes forms a way to understand the free, dominant, and authoritative behavior of an alpha chimpanzee, his erect posture and erected hair. It is also what losing a fight with a contender for alpha status clashes with, with the loser shrieking out in manifest misery, his posture shrunk.[76]

At a different plane of evaluating one's competences lies the impact on well-being of fulfilling a role in one's social surroundings, as Cantor and Sanderson[77] showed. In the negative, it appears from alienation, and from compensatory search for function in small social units such as terrorist groups.[78]

Desire for functioning well is probably the most adequate way to understand the driving power of something seemingly trivial: avoiding fatigue. Fatigue, of course, is usually unpleasant, but why? Because functioning occurs at the cost of resources. Fatigue is functional: it signals the action of taking a rest, and its being unpleasant merely conducts the signal. But its operation goes further. The very general desire for "escaping the self",[79] in alcohol, submission, or mystical fusion, may well be fed by a desire to get rid of the burden of being separate and seeking to be in control.

And well-functioning appears relevant in a seemingly odd concern: that for submission. Submission is not only a strategy to avoid punishment. It also is a concern, as appears from the frequent and avid seeking to submit to religious or political authority and lore, and to humble oneself before leaders, prophets, and gurus, and resultant emotions of awe.[80] Humility indeed is one of the values in Table 5.2. Submission again provides guidelines for action and for evaluating one's world, indicating one's stable place in that world, underlined by ritual.[81]

Many or most major surface concerns may be added. Attachments and life goals involve representation of persons, objects, and situations to be reached or maintained—their target objects. The concerns are about availability and integrity of these objects and goal states. They tend to have obtained functional autonomy. However, the mechanism of their formation is not very clear. Most plausibly, initial hedonic or other source concern satisfactions provided the relevant representations with their considerable incentive value, and embedded them in intricate webs of instrumental actions, subgoals for obtaining and maintaining the target objects. This is the mechanism suggested by Berridge's[82] account of incentive-instigated wanting and craving for drugs that have lost their capacity to elicit pleasure. The strong connection with such intricate action webs may form their core. This is plausible for attachments, and notably for being in love or infatuation. It may define major life goals. Wanting to establish God's kingdom on earth is, of course, tied in with numerous interpersonal practices and guidelines for selecting everyday behavior and for what to expect from other individuals, apart from the rewards of paradise such as seventy-five dark-eyed virgins. Wanting to become a dancer at an early age, and pursuing that into adulthood, may stem from images of the sparkling fame of Margot Fonteyn, but rapidly accretes the skills from exercise and training, the incentive values of tights and ballet slippers, the habit to spend effort, and so forth. Both concerns, with their valued objects and goals, are thereby integrated into one's conceptions of oneself. The life goals may, as a consequence, persist as ambitions even in the face of continuous failure to achieve them. The example, incidentally, suggests that a motive for self-actualization[83] is an unnecessary and unwanted supposition. Powerful motives exist for which there is no endowment is to be actualized.

VALUES

The duality of concerns about what you get and about what you do may clarify why and when cultural values, and suprapersonal values in particular, represent concerns. They often are: sources of striving to maintain or realize them, and of emotions when infringed upon, to the extent of willingness to die for them, or have others die for them.

Most values listed in Table 5.2 have a double face. They pertain to conditions of the world that may yield pleasure or pain, and also to conditions for functioning well and smoothly. The value of security draws from the desires to forestall pain, but also from ease in going one's way. Personal autonomy draws from the desire for unencumbered exertion of goals and competences, and control of one's actions, as well as from safeguarding the profits from one's other concerns and competences. Power is valued both because it yields access to resources and services, and because power is seductive as such when one possesses the competences to exert it. Conformity or conservatism implies smooth functioning that tradition and knowing one's place allow. It decreases the efforts of daily adaptations; you know what to do when, and you know what to expect.

Suprapersonal values, like liberty, democracy, justice, respect for human life, social harmony, obedience and recognition of authority and parents, and respect for tradition and divinity, share in that double face. Offense to those values implies actual or future elementary pain to oneself or others. Indeed, negative definitions of values are in general more easily given, and less ambiguous, than positive ones.[84] Conformity to them may imply elementary pleasurable effects: reaching desired goals, social harmony contains smooth and agreeable social contacts, rights to decide one's fate.

But that may not be the main source of their emotional role, their nature of concerns for those to those who hold those values to heart. Suprapersonal values relate to sectors of the world as a whole, and the conduct of life as a whole, of oneself and everybody else. Conformity and offense affect acting and striving in general, rather than pleasures when some people adhere, and the pains when they do not. They all represent guiding principles for action. They function as standards. Their being upheld by oneself and by others enables actions, diminishes effort in choosing actions, and decreases the need for being watchful for possible harm. For some people, a world without freedom or justice is a world one would not care to live in, or try other than to survive. For others, this applies to subservience to a divinity, respecting religious beliefs and obligations, or fulfilling one's assigned role in life. Infringements affect one's sense of the meaning of life.

These implications lift those values to a conceptual level, and thereby provide them with functional autonomy with respect to the pleasures and pains at their roots. One values adherence to such values, not only because that promises pleasure or escape from pain, but because the values embody states of the world that are anchoring points for action and orientation.

Concurrently, as guiding principles they form part of one's conception of oneself. Offending one's own values offends self respect. Avoidance of offending one's values forms a motivation for altruistic behavior with risk. Take the recollection of a man who took a Jewish child into his house during World War II: "But then the woman said, 'It's a Jewish child.' Janke [his wife] said, 'Oh, I'll have to talk it over with my husband.' We talked for some time, but we decided, 'When you would close the door on someone like that and you heard later that he was destroyed, how would you feel the rest of your life? I think I would be destroyed myself'".[85] As others said: "If I had closed the door, I could not have looked myself in the eye." The stories are typical. A penetrating account comes from the Hungarian writer Kertesz.[86] In the Auschwitz concentration camp, a fellow inmate who first stole Kertesz' daily ration returns and replaces the ration. The act harms that inmate's own chances to stay alive. However, returning it, as Kertesz concluded, represented his only chance of really staying alive, which weighed more heavily than just staying alive.

SELF-INITIATED FUNCTIONING

The incentive motivation model has replaced need and drive models of motivation. Yet, as we discussed, on occasion striving and actions do occur spontaneously, due to inner conditions of the individual. On occasion, the inner determinants suffice.

Wheel running in rodents was mentioned in chapter 3, when discussing pleasure. It is undertaken for its own sake. It is enhanced just by lack of opportunity to engage in exploration.[87] Spontaneously arising inclination for exploration is suggested by the behavior of animals that can freely range in a novel situation. They manifest periodic bouts of activities like locomotion, sniffing, investigating, grooming, and on occasion freezing.[88]

Propensity to manifest competences generally varies from moment to moment. Being interested goes up and down with general activation level, for instance, as when an individual is depressed, exhausted, or seriously sick. Potent inner conditions may suffice in the absence of any incentive stimulation. Konrad Lorenz[89] described how a starling that had been confined to a cage, when freed indulged in "vacuum movements": performing insect-catching actions with no insect flying around.

When potentiated by inner determinants, action dispositions are readily activated when opportunity presents itself. A clear example again comes from Lorenz. He describes a jackdaw that had been imprinted on him when hatching. The jackdaw always followed him around, walking after him. But one day a flock of jackdaws passed overhead: Lorenz' jackdaw took to its wings, and disappeared.[90] In running a maze, a rat spontaneously alternates when alleys allow that.[91] There often is spontaneous search for opportunities. Rhesus monkeys learn to open doors when rewarded by watching a toy train or permitted to take a puzzle apart.[92] Their reward is occasion to exert and satisfy the competences involved, watching and puzzling.

Potentiation of competences from inner determinants paradigmatically occurs during and immediately after birth. Butterfly pupae "want" to get out of their cocoon, and once out spread their wings; chickens are driven to hatch out. The foal struggles—truly struggles—to get to its feet within minutes from being born. A baby, shortly after first opening its eyes, opens them widely so that information streams in.

Concern for exerting competences is particularly evident from the experiments by Premack discussed in chapter 3.[93] Performing an action that has not been performed for some time serves as a reinforcer for performing an action for which that is not the case; propensity to exert appears potentiated. Exerting competences appears driven by something akin to a limit cycle attractor, at two levels. They are caught between the satisfactions of exerting them and habituation that takes the satisfaction away. McSweeney and Swindell[94] have proposed this principle as explaining the rise and fall of motivations. It may probably better be called satiation, following Harlow,[95] who took it from Lewin:[96] decreased propensity for exerting competence rather than blunting sensitivity to stimuli.

Wheel running is not the only competence exerted for its own sake. Foals perform antics in spring, and run their fields. Children hop, kick stones, and just bump in to each other. Both children and adults may enjoy dancing, singing in the kitchen, and going for a walk, sometimes even when it rains. When not finding occasion for any of those things, people may search for things to do. They rumble their bookshelves. They pick up yesterdays newspaper to read, for want of today's. They seek to keep themselves busy. If all that does not succeed, they feel bored and may shatter the windows of a telephone booth or otherwise try to become a nuisance. One even may get bored when there is plenty to do but it offers no novel challenge to whatever the competences involved. You don't do jig-saw puzzles the whole afternoon. All this has been put together as expressing a "need for variety," which is but a variant of need for exerting competence with some degree of challenge or uncertainty about success.

Self-sufficiency of motivation to exert competence-with-challenge without further or deeper sources may have much less innocent instantiations. Reports of the mass killings of Jews in Poland by a battalion of ordinary policemen suggest that what moved them to do what they did was not sadism, nor hatred of Jews, nor fear of punishment for noncompliance. Apart from their monthly salary, they appeared motivated just by propensity to perform tasks that were part of their duty, and to perform them as well as they could.[97] That motivation, as that in joyless addiction, appears enough to make one engage in strenuous behavior.

As the examples indicate, all so-called intrinsic motivations[98] come under this perspective of functioning well. Competence motivation[99] indeed is another name for them. They all involve competences that are rewarding when challenged and successfully exercised, and engender distress when unable to function properly. Adventure seeking aims at exercising the capacities for sustained and effortful goal orientation and for surpassing one's limits. In climbing mountains, parachute-jumping, or stunt-riding, one tests one's ability for performing difficult tasks, sustaining concentration, and withstanding threat and fear.[100]

WHENCE CONCERNS FOR WELL-FUNCTIONING?

The above variety of evidence suggests operation of a concern for exerting one's competences: for exerting them smoothly, in particular if there are instigations to do so and when there are challenges involved, and up to their completion. For short: there is a concern for the well-functioning of one's competences.

Why would this be so? The answer that was given in chapter 3 was simply that organisms are provided with a provision to monitor their functioning. Functioning well occurs when any given action disposition is enabled (as with the sparrow), or when progress matches or exceeds what the action instigation has set the action provisions for. Ill-functioning exists when progress falls short of the settings. In chapter 3 I argued that well-functioning of one's competences is the common denominator of a very large class of antecedents of pleasure and pain. I added the refinement that such monitoring goes on unnoticed when all goes well, or when ill-functioning is resolved automatically, as when vasodilatation corrects for body temperature that is too high or too low. Real ill functioning is signaled by signals for change that include unpleasant affect. Functioning well is being noticed when functioning proceeds smoothly but meets or has met calls for attention or effort. It is signaled by signals for continuation or for termination of action, that is, pleasant affect. Process monitoring is of course a central element in all goal-directed action, for it is what regulates effort expenditure, corrective action changes, and abandoning action that does not yield progress.

The pleasures and pains evoked by well and ill functioning, by what you do, have a different function from those contingent upon stimuli or other outcomes, by what you get. Affects have a dual role in motivation, as Reisenzein[101] argued: as regulatory principles of ongoing and potential action, and as motivational goals. I think that the former outperform the latter by far in frequency and motivational impact.

Function monitoring occurs at different levels. It occurs during the execution of individual actions and when achieving their aims; with regard to the functioning of particular competences or action systems; and with respect to person's functioning as a whole. The first is illustrated by the anger when one's pencil point breaks during writing, and the good feeling when relaxing and restful after a good meal. Satisfaction of competent mountain climbing, during the climb as well as when at the mountain top, illustrates the second; boredom when no competence can be exerted properly the third. Big cats in traditional zoos get restless and indulge in aimless movements, or so it seems. By contrast, a house cat that moves from an upstairs apartment without a roof exit to a house with a garden changes personality, and becomes lively, more interested and more interesting.[102] Extreme boredom occurs in prisoners in solitary confinement, as well as in battery chickens and cattle that become disorganized and may self-inflict serious harm by crib-biting, which presumably serves to enhance misery-blunting endorphin activity.[103] Presumed ill effects of absence of personal warmth have been mentioned above as partly due to absence of occasion to engage innate social skill propensities. Of course, these various adverse consequences of ill functioning have been discussed during the 1960s as the effects of sensory deprivation, and not reaching an optimal arousal level.[104] Monitoring well functioning thus may have direct consequences. Perhaps, diminished well-being is the readout of these consequences.

Concern for beauty may well just be rooted in an extension of the inclination to exert one's competences. Beauty involves finding unity in complexity, expanding meanings, grasping spectacles for no other purpose than grasping them. Functioning well does not explain why all this renders things beautiful; but it may explain why we desire it.

Considering functioning of competences in general a concern has an implication for interpretation of motivation generally. It leads to the prediction that propensity for exertion of all competences is a general variable—a variable that shows moment-to-moment variations, as well as, probably, forming a personality trait. It would be something like "mental energy." There is some evidence for such a general variable and trait. Lykken surmised something of that kind, and it is what shines through Nietzsche's "Will to Power".[105] The evidence is not strong, but worth looking for.

WHICH ARE THE HUMAN CONCERNS?

Recall that the mechanisms involved in serving the major biological necessities—eating and drinking, sex, affiliation and bonding, orientation, dealing with dangers and threats—all have been phrased here as competences: collections of skills, together with sensitivities for situations that call for their deployment. Notice that they all, at one time or another, have been conceived of as "needs" or "drives"; they were so phrased by Murray:[106] n Achievement, n Affiliation, n Sex, with n representing *need*. They may not all qualify for being considered to involve a competence; n Harm avoidance has more of a mini-concern, with moving away along the lines of force being the only skill needed. But most of them would. Which needs or drives there are, in the sense of deficits, presses, or activating conditions do not operate as forces that drive striving. They set sensitivities that set striving and driving in motion.

The preceding considerations lead to a conclusion about how many concerns a human being has. The conclusion: human concerns are not enumerable. Neither, therefore, are the final reasons for emotions. They are not enumerable because the number of competences a human can have or develop is unbounded. So is the number of possible surface concerns. Neither can these latter be reduced to the sum of their underlying source concerns. They have functional autonomy, if only because each surface concern—each attachment, each interest, each value—may differ from the next in the source concerns at its origin. Which competences there are depends on individual endowments, individual propensities, and on what the environment—material, historical, technological, cultural—offers and prompts to build competences for.

The large number of concerns consists of innate and acquired concerns. Acquisition does not only result from learning what to like, cultural or otherwise. More importantly, it results from life experience and developing competences. At the same time, such acquisition, as well as the innate fund, are constrained by the individual's, and the human species' architecture of mind:[107] its innate stock of sensitivities and competences, including cognitive competences. Humans are capable of foreseeing and recalling, of extensive object recognition and discrimination, as well as of bonding to individuals. Sloman once wondered whether a goldfish can love its mother.[108] It cannot, because it does not have the required mental architecture. Fish have little more than a reptilian brain, if they have that. And come to think of it, human mental architecture of course also has its limitations. Time discounting is one; we destroy our present world because its effects are in the future. And who knows what evolutionary or artificial progress is possible, assuming that there is such a future.

WHAT IS CONCERN RELEVANCE?

The preceding efforts allow specification of what is meant by "appraisal of concern relevance" and how primary emotional appraisal might proceed.

First, events as appraised—the representation of events together with that of their associated meanings, implications, consequences—correspond with a sensitivity, sufficiently so as to impinge on it. If they do, they then may match or mismatch with it.

Second, events as otherwise appraised may enable or obstruct the progress and completion of competence activation or the execution of action programs involved.

Third, events may match or mismatch action outcome expectancies or other conditions for action termination, such as the efferent copies of activated actions.

Fourth, events correspond with any sensitivity signaling likelihood of any event of the three previous kinds.

WHAT COMES FIRST, HORMICS OR HEDONICS?

The previous analysis shows that hormics and hedonics are closely intertwined. Hormic and hedonic processes appear difficult to separate. Concerns consist of sensitivities that largely lead to pleasure or pain, and that are the entry points of competences—response processes, often resulting in actions or encounters that produce pleasure or diminishment of pain. These form major grounds for caring. Progress of competences is often guided by pleasure, or adjusted by seeking to minimize pain. Again, the questions "are strivings to be explained by hormic or by hedonic principles?" and "what comes first, pleasure and pain, or more specific goals of striving?" thus are like that whether a glass is half-full or half-empty.

Well, -almost! Because concerns come first, the sensitivities and the endpoints of the competences that the sensitivities lead into. Pleasure and diminished pain are outcomes that guide continuation or termination, rather than ends that the system strives towards. The endpoints of concerns generally form setpoints that striving converges upon, if it can. In the simplest concerns, these endpoints indeed are the increase of pleasure or diminishment of pain that the situation allows. In most other concerns, they are not.

In major other concerns, the setpoints correspond to events that annul what the sensitivities responded to, or to termination of the last of the concern's action segments. Closing the hole in which she laid her eggs with a little stone terminates striving for the egg-laying concern in a digger wasp.[109] Sexual satisfaction momentarily stops desire in male animals, and decreases the partner's incentive value. Pleasure may result from what happens at that endpoint, but again it was not necessarily what instigated the striving. How else could a male dayfly find a mate? To show the role of striving without foresight was the reason for my emphasis, in this chapter as well as in that on passion, on processes in simple or naïve animals. They strive, but they know not what for, let alone for final pleasure.

The same for concerns for good functioning of competences. Their strivings arise because opportunities are met or looked for, but more basically, I think, because animals happen to be spontaneously active, most of their time. In lower animals like protozoae, spontaneous activity amounts to randomly moving about.[110] In higher animals, it amounts to being interested: having sensory and thought systems ready to operate, at least in the awake animal. And it amounts to wanting to play; and to obey inner activation of competences; and to seek opportunities. I repeat: is it not something like that which moves the new-born foal to try to stand, and what makes a healthy baby have its eyes opened widely when a few days old?

In all this, pleasure results, at the beginning when stimuli or other opportunities are met, and on the way, and at completion. However, at all three locations, it monitors and energizes action; it is not necessarily what one strives toward. True enough: even the male dayfly might be driven by pleasure. One may assume that a female smells good to him. But it is the pleasure itself that drives, and not its anticipation. It serves as a push, not as a pull. This is not restricted to naïve animals. It is common in human life. Friendship and love were mentioned as often showing a similar pattern. Vague dissatisfaction, nonspecific loneliness, facing an undefined pointlessness in life happen to dissolve with obtaining warmth. Pleasure tends to follow because it is the signal of having reached the end-point; it was not toward which the system tended. Affiliation, friendship and love strive for warmth, not for the pleasures of warmth; not primarily. That does not make such pleasure pointless. After reaching striving's endpoint, it does make the obtained situation stand out, and has it enter learning, building up the competence. Balleine and Dickinson proposed that this may well be the main function of conscious pleasure in striving and emotion.[111] It does not serve goal pursuit; it serves to know what to pursue the next time, and how to do it.

Such roles also apply to surface concerns, sentiments, and values. They have functional autonomy: Pleasures and pains at their origins have become secondary. Availability and integrity of their targets form their aims. They form a sort of set-points: They form standards because they allow, and often prescribe, networks of actions and social relationships. Reaching the set-points gives pleasure; but such pleasure is not what they are about.

Of course, this does not lose sight of the fact that animals and humans learn to anticipate and foresee future pleasures and pains, and select striving and behavior accordingly. Hedonic motivations are of major importance. They sponsor greed; they help seeking opportunities; they fill spare time. But they are not the only driver, and not the most fundamental one. Hedonic striving is parasitic on blind striving and driving.

As regards striving: The pleasure principle thus is not what governs it. Concerns do. Pleasure nevertheless does play a central role in governing striving under one very general condition, at least in humans. It is the guiding principle for choosing when there is anything to choose. When it comes to deciding between options, one must be weighed against the other. Then hedonic outcomes are envisaged, and is a common currency needed.

But in choosing options, the nature of the concerns again is decisive. Recall that various pleasures and pains are not equivalent. One pleasure is not like another, and the same for pains. Also, pleasures and pains do not simply add up or subtract. They are not mere qualia but carry what they are pleasures and pain of; chapter 3 elaborated on this. In the present analysis, the source concerns are largely treated as givens. They receive no functional interpretation here. Concern for sex, for affiliation, for no pain or for safety, and so forth, just happen to be there, at the level of process analysis. That is: their explanation comes from outside the process level, from evolutionary analysis, exploration or speculation.

This translates into a basic and general problem: that of conflict between concerns. Concerns are often incompatible; Berlin[112] extensively argued so. One often cannot pursue them simultaneously, or cannot easily do so. It is difficult to remain decent and become powerful; it is impossible to fully pursue individual liberty and be considerate for the liberty of others; and so forth. Resulting conflicts often cannot be resolved, neither by weighing satisfactions or pains, nor by compromise. Seeking to follow the pleasure principle is then inherently unstable. It is the more so since how future expected pleasures appears, and how they will look like when actually arrived at, the problem of time discounting again.[113] Both conflict and time discounting tend to cause post-decision regret; the alternative not chosen keeps nagging.

Still, hedonic concerns do exist. There *is* pursuit of happiness and desire to diminish pain. As a prostitute replied to a man she accosted, and who said that he never paid for love: "I do not offer love; I offer fun."

NOTES

[1]Examples of current theories include Frijda, 1986, Lazarus, 1991, Mandler, 1984, Oatly, 1992, Scherer, 1984, Stein and Trabasso, 1992.
[2]Solomon, 2004.
[3]Aristotle, 1941.
[4]Mesquita, 2003; Schwartz, 1992; Shweder & Haidt, 2000.
[5]Baumeister & Leary, 1995.
[6]Murray, 1938.
[7]Schwartz, 1992.
[8]Frijda, 1986.
[9]Shand, 1914.
[10]Duncker, 1941. Karl Duncker was a Gestalt psychologist, famous for his fundamental work on induced movement and on problem solving. The article referred to here, however, is in a different domain.
[11]I owe this to R. Reisenzein, personal communication, 2005.
[12]Numenmaa, 1997
[13]MacDougall, 1923.
[14]Reisenzein, R., 1996.
[15]Aristotle, 1941.
[16]Hume, 1739/1740/1969.
[17]Bentham, 1823.
[18]Rolls, 1999.
[19]Plato, ed. 1994.
[20]Batson, 1991.
[21]Batson, 1991
[22]D. T. Miller, 1999.
[23]Güth, Schmittberger, & Schwarz, 1982.
[24]Reisenzein, 2001.
[25]Hume, 1739/1740/1969.
[26]Berridge, 1999; 2004b.
[27]Berridge, 2004a; Mook, 1996.
[28]Gallistel, 1980; Mook 1996.
[29]Sloman, 1999.
[30]Bindra, 1978; Gallistel, 1980; Toates, 1986.
[31]Brooks & Hochberg, 1960.
[32]Depue & Morrone-Strupinsky, 2004.

[33]Gottlieb, 2002; Loewenstein, 1994; Piaget, 1936.
[34]Keverne & Curley, 2004.
[35]Keverne & Curley, 2004; L. J. Young & Wang, 2004.
[36]Baumeister & Leary, 1995; the definition is on p. 497.
[37]Tomasello et al., 2004.
[38]Harlow, 1960.
[39]Meltzoff & Moore, 1989.
[40]Zajonc, 2004.
[41]Goldschmidt, 1996.
[42]On Victor, see Mook ,1996, p. 134f; on Genie, see Curtiss, 1977, and Mook, 1996, p. 135f; on mate preferences, see Buss, 1994, and Hatfield and Rapson, 1996.
[43]Harlow, 1958; Depue & Morrone-Strupinsky, 2004.
[44]Berridge, 1999; 2003' 2004a; Panksepp, 1998.
[45]Dickinson & Baleine, 2002.
[46]For instance, see Schroeder's ,2004, survey.
[47]Dickinson & Baleine, 2002.
[48]Berridge, 1999; Dickinson & Balleine, 2002.
[49]Dickinson & Balleine, 2002.
[50]For more on restlessness in animals under food deprivation, see Bolles, 1975.
[51]Leitenberg & Henning, 1995.
[52]Keverne & Curley, 2004.
[53]Bargh, 1997.
[54]Berridge, 2003a; Dickinson & Balleine, 2002.
[55]Depue & Morrone-Strupinsky, 2004; Keverne & Curley, 2004.
[56]Kosfeld, Heinrichs, Zak, Fishbacher, & Fehr, 2005.
[57]Lykken, 1999.
[58]Groves & Thompson 1970; McSweeney & Swindell, 1999.
[59]Higgins, 1997.
[60]Schachter, 1959.
[61]Fiske, 1982.
[62]Depue & Morrone-Strupinsky, 2004.
[63]Allport, 1937.
[64]See J. B. Watson, 1929, where it is considered the original anger elicitor.
[65]P.Ellsworth, personal communication, july 3, 2005.
[66]Zajonc, 1968.
[67]Zajonc, 1994.
[68]Winkielman & Cacioppo, 2001.
[69]Loewenstein, 1994.
[70]Kruglanski & Webster 1996.
[71]Berlin, 1969.
[72]Kling, Shilby Hyde, Showers, & Buswell, 1999.

[73]Lagerspetz, 1961.
[74]Leary, 1999; Tesser, 1988.
[75]See Greenberg, Solomon, and Pyszczynski's, 1997, terror-management theory of self-esteem.
[76]De Waal, 1982, 2004, fig.3.
[77]Cantor & Sanderson, 1999.
[78]Stern, 2003.
[79]Baumeister, 1991.
[80]"Humble" is indeed one of the values in Schwartz's list (Table 5.2).
[81]This is in line with the theory of ritual advanced by Staal, 1990.
[82]Berridge, 1999, 2003.
[83]Maslow, 1954.
[84]Margalit, 2003.
[85]Block & Drucker, 1992, p. 49.
[86]Kertesz, 1997.
[87]Bolles, 1975.
[88]Bindra, 1961.
[89]Lorenz, 1937.
[90]Lorenz, 1952.
[91]Montgomery 1952.
[92]Butler, 1957; Harlow, 1950.
[93]Premack, 1962, 1965.
[94]McSweeney & Swindell, 1999.
[95]Harlow, 1950.
[96]Lewin, 1937.
[97]Browning, 1993.
[98]Deci & Ryan, 1985.
[99]White, 1959.
[100]Piët, 1987.
[101]Reisenzein, 1996.
[102]personal information, M.H.Frijda.
[103]Wiepkema, 1990.
[104]e.g., Hebb, 1972.
[105]Lykken, 1999; Nietzsche, 1901; for the latter, also see Solomon, 2003, chapter 3.
[106]1938; see above, Fig. 5.1.
[107]Sloman, 1987.
[108]Sloman, 1999.
[109]Tinbergen, 1951.
[110]Jennings, 1904.
[111]Balleine & Dickinson, 1998.
[112]Berlin, 1969.
[113]Ainslie, 2001.

6

Strength

Emotions differ in intensity. Some whisper, others are passions. There are wishes and cravings. There is passing anger, as when you overhear a mean joke on the streetcar, and there is rage that seeks to destroy its target. "Intensity" is a bleak term to refer to these differences. It biases attention towards heartbeat and feeling only. Better call it the strength of emotions, as Spinoza did.[1] The strength of an emotion is its degree of being a passion. It is what makes emotions socially relevant, and what calls for self-control.

What makes one emotion more passionate than another? That question only allows of an answer when the notion of emotion strength has become clearer. The question is not just academic. Emotion strength is involved in questions of responsibility, in a legal context or otherwise. It is important in judging therapy outcomes: do anxieties or depressions indeed have become weaker? It plays in daily contexts: which of the choices will make me happier or make me suffer less?

So: what precisely varies in strength? Emotions are multicomponential phenomena. The components do not all neatly vary together: by what token should one emotion be judged stronger than another?

Strength or intensity hardly forms a subject of research in emotions research. That is odd. The problem of understanding strength is old. The story of the Egyptian king Psammenitus, recounted by Herodotus, famously illustrates it. For brevity, I give Montaigne's version.[2]

> The story goes that Psammenitus, king of Egypt, having been beaten and taken prisoner by Cambyses, king of Persia, seeing his captive daughter pass by, dressed as a slave and sent to haul water, and all her friends weeping and lamenting around her, kept himself straight without a word, eyes fixed to the ground; and then seeing that one led his son to his death, kept the same posture; but having noticed one of his servants led among the captives, he began to beat his head and showing an extreme sorrow. Asked why this difference by Cambyses, Psammenitus answered: "Only the latter suffering can show itself in tears, the first two going widely beyond any means for expressing themselves."

What, then, is emotion strength? In most empirical studies, it is measured by the answer to a simple question like "How intense was your emotion?", or by one or a few selected physiological measures, like heart rate or galvanic skin response. Until recently, the only in-depth treatment was by Spinoza. Part IV of his *Ethics* is devoted to the subject: *"De affectuum viribus,"* or "The Strength of the Emotions."[3] Only during the last decades of last century it began again to receive explicit attention.[4]

WHAT IS EMOTION STRENGTH?

The Psammenitus story and multicomponential theory preclude a simple index of the strength of an emotion. Expressive behavior does not yield it: Emotions may be strong without it. Experimentally induced self-reported surprise, for instance, led only in 9% of cases to lifting the eyebrows, and in fewer still to widely opening the eyes.[5] Neither does felt emotion always accompany autonomic upset. As mentioned earlier, the discrepancies between intensity indices led Lang to his three-systems theory:[6] emotions represent activity of three discrete systems, those of feeling, behavior, and autonomic reaction. After treatment of phobic anxiety, the patient may without hesitation pick up the spider, may declare to have lost the fright, but heart rate still goes up steeply when seeing a spider close by. Such lack of covariation led to doubt that even autonomic arousal is a meaningful concept.[7] Correlations between felt intensity and expressive behavior, for instance, are found to be weak.[8] True enough, felt amusement by jokes and intensity of laughter correlate strongly, but this is not the case for joy in general.[9] Moment-to-moment changes in facial expressions in an individual person do correlate more closely with strength of feelings;[10] but this does not hold across participants. And perhaps the most distinct instance of discrepancy: nonconscious stimuli that do not arouse feelings nevertheless can influence affective judgments and preference behavior, as discussed in chapter 4.[11]

The difficulty of defining emotion strength becomes even greater when attending to other than immediately accessible response components. The range of response components that can vary in strength is very much larger. It includes those response aspects that suggest the notion of emotion strength in the first place, and that are responsible for emotions to be passions. Different emotions importantly differ in these regards. One of these is strength of action readiness, its sheer power to overcome obstacles and produce impact. It differentiates rage from anger. Another is drasticness of action: the impact that emotional action aims at or achieves. Aristotle pointed out that anger aims at retaliation or removal of obstruction, but that hatred aims at annihilating the person as such. A third aspect consists of control precedence, that includes domination of thought, such as having obsessive thoughts or incessant rumination. Control precedence is used as a telling experimental index of emotion strength in observing long latencies in word association tests, and in animals in the Conditioned Emotional Response CER:[12] suppression of bar-pressing for food by a signal for forthcoming electric shock.

Of course, in human work the most straightforward measure is to ask people to rate felt intensity. Intensity of feeling may seem an elementary quality of the experience of emotions, but it is not. It is not something elementary like the loudness of a sound. Verbal reports of emotional feelings show that feelings are usually composite;[13] chapter 8 will detail this further. Also, felt emotion intensity, like all other intensity judgments, is highly context sensitive. How intense an emotion is felt to be depends on the range and frequency of the other experiences that went before and to which the person may have adapted.[14]

To obtain more insight in the structure of all those parameters, a questionnaire study was made of the subjective intensity of potential strength variables in recalled emotion incidents.[15]

There is a hitch to studying felt intensity of recalled incidents. Kahneman[16] pointed out that what he labels *instant utility* should not be confused with *remembered utility*. Asking participants for on-line moment-to-moment ratings of feeling intensity measures instant utility; asking them to give overall ratings of an emotion episode provides remembered utility.

Remembered utility—emotion strength as recalled or reconstructed—was what was obtained in Sonnemans's study.

THE STRUCTURE
OF SUBJECTIVE EMOTIONAL INTENSITY

Thirty-seven participants were asked to recall a specific emotion incident and then to answer a questionnaire about it. The questionnaire included a question on overall felt intensity ("How intense was your emotion?"); on peak intensity; on various temporal aspects, such as latency of response; on various intensity aspects; and emotion duration. Table 6.1 lists the major questions. In addition, they were asked to fill out a 15-item appraisal questionnaire of the kind described in chapter 4. They also answered questions on whether they had tried to regulate their emotional feeling or behavior and on the amount of effort needed for control, and questions on the concerns they thought the emotion eliciting event had touched upon by. Participants were also asked to draw a graph of the intensity of their emotion over time on the computer screen.

The intensity questionnaire was presented on the computer screen. Multiple-choice answers were given by tapping the relevant keys. Each participant came for six sessions. At five sessions, they had to recall an emotion incident from the past week; at the sixth session they were asked for the most intense emotion from the past year. This thus yielded reports on 222 emotion incidents. At each session they wrote a brief description of the incident, chose a label for the emotion, and typed their answers. In the first session, prior to emotion recall, they filled out several personality questionnaires and a concern questionnaire. That latter listed 37 concerns, derived from the work of Hofstede and Schwartz.[17] It contained items such as "my need for privacy" and "my need to have influence on others." Each item was rated for how important it was for him- or herself on a scale from 1 to 7.

Correlations between the intensity questions were factor analyzed. Oblique rotation (rotation permitting correlation between factors) produced six factors that explain 68.1% of the total variance. The factors, in order of percentage of variance explained, are named as in Table 6.2.

Six major aspects of emotion strength appeared. Five of these, it turned out, were more or less independent of each other; they correlated .39 at most.[18] Duration, strength of action tendency, bodily effects, and recollection and changes in beliefs, and long-term behavior each represent almost independent aspects of the felt impact of an emotional event. An emotion can thus be intense in one way without notably being so in another: first conclusion.

Four of these above aspects correlate strongly (that is, over .50) with overall felt intensity. There appear to exist four largely independent emotional intensities. That is the second conclusion of this study. Duration of emotion formed an exception. It produced the only near-zero correlations in the correlation table. Duration, as rated by the participants, correlates weakly or not at all with the other factors, including overall felt intensity. Estimated duration of emotions thus appears to be nearly independent of felt intensity. That is the third conclusion. The same independence applies to duration as measured on-line. Kahneman and Fredrickson[19] found that actual duration and intensity ratings

TABLE 6.1
Major Questions in Intensity Questionnaire

Onset latency	How long was the interval between the eliciting event and the first emotional response?
Peak latency	How long was it before the emotional response reached its peak?
Felt peak amplitude	How intense was your emotional feeling at its peak?
Average felt intensity	How intense was your emotional feeling over its entire course?
Duration	How long did the entire emotional experience last?
Felt arousal strength	To what degree was your emotion accompanied by bodily symptoms?
Arousal duration	How long did the bodily effects last?
Recurrence in thought	After the initial emotional reaction, did you how frequently think of the event and reexperience the emotion?
Associational width	Are there events, things, or persons that trigger the original emotion? How many?
Felt impulse drasticness	How drastic was the action impulse that you felt?
Felt action readiness strength	How strong was the felt action impulse?,
Felt loss in action readiness	How strongly did you experience an incapacity or aversion to act?
Action drasticness	If you did something during your emotional response, how drastic was your action?
Action contentment	How satisfied were you, after the emotion was over, with your behavior?
Felt control strength	To what extent did you try to control your emotion?
Experienced (un)pleasantness	How pleasant or painful did you feel your emotional experience to be?
Life change	To what extent did your emotional experience (not the eliciting event) change your life?
Overall felt intensity	How intense was your emotional experience as a whole?

Note. Adapted from Sonnemans (1991)

of emotion episodes also were independent. They summarize their findings under the heading of "duration neglect." Independence of duration and strength appear to be general. It even applies to emotion strength in animals: frequency of intracranial self-stimulation—presumably indicating its attractiveness—is independent of the duration of each such stimulation pulse.[20] Duration thus is not an aspect of emotion strength, as measured by immediate response aspects.[21]

TABLE 6.2
Emotion Strength Factors (Oblique Rotation)

1. Frequency of recollection and re-experience of the emotion.

2. Duration of the emotion and delay of its onset after the event.

3. Extent of belief changes and changes in long term behavior.

4. Overall felt intensity.

5. Strength of action tendency, and drasticness of actual behavior.

6. Strength and duration of perceived bodily changes, or degree of passivity.

Note.   Adapted from Sonnemans (1991).

On the other hand, important longer term aspects of the emotions did relate to felt intensity as well as to duration, in Sonnemans's study, namely, frequency of recollections, and belief changes and long-term behavior (factors 1 and 3). They formed the largest factors, together with duration. They appear more strongly related to felt emotion strength than the more traditional aspects of bodily upset and strength of action tendency: conclusion four.

Fifth conclusion: overall felt intensity is itself a distinct aspect of experience. It forms a separate factor that is composed of the explicit overall felt intensity rating ("On the whole, how intense was the emotion that you described?"), peak intensity rating ("what was the intensity of the emotion at its peak?"), rating of "How intense was your emotion during the whole emotion episode?", and the area under the curve in the drawn intensity diagram. Overall felt intensity is virtually the same as peak intensity and as the intensity "during the whole episode": The first two questions correlate .72, and the first and the third, .80 (which are both about as high as the reliabilities of the questions allow). The close correspondence between overall and peak intensity corresponds with what Fredrickson and Kahneman[22] found: Overall pleasantness or painfulness of an episode appeared to be the average of peak intensity and intensity at the end of the episode. Intensity of an episode, they argue, is "evaluated by moments," by peak and end values in this case, rather than resulting from a computed time integral of the continuously varying instant intensities. End values may seriously bias estimate of such an integral, as experimental introduction of a weak unpleasant stimulus after a stable more unpleasant period has shown.[23] In our study, end values almost always were zero, and perhaps for that reason overall felt intensity correlated rather strongly (.58) with the area under the curve in the diagram, which is equivalent to the time integral; but indeed, that is much lower than full correspondence.

Overall felt intensity, because it correlates with all variables other than duration,[24] may perhaps be understood as a weighted sum of the strengths of the variables in the four other factors. Variables from these four factors were combined to examine their multiple correlation with overall felt intensity. Six variables entered to yield a multiple correlation of .69; Table 6.3 gives the variables and their contribution to multiple correlation.[25] These six variables thus explained about half of the variance in overall felt intensity. Note that all four factors other than duration participate (duration of bodily change is correlated with strength of bodily changes, and not with overall duration).

Overall felt intensity thus appears to be a compound of the felt intensity of various response aspects, notably felt re-experiencing the event, felt action tendencies, and felt bodily arousal. These three all can be regarded as contributing to experienced control precedence. Note that the role of felt bodily arousal comes third, and not first, as traditional theories have it.[26]

Different emotions differ in various response aspects. They thus indeed may appear intense for different reasons. The multiple regression analysis just described was repeated separately for the emotion groups for which enough cases were available: fear, sadness, anger, disappointment, and the positive emotions. Felt intensity of different emotions indeed was determined by different aspects. Felt bodily upset was important for fear ($r = .53$), but not for the other emotions. Strength of re-experience was not important for the felt intensity of anger, but strength of action tendency and belief changes were, as they also were for the positive emotions (mostly joy). The findings on fear and anger confirm those by objective studies.[27] Intensity of joy also correlated strongly (.54) with strength of re-experiencing. The intensities of sadness and disappointment are related to strength of re-experiencing the event; disappointment correlated, in addition, with the envisaged drasticness of action. Not too much weight can be placed on these differences, because the number of cases was small. Yet they indicate that it is problematic to measure the intensities of different sorts of emotion

TABLE 6.3
Correlations of Strength Variables With Overall Felt Intensity

Strength measure	r	R^2
Strength of re-experiencing the emotion during first 24 hours	.53	.28
Strength of action tendency	.49	.39
Strength of bodily change	.50	.43
Belief changes about people	.36	.46
Duration of bodily changes	.35	.47
Drasticness of envisaged action	.33	.48

Note. Source: Sonnemans (1991). R^2 = cumulative explained variance (squared multiple correlation).

all by the same measure. They also suggest that emotional intensity may not be transitive. Emotion A may be felt to be more intense than Emotion B, because of its greater autonomic upheaval, and B than C for making life appear more meaningless while the heart was going steady. C may still be felt as more intense than A.

A remarkable finding was the prominence of frequency and strength of re-experiencing the emotion after the event. It is the biggest factor, and it explains over one fourth of the variance of overall felt intensity. It is a major aspect of control precedence. The connection between felt intensity and rumination is known from other research, notably by Rimé.[28] Emotion strength is more than bodily feeling.

Rated overall felt intensity (and rated peak intensity) thus can be regarded as the weighted sum of all other aspects except duration. That indeed is implied by the use of multiple correlations, because these examine linear and additive relationships. However, this may not in fact be the appropriate model, as Sonnemans remarks.[29] Felt intensity may just correspond to the most salient variable. Indeed, the correlation between overall felt intensity with the magnitude of whichever happened to be the strongest of the three major variables, strength of bodily change, strength of action tendency, and strength of re-experiencing, (.65, or an R^2 of .42), was almost equal to their multiple correlation of .48.

HOW TO VIEW "EMOTION STRENGTH"?

Sonnemans's study was concerned with self-reported emotions only. On-line objective measures of autonomic variables, of behavioral force, amplitude and scope, of ruminations, belief changes, and changes in the conduct of life will probably yield similar findings of more or less independent response dimensions.

Assuming that to be so, the findings just given can be interpreted in several ways. They may be taken to indicate that independent and independently varying motivational and support mechanisms are in operation in emotions-the mechanisms, such as those of affect, attention, general activation, the specific action readiness systems, and autonomic system arousal. "Emotion strength" would not be a meaningful notion, just as "autonomic arousal" may not be. Different sorts of emotion strength would have to be measured independently, and labeled distinctively.

On the other hand, the response components were shown to converge on felt overall intensity. All variables except duration correlated positively—they all load on the first unrotated factor—and the same may be the case when objective response components are included. This might point to some basic process that affects the intensities of all components. The intensity of that process might represent "the" emotion strength. Separate parameters will also be influenced by specific functional and situational determinants. This, of course, would fit nicely with the dual model of motivation described in chapter 2. It would also fit meaningfully with evidence that the correlations between components are stronger with intense emotions. The higher the intensity of one of the manifestations, the larger the likelihood that other components participate. Rosenberg and Ekman[30] indeed adduce this latter finding as support for the basic emotions notion.

Under that interpretation, "emotion strength" is a meaningful concept. It might reflect the overall impact of the emotional event. It is not an implausible possibility. Whether overall felt intensity is the best index of that strength is thereby doubtful. In Sonnemans's study, it was the only variable employed as the dependent variable of multiple regression analysis; any other variable (e.g., recurrence in thought, or influence on the conduct of life) might also have been employed. But most importantly: overall felt intensity has an important drawback. It comes from retrospective rating of emotion episodes. We know that such ratings are fallible, because they are biased by end values.[31] For this, there are two alternatives. One is by self-reports during episodes; Stone and colleagues developed the Ecological Momentary Assessment procedure for the purpose[32] that, however, is little suited for many relevant episodes. Another is developing objective assessments of the variables that would appear to reflect control precedence: prolonged thought about the incidents and strength of action tendency, in addition to bodily arousal. Further parameters can easily be thought of, notably interference with ongoing activities. But whether that would help depends on how solidly such measures would hang together when objectively assessed, or are amenable to constructing a stable additive or disjunctive measure.

The two models correspond with two of the models of the organization of emotions, discussed in chapter 2. One may also develop a model in line with the third form of organization considered there: strength of action readiness and/or control precedence as the central variable, that interacts with the separate contributions of all other components. Which of the three comes closest to the facts can only be judged when the facts are there.

Pursuing research in this direction would be useful. It could show whether some notion of "basic strength" is really meaningful. It would then allow one to compare the strength of one emotion with that of another, or that of someone else. If research like this succeeds, it might allow to develop a measure of emotion strength, an *emol*, let us say, a unit of emotion strength, comparable to the *util* in utility theory.[33] It might allow to say that my rage is stronger than my despair and that my happiness is stronger than yours. Note that we often make such comparisons in everyday decisions and discussions.

DETERMINANTS OF EMOTION STRENGTH

What makes one emotion stronger than another? The preceding did not make answering that question easier, so I will neglect most of it. Relevant data on measures and determinants of separate strength dimensions are too sparse. I will use measures of felt or other intensity as if they simply indicate strength.

The question of what makes emotions strong has not often been studied in any detail. Its only truly systematic discussion, as far as I know, again was that by Spinoza.[34]

For Spinoza, the strength of emotion derives from the strength of striving or *conatus*. Emotions differ in strength with the strength of the concerns or desires at stake in the emotional event.[35] But given a particular desire, strength also depends on the strength of the external cause,[36] that is, upon the magnitude of the affecting event. Importance and impact depend on strength as well as number of the desires that are thwarted or gratified,[37] and thus also on the magnitude and number of meanings that a given event possesses.[38]

Event magnitude, in Spinoza's view, is increased by concurrent pleasures and pains; so does emotion strength, because pleasures as well as pains, in his treatment, summate. Their concurrence stems from the cognitive activities of remembering, foresight, and imagination. Pleasures of recollection add to actual pleasures, and pains of imagination to actual pain. In jealousy the pain of loss is augmented by the hatred inspired by the rival, and again by the pain induced by the pleasure he is supposed to have.[39] Simultaneous pleasure and pain tend to subtract, or else give rise to ambivalence, the wavering of mind.[40] Nostalgia (*regret* in Parkinson's translation), for instance, consists of the mixture of pleasure coming from the recollection of something loved, and the pain caused by that event being irrevocably gone.[41]

Emotion strength is further seen to depend on the emotional effectiveness of the emotional object's representation. Representations are emotionally effective when they posit the existence of a given thing.[42] Effectiveness is weakened or annulled by (and can only be weakened or annulled by) representations that posit the non-existence of the thing, for instance by positing that a contrary event might occur. Net emotion strength, depends on the proportion of representations that posit to those that contradict the thing's existence. Due to this proportion, an emotional event is more potent when it is actually present before one's eyes than when it is merely known about or imagined,[43] and when it is close by, rather than remote in space or time.[44] Likewise, emotion is stronger when events are conceived as necessary or probable, rather than as merely possible,[45] or when having occurred in the past. The variability of this proportion explains the inconstancy of hope and fear.[46]

This is a fine analysis of what current investigators call the effects of appraisals of reality and proximity of the event on emotional intensity, as these were condensed in the Law of Apparent Reality in chapter 1; they are extensively discussed by Ben-Ze'ev and by Ortony, Clore, and Collins.[47] Spinoza's formulation of the above principles stressed belief strength as their common denominator. Belief strength can vary with respect to different event aspects. One such aspect is the event's probability of occurrence, or the probability of a particular consequence. Another is the *indubitability* of the event: the certainty that a given interpretation of the event's meaning applies.[48] Such certainty depends on the individual's belief system and manner of thinking rather than on the actual evidence. It differs between individuals and with cultural habits. When Creole Dutch participants of Surinamese origin were asked whether other people would agree with how they viewed an anger-provoking event, they thought they would; autochthonous Dutch participants, by contrast, were much less convinced of that. Drasticness of action differed accordingly. The Surinamese had more frequently broken off relationships that had provoked the anger than the autochthonous Dutch.[49]

Spinoza thus located the causes of emotion strength in strength and number of relevant concerns, in event magnitude, and in the cognitive processes that current psychology calls appraisal. Emotion strength thus appears to be the result of complex influences. The complexity probably goes further than these three kinds of influence. I expect there are at least three more: degree of readiness to respond in a particular emotional fashion-propensity for a particular form of action readiness such as anger or sadness; individual differences in temperament or personality; and emotion regulation that dampens or enhances one's emotion. These expectations can be represented somewhat pompously by the following formula:[50]

$$S = f(C, E, CA, A, P, R),$$

in which S represents Strength, C represents Concern strength, E represents Event magnitude, CA represents Context Appraisal, A represents Action Potential, P represents Personality, and R represents Regulation. I briefly discuss each.

Concerns

Most people would share Spinoza's view that emotion strength depends on how important an event is to the person and that this may well, in turn, depend on the strength of relevant concerns. Concern strength is not easily measured, although efforts have been made; for instance, one might measure risk taken and effort spent in reaching a goal.[51] One may also expect that number of relevant concerns plays a role. Empirical findings agree. As already mentioned, Sonnemans obtained the participant's ratings of the general importance that each of a number of concerns had, to him or her. With each recalled emotion incident, the participants also indicated the concerns for which that incident had been relevant, and how strongly so. This yielded the number of concerns deemed relevant, among other things. The outcome was striking. Almost always (in 96% of the emotion instances), more than one concern was considered relevant. In 74%, five or more concerns were checked. Most emotional events have complex meanings.

Both number and strength of the relevant concerns correlated with the overall felt intensity of the emotion incidents. The outcomes merit a table, Table 6.4. Concerns appear importantly related to felt emotion intensity. The number of concerns that an event touches upon correlates significantly with felt intensity. So does the strength of the relevant concerns. Event relevance—the importance of the concerns in the emotional event—also contributes, and adds somewhat to the effect of the mere number of concerns. Some of these relationships were confirmed in other studies. "Commitment to achievement," for instance, appeared to correlate with perceived motivational relevance of achievement-oriented events.[52]

Strength and relevance of the various concerns might combine in different ways. They might add, or multiply; their average might be what determines felt intensity, or the one with highest strength or relevance may carry the day. The evidence from Sonnemans's study favors the latter. As the bottom line in Table 6.3 shows, felt intensity depended most strongly on the concern with the highest product of strength and relevance; the correlation is a trifle higher than with the sum of the products. But of course these differences are not significant, and come from just this one study.

Event magnitude

Serious illness of someone one loves will cause more severe upset than a passing indisposition and a scathing insult more than just a slighting re-

TABLE 6.4
Correlations of Concern Measures With Overall Felt Intensity

Strength measure	r
Number of concerns	.40
Summed strength	.40
Summed relevance	.45
Summed product of relevance and strength	.47
Highest product of relevance and strength	.49

Note. Adapted from Sonnemans (1991).

mark. Such magnitude is not an objective fact. It comes jointly from objective aspects of the event, and from how it is appraised. How serious an insult is taken to be depends on social norms with regard to insulting, on who does the insulting and in what tone of voice, and on the individual's history with being insulted. The tenth insult in a row may lead to an unstoppable rage; it may also elicit a shoulder shrug: "He is at it again." Seriousness also strongly depends on how seriously one takes it—as nasty or as a joke, reality appraisal. In Sonnemans's study, appraised event reality correlated significantly with felt intensity, particularly in fear incidents.

A major influence on appraised event magnitude comes from the event's context of comparison, in accordance with the Law of Change and, generally, the Law of Comparative Feeling. Part of such comparison is with the magnitudes that one is used to, as best approached through adaptation level theory or Parducci's (1995) range-frequency theory.[53] A major, overlapping, part is due to comparison with norms, expectations, and other reference points, as caught in Norm and Prospect theories.[54] Comparisons have additional consequences: they may let additional concerns enter the game. If I get a smaller salary increase than my neighbor, not only does the "increase" turns into "less than he," but it engages the concern for comparative social prestige and for daily status display.

Context Appraisal

Most of the cognitive aspects discussed by Spinoza—proximity of the event.[55] Some of these aspects affect the strength of any sort of emotion; they are "global variables".[56] Others are "local variables," specific to particular emotions. One of the major global context variables is appraised difficulty of dealing with the emotional event, the inverse of appraisal of low coping potential discussed in the chapter 4. Urgency is a simple variant;[57] more complex is finding there is no way out of misery, and no resources remain. Panic occurs when there is serious threat but ways of escape are closing; despair when they have definitely closed. Difficulty gone gives rise to the joys of relief, and the flow experiences of smooth progress under challenge.[58] Obstacles on the way to one's goals increases desire. The harder to get, the harder we strive; this relationship has been a cornerstone of Brehm's theories of reactance and motivation strength.[59]

Another global context variable is the salience of event features. Salience readily results from change and from prominence of a standard of comparison. Both give rise to "focusing illusions":[60] higher appraised event magnitudes for that reason. People are "loss aversive" because loss contrasts saliently with having had what is lost; losing money is more painful than never having received it. The ease with which counterfactual alternatives can be constructed for missed or lost opportunities likewise enhances felt

intensity.[61] Intensity of grief, regret and disappointment indeed varies with
how acute the loss, how near the miss, how vivid the expectation.[62]
Kahneman and Miller (1986) formed their Norm Theory, "a hypothesis of
emotional amplification, which states that the affective response to an event is
enhanced if its causes are abnormal".[63] Empirical support has been obtained for all these generalizations. True enough, in all of them it may not be
only salience of unexpectedness or abnormality as such that caused the am-
plifications. Every unexpected event not only stands out, but also requires
acute readjustment, cognitive or otherwise.

   Salience is counteracted by decrease of apparent reality appraisal. Time
discounting does just that, as I proposed in chapter 4; but it can also be
achieved by turning away from cues and sheer disbelief.

   Local appraisal aspects contribute to the intensity of particular kinds of
emotion. Several of them have been subtly described by Ben-Ze'ev as
"background circumstances." They include appraised accountability with
its variants like "blameworthiness," "arbitrariness" and "unfairness" of
harm, relevant mostly to anger and guilt and the deservingness or
undeservingness of objects of harm and praise in sympathy, pity or envy.[64]
Sonnemans's study provided clear evidence for the effects of some of these.
For instance, difficulty, novelty and blameworthiness correlated significantly with overall felt intensity—novelty particularly within sadness and
the positive emotions (.39 and .29, respectively), and blameworthiness of
someone else with the intensity of anger (.35).

   I will be brief about the entries *Action Potential* and *Personality.* The
strength of an emotion depends not only on aspects of what elicited the
emotion but also on the proclivity of the individual for that sort of emotion.
One can at some moment of time be inclined to anger, due to mood or to previous irritations; or one can be inclined to sadness, again due to mood, to
previous stimuli, or to biochemical state. But proclivity for a particular kind
of action readiness or action may also be a function of the individual's action repertoire: his or her expectations that particular actions are effective in
dealing with emotional events. Arguably, anger is more easily evoked
when it has proved effective in the past, or can be expected to be effective
for technical reasons such as possession of weapons or social power.

   Personality, thus also influences emotion strength by favoring or enhancing, disfavoring or weakening, certain appraisals and states of action readiness. As mentioned in chapter 2, emotion traits like Positive Affect and
Negative Affect, Neuroticism or Trait Anxiety, Trait Anger and Impulsivity
are stable personality traits that influence the frequency of their corresponding emotional states. They are in fact defined by them. They do so by
lowering the thresholds for the given appraisals and/or states of action
readiness and, thus, thereby influencing the strength of the corresponding
emotions.

A general relevant personality attribute is affective responsiveness. Stable individual differences exist in average emotion intensity as measured over a given time span, called Affect Intensity. The trait predicts higher intensities of emotional responses to standard events.[65] In Sonnemans's study, overall felt intensity of each emotion incident correlates significantly with mean overall felt intensity of the five other emotion incidents that each subject reported. The trait of impulsiveness[66] may correspond to relative weakness of emotion regulation.

EMOTION REGULATION

The Law of Care for Consequence discussed the ubiquity of emotion regulation in normal circumstances. Almost all emotions are controlled and attenuated to some extent, except when drunk or brain damaged. Regulation can affect all components of the emotion process: not merely outward expression, but also feeling, attention for emotional events, emotional appraisal, affect and action readiness.[67] Regulation can affect each of these components separately: only outward expression, only feeling, only autonomic response, or only action readiness. It operates by processes of different sorts. Some are automatic and autoregulatory, such as numbing under traumatic stress.[68] Others are more deliberate, such as avoiding stressful encounters, seeking diversion, emotional detachment, considering harmful events as unlikely or untrue, and use of beta-blocking drugs and anti-depressants as examples.[69]

Emotion strength is always the outcome of an interplay between excitatory and inhibitory or enhancing regulatory factors. Regulation arises largely in response to excitation or to anticipation of excitation to come. It is to a large extent instigated by feedback from the emotion process and its actual or foreseen external effects, although it is also a result of personal habit and temperament.[70] Enhancing one's emotions is instigated by perceived or hoped-for success of one's emotion displays, such as intimidation, compassion, or evoked sympathy.

Regulation varies in specificity. Instructions to reappraise an emotional situation can have effects on decreasing the intensity of many components.[71] Suppression of one's facial expression may have no other intensity consequences, or it may even enhance other strength indices such as physiological arousal.[72]

The effects of emotion regulation on overall emotion strength are not easily assessed because of their reciprocal relationship: one may expect stronger emotional impulses to generate stronger regulatory efforts. This is indeed what was Sonnemans found.[73] His questionnaire included two major regulation questions: "how much effort did you need to lessen your emotional feeling?" and "how much effort was needed to control your emotional behavior and expression?" In 48% of the reported emotions the subject had tried to control his or her feeling, and in 69% his or her behavior and expression. Correlations with overall felt intensity were indeed substantial: .58 for the feeling, and .37 for behavior and expression. Seeking to examine the effect of regulation efforts on intensity, Sonnemans reasoned that a linear combination of intensity and regulation should correlate higher with the intensity determinants than did intensity alone. This amounts to calculating the canonical correlation between overall felt intensity plus regulation effort with the determinants found to correlate with overall felt intensity, namely concerns (the maximal product of strength and relevance), the appraisals of difficulty (anticipated effort) and of reality character, and the individual's mean overall felt intensity. That correlation turned out to be significantly higher than that with overall felt intensity alone (.60 when including regulation of feeling, and .59 when including regulation of behavior and expression, as compared with .56 with overall felt intensity alone).

But the effects of automatic regulation processes can cause discontinuities in the determinant-emotion strength relationship. People may dissociate, or more voluntarily distance themselves, and transform their emotions into virtual emotions,[74] to which strength measures not easily apply. One may suppose that something like that happened with Psammenitus.

EMOTION STRENGTH
AND ITS MANY DETERMINANTS

The various classes of determinants summarized in the formula indeed appear to make independent contributions to the strength of emotion. A stepwise multiple regression analysis to overall felt intensity resulted in significant contributions of determinants from the three groups of determinants concern/event, context appraisal, and personality.[75] Table 6.5 gives the results. The obtained multiple correlation is .57. The examined determinants thus explain 31%, about one third, of the variance of felt intensity.

Amount of control effort was also related to emotion strength, as just shown. The control questions correlated .58 and .37 with overall felt intensity of all emotions, and .69 and .44 for that of the negative emotions only; evidently and understandably, negative emotions are controlled to a larger extent than the positive ones. The joint effect of the determinants indeed rises from 31% explained variance (in the multiple correlation) to about 36% explained variance (in the canonical correlation) when regulation effort is included.

The various determinants determine most of the strength dimensions more or less equally. Only the multiple correlations for the strength of felt bodily changes and for duration are somewhat lower than the others. Interestingly, concerns affect the cognitive and more enduring effects of the events more strongly than the acute emotion manifestations. These appraisal vari-

STRENGTH

169

TABLE 6.5
Correlations Between Determinants and Intensity Variables

Strength measure	Recollection & re-experience	Duration & delay	Action tendency & behavior	Belief change, long-term behavior	Bodily changes	Overall felt intensity
Number of concerns	.423	.290	.343	.457	.308	.417
Sum product relevance and strength, group	.440	.261	.412	.467	.353	.473
Maximum product relevance and strength, group	.380	.170	.381	.397	.295	.488
Anticipated effort	.251	.278	.332	.382	.295	.297
Experienced before	−.308	−.184	−.102	−.232	−.223	−.242
Well-being others involved	.330	.139	.224	.349	.136	.234
Felt unreality	−.224	−.068	−.110	−.156	−.151	−.215
Mean overall felt intensity	.283	.188	.235	.271	.160	.247
Multiple correlation of underlined items	.546	.406	.499	.602	.436	.565

Note. $N = 219$; 3 cases are missing because of missing concerns. The italicized variables are those that entered the stepwise regression analysis resulting in the multiple correlations in the bottom row, $F > 4$. From "The Determinants of Subjective Emotional Intensity," by J. Sonnemans and N. H. Frijda, 1995, *Cognition and Emotion, 9*, p. 494. Copyright 1995 by Lawrence Erlbaum Associates. Adapted with permission.

ables equally influence the latter. Strength of action tendency and drasticness of behavior are mostly determined by the apparent difficulty of the emotional situation (anticipated effort). The strength of bodily changes, too, appears related to difficulty and novelty, and to some extent to the concerns.

Some evidence is thus obtained that the strength of an emotion indeed is the joint effect of a number of determinants. They explain about one third of the variance in emotion strength. This is not too bad a result, considering that questionnaire answers are not very reliable indicators of what really was going on. What outcomes would be obtained when behavioral and physiological data are used, together with subjective data is difficult to foresee. Higher reliabilities may yield more substantial explanation, but objective measures may also show less coherence among strength measures.

SHAPES OF FUNCTIONS

The formula that summarized potential strength determinants did not specify the kind of relationship of these determinants and strength. It will not be easy to specify them, because that would, first of all, require mean-ingful metrics of the determinants, and notably of the concern strengths and event magnitudes, the major determinants. Only in a few instances, such metrics might be available, such as magnitudes of and distances from or to a reward. Even there, there are problems. For instance, Cacioppo, and colleagues have argued[76] that positive affect shows "negativity offset." Zero input evokes a little bit of positivity: an animal will approach an unfa-miliar neutral stimulus from a long distance. But a stimulus at a distance still does not form zero input, nor does approach prove non-neutrality ex-cept by circular definition. For less simple stimuli, the problems are com-pounded. How to scale the seriousness of losses separately from the sadness they evoke?

Anyway, in general, one may expect nonlinear relationships between subjective and objective measures of event magnitude and emotional ef-fects. Experienced or effective magnitude, plotted against stimulus magni-tude (palatability against number of sweets consumed, for instance) often shows a negatively accelerated function; so does running speed against proximity to the reward. It forms a standard finding in the relationship be-tween pleasant and aversive stimuli and rated liking and dislike.[77] But such a function holds only within the limited ranges of likes and dislikes of sim-ple stimuli, or concepts. Rated intensity of electric shock to the finger shows a positive coefficient in Stevens' power law[78] and thus a positively acceler-ated function. Would painfulness be measured, the same will probably be found. However, when stimulus range is extended, Brehm's saw-tooth function will most likely be found:[79] The subject will faint, dissociate, or tumble into apathetic helplessness.

Brehm's studies of strength of motivation plotted against difficulty of approach shows that determinant-strength relationships can be nonmonotonous. Motivation strength rises to a peak when difficulty mounts, but then drops off steeply, and motivation will be abandoned. One tends to abandon desire when it becomes unrealistic, not worth the effort, or abandons hope. Brehm argues that this holds for emotions generally. Whenever the emotion meets with a deterrent—"any factor that resists or opposes the function of the emotion"[80]—the same nonmonotonous, cubic relationship between deterrent magnitude and emotion intensity should appear. A small deterrent will appreciably reduce intensity, a larger deter-rent hardly do so, and a strong deterrent abolish striving. Confirming evi-dence has been obtained in a sizable number of experiments, with emotions of sadness, happiness, anger, and sympathy.[81] Non-monotonicity was, of course, earlier argued by Hebb in the inverted-U-curve hypothesis.[82]

Changes may also be qualitatively discontinuous. When events get gradually closer, or stimuli get gradually more intense, behavior may sud-denly flip over from one to a different kind. A cornered animal suddenly switches from fearful withdrawal to fierce attack. This example given by Zeeman[83] was perhaps the first illustration of catastrophe theory in emotion psychology: discrete jumps occur as a result of continuous input changes that often are not precisely reversible. Once an animal became enraged, it will not readily shrink into a corner again. Scherer[84] has recently argued that such nonlinearities of chaos and catastrophe theory may well recur more generally in emotional determinant-strength relationships.

CONCLUSIONS

So what do we conclude, with regard to the strength of emotions? I am tempted to conclude that emotion strength is a meaningful and unitary notion, but that it is difficult to find appropriate measures, apart from overall feeling ratings, that are not applicable to animals and suffer from end-value bias. What one can measure are intensity aspects that are only partly dependent on that basic strength. Among the determinants, event importance—the nature and number of event-relevant concerns, and the magnitude of the event itself, as appraised—appears to carry the heaviest weight. Appraisals such as unexpectedness, difficulty, those due to the individual's history with particular event types, and impact on the conduct of life provide nontrivial contributions. But the shape of the functions relating emotion strength to determinant magnitudes represents a domain largely to be explored.

NOTES

[1]Spinoza, 1677/1989. I adopt "strength" in agreement with Parkinson's Spinoza translation, p. 141.
[2]Montaigne, 1580/1965 Ch. 2. (p. 58/59). My translation from the French.
[3]Part IV of the *Ethics* carries the title "On the Strength of Emotions."
[4]In temporal order: Ortony, Clore, & Collins, 1988; Sonnemans, 1991; Frijda, Ortony, Sonnemans & Clore, 1992; Reisenzein, 1994; Brehm, 1999; Ben-Ze'ev, 2000;
[5]Reisenzein, Bördgen, & Holtbernd, 2001.
[6]Lang, 1993.
[7]See Frijda, 1986, Ch. 3.
[8]Ekman, Friesen, & Ancoli, 1980; Ruch, 1995.
[9]Ruch, 1995.
[10]Rosenberg & Ekman, 1994.
[11]Bargh, 1997; Berridge, 2004b.
[12]e.g., Hunt & Brady, 1955.
[13]Davitz, 1969.
[14]Parducci, 1995.
[15]Sonnemans, 1991; Sonnemans & Frijda, 1994.

[16]Kahneman, 1999.

[17]Hofstede, 1980; Schwartz, 1992, see also Chapter 5.

[18]In a preliminary classroom study in which 360 participants answered an earlier intensity questionnaire, the factors were in fact almost independent (see Sonnemans, 1991; Frijda et al., 1992).

[19]Fredrickson & Kahneman, 1993.

[20]Shizgal, 1999.

[21]One may therefore disagree with Ben-Ze'ev, 2000, who considers it an aspect of felt intensity.

[22]Fredrickson & Kahneman, 1993.

[23]Kahneman, 1999, for references.

[24]All variables load on the first unrotated factor, which explains 52% of the common variance.

[25]Essentially similar results were obtained when scales were constructed for all six factors, by adding the highest-loading variables from the orthogonal rotation, and regressing the scales for the first five factors onto the scores for overall intensity. The figures are given in Sonnemans & Frijda, 1994.

[26]e.g., Damasio, 2003; Mandler, 1984 and the venerable Schachter and Singer theory.

[27]e.g. Oatley & Duncan, 1992; Lambie & Marcel, 2002.

[28]Rimé 2005.

[29]Sonnemans, 1991.

[30]Rosenberg & Ekman, 1994.

[31]Kahneman, 1999, p. 20.

[32]Stone, Shiffman, & DeVries, 1999.

[33]Fischer, 1892.

[34]See Frijda, 2000, for a summary of Spinoza's emotion theory.

[35]The s refers to the scholium added to the proposition.

[36]ibid., IV, prop.5.

[37]ibid., e.g., III, prop. 38.

[38]ibid. III, prop. 17s.

[39]ibid. III, prop. 36s.

[40]ibid. III, prop. 17s.

[41]ibid. III, def32.

[42]My English translation of the *Ethics* here uses the term *imaginations* where I use *representations*.

[43]ibid., IV, prop. 9.

[44]ibid., IV, prop. 10.

[45]ibid. IV, prop. 11 and 12.

[46]ibid., III, prop. 18.

[47]Ben-Ze'ev, 2000; Ortony et al., 1988. See also Frijda, 1986.

[48]Ben-Ze'ev (2000) gives a related distinction between probability of existence and vividness as meanings of "reality."

[49]Mesquita, 1993.
[50]It differs slightly from the one in Sonnemans & Frijda, 1995.
[51]e.g., see Richter, 1927.
[52]Pope & Smith, 1992
[53]Parducci, 1995
[54]Kahneman & Miller, 1986; Kahnman & Tversky, 1984.
[55]Frijda, 1986.
[56]Ortony et al. 1988.
[57]Robinson, 1998; Scherer, 1984.
[58]Csikszentmihalyi. & Csikszentmihalyi, 1988; Piët, 1987.
[59]Brehm & Self, 1989.
[60]Kahneman, 1999.
[61]Kahneman & Tversky, 1982.
[62]From the large literature: bereavement, for instance, Parkes, 1972; disappointment: Van Dijk, 1999; regret, Kahneman & Tversky 1982; Zeelenberg, et al. 1996; surprise: W. U. Meyer, Reisenzein, & Schützwohl, 1997.
[63]Kahneman & Miller, 1986, p. 145.
[64]For anger and arbitrariness, see, for instance, Ortony et al., 1988; for guilt feelings, see McGraw, 1987; for accountability and deservingness and pity and envy, see Ben'Ze'ev, 2000, and Ortony et al., 1988.
[65]Larsen & Diener, 1987.
[66]Gray, 1987.
[67]Frijda, 1986.
[68]Horowitz, 1992.
[69]For details, see Bonanno, 2001; Gross, 1999.
[70]Gray, 1987; Kagan, 1994.
[71]Gross, 1999.
[72]Lanzetta, Cartwright-Smith, & Kleck, 1976.
[73]Sonnemans 1991.
[74]see Chapter 2.
[75]Concern strength and event magnitude could not be separated in this analysis.
[76]Cacioppo, Larsen, Smith, and Berntson, 2004 have argued.
[77]Cacioppo et al., 2004.
[78]Stevens, 1971.
[79]Brehm, 1999.
[80]Brehm, 1999, p. 5.
[81]Brehm, Brummett, & Harvey, 1999.
[82]Hebb, 1972.
[83]Zeeman, 1976.
[84]Scherer, 2000.

7

Time

Emotions are events over time. They also vary over time. They are embedded in sequences of feelings, thought, and behavior over time, and they embed lower order processes that also vary over time. The various time courses carry information. In an old study that compared judgments of film clips of naturally occurring facial expressions with those of photographs giving these expressions' apex (when the expressive movement had one), correctness scores for the film clips were about 50% higher than those for the photographs.[1] More recent, better controlled studies confirmed the gain.[2]

There are, however, many more temporal aspects of emotions that merit study. They are informative for underlying processes and intentional content, and are so at different levels.

PROSODY

In chapter 2, I called the time course of individual reactions the *prosody* of behavior. Under *prosody* I included degree of fullness of behavior—grasping with two fingers or with a whole hand, or together with reaching over—because fullness and time course are mechanically and motivationally linked.

Varying the time course of a given facial expression can drastically modify its apparent meaning. A slowed-down startle reaction may look like a moment of mental concentration.[3] Smiles with speeded-up onsets, apexes, and offsets appear as inauthentic, polite, or false, rather than happy and spontaneous; natural ones with those temporal characteristics indeed are, confirming hypotheses by Ekman and Friesen.[4] Not only expressive behaviors have informative prosodies; every single item of behavior, feeling, and thought has its prosodic aspects. Prosody gives instrumental behavior expressive quality. One can grasp reluctantly, greedily, or listlessly, or just grasp. It largely is what underlies the emotional content and impact of music and ballet dancing.

Affinities exist between prosodic patterns and particular emotions. Recognition of emotion from vocal intonation is almost as good as from facial expression.[5] Graphic expression suggests similar differentiation. Participants, asked to draw simple lines that express given emotions, produced different patterns that tended to be consistent for the different emotions; judgments of the expressive content of such lines showed considerable interjudge agreement.[6] A line depicting joy generally is curved and goes upward, that for sadness is thin and bends downward, for anger it is heavy and angular. The lines for joy and sadness tend to show the same pattern as the voice intonations in those emotions do.[7] Clynes[8] demonstrated differentiation between emotions in patterns over time of pressure on a kind of piano key. Systematic analyses of emotional behavior prosody are scarce, though. The field is almost uncharted, its central place in music and dancing notwithstanding.[9]

Behavior prosody varies along many dimensions. There are the obvious ones of speed and amplitude. There is fullness, defined in chapter 2 as the extent to which the body participates in a given type of expressive reaction or action. There are rate of change, as well as shape of change. Changes in speed, amplitude and direction can be gradual or brisk, rounded or angular. Sudden changes, for instance, either in behavioral onset or offset, or in switching from one pattern to another, suggest willful intervention or impulsiveness and loss of control.[10] There further is the important dimension of coherence among movement components. Their changes, in a given movement sequence, can occur in parallel or in orderly sequence, or more or less independently. Orderly sequence for instance, is illustrated by the development in time of the startle response: first the eyeblink, with a latency of about 40 msec, followed by mouth opening and an overall flexion movement with latencies of between 50 and 120 msec for the various components and individuals, and then bending of the knees.[11]

Many expressive movements appear to have a natural prosodic structure and component coherence, at a given level of amplitude. They form "coordinative structures," both temporally and spatially.[12] The features that make for an authentic smile, referred to above, provide an example, and deviations strike as not authentic. Lack of coherence or of being coordinative can be seen in bad amateur acting: some components are disproportionately more outspoken than others; one shows surprise with eyes opened widely only, without stretching the neck or movement arrest. Variations in temporal relationships can carry different sorts of information. In grasping an object, the hands may open and the fingers spread right when the arm begins its forward movement, or they may do so when the hand is near the object; the variations probably have to do with movement impulsiveness, deliberate intent, or haste and greediness. Coyness, embarrassment, and shyness owe their distinction to different time relationships between smiling and turning away the head.[13]

Coherence with external events is similarly variable. Actions may precede those of someone else, coincide with them, or follow them. Interrupting someone else's talking is an example; it may have instrumental but also motivational significance. Motivational significance is pertinent when action continues after having obtained its effect, as when violence goes on after the antagonist is down. Equally significant, it would appear, are overall temporal properties: pauses between action occasions and actions, such as waiting a moment before consumption, in order to relish the moment and the suspense, lingering as a telling aspect of acceptance wriggles, acts of savoring, and emotions of enjoyment. Temporal aspects of action obviously are guided by desires to reach the aims of action readiness, and desires to consciously experience the actions and their outcomes.

Many prosodic features would seem to be able to vary more or less independently. The only clear evidence that I am familiar with, however, so far comes from the analysis of respiration and from voice intonation. As regards respiration: rate, amplitude, pause duration, inspiration time, inspiratory duty cycle (the inspiration time/total cycle time ratio), angularity of inspiration-expiration transitions, and roundness of inspiration and expiration movements are distinguishable. In factor analysis, they are represented by at least three independent factors: amplitude, cycle time or frequency, and inspiratory duty cycle,[14] of which two are prosodic aspects. Emotion ascriptions on the basis of voice intonation patterns also yield three orthogonal dimensions.[15] The low correlations between acoustic intonation parameters likewise suggest separate dimensions.[16]

Prosodic patterns are, in general, not directly linked to particular modes of action readiness or emotions, even if voice intonation and expressive lines allow to distinguish them. The simpler prosodic features would seem to reflect dimensions of activation or degree of action readiness only, together with control of expression and action, be it deliberate or by concurrent emotional aims. Analysis of intonation indicates that "activation" or "degree of action readiness" exists in kinds, though. The several factors found in intonation-emotion linkages suggest that each factor represents some different sort of activation variable.[17] More complex intonation aspects—wailing and plaintive tones of voice, for instance, and of course the time flow of laughter[18]—can be expected to be more specific to particular modes of action readiness, with particular communicative aim.

The most interesting and informative aspects of prosody: those that give rise to the passionate character of passionate movements, the aspects that reflect or suggest urge, desire, wanting, or being gripped. World Press Photo recently gave its annual award to Arko Detta for a photograph of an Indian woman lying in the middle of the street, motionless, arms spread wide, palms up, fingers spread, whose child or husband had just been killed in the tsunami. The major reflections of passionate power, though, consist of simultaneous signs of engagement and restraint, of letting go and control, that mutually emphasize each other. Kreitler and Kreitler[19] write about the "play of tension and counter-tension" as the main emotional feature of both dancing and music. Tension comes from what seeks to reach some aim, to establish some relationship, or to abandon to seeing no way out. Countertension is what holds this back, for modesty, for retaining inner balance, for better reaching one's aim, or for savoring, not to take those lips at once. What the precise prosodic features are, I can only intuitively guess. Behavioral fullness is one; it would seem to be the most direct reflection of engagement. Temporal features that reflect that the action is "driven," and not "willed" would seem important. The contrast between tension and countertension may well be a further major feature: two trembling fingers and overall rigidity that may form the most passionate caress, or a whispered endearment amidst immersed attention. But as I say, these are intuitive guesses. Kinesics, music theory, and ballet theory no doubt have better-thought ones. Truly exploring the domain appears a worthwhile endeavor.

EMOTIONS OVER TIME

Emotions as such also change over time. In Sonnemans's study, described in the last chapter, participants had to draw a graph of the course of their reported emotion and to indicate the moment and meaning of each cardinal point such as an intensity peak. One kind of curve is given in Fig. 7.1. It more or less reflects the paradigmatic shape of emotions, as usually described in the literature: a single-peak event, with a certain onset latency, a steep rise to a peak, and a gradual offset back to base level.

However, that shape is not typical as actual occurrences go. Single-peak emotions lasting less than 10 minutes make up about 5% of the graphs in the study.[20] Almost one half (44%) show a single peak, but most often as that in Fig. 7.2: more a hill with a summit. They indeed emerged from preceding

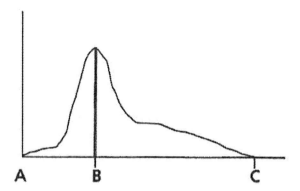

Figure 7.1 Single-peak emotion. Menaced by a guy with a screwdriver. "Weirdness." Duration: 2'30" + 45.'" Last night I walked to the station with two friends, a little after midnight. Then we were bothered by this guy. First he babbled away some nonsense, until he started talking like "I'd like to see the blood pouring out of you." He gripped this big screwdriver, which he took from his coat pocket. After that he again started talking nonsense, until he asked everyone a handshake and a cigarette. Then he walked a little distance with us, and then left. (J. Sonnemans, personal communication, 1994).

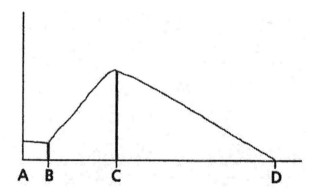

Figure 7.2 Extended single-peak emotion. Giving a talk. "Nervousness." Duration 1h + 10' + 20' = 1h30'. "Only nervousness. I had to give a talk at our seminar, with my girl-friend. In the morning we got up, had breakfast, took our things, and cycled to the laboratory. When everyone was there we started our presentation. We already had made one another nervous at breakfast. I was too busy with other things to really get nervous. Only upon arriving at the meeting room it began in earnest. Once talking it dropped somewhat, and when it was over I felt relaxed, and in any case very much relieved." (J. Sonnemans, personal communication, 1994).

suspense or watchfulness. The remainder of the graphs shows a more or less extended plateau, with one or more peaks superimposed, as in Fig. 7.3. That probably is the time course typical of emotional incidents that result from events with any true personal relevance. Thirty-four percent of the 222 graphs in the study showed multiple peaks. In an additional 22% of the cases, multiple peaks were indicated in the questionnaire, but did not show in the graphs.

As the graphs suggest, emotions are not generally brief, fast, flashlike responses. The questionnaire confirmed this. Table 7.1 gives the distribution of the answers to the five-category scale. Only a few emotions had been really brief. Two thirds of them lasted for more than 1 hour. Durations indicated with the graphs also ranged from under 1 minute to over 1 week. Thirty percent indicated more than 24 hours; only about 10% reported 10 minutes or less. These figures match those of other studies.[21]

The fashion to consider emotions as fast emergency responses, made to measure by evolution to grab prey or mates or vanish from predators, is wrong. It is a romantic stereotype. Such emotions may occur and do occur, but they do not form the rule. Anger responses in animals, too, very often build up slowly; fears grow from watchfulness over apprehension to flight; mating follows lengthy courting, except, maybe, among ducks in a pond.

The shapes of the intensity contours vary greatly. In 22% of the diagrams, peak latencies (times to the graph's peak or first peak) are less than 1 minute. The longest were over 3 days (in 3%). The rest falls in between and thus

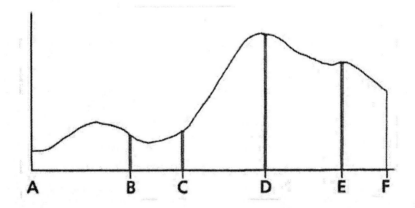

Figure 7.3 Multiple-peak emotion. Watching a friend at TV. "Happiness." Duration: 1 h + 30' + 1 h + 1 h + 2 h = 5 h 30'. Participant watching her friend participating in a TV contest. They went to the studio by A. From B to C they waited for the session to begin. The contest started by C, and at D he won. They stayed in the studio till E; going home till F. (J. Sonnemans, personal communication, 1994).

TABLE 7.1
Recalled Emotion Duration

Recalled duration	N	%
Less than 1 min	4	2
1 min–10 min	16	8
10 min–1 hour	36	16
1 hour–6 hours	96	43
More than 1 hour	70	31

Note. From Sonnemans, (1991).

shows gradual growth. Average latency differs between emotions. Sadness peaks fast only rarely. Fear comes fast more often than the other emotions, but slowly growing fears are not uncommon.

Much is going on during "peak latency." Information is assembled and processed, by which appraisal grows until it has stabilizes sufficiently to allow definite response. Appraisal growth and stabilization and action selection are reciprocal: each may amplify the other, very much as Lewis[22] suggests. Meanings are recruited, response components that are already called up are overwritten or decay, like initially being dazed by an unexpected event. The moment of stabilization, the extent of processing, presumably, depends on urgency, event suddenness, and the like. But research on what happens during the first milliseconds of an emotional encounter—research like that of Stapel and Koomen[23] mentioned in the Appraisal chapter—still is in an early stage.

What participants report as "an emotion" in retrospective studies usually were complex sequences. The incidents were more complex than just unexpected appearance of a predator in a safe savanna. Most of the reports, moreover, mentioned more than one emotion. Incidents of anger included feeling hurt, hopeless, or afraid of retaliation, and satisfaction about the harm one inflicted on the antagonist. Incidents of sadness mention despair, anger, and bewilderment, besides sorrow and distress. Instances of jealousy include mention of distress, anger and sheer anguish, besides what people label as pangs of jealousy. As an instance of sorrow, a girl gave the story of what she felt when she began to live away from home. It included feelings of loneliness and despair. Instances of an emotion thus were described in terms of other emotions. Emotion "mixtures" are the rule in reports of emotion incidents, even if these are presented as instances of particular emotions.[24]

The complexity is not well described as "emotion mixture," however. Sometimes, different emotions followed each other, and sometimes they were more or less simultaneous; Oatley and Duncan[25] found the same. Yet in all cases, the entire sequence in some sense constituted one emotion. In no instance did the graphs return to baseline between peaks. They did not, even in the cases of emotions with stated durations of over 24 hours. In Sonnemans's study, these formed almost one fourth of the reported incidents. This is not particular to this study. Fifty-five of the sadness instances, and 29% of those of joy, in the study by Scherer, Walbott and Summerfield,[26] were reported to have lasted for more than 1 day. In all those cases, the emotions thus spanned interruptions due to sleep.

Emotion Episodes

One of the participants, a woman in her 20s, told the following story. "One night I walked home from putting a letter in the mailbox. Two boys were leaning against a car, and one said to the other about me: 'tasty piece, that, I would like to get on top of her.' The remark almost made me vomit, it made me shiver. When coming home I became very, very angry, I felt it a dirty thing, so to humiliate someone. I threw something through my room. That night I dreamt about girls carrying their sex parts in their face and I woke up, feeling like one of those girls.... After an hour or so my feeling turned around, though, I thought the boy who had made the remark just ridiculous, it made me laugh, and I felt above it. A little later I went out shopping, and that was the end of it." The intensity peak of the experience, as she drew it in her graph, occurred upon coming home. The laughter came after 10 hours, after which the graph went steeply down. Duration from beginning to end was 11 hours.

The intensity contours of the reported incidents thus envelop a number of events, both external and internal. I will refer to emotional incidents as *emotion episodes*. I will reserve the term "an emotion" for parts of such a sequence to which a separate emotion name would seem appropriate, as in the examples. An emotion episode is a continuous emotion sequence resulting from the more or less continuous transaction with one given event or issue. The episode may begin before events actually occur, for instance, with expectations, or apprehension in surroundings where a predator may appear; savannas, presumably, were not that safe. One enters a context charged with meaning, very much as Prospect Theory describes.[27] The episode continues till events have been processed and the person has emotionally come to rest. Participants in self-report studies of emotions typically report emotion episodes. When episodes in Sonnemans's study were defined by the presence in the drawn diagrams of more than one peak or a duration of over 3 hours (or both), 66% of the reported incidents were episodes.

This notion of emotion episode seeks to catch two basic facts. First, the continuous emotional impact of one given transaction is felt to possess some sort of unity or coherence. Second, multiplicity of emotions may be engendered in that one transaction. The participants in Sonnemans's study were asked to check a list of emotion labels, regardless of the label they had chosen for the incident as a whole, and to indicate the intensity of each on a 10-point scale. The woman whose insult report was just given checked anger, 5; disgust, 5; and hatred, 2.

The following was also told as an instance of anger. The participant, male, had helped his mother remodel her house; now that he himself needs help for moving, his mother has no time because she has her tennis appointments. The participant reports having been disappointed, quite sad, and angry: "I tried to explain to her her egoism and unreasonableness, but she didn't even hear me." There are three phases: the mother's initial refusal, her continuous refusal during the participant's explanations, and the latter's subsequent rumination. Emotional arousal was present during all that time, as his graph showed. The participant checked anger, 9; sadness, 9; shame, 9; contempt, 8; disgust, 10.

These are not mere sequences of separate emotions. Each episode forms one emotional whole. The various phases are felt to hang together. What makes them hang together? Is it more than being confronted with one continuous event?

There is. The emotion episode as a whole forms a protracted transaction. It forms a coherent "narrative." The person is dealing continuously with a particular event or state of affairs. The word *transaction* is used to emphasize the reciprocity between person and event that is usually involved, be it only in the person's thoughts.

In spite of ongoing changes, one thing remains more or less the same during the narrative: the core meaning that the transaction is about. Lazarus[28] described them in terms of "core relational themes," such as threat, loss, opportunity, and achievement. The story of the woman going to the mailbox was about the theme of offense and insult. Episodes of mother–infant interaction may change from minute to minute, but each aspect is colored by the core appraisal of the warm and intimate, trusted interaction.[29] Conversely, each element in an episode is profoundly colored by that core appraisal, and by what precedes it in the episode. Enjoyment smiles differ according to what the enjoyment is about, and in what interpersonal context it occurs.[30]

The unity and continuity of an episode obtains emotional substance from the development of emotional engagement and control precedence; Solomon, with very good reason, gave engagement a central place in understanding emotions.[31] Rise, peaks, plateau, decrease are the life stages of an engagement: onset, peak confrontation, decay or solution. Even when appraisal changes drastically, and affect turns color after overcoming the emotional problem, winning the game, or shrugging off one's being offended, engagement provides coherence among the successive emotions.

When engagement dissipates, the overall process ends. The graphs drawn represent the course and strength of the engagement. The story of the insulted woman again provides an illustration. Her disgust and anger mounted; the upset continued into her dream and emerged in the morning in her thoughts and was rendered by a plateau of relatively high level in her graph. Her laughter initiated the decrease of involvement, and rounded off the excitement of the earlier emotions. There is one curve over apprehension, expectancy, worry, anxiety, despair, and relief. It is, in fact, the characteristic curve of any suspense episode.

This analysis of episode unity offers insight into that peculiar fact: so many emotions are reported to have lasted for more than a day, and thus to have spanned interruptions. Thirty-one percent of the participants in the study reported such long durations, as Table 7.1 shows. Participants said they were angry for days, or grieved for months, and that after sleep or diversion the emotion still was present or was felt to return. These are not figures of speech. The episode's continuity and coherence actually survive interruptions. The emotional event is found upon awakening, and its impact is still there. The self-report by the insulted woman provided an illustration; so do many stories of grief upon loss. And aspects of action readiness may just remain in force. Emotion urgency, its control precedence persists during interruptions. Control precedence was defined as readiness for a given action tendency to take control whenever circumstances permit; it thus is in effect while circumstances do not permit. In the morning one finds oneself with the same hopeless apathy or restless agitation with which one went to bed. Action readiness in fact during sleep caused dreams, and the sleep to be restless; during diversion it formed the background of flatness or restlessness in the amusement or being busy with other things. Here, too, the woman's story illustrates the point.

Core meaning remains the same over an episode, but only more or less so. True changes in the transaction may occur. Appraisals may jump from one to another when different aspects are focused on, or different implications come to mind. Action tendency may briskly change from defensive withdrawal into attack—from fear to anger; or from anger to submission, to giving up. New information may be brought in, a different issue appears behind the current one. The subject's appraisal of the event may vary during the transaction. In a response to personal loss, the finality of the loss may grow or decrease in cognitive and affective effectiveness. In the example of the insulted woman, appraisal of an offense against personal integrity remained constant, but the feeling of having being intruded upon varied, as did focality of the act and, finally, even its offensiveness. Thus, some appraisal aspects remain persistently present over the episode; the willful offense, in the example. This constitutes the core appraisal, the second element that binds the phases of an emotion episode. Core appraisal—"this is an intrusion that I don't want"—may get successively filled in in different ways—"it is vulgar," "they intruded actively," "it does not really touch me"—but the framework remains. It binds the phases of an episode quite strongly, because core appraisal is linked to action readiness at the strategic level: action readiness to achieve that the situation at hand may terminate or continue. Modes of activation, too, may persist for relatively long periods, and over changes in specific emotions. The same excitement or active stance was present in the various emotions felt by the insulted woman, as well as by the subject who was angry with his mother. They have their counterparts in physiological reactions such as increased blood pressure, hormonal level, neural and neurotransmitter activity, that may endure for similar extended periods.

TIME SCALES

Emotion episodes embrace a hierarchical structure of component processes. Even one-emotion episodes do. Component processes at different levels have different durations.

At the highest level there thus is the emotional engagement in a given transaction, implemented by its life history of waxing and waning, but continuous, attentional involvement and control precedence, and the waxing and waning of cortical and autonomic arousal. Such engagement may last for days, probably longer. The gross quality of that engagement, in affective relevance, in core appraisal, and in action readiness at the strategic level, may last as long, while showing major changes in the processes one level of analysis down. Development of a transaction of threat may turn into the sense of gaining the upper hand, and then into relief.

These major changes correspond with the sequencing and intermingling of emotions, as defined by changes in appraisal and mode of action readiness. A hostile encounter gets appraised as involving being slighted, then by not advancing an inch in being heard. Defensive alertness then switches over into actual hostility. Periods of hostility, in turn, contain less acute phases when hostile action readiness is merely felt, and perhaps show in an edge creeping into one's tone of voice, which phases alternate with more acute phases and affect bursts. These latter are manifest in expressive sequences: frowning, shouting, facing each other in enraged attitudes. The elements in those sequences, finally, consist of specific expression patterns, such as "facial expressions of anger," and clenching and declenching the fists.

At a still lower level are the constituent covert processes such as reception and processing of stimuli, activation of stored information, and activation of response processes. Time scales decrease as one goes down the hierarchy. Duration of those lowest processes is hard to define because they blend imperceptibly with feedback from their effects, and their dependence upon higher level context. The flow of processes is best represented by the models of cascading processes by Bradley et al., by Scherer, and by Lewis.[32] But the processes can be rapid, and short. Stimuli can produce evaluative and other effects related to meaning after exposures of 4 msec[33] in the suboptimal exposure experiments mentioned in chapter 3. The processes and their effects are continuously modified by further incoming information and more extensive processing—100 msec exposures produce effects that differ from those of, say, 30 msec—and from their own feedback, as evident in the effects if longer exposures and conscious awareness.[34] They continuously modify their outputs till these, presumably, are stabilized by overt response or conscious awareness, or their decay when neither takes place.

Appraisals that use more information than coming from the stimuli alone will take more time. Conscious awareness effects on evaluation were obtained with exposures of a full second[35] and may extend indefinitely, concurrently with ongoing outputs. Overt response preparation may take times from 300 msec upward.

The facial expressions and other phasic responses at the next higher level are still brief. Ekman reported that "the great majority of expressions of felt emotions last between ½ and 4 seconds, and those that are shorter or longer are mock or other kinds of false expressions."[36] I am not familiar with the data upon which this conclusion is based; however, almost certainly the conclusion needs qualifications. Smiling may rarely last longer than 4 sec, and "single acts of laughter rarely exceed 7 seconds".[37] But a fear grimace while looking at a frightening or horrifying scene may well do. Crying, too, may last longer. Vingerhoets[38] reports that among the self-reported durations of the participants' most recent crying fit, 36% lasted between 5 and 15 min, and 15% lasted more than 16 min. True enough, these last data come from self-reports and not from observations.

From his data, Ekman concludes that emotion duration is within the few-seconds range.[39] I do not agree. Duration of single facial expressions is an arbitrary criterion for emotion duration. It may be indicative of the duration of elementary single-peak emotions that consist of prewired and fixed motor responses. The startle response lasts for between 300 msec and 1.5 sec, depending on stimulus intensity and the individual.[40] Similar reactions are found among other prewired reactions to sudden and/or brief stimuli, such as the defensive response of newborn kittens (hissing, teeth-baring, and claw protrusion) to unfamiliar animate stimuli, and jolts of fright upon a noise when walking apprehensively in the dark. The durations may be somewhat longer when autonomic response and other response components are taken into account. Temporary postresponse decrease in threshold for response to subsequent stimuli is one of these latter. So is cognitive tuning: cognitive realignment after startle may take awhile.

But the duration of individual expressive patterns is not a good indication of the duration of underlying emotion processes such as arousal of action readiness. These are manifest in extended sequences of facial expressions that each are variations on a common theme. Different facial expressions that are indicative of anger follow each other for as long as an enraged harangue lasts. Facial and postural behavior indicative of sadness can probably persist for hours when a person turns a grieving event over and over in her or his mind: a dejected look, silent staring, biting the lips, weeping, and looking into the corner of the room with a frown or depressed corners of the mouth. Facial expressions indeed are elements in behavioral sequences that also contain postures, locomotion patterns, and vocal behaviors. Likewise, for instance, for fear. Facial expressions in fear tend to be accompanied by movement arrest, head aversion or a retreating movement of head and shoulders, and often by signs of adopting a crouching posture.[41]

Sequences of behavior elements with a common meaning are among the phenomena that led to the notion of action readiness in the first place. States of action readiness often last longer than such sequences. They often precede behavior; motive states are present before translating into action. They also may outlive that action. Self-reports on emotional urges, small behavioral manifestations such as the trembling lips before crying bursts out, irritability when action has died down, and emptily looking out in space after the burst is passed support both assumptions. So does the fact that planned behavior may occur on the wings of emotion. It may merit to illustrate this by a state of readiness lasting for hours, taken from the self-report of an instance of joy.

The participant is a male Turkish immigrant who succeeded for his examination as a driving instructor. "I was so happy, so happy. My joy just drowned out everything else. There was no room left to think anything else. As if the man who gave us our diploma's had done so from his own pocket, I thanked him a hundred times." He drank something, then called his mother. Then he goes home, is welcomed by his mother, who embraces him and tells him she had always thought he would pass, he had always succeeded in what he did. After dinner, he goes into the coffeehouse to celebrate with his friends. The joy was manifest in feeling and in the urge for expansive behavior. It continued at least until the end of his having had his drink and probably continued without interruption until his celebration in the coffeehouse. The duration was from something like 11:00 a.m. until 9:00 or 10:00 p.m.. Don't call it a mood. All feeling and action were focused on the success, and conspicuously linked to it.

The duration of given states of action readiness are clearly influenced by the duration of the emotion-arousing events, and of the transactions that follow. Joy tends to die down if nobody shares. There also is, however, spontaneous decay of states of action readiness to brief events and in the absence of actions or thoughts by the subject that prolong the actual interaction.

States of action readiness can themselves be distinguished at different levels. Bradley, Lang and colleagues[42] distinguish between *strategic* and *tactical* levels. Unpleasantness, readiness to discontinue a given interaction, is at the strategic level. Readiness to actively remove a person or object (defining anger) and to protect oneself (defining fear) are at the tactical level. Readiness at a strategic level may persist for hours, meanwhile changing its tactical specification several times.

Many of these things said about action readiness also apply to appraisal. Awareness of successful achievement can remain on someone's mind for a day, as in the example of the driving instructor. It may meanwhile change its focus and context, from focus on one's worth to focus on that of one's family, on one's achievement or on one's friends who share in it.

I only need to mention that physiological reactions, too, have temporal properties that may be quite different for different reactions. Different reactions have their specific latencies and decay times. They often continue in time beyond the emotional stimuli and overt emotional responses, due to restabilization and compensatory processes. Durations of central and peripheral neurohumoral processes may extend considerably beyond that of stimulus impact, and may then influence thresholds for subsequent emotional stimuli and, for instance, cause protracted irritability and jittery feelings.

Affect, a response aspect at the strategic level, may exist independently of autonomic response and expressive or other behavior. It has interesting temporal properties. Affect shows, or can show, very short latency. In old introspective studies by Lehmann,[43] the reaction time for affective response to sensory stimuli was found to be shorter than that for physiological responses like heart rate and respiration change. In current studies of the automatic evocation of affective valuations, latencies can be under 100 msec.[44] Affect can go on for long unbroken stretches of time. When of long duration, it may correspond to mood.[45] However, there also exist affective states of long duration that do involve a continuous felt bearing on an object or situation and thus, by definition, represent emotions. They may go on for hours, days, and perhaps longer, in the days or weeks after loss or during infatuation, or when living in a political prison or other condition of incessant threat. Objects, relationships, and conditions can be continuously present to one's mind. In a television interview, an ex-inmate of a German wartime torture center said "Fear? Yes, it felt like a strangling grip, day and night."

EMOTION EXTENSIONS

Several behavioral and mental phenomena extend the duration of emotions indefinitely. Whether to view them as consequences or as parts of the emotions is largely a matter of taste. Two of the most important of these are goal formation and belief changes, mentioned when discussing emotion strength.

The urge to hurt the target of one's anger may shift from the desire to shout and hit and kick to subtle scheming for damaging his or her good name. Joy may lead to the goal of sending a telegram. These goals complement the urges to oppose or to be with the other. Self-reports of emotions are rich in mention of planned actions, and the resulting actions are the major grounds for attributing particular emotions to others, as Planalp showed.[46]

Emotions also generate belief changes. As discussed in the chapter on appraisal, changed beliefs are part of emotions. Such changed beliefs may, however, persist over time, and the appraised event properties may turn into dispositional attributions to people or kinds of events. They then form sentiments.

Similarly for goal formation. Execution of these goals may not itself be part of the emotions, but it keeps the action readiness alive. Continuous action readiness is what gives plan execution its vitality and vigor. It also keeps the emotion alive by producing new confrontations, and recollection of earlier ones. The goals may, moreover, obtain independent emotional existence, and become true passions: passionate goals that endure indefinitely, such as taking revenge for former wrongs, or obtaining satisfaction of an infatuation.[47] I will further discuss sentiments and passions later.

Other extensions are more immediately linked to the acute emotions. Emotions engender trains of thought that seek to get a grip on the meaning of the emotional event or that seek to resolve the emotional problem: Why this failure, why this loss, why this infatuation, who am I after this has happened? Emotions may extend to rumination: prolonged and recurrent thoughts turning on why it happened, what meaning it may have had,[48] what the consequences are, and what could have been done differently. It not only extends emotions: it maintains them and by their feedback may enhance them. Rumination has been extensively investigated by Rimé and his colleagues.[49] As mentioned earlier, its duration correlates with the initial emotion intensity. A further extension consists in social sharing of the emotions.[50] People share by far the majority of their emotions, mostly with friends, partners, and parents. The interactions again may entertain and prolong the impact of the events, adding to them when the emotions are pleasant, and attenuating them when unpleasant.

The most important extension is by memory of the emotional events and their impact themselves. Emotional memory is not inert. It influences novel experiences and may vibrate, consciously or nonconsciously, with novel impressions. Intrusive thoughts may arise, unbidden recollections, vehement emotions elicited associatively by innocent stimuli such as a toy turned up when digging one's garden, or seeing a smoking chimney. Loss of a child, incest and rape, torture and severe humiliation may return until the end of a person's life.[51] Psychological functioning as a whole may be affected, in what is nowadays called the post traumatic stress disorder. All this is beyond the topic of emotion duration, and this book as a whole, and treated profoundly by others.[52] No discussion of emotion duration is meaningful, however, without indicating in what ways, and for how long, emotions can be said to endure.

WHAT DETERMINES HOW LONG AN EMOTION LASTS?

We have seen, in the last chapter, that emotion strength and duration are virtually unrelated. Then what determines how long an emotion lasts? Most likely, the main determinant of emotion duration is the duration of the emotional event and its aftermath. There are small threats—a policeman turns the corner when you are driving without a license, and when he drives by, the emotion is gone. But there are standing threats, as in prison as a political prisoner, with concomitant continuous fear, as in an example given earlier.

The graphs in Sonnemans's study rather generally follow the course of events, as the three figures in this chapter illustrate. Interaction with the responses of others also influences duration, by maintaining and extending the episode. Take the story of the Turkish driving instructor. His mother's welcome and admiration, and the celebration with his friends, extended the emotion episode. Or take marital quarrels, in which responses recruit enhanced further response. Then, major emotional events have major and long-lasting aftermaths. Some of these were just mentioned. Losing may be brief, but having lost has no end. Personal loss leaves one alone indefinitely; the 2005 tsunami left the survivors amidst devastation and a life without meaning. Severe or prolonged humiliation can have harmed self-esteem for years or forever. As mentioned before, forced emigration uproots and may shatter sense of identity.[53] By contrast, fulfilled desires may entail long-lasting, satisfying, and happy interactions and formation of a life goal. Extended durations of this sort are not absent in animals. Long-lasting emotions of loss have been observed in chimpanzees;[54] De Waal describes an elephant that lost her child, and, each time when passing the skeleton in the woods, touched it with her trunk.[55]

It has been found in the literature that emotions differ in average duration. In Sonnemans's study, and in the cross-national study by Scherer et al.,[56] both sadness and joy tended to last long; anger was shorter; fear rarely lasted longer than an hour (only 18% in Sonnemans's study), and in a large number of cases less than 5 minutes. The relative durations of several different emotions were consistent over various cultures. But these differences appear largely due to the ecology of these emotions, rather than with the kinds of emotion as such. Joy and sadness, in these studies, mostly concerned personal relationships that usually extend in time; and fear mostly concerned fear from transient events.

In continuous circumstances, durations are curtailed by habituation. Sexual pleasures with a particular partner diminish with repetition, at least in men.[57] One gets used to, or adapts to, adverse circumstances,[58] at least up to a point. Emotional habituation to continuous averse circumstances probably proceeds more slowly than does that to pleasant circumstances, and in many situations it does not adapt at all, as argued in chapter 1 under the Law of Hedonic Asymmetry.

The lack of correlation between emotion strength and duration may not invariably hold. Rimé[59] found, at least in one study, that emotion intensity correlated with the time spent in rumination. Duration of episodes of depressed mood parallel both the extent of rumination and severity of the depression.[60] Sonnemans found significant correlations between emotion duration and the number of concerns at stake in the emotion incident ($r = .36$). Mention was made above for the extended duration of emotional consequences of truly incisive emotional events, like incest and loss of a child. How these various pieces of evidence should be combined is unclear to me.

For completeness' sake, mention should be made of more intrinsic influences on the duration of emotional reactions,. Startle has its proper duration that parallels stimulus intensity. Fits of laughter and weeping, and outbursts of blind anger, panic and desire appear to have particular built-in time courses. Neither of these can be stopped at will by the person, once overt expression has gone beyond a certain "point of no return." Sometimes, in blind anger, the actor in a frenzy continues stabbing the victim after the latter is motionless.[61] Anger needs not to be very intense to have a sort of inertia. People tend to continue to shout and scold for some time after the antagonist has explained or apologized; often, the shouting peters out miserably. There is, of course, old lore that anger, laughter and weeping "discharge" tension states. That metaphor does not say more than that an activated response is gone when executed; but the activation may prescribe execution's course over time. Yet, other, obscure variables are also involved in such time courses. The fits of laughter sometimes called "the giggles" appear unrelated to the intensity of what caused them; the fits of weeping unleashed by alcohol also often seem to depend on some internal dysregulation rather than release from pent-up sorrow. At a different level, love and desire for revenge are not matters of hours or days, presumably because (or when) they are sustained by incisive belief changes: by sentiments.

SENTIMENTS

Sentiments were introduced before. They were defined as dispositions to respond emotionally to a particular object (person, object, kind of event, issue). Affections and aversions, sympathies and antipathies, loves and hatreds, are sentiments, and so are emotionally charged attitudes towards issues and political entities. Fears and phobias, in which harmless objects like dogs, spiders or crowds elicit strong fears, too, fall under the category.

The dispositions are affective schemas with features similar to those of emotions. The schemas include appraisals of the objects, including affective valence—they are liked or disliked—and often further valenced properties ("dishonest," "always interesting!," "a dangerous animal"). Sentiments thus contain beliefs, and like or dislike is felt when the object is merely mentioned or thought of. The schemas also contain latent action readiness to seek or avoid the object, or to affect it in some other way. Hatreds include propensity to inflict harm, and to applaud harm done to the object. Sentiments may lead to action when confronted with their object, including avoidance. The sentiment that public exposure is shameful causes women in some Muslim cultures not to go out unveiled or unaccompanied, so that they don't feel shame; sentiments of admiration may make admirers flock to a star's concert.

The corresponding evaluations arise automatically and rapidly when the object is seen, or mentioned in conversation. The automaticity is evident in priming studies.[62] This has further cognitive implications. Properties that are consonant with the affective value are accepted with less reserve than other of the object's properties, and they are more readily thought of, as has been shown in attitude and prejudice research.[63]

Sentiments are often conscious. One often knows about them. When talking about an object of a sentiment, one often go through the motions of mock affect, speaking in tones of rapture or revulsion. Thoughts about the object, and how it is appraised, may come up spontaneously. "It remains there to bother you; it keeps pursuing you, more or less." Sentiments affect the conduct of life in many ways. Designation as dispositions is therefore not entirely appropriate. They can be occurrent. One is aware of one's sentiments, not merely through emotion, but also through conscious affect and thought.

Sentiments can be regarded as latent emotions. Emotions and sentiments only differ in that the former are occurrent and the latter largely dispositional. Sentiments thus lack control precedence and actual action readiness in between encounters with their object in reality or thought. The moment these latter arise in some encounter, sentiments become manifest as emotions. But structurally they are the same.

Sentiments resemble attitudes. In fact, they *are* attitudes. Most authors, for instance Asch,[64] felt the difference to be merely one of emphasis. Sentiments are those attitudes in which the person cares about the attitude object, whether for good or for bad. Sentiments also *are* concerns: events obtain meaning from being relevant to their target object. As Shand[65] expressed it: "A sentiment is a system of several emotion dispositions, having different conative tendencies, connected with a common object, and subordinated to a common end." Sentiments are concerns of which the fate, existence or presence of a particular specific person, object, or issue forms the target.

Many sentiments are formed by social transmission: other people, authorities in particular, and media tell you what particular persons, objects, or issues are like. But very often sentiments are the precipitates of emotional encounters. Event appraisals turn into object properties, and thus obtain both permanence and generality; they turn into enduring truths. A man whose woman friend married another without having told him said: "one must not take every friendship seriously." A woman who had had a relationship with a man who also had other relationships related the following, containing a sentence just quoted. "One day, when we were dining out, he told me: 'Listen, it is very unpleasant, but I probably have a venereal disease, and most likely it comes from you.'" She couldn't bring out a word, but only thought: "I do not hear properly." Then she became amazed, disgusted, angry, and excited, and went home. She at once ended the relationship. When people asked why they did not see her with her friend anymore, she had answered: "Him you'll never see any longer. I don't want to see him, because he is a dishonest person. It remains there to bother you. It keeps pursuing you, more or less. Of course you meet people you like, but you also have become distrustful."

Emotions thus can turn into sentiments, and emotional appraisals turn into enduring belief changes. They certainly not always do. Marital quarrels often include the emergence of beliefs in one's spouses nastiness, that dissolve when the quarrel is over. I will not speculate about the conditions under which emotions precipitate into sentiments; I will briefly touch upon the issue in chapters 10 and 11.

PASSIONATE GOALS

Emotions, on occasion, generate long-term emotional goals. An interest, an attachment, a worry or indignation may expand from the transient aim of emotional action tendency to a stable and enduring concern for achieving the action tendency's specific end-point. The concern obtains high priority within the individual's concern structure, to the extent of absorbing much of the individual's resources in time, money and energy, and readiness to face risks and other costs. That is what I mean by *passionate goals*—what usually are designated as "passions" for short, as I did in my 1986 book. Examples include some loves, absorbing interests in a particular domain of knowledge, expertise, or craftsmanship; devotion to a particular ideological cause, belief system, or set of suprapersonal values.

Passionate goals are goals with high emotional value; they form major, prominent, and dominant concerns. At the same time, like sentiments they have the structure of emotions. But whereas sentiments have that structure primarily through the appraisals that they harbor, passionate goals have it in harboring aims for action. At the same time, as with sentiments, there is a major difference with emotions. Emotions are occurrent states; passionate goals are dispositional ones that, when opportunity is there take center stage. The collector of pre-1900 postage stamps gets a shine in his eyes when looking in a precious album at an auction; the passionate ideologue may get enraged when hearing that his party or faith has been offended.

But, as another difference with emotions, passionate goals can be pursued coolly, without a sign of control precedence in the sense discussed in the Passion chapter. One can plan one's political strategies and tactics without excitement. Risks are weighed—not the personal risks, but the goal-related ones—without emotion-instigated cognitive biases, without neglect of consequences. Action readiness is not their motor of action, but intention, anticipation, and reflective control over action are. All this, nevertheless, owing to one's emotional engagement.

An example of a cold passion is that which brought a man to murder the vice president of a major Dutch supermarket chain that I will relate in some detail in chapter 10. As far as the available information goes, the goal was set and followed with little actual emotion. An example of a somewhat hotter passion was Hitler's hatred of Jews. It can be considered a hot passion because of the violent emotions manifested when he spoke about the presumed role of the Jews in losing World War I and in polluting the German people. His paroxysmal outbursts, with foaming mouth, in this and other connections, are well documented.[66] The passion led to inciting others to this hatred, organizing intimidation raids, conceiving of the idea of total destruction in January 1939, and ordering the implementation of that total destruction in the spring of 1941. But much of this again was planned coolly, or made to be planned coolly by others, and executed coolly by again others.[67]

The notion of passionate goals (and the word "passion") is more readily connected to benign goals. Biography gives descriptions of emotionally motivated life long strivings for achieving the freedom of one's group; Gandhi, Martin Luther King, Jr., and Nelson Mandela are cases in point. Devotion to truth, as one sees it, or to God's Glory, as with the Fathers of the Desert and many of the Christian martyrs and Muslim sages, provides other cases; but this, too, has very cruel, and sometimes cool, variants.[68] Then of course there are the erotic passions, some over shorter and others over longer time periods. Tristan and Isolde and Romeo and Juliet are classic stories; but true ones abound.[69]

WHAT IS "AN EMOTION"?

The durations of emotions are ill-defined. There are few brisk transitions within episodes, and many single-emotion episodes have neither a precise beginning nor a precise end, since they begin with expectations or apprehensions. The time courses of constituent processes are not neatly coordinated, but overlap and mutually influence each other. Also, emotions can be said to endure until feeling turns elsewhere, until an episode is over, or they can be said to endure as long as the emotional event emotionally colors the individual's life.

"An" emotion thus is a slippery notion. Successive emotions within an episode share some components and vary in others. It still makes sense to say "I first was amazed, then it turned into anger, then into utter confusion," because, at that level of analysis, the terms refer to the temporary predominance of a given appraisal and/or a given action readiness. "An emotion," in this sense, may last as long as a given mode of appraisal or a given mode of action readiness is maintained; but how long that is can only be indicated by approximation because of the blendings-over and thinkings-back. At the same time, the nature and composition of each emotion is shaped by the temporal event context in which it occurs. Each individual emotion occurrence carries the stamp of that context, just as every pleasure does.[70]

It thus is sheer desire for order to reserve the word "emotion" for an episode concerned with a particular relational theme, or for a phase dominated by a given form of action readiness, or, a little more restrictively, for an acute phase within occurrence of such a state of action readiness. But it is also meaningful to consider longer enduring appraisals and goals, the sentiments and true passions, as "emotions," as many investigators, in particular those with a philosophical or sociological bent, tend to do.

NOTES

[1]Frijda, 1953.
[2]e.g., Wehrle et al., 2000.
[3]Frijda, 1953.
[4]Krumhuber & Kappas, 2005; Krumhuber, Manstead, & Kappas, in press; Krumhuber et al., 2005. Hypothese tested came in particular from Ekman & Friesen, 1982.
[5]Banse & Scherer, 1996; Johnstone & Scherer, 2000.
[6]Krauss, 1930; Poffenberger & Barrows, 1924.
[7]Owren & Rendall, 2001.
[8]Clynes, 1977.
[9]but see L. B. Meyer, 1956.

[10]Frijda, 1956.
[11]Landis & Hunt, 1939.
[12]Camras, 2000.
[13]Reddy, 2000.
[14]Boiten, 1993a, 1993b; Boiten, Frijda, & Wientjes, 1994
[15]Van Bezooyen, 1984.
[16]Banse & Scherer, 1996.
[17]Van Bezooyen, 1984.
[18]Ruch, 1993
[19]Kreitler & Kreitler, 1972.
[20]Frijda et al., 1991; Sonnemans, 1991.
[21]Gilboa & Revelle, 1994; Scherer, Walbott, & Summerfield, 1986.
[22]Lewis, 2005.
[23]Stapel & Koomen, 2000.
[24]Oatley & Duncan, 1992.
[25]Oatley & Duncan, 1992.
[26]Scherer et al. 1986.
[27]Kahneman & Tversky, 1984.
[28]Lazarus, 1991.
[29]Fogel et al., 1992.
[30]Fogel, 1993.
[31]Solomon, 2004a.
[32]Bradley, Codispoli, Cuthbert, and Lang , 2001; Lewis, 2005; Scherer, 2000.
[33]Murphy & Zajonc, 1993.
[34]Murphy & Zajonc, 1993; Rotteveel et al., 2001; Stapel, Koomen, & Ruys, 2002.
[35]Murphy & Zajonc, 1993; Rotteveel et al., 2001
[36]Ekman, 1984, p. 333.
[37]Ruch, 1993, p. 607
[38]Vingerhoets, Cornelius, van Heck, & Becht, 2000.
[39]Ekman, 1984.
[40]Landis & Hunt, 1939.
[41]Frijda & Tcherkassof, 1997; Grammer et al., 2004.
[42]Bradley et al., 2001.
[43]Lehmann, 1914
[44]e.g., Fazio, 2001; Rotteveel et al., 2001.
[45]Mood can be so defined when one does not want duration to be the defining characteristic (Frijda, 1993a).
[46]Planalp, 1999.
[47]See chapter 10 for the example of revenge.
[48]Silver, Boon, & Stones, 1983.
[49]Rimé, 2005; Rimé et al., 1992.
[50]Rimé, 2005; Rimé et al., 1992.
[51]e.g., Silver, Boon & Stones 1983; Wortman & Silver, 1989.

[52]Horowitz, 1992; Rimé, 2005.
[53]Apfelbaum, 2000.
[54]Hamburg, Hamburg, & Barchas, 1975.
[55]De Waal, 1996
[56]Scherer et al. 1986; Scherer & Walbott, 1994.
[57]Ford & Beach, 1951.
[58]Brickman, Coates, & Janoff-Bulman, 1978.
[59]Rimé, 2005.
[60]Rimé, 2005.
[61]Mergaree, 1966
[62]Bargh, 1997; Fazio, 2001.
[63]Fiske & Taylor, 1984
[64]Asch, 1952.
[65]Shand, 1922.
[66]Fest, 1973
[67]Browning, 1993.
[68]Stern, 2003.
[69]Fisher, 2004.
[70]Fogel, 1993.

8

"Feelings"

WHAT ARE FEELINGS?

What is the nature of feelings? The word *feeling* is ambiguous. It is used for tactile sensations and inarticulate thoughts ("I feel that he is right!"), as well as for emotional feelings. In this chapter—in this book as a whole—it refers to the latter only. But even so restricted, what it refers to is unclear. *Feeling* has the overtone of something "within" the individual. It has the overtone of being the feeling of a particular emotion, of anger or fear or love. But that may not always be what is meant. Emotion experiences, most of the time, are not experiences *of*. They are experiences *that*. They mostly are experiences that I perceive a lovely person; that I perceive a nasty bastard; that I know to be in a frightful predicament, or faced with a loss, a loss, a true, terrible loss.

Let there be no misunderstanding. Experience of terrible loss is subjective. It cannot be measured from the outside. I only can tell you that I experience a terrible loss and, yes, that my steps are slow, not because I am tired, but weighed down by the experienced loss. That is the emotional experience. In what follows, I will mostly talk about "emotion experience," to escape from this ambiguity. But I begin with feelings because of the problems that the word and its analysis have created.

So, indeed: what are (emotional) feelings? It is puzzling. Very different answers have been given. The issue has been touched upon in chapter 3. Feelings have been described as ineffable *qualia*, as body feelings, or as states of pleasure or pain and felt activation. All three descriptions have something that speaks in their favor, but all three encounter problems. In the qualia view, different emotions correspond to different such qualia; at least, different basic or elementary emotions do. Each *quale* is unanalyzable, in the same way that color experiences of red, green, blue, and yellow are.[1] However: there is no criterion for identifying them. How many different qualia are there, and which are they, among the many feelings that we have words for? The only criterion that was proposed is that words may exist for a small set of basic feelings that correspond to the qualia[2] and that all other emotion words can be unambiguously defined in terms of them. This implications, however, is not supported by the evidence.[3]

The second view characterizes emotion experiences as body feelings. It does justice to the prominence of such feelings during emotions. They result from feedback from muscles and inner organs that are active during the emotional reactions. That of course was James' proposal, recently renewed, in a fashion, by Damasio.[4] But this fails to accommodate the feelings of pleasure and pain that are so basic in emotions: they are not body feelings, as was argued in chapter 3.

The third answer focuses on that pleasure and pain. Feelings are variations of pleasure or pain, combined with felt overall state of activation. The answer goes back to Wundt.[5] Russell presents a modern version: Pleasure and pain, and activation form "core affect attributed to something, plus various nonemotional processes."[6] Yet how that feels does not become clear. The view thereby shares its major problem with the other two.

That problem is that none of the three answers does justice to how people describe their emotion experiences. When asked, they can and do give such descriptions even of so-called elementary feelings.[7] No unanalyzable qualia there. The descriptions have an entirely different flavor. They hardly present feelings as "feelings." They present them as experiences of the world or of oneself. The world or oneself is experienced as carrying meaning, involving one's relationship to them, and their relationship to oneself. Felt depression is not just described as pain, apathy, and heaviness in the limbs, nor is first of all labeled "sadness" or "depression." Rather, it is described as feeling to be living in hell, from which there is no escaping, or of being faced with one's utter worthlessness. Anxiety is reported as experiencing a world that offers no hold, with threat lurking everywhere, and with no means to obtain a hold or get away. A given feeling of love consists of witnessing the twins of a gazelle, to quote the Song of Songs, and of the longing to be close to them. Such emotion experience is best characterized as perception of a meaningful world that is filled with calls for action.

How can it be that something as common as emotion experiences can lead careful investigators to such starkly different descriptions?

EXPERIENCE AND ATTENTION

Lambie and Marcel[8] provided an illuminating explanation. All mentioned views, they argue, are on occasion correct. Emotion experience can take different forms, just like any other experience. Which form it takes depends on the involvement of attention, and on one's mode and direction of attention. Visual experience, for instance, exists before attention is aroused, but cannot be reported or recalled.[9] It can be integrative and synthetic, and then yield size, shape, and color constancy. It can also be analytic, when attention is focused on one aspect of a viewed scene only, and then the constancies are largely lost. Similarly for emotion experience.

Lambie and Marcel outline four kinds of variation that shape emotion experience. First, there exist two orders of consciousness, characterized by the absence or presence of focal attention. Second, attention can be directed either toward the "world," to external objects of perception or thought, or toward oneself: toward "the self," that is, toward one's body, one's location in space, or oneself as the conceptual entity that "has" experiences or is the agent of actions. Third, attention can be directed to how the emotional object, whether world or self, appears, or to one's action (or, I would say, one's action readiness), whether in the form of perceived action targets in the world or as body states and strivings of oneself. Fourth, attention can vary in mode: it can be analytic or synthetic, and detached or immersed.

Emotion experience thus is likely to differ according to the circumstances under which it occurs or is examined, since circumstances differ drastically in their attentional demands. Emotions often arise in direct confrontations with an object or event, with which one urgently has to deal. Attention is tied to what the event means. There is little or no latitude to be aware of one's feelings: one is aware of their object. Attention is quite different from when one can sit back, and wait or watch, or when asked "what do you feel?," and when engaged in self-observation in safe surroundings.

Examination context thus influences the resulting account of emotion experience. Urgency to act in an emotional confrontation is not readily compatible with the awareness of "having" an experience. Emotion experience, in such a confrontation, is indeed not well designated as a "feeling," with its connotation of inner or subjective experience—the main reason to put this chapter's heading between quotation marks. When attentional focus is on the world, the experience is in a sense an absence of feeling. One is coping with a difficult situation. One is immersed in dealing with a meaningful event. One may not even identify one's experience as an emotion. Take infatuation: One is enthralled by a person's attractiveness, which may be taken for an objective fact. No subjectivity, no reference to "the self" is involved. Or take envy. One may merely perceive someone who has received a ridiculous prize, which he or she accepted with foolishly naive pride. One is surprised when others label one's experience envy, instead of amusement caused by people so naive. And let there be no mistaking: there is nothing unconscious about these emotions. One is aware of someone very attractive, of a person acting in a ridiculous way. One is having emotion experience.

Feelings as experiences that stand more or less apart are the products of a particular attentional direction: towards one's experience, rather than to the world or oneself as a person. Only when one has an eye on one's experience, and not on the pleasant or unpleasant object, does "a feeling of pleasure" or "a feeling of anger" emerge. When attention is towards objects, however, with their demand characters of what they want from you, may do to you, or seem to offer, they are not there.

I will briefly seek to characterize experience under some of the attentional directions. The analysis owes importantly to that of Lambie and Marcel[10] but in several aspects goes its own way. It also tries to probe a little further into the details of the various aspects of experience.

FIRST- AND SECOND-ORDER EMOTION EXPERIENCE

Attentively observing an object introduces something that was not there before paying attention: the awareness that the object is there. Being aware that one sees an object comes on top of seeing that object. Consciousness has indeed been characterized (I cannot retrace by whom) as "awareness of awareness." And indeed, often one sees an object without being aware that one does. Dennett[11] describes this as "rolling consciousness," nicely illustrated by the common experience of driving one's car over a not too difficult road, while engrossed in conversation. One drives adequately, and the surrounding landscape is seen because one hits no trees, and turns when needed. But attention goes elsewhere. Road and landscape are not really noticed. One cannot recall them. That was first-order perceptual experience.

A distinction between two modes or levels is common in studies of consciousness, under various names and with different emphases. Sartre distinguished irreflexive and reflexive consciousness, Farthing primary and reflective experience, Damasio core and extended consciousness, Zalazo minimal and recursive (or still more complex) consciousness.[12] Lambie and Marcel use "first-order" and "second-order" experience, to which they also refer to as "phenomenology" and "awareness," respectively. I prefer their distinction, as it is the most elementary. Only it may not so much involve focal attention, as well as "paying" attention, that is, staying with the phenomenology at least a trifle longer, not letting it fade at once or evaporate in response. The content of first-order emotion experience is approximated in the immersed mode of awareness, more of which later. It occurs in states of ecstasy (not the drug), and love and other raptures. It also occurs during "flow," under extreme concentration.[13] The distinction between the two modes of consciousness come to the fore when the two are dissociated. This can occur during hypnosis, when a "hidden observer" coolly observes the pain that the manifest "me" does not feel.[14] It is also frequent during traumatic experiences. Under torture, the victim may observe him- or herself writhing and shrieking on the floor, but as from afar, as if pasted to the ceiling, looking down on him- or herself in a somewhat ironical and distant fashion. Aloof, he or she may coolly scan for ways of escape from a situation experienced non-coolly as unbearable.[15]

First-order experience is of a piece, and only concerned with the object and its here and now. As such, human first-order experience is not reportable. It suffices to determine behavior. First-order emotion experience can lead to expressive behavior, without being reportable. If attention does not cling to the experienced object, it is difficult to recall, even only a few seconds after. It is reportable only when focused attention intervenes or clings, and a shift to second-order experience occurs. Then, one realizes that there is a road, trees, the landscape, one's pain. Words may arise, and thoughts elicited by what one sees and experiences. It may shift and extend into awareness that these are *my* experiences. Then, and only then. First-order experience is conceivable (and plausible) in nonhuman animals and infants. They can be said to feel, but not to be aware that they are feeling.

First-order emotion experience has interesting structural properties. One of these is the "objectivity" already hinted at. In first-order emotion experience, the experienced meanings are felt as properties of the objects or events perceived. With focus on the world, the properties are out there: frightening, evil, or attractive. When focus is on oneself, the properties are felt as facts. One is worthless, diminished, or dwindling to nothingness. This objectivity of emotion qualities often remains in second order experience. In infatuation, one's love object just has all those admirable qualities; there is no doubt about them, until the infatuation is over. In hostility, the enemy just is evil, and so are his views and intentions. Politicians are proficient in this.

EMOTION EXPERIENCE AS EXPERIENCE OF THE WORLD

Emotion experience can have the form of affectively meaningful perception of the world: of an object, an event, or the external world as a whole. One perceives a threatening object, a lovely person, an offensive event perpetrated by a nasty offender who blocks ongoing action. If attention is fully focused on the world, emotion experience is out there. The meanings are out there, phenomenally. Experience is of "situational meaning structure".[16] Different emotions correspond to different such meaning structures.

This way of characterizing emotion experience comes from phenomenology, notably from Sartre and Arnold.[17] It emphasizes the intentional nature of emotion experience: the experience is *about* something, not just *of* something. This characterization appears valid. Descriptions of emotion experiences, in self-reports, for a large part consist of descriptions of the meanings of objects or events; different emotions (as named by the subject) tend to correspond to different patterns of meaning.[18] As mentioned in chapter 4, ratings of recalled emotion incidents in terms of appraisal questions that seek to catch those meanings are distinctively linked to the emotion labels used for these incidents.

But situational meaning structures first of all do not lead to assignment of emotion categories or labels. They consist of perceived felt qualities that lead a person to use epithets like "attractive," "fantastic," "repulsive," "uncanny," "weird," "open," and to identify the event as a threat, a loss, or an invitation, as confusing, oppressive, or yielding. All these are the conscious outcomes of appraisal processes that themselves are largely nonconscious. When explicated, the felt qualities appear to fuse the four primary aspects of emotional reactions: the event's, object's, or action's pleasant or unpleasant nature, its affective valence; what the event, object, or action appears to do or offer, and to allow or prevent dealing with it—its context appraisal; what the event actually invites or incites one to do—one's state of action readiness; and *that* the event affects one, the felt precipitate of control precedence.

I rapidly peruse those four aspects. Pleasantness or unpleasantness may appear intrinsic in the perceived object, as in pleasant tastes, or in what it signals or may bring about. Felt context appraisal includes what Gibson[19] called *affordances*. Sirens (not the winged kind) sound alarming; big, sharp teeth look grisly; ravines look as places to fall into; a friendly face as one that allows approach. It also includes what Lambie and Marcel, following Lewin,[20] call "hodological space": the paths for reaching what is desired and barriers to avoiding what is disliked, their openness for approach and resistance to being overcome. Panic, for instance, contains the experience of a world of threat that offers no way out, or with its exits rapidly closing. Perceiving paths and barriers, too, results from interaction between properties of the event and one's actions. "The phenomenology is of the physical relationship between the body and the world".[21]

As to states of action readiness: situational meaning structure includes the world-focused precipitate of one's state of action readiness. It reflects what the event is inciting, ordering, and guiding one to do. When having hit one's head against a kitchen shelf, that shelf is seen as a blameworthy agent, and treated as such: One may smash it. The felt qualities include those of being targets for action, their perceived instrumentality for ongoing or planned actions, their nearness for grasping. They are related to what Lambie and Marcel set apart as "gerundival properties."[22] Action readiness transforms a neutral world into one with places of danger and openings towards safety, in fear, with targets for kissing, and their being accessible for it, in enamoration, with roads stretching out endlessly before one in fatigue, misery, and despair, with insistent calls for entry or participation or consumption, in enjoyment. And to do all that *now*. Action readiness is reflected in the objects' and places' demand characters of "to be removed," "to be distanced from," or "to be united with." The demand characters differ subtly from the affordances and hodological properties. The latter reflect appraisal of what one *could* or *could not* do; the former reflect one's being set to do or actually doing, with its control precedence. During emotion, the felt quality "desirable" changes into that of "desired!," of "an object-to-be-possessed-not-in-possession" into "the object-to-be-possessed!" With joy, experience shifts from "the world as open and available" to "the world within reach," "at one's fingertips," "to-be-participating-in."

Control precedence shows in situational meaning structure as the urgency of the action calls that targets emanate, the violence of their call as incentives, their appearing irresistible, overpowering, unbidden, not to be lost track of.

SELF-FOCUSED EMOTION EXPERIENCE

When attentional focus moves from the world to oneself, experience changes accordingly. The objects now are aspects of *my* body, *my* states, or *my* person. *My* does not mean the same in each instance. It refers to belonging to the totality of the proprioceptive or visual image, to oneself as an agent or subject, or to the conceptual entity on the same level as other persons seen and interacted with.

In emotion, attention may go towards one's responses, perceived from the inside, so to speak: the sensations from one's muscles and inner organs, or one's appraisals of one's competence or incompetence in the particular situation, or of being attracted, of having lost part of oneself, upon personal loss, or as being diminished by failure or insult, or, at a global level of synthesis, as one's feeling of sadness or shame, if one would come to categorize it. In all these variants, attention towards oneself generates the subjectivity of felt emotion, the notion of "having" an emotion, and awareness of entertaining some state of action readiness.

In self-focus, action readiness becomes articulate as felt urge—urge with a particular aim, such as for self-protection, or to broaden and build the scope of one's interactions. Felt anger turns from seeing a bastardly offender into felt urge to strike out, to harm him and remove him from one's field of action.

Other aspects of perceiving oneself may also become emotional objects, and at various levels of synthesis: from feeling muscle twitches to perceiving oneself as a person of high worth or as worthless. Attention can be usurped by the body sensations, or directed to one's body as ugly or sinful. It can focus one's smallness in relation to someone else. It can focus one's emotion experience, and categorize it.

Many of the mentioned aspects exist as objects in irreflexive first-order experience, without awareness, notably when laying down in pain, the body burning, or unable to move, or when disinclined to face the world in hopelessness in depression and feeling small and diminished after loss. Categorizing, though, needs second-order experience, attention for one's current state.

What makes attentional focus shift from the world to oneself? One major condition is salience of some aspect of oneself. The body may cry out loudly, or is perceived as the target of other people's actions. Action urges call for attention when nothing can be done, or action has to be held in abeyance. Fear presumably is felt most strongly when you cannot flee. One also can become oneself the emotional object: how one appears to others, what effects on body or self-image an event has or may have, how one evaluates oneself. Second-order experience shapes further sources. A true notion of self arises, a self-image, the awareness of one's unitary point of view on the world, and of being an autonomous being with a particular set of properties.

WORLD, ACTION, AND BODY
IN EMOTION EXPERIENCE

Note how different experience is under world- and self-focus. Having a feeling of horror or feeling the shivers down one's spine are vastly different from perceiving a horrible event. In one, one's glance goes inward: One feels miserable or shivering. In the other, it goes outward: there is a very evil thing.

And yet awareness of the world and of oneself are strongly intertwined. What is not focused is still in some way present in experience. As Lambie and Marcel[23] formulate it, world and oneself are related as figure and ground. The focused pole becomes the figure, and the other one the ground. Something is seen as looming but, parenthetically, it is because it towers up over oneself.

In self-focus it is the other way around. Awareness of action readiness includes the felt urge to approach or flee, but still toward or away from somewhere. It is awareness of desire and striving to establish or modify a relationship. Action awareness by necessity is situated; otherwise it becomes mere awareness of muscle tension. Take the experience of pointing one's finger: it feels different from stretching one's finger, because the action is guided by orientation towards a point in space.

Shifting focus shifts figure and ground, as they do in visual perception. It modifies the feeling. Perceiving a looming object changes into perceiving oneself as small and vulnerable, or modest and humble, according to degree and kind of synthesis. In world-focused grief the world is an empty place; in self-focused grief, part of oneself is missing.

Conceivably, focus and its shift may be absent. Elements from world and self may be fused. This may be so when attentional focusing has yet to develop, in lower animals and newborn infants, or when world and self dissolve in ecstasy or meditation. Then there only is a dim and inarticulate sense of free-floating pleasure and pain, of stability or instability, of acceptance or non-acceptance. This may well be the most primitive form of feeling, that even an octopus or slug may be capable of.

Experience of action readiness is assumed to be crucial in emotion experience, in world or in self-focused form. This assumption is supported by the evidence on neural activity during emotions, in body sensing and action organizing brain regions such as insular and anterior cingulate cortex.[24] That activity reflects engagement of representations of one's body state and action readiness of the moment. It also suggests that those representations do not primarily derive from peripheral feedback, as James surmised, but from central processes.

The present analysis converges with the analyses of Lambie and Marcel and of Damasio,[25] in concluding that feelings are closely tied to information involving the body. Emotion experience is embodied experience. However, at the same time one has to take issue with Damasio's general formulation of "the stuff that makes a feeling": "the idea of the body being in a certain way" or "the perception of a certain state of the body along with the perception of a certain mode of thinking and of thoughts with certain themes."[26] The formulations are imprecise, and even somewhat misleading. They suggest peripheral feedback, which is secondary when playing a role at all. More importantly, they distract from making explicit that major aspects of feelings are not properly bodily, which would have come out if what is meant by "state of the body" were specified. One of those aspects is affective valence: pleasure and displeasure. A long controversy ended in the conclusion that pleasure and displeasure cannot be reduced to body feelings.[27] Pleasure and pain are not aspects of body states but *glosses* to such and other states, that is, experiences linked to acceptance and nonacceptance tunings, as set out in chapter 3. They may occur when thinking proceeds smoothly or unsuccessfully, which also would not seem to fit "the idea of the body being in a certain way."

Another major aspect that Damasio's formulations fail to point at explicitly is that the representations underlying feelings correspond to appraisals and to action readiness and action. Both go beyond body state as such. Experience of pleasure and pain, most of the time, is *about* some object, and not just accompanied by, or even attributed to it. Action readiness and action, too, include the momentary relation of the body to the world, like in pointing the location one's finger is pointing to. As mentioned in chapter 2, the neural representations of body states and movements reflect this. They covary with the body's location with respect to relevant objects, and its relation to movement targets,[28] and they appear to correspond closely to the phenomenology of awareness of acting.[29] They include the relationship of current state to projected future state, as present in the aim of action readiness. Awareness of the aims of non-planned actions and of urges stems from information termed "reafference" or "preafference" in behavioral and neural control theory.[30] One may indeed expect that activity in the cortices mentioned—ventral premotor cortex and insular cortex—is influenced by those information sources. The evidence suggests that indeed they are.[31]

Characterizing emotion experience as body experience makes what James called the "psychologist's error"; perhaps it should be called now the "neurologist's error": characterizing experience by what one knows about the information leading to that experience. It makes a category error. Emotional feeling is hardly more body feeling than experiencing visual distance is. For the same reasons, Damasio's somatic marker theory[32] should be considered superfluous and confusing. One should just substitute *emotional feeling* (or even *emotion*) wherever *somatic marker* is invoked, because it is uncertain what Phineas Gage–like patients and psychopaths lack in response to affectively competent stimuli: body engagement proper, or arousal of pleasure or pain, or responding with a change in action readiness.[33]

ATTENTIONAL MODES: SYNTHESICISM VERSUS ANALYTICISM, DETACHMENT VERSUS IMMERSION

In the descriptions of world and self focus, I emphasized the more synthetic and immersed variants. These instantiate the intentional nature of the most characteristic forms of emotion experience. Such experience is about objects or events, in the world or of oneself; and the "aboutness" implies their meanings and their being targets of action readiness and action.

However, both sense of meaning and felt intentional nature depend on the current mode of attention. They are most distinct in synthetic mode and immersion, and may be destroyed with increasing degree of analyticity. In first-order experience and in immersion, you are all in it. There is no separate awareness of here and there, of me and the object. It is a major form of emotion experience, since most immersed experience *is* emotion experience. At the end of working in a state of flow, you come out of it, and "come back with one's feet on the ground," or "back to oneself."

Second-order self-focused awareness strongly varies in analyticity. Analytic attention may reduces felt bodily engagement to just that. One may become aware of one's heartbeat or one's wetted pants. Felt impulse to shrink back from a threat is transformed into felt muscle tension. Under threat, one can come to feel dizzy, one's heart racing, instead of feeling anxious or upset. The differences can be consequential. When dizzy or having spells of a racing heart, one visits the general practitioner and not the psychiatrist. Analytic isolation of information sources robs experience of its emotional character. Recall also that analytic attention is favored by introspection. It directs attention away from the links between responses and events, and away from what the movements aim at, their intentional content. Hence the effects mentioned of conditions of observation on the nature of emotion experience. Hence also, I think, the dominant place of body feelings in the history of theory about such experience. Cultural schemas may help in analytic focus, and may explain why Tahitians do not experience sadness, but only fatigue.[34]

One of the most synthetic forms of emotion experience is having feelings of a particular emotion—feeling joyful or angry or jealous. Such feelings are second-order ones, occurring outside immersed confrontations. I return to them presently.

Detachment was briefly mentioned in chapter 4. It can occur in both self-focus and world-focus. It can occur during enjoyment, when holding back from throwing oneself into the pleasure and adopting the attitude of savoring. Detached second-order experience can go all the way from empathically following a target object's movements and strivings, to cool or hostile observation and, in the extreme, to depersonalized feeling: "this does not happen to me." In world-focus, that may lead to feelings of unreality, so frequent during traumatic events. You watch your skidding car slide towards the trees, without fear, and not towards the coming pain. Or you watch that man there on the street falling backwards with a red patch spreading on his head. The experience is cold, although the meanings may be present in first-order experience and arouse reactions such as wetting one's pants, and biting one's lips till they bleed.

During trauma, detachment is automatic. In observation, as a witness at the sidelines, and in savoring it is controlled by voluntary disengagement. It may constitute "emotion refinement," in which one seeks experience and its variety for its own sake, or for deepening emotional insight into a phenomenon or event.[35] Detached emotional experience involves mentally transforming appraisals and states of action readiness into mental images of what the perceived or thought-of event might imply, and how one might respond to it in action; the focus of attention, however, is one's feeling, not the event and how to deal with it. It can extend to an aesthetic attitude towards everyday life.

FEELINGS

At this point, I use the word *feeling* for the qualitative aspects of experience: "feelings of anger," felt qualities, and the like.

Notice that emotional feelings do not have to do in the first place with assigning experience to some category. Experiencing emotions as instances of anger or joy do not form the primary datum; nor do they form the primary datum in recognizing emotions in others.[36] Barrett and Russell are not on the right track when focusing their analyses of emotional feelings on what may underlie assignment of verbal emotion categories.[37] Emotion experience is more interesting than that, and merits reflection on conscious experience as such.

Indeed, the fact that attention shapes emotion experience reveals a basic property of consciousness: its "creative" nature. Conscious experience is not the immediate outflow of information processes of a given intensity. I think it is incorrect to say that "to experience an emotion is to perceive it".[38] Conscious experience is not isomorphic to the underlying information, but involves a transformation.[39] It is creative in that some of its properties could not have been predicted from knowing that information, or from the nerve impulses carrying it. Coming from Mars, observing nerve impulses induced by electromagnetic waves of 660 mμ would in no way predict something like a color red.

Feelings point to another creative aspect of conscious experience, and a basic one at that. Not all such experience comes from the senses. A sensorialist bias has pervaded psychology. It was and is present in the efforts to reduce all experience to sensations or images, and pleasure and pain to body sensations. But there is imageless thought. In feelings, there is awareness of urge. There is awareness of what one wants to do before doing it, and of being set for a given action. There is feeling that feelings are about something. There are feelings generated by failure or successful completion of one's actions. There are feelings coming from the proper functioning of one's information processes, as argued in chapters 3 and 5.

Moreover, experience in general, and feeling in particular, as Scherer argued,[40] present amalgams, or rather syntheses and integrations of the complex information that enters the meanings of emotion words.[41] Conscious experience does not point for point correspond to the underlying sources, even if it reflects them. That is evident even in simple and basic aspects of visual perception. Perceived objects appear to "exist," they are "out there," and will still be in a minute or two. They are felt as "real," except when one is in fever. It applies to basic elements of one's sense of self, such as awareness of agency. These experiences all integrate diverse sorts of information. One can walk around objects, they will still be there when one closes one's eyes, they may hit your head: in experience they blend in the sense of reality and of "out there." Visual impressions *per se* are integrated with motor components and expectations. Motor information of course pervades visual perception, in depth perception, in the perception of close distances, in that of affordances, and thus in one's sense of reality. That is the core of embodied perception.[42]

Synthesis and integration show most clearly in what I referred to as "felt qualities": weirdness and uncanniness, perceived affordances, hodological and gerundival properties. They also show in the "feelings of sadness," of joy, anger, and so forth. They all integrate diverse information "in a single integrative blend";[43] it is the view of most current investigators.[44] The felt qualities are amalgams from nonconscious representations of what events can do to you, allow you to do, incite you to do, or are in the process of doing. As just indicated, "feelings of sadness" and of other emotions that language distinguishes somehow synthesize and integrate sensed appraisal, affect, action readiness and autonomic reactions, helped by available verbal categories.

Following the integration processes in the inverse direction, feeling and felt qualities appear to be pointers to the information at their source. The feelings represent a dim sense of the paths to those sources, or of the mere existence of such paths and sources. Feelings generally do, even nonemotional ones. Their paradigm instances are the feeling of knowing, and one's awareness that one understands a verbal message. These clearly are pointers. Consider that someone speaks a sentence, and you nod: you understood what he said. What is it that you nod to? In his research on imageless thought, K. Bühler[45] studied people's understanding of complex texts. A proverb was read to them; they had to press a button when they understood its meaning, and report their experience. Subjects generally acknowledged that "understanding" did not imply explicit thoughts or images representing meaning. No such thoughts or images were yet present when they pressed their button. Bühler called these experiences *Bewusstheiten*, "consciousnesses," and, in later studies, simply *thoughts*. Subjects were able subsequently to explicate the meaning. The feeling of understanding thus can be considered a pointer to the possibility of explicitation.

Emotional feelings and felt qualities can be regarded as similar pointers. If the conditions are right, and the subject has the necessary cognitive abilities, the sources (or presumed sources) can be retraced by processes of explicitation. The diffuse and "ineffable" feelings of anger, joy or sadness then can yield articulate awareness of appraisal and action readiness. Felt qualities can likewise be taken apart, in principle at least, in terms of the four aspects mentioned earlier. Importantly, the pointers do not primarily point to declarative information. They point to affectations, bodily for a large part (going to be hurt, satisfaction etc.), to access (or lack of access) to action programs, and to their actual activation and progress, or lack of it. These are, I think, the most elementary targets of their pointing.

Feelings of pain and pleasure may form an exception. As mentioned in chapter 3, they may form the only irreducible affective qualia. But I have to admit: feeling of pleasure, or the felt quality of pleasantness, is a pointer too: a pointer to the action tuning of event or state acceptance; that of pain is a pointer to tuning to event or state change. The pointing persists until the thing pointed to has emerged: the thought, the perceived appraisal, or the relevant action.[46]

SECOND-ORDER EXPERIENCE: EMOTION EXPERIENCE AS EXPLICABILITY, EXPLICITATION, AND ELABORATION

Second-order awareness considerably adds to first-order experience by awareness, permitting attention change, and reporting and naming. Feelings of pleasure, and those of core affect in Russell's sense,[47] are second-order experiences. They only exist by virtue of this little bit of attentional deflection. So do, of course, the feelings of anger and so forth.

Awareness is not always very articulate. That of core affect is not: it fuses pleasure and activation, and the component of activation is an inarticulate blend (and abstraction) of felt action readiness and felt autonomic arousal. More complex feelings still can be inarticulate. Think of moods. Recall the small emotions mentioned in chapter 2. They are brief, and small in action readiness: just a moment of felt disturbance, just a little feeling behind the eyes, just a moment on wants to sit down, or a flash of thought to go after something. There hardly is appraisal awareness: just the inarticulate thought of how terrible that was, what passed one's mind. Still, this was emotion awareness. It held the felt qualities with their sensed explicability.

But all this can be fuller in full-blown emotion, it can be attended to, and it can be made truly articulate by explicitating the feelings and felt qualities—that is, by following up the paths that these are pointers to.

Explicitation yields the main substance of full second-order emotion experience. In that, its forces are joined by elaboration, thoughts and images generated by the phenomenology and what it gives access to. Thoughts roam around the event and one's reactions: what more could happen, what might one do, what might the consequences be. Experiencing the grisliness of a spider may expand by noticing the crawling legs, the shivers that may be forthcoming when feeling it crawl over one's skin, the idea of its getting into one's hair. The outcomes of explicitation and elaboration, in turn, modify the phenomenology, deepen or change the felt qualities—say, making them horrid or horrible or awful or revolting or unnameably different—modifying action readiness. Take perceiving something that stands out as unique, say a different pencil among a set of similar ones. One may realize that the uniqueness confers distinction or, by contrast, that choosing it makes one conspicuous. It leads one to either prefer or reject the unique pencil, depending on one's concerns. In fact, in an experiment in which students were offered a pencil as a present, American and Korean American students indeed tended to choose the unique one, but not so Korean students, and Korean Americans after a five weeks stay in Korea. Their preference shifted toward one of the identical ones.[48]

Explicitation and elaboration merit attention not only because they provide a closer view of emotion experience. They also promise insight in how experiences of similar emotions may differ from each other. Emotion experiences differ between instances and individuals, not only because regulation and display rules may differ. Concerns also differ, and so do things appraised, the most available specifications of states of action readiness, the most available actions, and historical contexts, social contexts and expectations. All that results in experiences that differ, and most clearly so upon explicitation and elaboration.

Explicitation follows four main roads: downward, upwards, back- and forward, and around. Downward, in articulating the momentary appraisal and action readiness, and their influence on one's functioning. Upward, in seeking to articulate the concerns that give the event its meaning: why the threat, why the sadness? Backward into the past that was carried along in the appraisal, and forward towards the future, when exploring the likely consequences of the event and one's reaction. And around: the implications of one's appraisal and one's action readiness and actions for who one feels one is, and for one's relations with other people.

A few words to detail what those four roads contribute. "Downward" explicitation seeks to articulate experience of one's appraisal and action readiness. It leads to experiencing the appraisal and action readiness patterns like those described in self-report studies mentioned in chapter 4. It traces back the sources of hodological and gerundival properties, be it that outcomes of retracing them may well differ from the sources. It also yields awareness of restraint and inhibition: the flatness of one's anger, the discrepancies between what is felt and what is becoming manifest in actions and words. Downward explicitation deepens as well as clarifies the emotional event's meaning. Each hodological and gerundival property reveals both a potential of the world as well as a potential of oneself: what the world can do, and what one is vulnerable to. They each condense the emotional meanings of events and objects: what they brought me or did to me, could do to me or will do to me. Clarification extends those meanings and may in turn modify phenomenal awareness.

Explicitation of felt action readiness colors and specifies feeling. Take the hostile action tendency of anger, that changes shape with circumstances and concerns at stake. It can take the form of paying back or ending current interaction, or saving interaction for the sake of harmony. The prepared-for

actions are perpetrating physical or verbal violence, falling silent and silently turning one's back, or being polite and seeking some form of interpersonal harmony. Not only the sensed motor feedback of all these differs;
they also have different consequences for the social relationship and one's
self-image. The first modifies the power relationship; the second may protect one's sense of dignity; the third safeguards future social options. The
experiences differ accordingly, and coalesce in the phenomenologies of perceiving one's antagonist as "to-be-neutralized," "to-be-distanced-from," or
"to be reconciled with," the last differentiating the meanings of the words
anger and *boosheid* in Dutch, from *ikari* in Japanese.[49]

With *upward* explicitation I mean assessing which concerns were at stake
in the emotional event. Offense, promise, or loss with respect to different
concerns each have different implications for action selection, for the perspectives on how the event will develop, and for one's self-image. Fear for
one's safety feels different from fear for one's moral integrity. Finding out
the reasons for one's anger differentially influence regulation efforts, or the
direction of correcting action. This may lead to different felt qualities, like
"offensive," "insulting," "demeaning," or "humiliating." The differences
in concerns, and the consequences of actions for safeguarding those concerns, may make that close translations—say, *anger* and *ikari*—still denote
different experiences. *Anger* that is felt to upset social harmony by retaliation feels different from *ikari* that, by falling silent, respects the other and
keeps social options open.[50]

Explicitation and elaboration also go backward and forward, to past and
future. Appraisals are influenced by one's history of previous experience
with events similar to the present one. An insult may be a surprising first
one or the intolerable tenth in a row, or one that one knew to expect and is
resigned to, or that one grudgingly lets pass, but files for later reference.

Past and future may extensively affect emotion experience. An insult
known as the tenth in a row makes it suffocating. Depth of loneliness differs
between that due to this Sunday's absence of one's friends, or to having fled
one's country, being cut off from one's language, one's history, and the
sources of one's social identity.[51] It is not a matter of emotion strength only,
but also of the appraisals of finality of loss, of what could possibly lift the
loneliness, the impenetrability of the barriers to roads for escape.

Then, finally, explicitation can go "around." It may bring awareness of
important consequences for who one feels one is, and for one's relations
with others. These constitute what I have called the emotion's *significance*,[52]
which mediates emotion regulation. A dim sense of comfort or discomfort
may come to take the contours of feeling proud or ashamed of one's emotion. It may bring realization that it attracts or repels others, or conforms
with or deviates from shared values. Again the felt qualities change. An
emotion that one approves of feels different from one that one rejects, or one

that unites from one that leaves one alone. One may feel proud or ashamed of one's appraisals and for one's desires. The emotion may also attract or reject other people. In other words: there is much in emotion experience that is felt to unite with, or separate from others. Hence considerable differences in the experience of similar emotions when these are, or are not, supported by dominant cultural models or norms. Shame is not frequently a very strong emotion in the Western world; and where it is, it is a private matter.[53] It is, however, a strong dynamic force in the Muslim world, where shame may break a life course, and avoidance of shame is one of the guiding rules of daily life.[54]

DIFFERENCES IN EXPERIENCED EMOTIONS

The above descriptions show how emotion experiences can differ, even when sharing the core features of appraisal and action readiness, and on the whole labeled in equivalent ways. That what comes about in explicitation reflects variety in felt qualities—horrid, horrible, awful, and so on—and what comes out in elaboration may modify the phenomenology. The variety comes from variety in concerns that underlie appraisals, in details of the appraisals coming from differences in events as appraised, from variants in action readiness and the implications of resulting actions.

Let me illustrate this variety by examining a group of emotions, designated in English by one common name: *awe*. I borrow the gist of my description from Keltner and Haidt.[55] The core of emotions of awe consists of the appraisal of vastness, one's inability to fully grasp that vastness, and consequent inability to deal with it, and how to fit it among things one can handle. This situational meaning motivates the action tendency of submission, and actions with that aim. One approaches softly. One acts or handles with care. One may weep, which I view as an act of submission.[56] One does not speak unless spoken to. One feels unable to act as an equal, with self-confidence or defiance. One feels humble and small.

Variations in awe experience come from additional appraisal components, and entail variants in submissive action tendency. The additional appraisals specify the nature of the vastness involved: superior ability, beauty, charisma, extraordinary intellectual or technical intricacy, menace, virtue, and power—natural, social, or supernatural. These color the awe by simultaneous other emotions: admiration, fear, humility, respect, sense of the sublime, timidity, or desire to follow and emulate. The additional appraisals let the object impinge on different concerns, and each dictate different action tendencies. Threat comes from the object's vast power to inflict punishment or other harm; that awe borders on fear. It is evoked by individuals in superior power positions, like kings and the other mighty. The supernatural shares in it. God has been designated as *tremendans et fascinans*, fear inspiring and absorbing, although he can be felt to share the virtues of love, superior ability, and supreme goodness; after all, he is supposed to have created the world and to know all. Superior power and the supernatural also share the extension of power beyond physical proximity. The mighty and God possess the police and the All-Seeing Eye, respectively. Beauty incites different aims: careful treatment, sensory absorption, and possession. Virtue, threat and supernatural power may share instigation of further desires to participate in them, by exposing oneself to their abilities for spreading contamination.[57] One tries to emulate the objects, and to touch them. The rock at Lourdes is glossy from the millions of hands that touched it in passing; touching persons of stature, or their clothes, or their letters, is common and, I think, universal.

There exist other emotions with submission at their core, but that in English carry different names from awe: respect, humility, certain forms of shame, for instance. It would be worthwhile to spell out what appraisal aspects make them different.

I want to illustrate this variety of emotion experiences further. The variety may provide clues to understand cultural differences in such experiences, even among emotions considered universal and designated by words considered close translations. Mesquita has provided the lines along which the differentiation can be described.[58] I choose possible variant emotions defined by hostile action tendency elicited by appraisals of offense. Hostile action tendency is defined by the aim of terminating offense by inflicting pain. Offense is defined as any willful action that causes pain or harms a concern. The variants can be considered variants of experience of anger, *ikari, colère, boosheid,* or whatever related names; each may, in some language, correspond to a more specific label.

There are many sorts of offense, due to harm to different concerns. I give several variants in Table 8.1. Each, obviously, has different implications for the kind of concern or concerns it offends, the importance of those concerns, and the ways they interfere with striving.

The aim of hostility can take various forms, as a result of interplay between hostility and the concerns it may defend, promote, or protect. They need not all be the same as those offended. I list some of them in Table 8.2. Each has different repercussions for social interactions and self-esteem. Any of these aims may induce various types of action that, again, differ in personal and social significance: Table 8.3.

WHAT IS EMOTION EXPERIENCE GOOD FOR?

What is the function of emotion experience? That is: how would human behavior and beliefs be different if emotion experience were absent?

TABLE 8.1
Offenses

Someone's action harms one's health, safety, possessions, or access to resources.

Someone's action harms continuity of one's ongoing actions.

Someone's action disturbs social behavior habits.

Someone's action threatens one's power or status relative to that of the antagonist.

Someone's action carries the likelihood of repetition of the offense.

Someone's action damages social esteem and/or self-esteem.

Someone's action threatens values and the esteem for respected or loved others.

Someone's action threatens one's role as a defender of those others.

Someone's action threatens one's status in the eyes of others.

Someone's action threatens one's prestige in the eyes of one's children.

Someone's action opens the possibility of derision by others present.

Someone's action threatens confidence in respectful social interactions.

Someone's action threatens the "symbolic universe" as the sum total of values that give meaning to events and the world.

TABLE 8.2
Variations of Hostile Aims

Annulment of power inequality disturbance.

Achieving superiority or dominance.

Supporting social prestige.

Serving as a model to others.

Remaining human and civilized, and keeping self-respect.

Safeguarding the relationship to the antagonist.

TABLE 8.3
Offense-Instigated Actions

Physical attack.

Verbal attack.

Humiliating the offender and gaining social ascendancy.

Turning one's back and terminating the current interaction.

Turning the other cheek or doing nothing.

Leaving the field, abandoning effort to restore power inequality.

Doing any of these by mere hints and indications.

The question may appear silly. Feelings may seem to be what emotion is all about. It is not entirely silly, though. Emotion experience reflects nonconscious appraisal processes, states of action readiness, action, and physiological changes, that largely would occur whether experience follows or not. Emotions, if defined by these processes and their outcomes, can occur without consciousness; so, what does experience add?

That emotional reactions do occur without conscious experience appears from extensive research on automatic or nonconscious arousal of various such reactions. Some of the evidence has been reviewed by Bargh and by Öhman and Wiens.[59] Nonconscious arousal means that the subject is not aware of the eliciting stimulus or of its emotional valence or content. He or she may also be unaware of the responses, or of the fact that they were due to the antecedents they were in fact due to. The elicitors include affectively valent stimuli that were rendered nonconscious by backward masking or very brief exposure times, or of which the cognitive aspects were rendered largely inaccessible by cortical lesions.[60] The responses were enumerated in chapter 4. They include conscious affective judgments (liking or dislike) of subsequently presented neutral stimuli, slowing down extinction when the conditioned stimulus was a backwardly masked stimulus such as the picture of a spider or snake, freezing, startle, and autonomic upset, and enhanced consumption of a liked drink after masked priming by a happy face.[61] The effects may on occasion be even stronger for nonconscious than for conscious stimuli.[62] All this led Le Doux[63] to make his notorious remark that the study of emotion experience is a red herring in the investigation of emotion.

Is that remark warranted? No, it is not.

It would be foolish to belittle the role and impact of emotion experience, in particular as first-order phenomenology. Just look at the small range of reactions that follow suboptimal stimuli, as just summarized: evaluative changes of formerly neutral stimuli, retardations of extinction. Look at what is involved when actions are more complex: with increases of consumption of drinks liked anyway, in the mentioned Berridge and Winkielman study, perceived palatability was almost certainly involved; the drink was in full view. Look at the emotional reactions of split-brain patients when stimuli are exposed to the right hemisphere: giggles, vague disturbances. Look at the range of things undertaken by people with blindsight: hardly anything. Why should they undertake anything? Adequate actions with respect to objects in the blind field are possible when subjects are induced to act on "guesses," but they will not do so spontaneously.[64] They have no reason to act; a blindsight patient is deeply handicapped.[65] And imagine what people with affective blindsight might do—people who show neural signs of recognizing facial expressions without being aware of it, nor feeling anything when the expressions are shown.[66] Imagine people with entire affective blindness: no feelings of pleasure and pain, but at most immediate responses of increase or decrease in consumption, extinction delays and the like. They would show no hedonic concerns, as described in chapter 5; they would do nothing for fun or enjoyment. Neither would they act out of compassion.

Sure, the mentioned findings on nonconscious emotion-relevant processing represent discoveries of major importance. There are many things, in the emotion domain, that lower animals and brain-lesioned higher ones, and people after masked-priming stimuli, *are* capable of doing. The findings do show the nonconscious nature of the major emotion-generating mechanisms. But building emotional interactions and strivings on that basis is another matter.

It is, because the listed nonconsciously elicited reactions represent only a fragment of what emotions consist of. They consist almost entirely of rapid reactions to actually present stimuli. The preceding chapter showed, however, that sudden and brief emotional reactions form perhaps 5% of human emotional reactions, and probably not much more of those of other primates. Robinson[67] presented the generalization that all that preattentive processes may produce, are valence and urgency appraisals, together with automatic responses; Shizgal[68] came to a similar conclusion from analyzing midbrain dopamine function. Such appraisals may be all that is needed for those automatic responses and parameter changes. But it is not enough for nonstereotyped action, for actions guided by intention-in-action,[69] for action when stimuli are not present to the senses, and for controlled processing.

There is unlikely to be much striving for distant objects, even if within sight, if there is no affect drawing that striving, if there is no felt incentive value that draws. The butterfly may need no more, because the zigzagging and keeping moving along that line is automatic; but also, it is about all that a butterfly can do. Dogs or wolves circling, I would predict, need more: feeling threat when you turn your back, as well as when you lose sight, and therefore circling with their side and their eyes towards the antagonist.[70] Feeling appears needed for flexible action. Striving is even less likely when it is not towards an object present to the senses, but in search of something anticipated: Why search if there is no present reason, in affect or in fuller feeling?

In fact, there is little or no evidence to the contrary. Instrumental learning appears to be dependent on awareness of hedonic outcomes, as grasped as causally linked to one's actions. As mentioned in chapter 5, Balleine and Dickinson showed that hedonic experience may well form a necessary link in such learning, arguing that it appears as one of the major functions of conscious awareness.[71] Le Doux demonstrated that a conditioned reaction of fear or panic can only be established in a rat with cortex intact, though it can be maintained with cortex severed from limbic circuits.[72]

All this is not surprising. Many psychological functions depend on attention, and drawing attention is one of the major effects of affects.[73]

Beyond the rat, the causal effects of affects are perhaps more transparent. Feelings represent information, as Clore and Schwarz demonstrated, they form a basis for judgments and decisions, and extensively influence value attributions and searching for their possible reasons or justifications.[74] They may well form the basis for the superiority of "intuitive" over well-reasoned decisions in complex situations.[75] "Intuitive" judgments may well result from inarticulate accretions to and decretions from global feelings about an object. You like it more or like it less with each piece of information, without having to wonder and ponder why.

No striving, no learning. One of the main functions of emotion awareness may precisely be to enable action when no automatic action—no hissing and barking and freezing—is available. That is, it recruits and enables controlled processing.[76] One goes in search; search is sustained over time, even when the eliciting object has gone. Action may be shown after a delay only; action readiness can be held in abeyance, and retaliation may follow minutes, hours, or years later. Complexities of this kind are shown not only by humans. As mentioned earlier, an elephant mother touches the bones of a deceased infant with her trunk, even when passing by years after the loss occurred.[77] No sadness or nostalgic feeling? Come on!

What feelings appear to do, in the examples, is calling upon wide arrays of processes and responses, in conjunction with specific event features. That is to say: emotions can only show these various features of action readiness and its widespread activation of other processes if the information eliciting and guiding them has the functional properties generally ascribed to consciousness. Baars and Dennett, among others[78] have outlined them. One is that conscious contents "broadcast" their message or, in Rozin's terms, exert "systemwide activation."[79] Pleasure and pain experience do so in particular, and Shizgal[80] considers that to be their function. They are distinct alarm bells, with their strongly attention-absorbing qualities that, for pain at least, have been abundantly demonstrated,[81] and that may be considered essential in establishing the powerful incentive values that elicit cravings and some other concerns. Conscious experience is "heard" by an indeterminate number of action dispositions. It may activate some actions, and stop or interrupt others. It modifies expectations.

Finally, conscious experience represents integrated and synthetic information from different sources. That information is kept available during delays in the planning and execution of actions. Consciousness may be related to working memory for planned action.[82] It allows the human ability to have emotions that are not expressed but only experienced, but nevertheless influence the conduct of life. Capacity for consciousness allows pondering, considering, and planning, on the basis of goal-settings independent from immediate action and of shifting future priorities after eliciting events have gone by.

All this is more or less standard functional theory of consciousness. It distinctly accounts for a functional role of conscious emotion experience. It indicates that role not just to be a human luxury on top of elementary responsiveness, but to go at the heart of emotions.

Unconscious emotions? They can be said to exist, but their range appears as extremely limited and perhaps hardly deserving of the term. There is no sign that someone would beat up someone who had harmed him, or would stalk a woman, or would offer her kisses and waste away when she refuses them, without experiencing anything about it.

BEYOND ADAPTATION

Moreover, the main functional role of experience may be elsewhere. It may not primarily be to render adaptation more efficient. Emotion experience provides novel motivations and new knowledge that lead to novel emotions and actions. And it creates future: the awareness of future that allows true intentions. Emotion experience extends the niches that people and animals seek to adapt to, rather than only improving adaptation to the niche that exists.

Going beyond adaptation is evident in seeking pleasure. The experiences of pleasure and pain instigate getting and getting rid of them; they become ends in themselves. Don't shrug this away as secondary offshoots of adaptational necessities. It makes human nature to be what it is: emotionally adventurous and inventive. And it is not restricted to humans. Mice self-administer morphine that produces experience that asks for more. Bonobos and dolphins masturbate, presumably for the same reason that we humans do.[83] Seeking pleasure and decrease of pain can only be conceived as stirred by feelings. There is independent evidence for that conclusion. Interference with the opiate system takes away sniffing and whisker-trembling in mice confronted with previously preferred foods.[84] Battery animals indulge in self-injurious behaviors and odd behaviors like crib-biting, presumably for increasing endorphin levels that presumably reduce felt discomfort.[85] Of course, pleasure seeking and pain reduction enhance reproductive fitness, but that does not explain how they operate. It certainly does not explain the prominent consequence of pleasure seeking: abundance or luxury motivation that seeks to get more than one needs, like gluttony, greed, seeking more possessions or more power, up to the unquenchable search for it in individuals like Nero and Stalin.

Experiences of pleasure not only expand motivation beyond homeostatic or similar concerns. They extend it to novel domains. Humans seek fine wine and chili peppers; evolution surely has not shaped taste mechanisms for them. They use cars not only to gain time but to lose discomfort and go for the pleasures of driving a Ferrari. Novel object domains are drawn into the individual's range for free. Climbing mountains may be useful for finding roads to food, water, and nice views; but the pleasure of doing it under difficult circumstances provides a motive on its own. It expands the domain of activities and skills actively sought. The same for interest and curiosity. Curiosity, again, is no doubt useful for getting one's bearings and detecting friends, foes, and resources, but that does not sustain it. The feelings self-reinforce by the outcomes of what they make one do. They lead to feeling at home in a wider environment, and to being thrilled by ever novel challenges and successes. The environment gets very much larger because it comes to include moving about in the worlds of knowledge and imagination. In the wake of all this, people may go and seek discomfort for the pleasure that follows: the icy wind on the mountain top, the suspense of a horror movie, the chili peppers again.

Such growth goes along with a growth in the world of emotions. Owing to experiencing them, pleasure and pain can turn from signals of well functioning into goals. Well functioning itself becomes such a goal. Death can become a sting, and love a glory. Many things that are stumbled upon as sources of pleasure or pain turn into objects of striving and desire. In several emotion domains this is prominent.

The first is that of self-conception. Much second-order emotion experience consists of making sense of one's emotions. One locates one's emotion within a causal nexus, with the incumbent discoveries about oneself and the world, and the bases of new emotions that these discoveries provide.

A second domain is that of beauty. Beauty only exists as experience, and it only leads to behaviors that serve to enhance experience. Very little if anything adaptive is gained in addition to that, except in the case of sexual beauty. Beauty is created as well as sought for the purpose of experiencing. Whence does the experience of beauty come? I do not know, except that experience of beauty satisfies concerns for certain other types of experience: of understanding, of perfection, of the well-functioning of the competences involved in grasping the beauteous event, and of coherence with the world.

COHERENCE

Achieving coherence with the world is a third domain in which emotion experience shapes behavior. Its most noticeable instantiations are love, friendship, and social belonging, maintaining intimate interpersonal interactions. The interactions are driven by their felt satisfactions, the felt suspenses and excitements when they are in the making, and the anxieties and loneliness when they are broken or out of reach.[86] Much of the behavior is directed towards obtaining or maintaining the positive experiences that range from the sensory experiences of body warmth and of staying out of the wind-stream (which, I am told, motivates geese to fly as they do) to mental exchange and felt mental closeness.

This is particularly prominent in emotion sharing.[87] Exchanging emotion experience is what much of social interaction is about; in social sharing it is explicitly sought. People share between 75% and 95% of their emotion incidents with at least one other person, within a few days after the incident. Emotion sharing does not aim at solving one's emotional problems, and it does not help in doing that. It appears primarily motivated by being inherently satisfying, and by maintaining or regaining the "symbolic universe." Likewise, much of the pleasures of sex derives from sharing the pleasures,[88] just as the joint pleasures of child rearing help to offset the burdens of such rearing. Pleasure is involved in all this: damage to opiate systems damages social inclinations.[89]

At a deeper level, emotion experience forms the very substance of what cements much social interaction: empathy. Empathy is defined by awareness of the emotions of others. It is what allows social sharing, but also comforting and helping others. Comforting and helping have been observed in non-human primates: a chimpanzee rescuing another chimpanzee trapped in a ditch, by lowering a ladder into that ditch. The subtle interactions in flirting and sex among humans and primates, too, rest on awareness of what the other feels, or may or should feel. Interestingly, empathy appears largely based on nonconscious processes,[90] but helping behavior is not.

Emotion sharing, love and friendship appear to be manifestations of a wider emotional aim: establishing a sense of coherence with others and the world. Sense of coherence is experiential by definition. It is pervasive but hardly noticed until it drops out during derealization experiences and loneliness. It makes itself felt when emotional meanings are absent. Emotional flatness is one of the major complaints in boredom and depression, and one of the reasons that a depressive may feel life to be meaningless.

Emotion experiences of any kind represent links with the world, as well as with oneself. Coherence is sought, both as a sense of external reality and as a background sense of self, even if only in the experience of the one bumping into the other. It is of course explicitly sought in a mystical sense of unity with the world.

How does emotion experience provide a sense of coherence? The explanation may lie in one of the basic function of pleasure, signaling well-functioning. Sense of well-being can be viewed as the superordinate level of monitoring well functioning. Loneliness indicates that social desires, propensities, and capabilities run on empty; boredom that emotional and cognitive functions do not function properly. Coherence mirrors high-level adequacy of functioning.

But perhaps the explanation is simpler and unsurprising. It is experience of actual coherence. The world impinges on one's body and actions, and one modifies the world in return, or sets to it, in action readiness and action. The world shows open roads for access, and action readiness prepares to dive into it: joy. Or the world blocks progress, and makes one push against the block, or withdraw from it, in anger and fear. Even hatred represents a relationship. Even one's sadness is a dear experience one does not willingly let go of, because as long as the sadness is there, the lost one is not entirely gone.

NOTES

[1]Izard, 1977; Oatley and Johnson-Laird, 1987; Plutchik, 1980.
[2]Johnson-Laird & Oatley, 1988.
[3]Reisenzein, 1995.
[4]Damasio, 1994; 2003; James, 1884.
[5]Wundt, 1902
[6]Russell, 2003, p. 145.
[7]e.g., Davitz, 1969.
[8]Lambie & Marcel, 2002.
[9]Lamme, 2003.
[10]Lambie & Marcel, 2002.
[11]Dennett, 1991.
[12]Damasio, 2000; Farthing, 1992; Sartre, 1939/1948; Zelazo 1996.
[13]Csikszentmihalyi, 1990.
[14]Hilgard, 1977.
[15]e.g., Langhoff, 1935
[16]Frijda, 1986.
[17]Arnold, 1960; Sartre, 1939/1948.
[18]e.g., Davitz, 1969.
[19]Gibson, 1979.
[20]Lewin, 1937.
[21]Lambie & Marcel, 2002, p. 238.
[22]For Lambie and Marcel, these are aspects of second-order experience only. As sketched here, they can also belong to first-order experience, to phenomenology.
[23]Lambie & Marcel, 2002.
[24]Damasio, 2003; Panksepp & Watt, 2003.
[25]Damasio, 2003; Lambie & Marcel, 2002.
[26]These quotations are from Damasio, 2003, p. 83, p. 85, and p. 86, respectively.
[27]Arnold, 1960.
[28]Gallese, 2005.
[29]Gallese & Metzinger, 2003.
[30]see Freeman, 1999; Gallistel, 1980.

[31]also: Panksepp & Watt, 2003.
[32]Damasio, 1994.
[33]Hare, 1976.
[34]Levy, 1973.
[35]Frijda, 2005; Sundararajan, 2005.
[36]Frijda, 1953; Frijda & Tcherkassof, 1997.
[37]Barrett, 2005; Russell, 2003.
[38]Barrett, 2005, p. 275.
[39]Marcel, 1983.
[40]Scherer 2004.
[41]Ortony, Clore, & Collins, 1988; Russell, 2003.
[42]Niedenthal, Barsalou, Ric, & Keith-Grauber, 2005; Varela, Thompson, & Rosch,1991.
[43]Russell, 2003, p. 148.
[44]e.g., Russell, 2003; Scherer, 2004; perhaps also James, 1884.
[45]K. Bühler 1908.
[46]Jim Averill, pointed out to me that this analysis of qualia was made earlier by Dennett, 1991. Of course.
[47]Russell, 2003.
[48]Kim, cited in Mesquita & Markus, 2004.
[49]Frijda et al., 1995.
[50]Mesquita & Markus, 2004.
[51]Apfelbaum, 2000.
[52]Frijda, 1986.
[53]Lewis, 1971; Scheff, 1988.
[54]Abu-Lughod, 1988; Bourdieu, 1966.
[55]Keltner and Haidt, 2003.
[56]Frijda, 2001.
[57]Rozin, 1999
[58]Mesquita, 2004.
[59]Bargh, 1997; Öhman & Wiens, 2004.
[60]De Gelder, Vroomen, & Pourtois, 2001; Moors, De Houwer, & Eelen, 2004; Murphy and Zajonc, 1993; Öhman and Wiens, 2004; LeDoux, 1996.
[61]Berridge, 2004a; Berridge & Winkielman, 2003.
[62]Murphy and Zajonc, 1993; Rotteveel, 2003
[63]LeDoux 1996.
[64]Marcel, 1988.
[65]Weiskrantz, 1997.
[66]De Gelder, 2005.
[67]Robinson, 1998.
[68]Shizgal, 1999.
[69]Recall the term used by Searle, (1983) mentioned in Chapter 2.
[70]Recall the description of circling wolves as cited in Fogel, 1993, p. 29–30.

[71]Balleine & Dickinson, 1998.

[72]LeDoux, 1996.

[73]Phelps, 2005.

[74]Clore & Gasper, 2000; Schwarz & Clore, 1988.

[75]Dijksterhuis 2004.

[76]Clore & Ketelaar, 1997; Oatley & Johnson-Laird, 1987; Robinson, 1998.

[77]De Waal, 1996.

[78]Baars, 1997; Dennett, 1991.

[79]Rozin, 1999, p. 113.

[80]Shizgal, 1999.

[81]e.g., Crombez, Eccleston, Bayens, & Eelen, P., 1998.

[82]Baars, 1997.

[83]See De Waal and Lanting, 1997, for bonobos; see Fisher (1992 chap. 9, note 25) for dolphins.

[84]Berridge, 2004a

[85]Wiepkema, 1990

[86]e.g., Shaver & Rubinstein, 1980.

[87]Rimé, 2005.

[88]Fisher, 1992; Hatfield & Rapson, 1993.

[89]Fisher 2004; Panksepp, 1998.

[90]De Gelder et al., 2004.

9

Sex

SEX AND EMOTION

Sex would seem a major topic in the psychology of emotion. Yet, in standard treatments of emotions it is strikingly absent. Sexual passion does not figure among the lists of basic emotions. It is not in Ekman's, not in that of Izard, not among those listed by Tomkins, not among the basic emotions discussed by Oatley and Johnson-Laird.[1] This is decidedly odd. It has not always been so. Lust was an important emotion for Thomas Aquinas. It belonged to the seven deadly sins together with other major emotions like anger, pride and envy. Nineteen-century psychologists like Bain did discuss the "sex emotion,"[2] but few have done so since. Luckily, the tide is turning. In 1988, Walter Everaerd published his paper "Sex as an Emotion."[3] Several current psychologists include sexual passion or sexual love among the emotions again. Hatfield and Rapson devoted several books to passionate love;[4] so, more recently, did Fisher;[5] Regan and Berscheid published a book simply called *Lust*.[6]

Then why was it dropped for so long from the study of emotion? Probably because it was delegated to the domain of motivation; perhaps also because lust and sexual desire have no distinct facial expression. But probably also because sex does not involve just one emotion, but a whole series of them. A number of different emotions result from the fates of sexual concern. They blend over into each other. They might be considered different stages or appearances of one sex emotion. Those I will here call the sexual emotions.

Each can be understood and described from the perspectives of emotion analysis, as developed in the preceding chapters. All sexual emotions result from events impinging on the sexual concern, that is, the sexual motivational system, rooted in neurohumoral dispositions, without which no sexual feeling or striving could occur. As any other concern, the concern has three sets of major components: sensitivities, which are responsive to particular classes of external events and thoughts; a set of response dispositions; and a set of properly motivational provisions that determine the ease with which response dispositions are potentiated.

By and large, sexual activity and emotions can be described in terms of the incentive motivation model described in chapter 5. Sexual emotions are aroused by stimulus events, but, as also discussed there, the concern can on occasion manifest itself more spontaneously, diffusely, as unrest, and more focally through fantasies and thoughts. In all, the sexual emotions are responses to the fate of the sexual concern: to events that activate it, and to those that allow progress toward its satisfaction. The different sexual emotions result from different events as appraised. They are distinct by different appraisals and by different states of action readiness. They are: being attracted; being charmed; being in love; sexual excitement; sexual desire; lust; sexual enjoyment.

BEING ATTRACTED

"Being attracted" is an ambiguous expression. One can be attracted to someone as a potential marriage partner, or as an attractive erotic or sexual target. The distinction needs being emphasized. It is not always made in empirical studies on mate preferences. There, the various sources of preference are frequently confused. Here, I use "being attracted" exclusively in an erotic or sexual sense.

The emotion of being so attracted consists of appraising a person as a potential target for erotic or sexual interaction. Often, that means no more than that he or she draws attention as a physical presence, catches the eye, and holds it. The calls to attention are manifest in many men in the rapid, almost reflex-like turning of the head when an attractive woman passes by.

Being attracted is often a small and fleeting emotion. One just notices attractiveness like one notices a smell. Yet it is an emotion: There is change in action readiness. At the least, attention is drawn and retained. Ongoing attention is interrupted, however briefly. There often is further bodily response. Just seeing an attractive person may cut one's breath, speed up one's heart. Humans like to sit on the sidewalk café or in the pub, watching the pretty boys and girls pass by. Viewing times for attractive faces are longer than for average ones, even in infants. One evidently is willing to spend effort to watch attractive people.[7] Even animals do. Male rats and female rats in estrus work to be allowed viewing a member of the other sex, even when no occasion for intercourse follows.[8]

Attention in being attracted is of a particular kind. It does not aim information intake. It does not seek to know more but to experience more of the same. It gives pleasure and potentiates the desire system. Attractive female faces enhance neural activity in men's nucleus accumbens, and erotica in the ventral striatum.[9] One also experiences the pull that leads to the label "attractive." The object calls to follow the attraction up. Approach indeed may follow. On the street, one may turn around and follow with one's glance. One may follow with one's feet, for a block or two, or one lingers in front of the window of the shop that she or he entered.

In being attracted, the target is somehow apprehended as a fit object for one's sexual concern. Attention is directed to its role as a sexual target, as male or female, or as fitting one's sexual action potentials. Attention usually goes toward the object as a person. On occasion, however, it focuses a sexual aspect of the person only. One is drawn to a breast, an ankle, a piece of skin. Proust gives a description of how the eyes of monsieur Swann, in the midst of the crowd at a *soirée*, are suddenly glued to the deep décolleté of the Marquess de Sursis. He is absorbed by it; he even puts on his monocle, so visibly that, "even if embarrassed, [she] suppressed respiring deeply, so much can desire sometimes be contagious".[10] Fascination by attractiveness is not restricted to men. I once was with two young women in a pub; both were having solid and stable affairs. Enters a youngish man, gipsy-like, a bit unkempt, walking to the bar with a slightly insolent gait. The women for a moment kept their breath, their eyes glued to him, then started to whisper excitedly.

But, again, attraction may target restricted aspects of the object only, and fittingness of restricted aspect of one's erotic action repertoire, as demonstrated by the not inconsiderable sexual attractiveness, to adults, of children. Pedophilia provides this demonstration in only extreme measure, Children of both sexes were strictly banned from the settlements of the Saints of the Desert in early Christian times.[11] The temptations of Saint Anthony were no legend; they may have faithfully reflected self-report.

Appraisal of attractiveness often stems from good looks and physical appearance. Women as well as men are sensitive to them, and to an almost equal degree; gender differences mostly are modest.[12] Good looks range among the six aspects most frequently endorsed in questionnaires that ask what the respondent finds important in a mate, in both sexes, and in a large number of different cultures.[13] In a study among Dutch students, it was the most frequently mentioned aspect (67% of the men, 70% of the women), and very often it was mentioned first.[14] Good looks and physical attractiveness do offer great advantage in a multitude of social contexts. Beauty makes the heart grow fonder. It makes that people more readily drop reserve, become more warm and friendly, and mellower in their judgments of personality and ability.[15] This, in turn, tends to render the beautiful person more relaxed and self-confident.[16] Good looks and physical attractiveness obviously function in erotic partner selection. They can be noticed from a distance, allowing to pick out and be picked out as a possible partners from across the street or the field.

But what are "good looks"? Obviously, they are in the eye of the beholder. The beholders indeed are sensitive to prettiness. Even young infants show longer viewing times to pretty than to average female faces.[17] These sensitivities thus most likely have an unlearned, innate basis. In itself, this is plausible, considering the fine tuning in animals, even fish, that are attracted to members of their own species and not by those of closely related and similar ones.[18] Humans show preference for facial symmetry, and for faces matching the cultural average (composite facial photographs are rated as more attractive than any of the composing ones); female waist–hip ratios of .70 are fairly generally preferred. All three preferences may be cross-culturally general, and are frequently being given evolutionary interpretations, as they relate to youth and health.[19]

True enough, appreciable cross cultural divergence with regard to female bodily attractiveness has been found. Ford and Beach gave an extensive review from anthropological data; Hatfield and Rapson provided a coherent interpretation.[20] Plump or slender body build may be preferred, pendulous or upright breasts, broad or narrow hips. But considerable cross cultural generality is also evident, and perhaps even more so. Human males rather generally prefer younger women over older ones. In almost all cultures investigated, married men are usually older than their wives.[21] No such age preference is evident in primates.[22] Moreover, those cultural preference differences that do exist primarily concern differences of a few centimeters at the same places, or in something like one unit on a rating scale. It would seem that a woman's breasts, and her hips contribute to her attractiveness everywhere, whatever their precise preferred shape or size. Hatfield and Rapson conclude: "In any case, we do know that people who are considered good looking in their own cultures are likely to be considered to be attractive in other cultures as well".[23]

But one major thing about sexual attractiveness has been almost neglected in discussions about universality, and its possible implications for evolutionary interpretations. Sexual attractiveness comes not only from good looks and shapes, but also from behavioral ones. In many animals, behavior patterns are decisive in evoking sexual interest. I mentioned the fickleness in female fish with regard to the "proper" male courtship dances. A human example of behavior as a source of attraction occurred is my "inso-lent gait" example above; such gait can be taken as an instance of "macho behavior." I think that a large repertoire of attractive behaviors exists, al-though relevant research should come from observational studies rather than from questionnaire surveys. Apart from machismo, the repertoire in-cludes coyness, mostly in women (and small children); seductive behav-iors, such as winking, inviting looks, and making secondary sex attributes prominent; suggestive and seductive tones of voice, of which the time pat-tern resembles that of caresses; and shows of "innocence," "timidity," and bashfulness that, in both men and women, would play on caring-for sensi-tivities. Flirting behaviors have much of these features.[24] Interestingly, most of these behavioral aspects work by way of their prosodic aspects, their time courses, rather than by their topographies.

In fact, sexual attractiveness resides for a large part in bodily and behav-ioral features implying or promising smooth intimate and reciprocal sexual interaction, by fitting one's sensitivities and action propensities. They are liked for that reason, and influence behavioral and morphological evolu-tion by sexual rather than natural selection. Many features are attractive just because they strike the eye. Other things appeal because they suggest pleasant things one can do or can have done to one. Most attractive female bodily features are nice to the touch. Seeing smooth or cool skin makes a men's fingers grow nervous or insolent.

This applies in particular to the female breast. The prominent shape of women's breasts is somewhat of a mystery.[25] It bears no relationship to their feeding function, and nonhuman primate females indeed do not show such breast-shape when not lactating. Of course, the female breast is the major cue for a distant human conspecific being a female. It may just be perceived as beautiful, as Fisher suggests. In addition, however, the human female breast does function importantly in stroking, squeezing, fondling, hugging and cuddling. All those are liked by both women and men, and this in-cludes women and men in cultures that keep the female bosom uncovered, such as on the Trobriand Islands.[26] Touching, fondling, or kissing the woman's breasts during love play does not occur in all cultures but it does so in by far the majority, whereas it is absent in other animals.[27] Evolutionarily, bosom development may have paralleled the development of hands fit for caressing, and, in turn, the development of emotional inti-macy between sex partners, when grooming had become meaningless in the naked ape. Intimacy in connection with sex is incomparably more im-portant in humans than in other apes, let alone other animals. The hypothe-sis is not at all implausible. "Nipple stimulation during lactation is one of the most potent stimuli for oxytocin release",[28] with its consequences for bond strengthening, and this might equally apply to stimulation during erotic interaction.

This focus on interactional significance of bodily and behavioral features extends to other aspects of attractiveness. Men may prefer younger women not only because in evolution these happened to bear more children, as Sexual Strategies Theory has it.[29] Youth is also linked to readiness for sexual play and perhaps to being more easily brought to compliance. Indeed, young men are equally attractive to men as are young women; recall their both being banned from saintly hermits' residences. Young men may also well be attractive to women;[30] Lou Andreas-Salomé had her first sexual relationship when she was 36 and her lover, Rilke, only 26.[31] In fact, the sexual preferences of men and women may not differ much when women are free to choose, and economical considerations irrelevant. Women from the nobility in France in the 16th century, and courtesans accepted in the higher classes, appear to have been remarkably free in tastes, initiatives, and practices, to judge from Brantome's account.[32]

All this applies forcefully to the outright interactional aspects of sexual attractiveness. Perceived warmth, and responsiveness to being given attention, are among the most frequent reasons given for being attracted.[33] Kindness is often the first reason mentioned in questionnaires, by men as well as by women.[34] In the Dutch student study, the frequency of "sweet, warm" comes second for the men, and third for the women; "accepting" comes fourth for the men and second for the women.[35] Propensity for such interpersonal behaviors is often suggested by physical features. Beautiful eyes are not those, I think, with pronounced color and remarkable size, but those that appear to look intently or with open acceptance, even if by belladonna. Women consider men attractive primarily when they are lively, alert, with "meaningful" manners of looking, attentiveness, humor, discernment, intelligence, competence, and being interested in them, but not too obtrusively so.[36] Obviously, the attractiveness appraisals are more complex than those rooted in the strictly physical ones. They presuppose some involvement of the beholder's own potential actions, the intuitions or rapid imaginings on how he and she, she and he, would fit in interaction. It will be obvious that I have my strong doubts about Sexual Strategy Theory. It is a bit facile. Moreover, we know almost nothing about the presumed Ancient Adaptational Environment, its opportunities, and its presses, not even how the social structures were.[37]

Sexual attraction indeed can originate in quite nonsexual attractions. A person may appear attractive as useful company, or as a possible marriage partner, or as commanding material resources. "Spending a lot of money on me early on" is mentioned as what made a person attractive for a brief erotic encounter.[38] There is no need for mockery here. Advantage forms a motive to search for sexually attractive features, and these can usually be found. Some old experiments illustrate this. Valins[39] showed that attractiveness ratings of female nudes were influenced by false heart rate feedback.

Barefoot and Straub[40] then found that the attractiveness ratings remained the same upon re-exposure without such false feedback. As the authors argued, the subjects probably managed to find sexual features that justified their prior judgments. Sexual responsiveness is flexible and wide, given proper readiness.

All this is of course relevant for understanding the origins of sexual attractiveness appraisals. Youth, skin, breasts, and resourcefulness all have interactional implications that, in the human species, as such are major conditions for reproductive success. They not only were back in the Ancient Adaptational Environment; they still are. They do not just provide "stimuli" that match innate sensitivities. They fit interactional propensities.

Anyway, preferences as examined in the anthropological and questionnaire studies are somewhat peripheral to what determines sexual attraction. Preferences are comparative judgments; attraction is an absolute response. Western men may perhaps, on the whole and right now, prefer younger women, and women may prefer men with a sense of humor, but each can perfectly imagine being attracted by an older or less slender woman, or a serious man. Most people have to do with what falls short of those cultural preferences and, presumably, have experienced attraction. And most people are quite content with that. As the Yiddish saying goes, every *schlemiel* finds his *schlimazel*.

BEING CHARMED

Attraction can gain grip on one's readiness for action. It may lead beyond just following for a moment with eyes or thought. Such grip may result from beginning interaction—a glance is returned, and lingers for a fraction of a second—or fantasy takes hold. The manner of doing or saying, erotic or otherwise, charms. It obtains individuality. There not just is a beautiful face, a breathtaking form, a pair of blue eyes, but something from which a person appears, and one that pleases. The attractiveness appears to epitomize a mode of being, physical, emotional or intellectual, that transpires in manners of doing or thinking, or rapidly spreads all over the physical and emotional manifestations. Being charmed consists of appraising someone as a person who fits interaction with intimate and erotic implications.

It also spreads to action readiness. One is charmed in the original sense of that word: one becomes subject to a spell. Attention becomes sucked up and dwells on the impression that the particular person made. It extends to readiness for maintaining and developing interaction. Charm appraisal motivates efforts to establish a relationship as a gateway to erotic interaction. The efforts contain more specific aims: to make oneself conspicuous to the target; to make oneself conspicuous as erotically interested; and to kindle the target's erotic interest in oneself. One promotes oneself and seeks to engage the other in an interplay. Appraisals and actions tug at the frontiers of casual or friendly interactions.

The emotion of being charmed includes the action readiness for courting, in its human form: flirting. Flirting is driven by the emotional desire to evoke interest and desire. It shares the functions of erotic warming up, kindling erotic interest generally ascribed to animal courtship.[41] Flirting can avail itself of a large array of "sexual influence tactics,"[42] ranging from just looking in the eyes and winking to kissing and uttering endearing words in a mellow tone of voice.

Of course, flirting can be a cold-blooded strategy toward seduction. But in principle it is emotional: stirred by the appraisal of charm, stirred on by signs of the target's interest—an enticing game with clear criteria of progress provided by encouragements, increasing reciprocity, and increasing erotic content. With appropriate appraisal and background mood, flirting often develops automatically and almost unwittingly. Men start sitting more upright and turn to prowess-demonstrating talk when a handsome woman appears; women change their postures, touch their hair, think of their makeup, and also start prowess demonstrations.

Being charmed may not be the best designation for this emotion. I know no better name for what stirs flirting, either in English or in Dutch (although English is on one occasion inclined toward the use of an emotion term: a peacock showing off its tail is said to be "in its pride").[43] The human flirting repertoire may well be using innate endowments. Elements of the flirting repertoire appear available to children, at least to little girls of 2 years and older. They can produce coy smiles, accompanied by looking-at/looking away sequences, and the slight head tilts described for embarrassment.[44] Many actions in the repertoire make one's erotic capacities and desires salient, and demonstrate appreciation of those capacities and desires in the target. They include explicit relationship-building actions such as eye-play, often beginning with the looking-at/looking away sequence just mentioned. Eye-play initiates flirting, and mutual eye-play seals it. When appropriately responded to, it extends to mutual glancing, to turning to straightly facing each other, and then proceeds further.[45] Mutual and prolonged gazing enhance feelings of love.[46] A study of observations of flirtation in bars shows that relationship-building in detail. Its authors could construct a flow chart of how one thing was conducive to another. You seat yourself next to an attractive person, or one who otherwise appears available. Mutual glancing may precede or follow such seating. Sitting shoulder to shoulder leads to turning face to face when signs of interest or willingness have been given off, in the event leading to kissing and, in the event, to leaving the place together.

The game of flirting has a more complex function than only advertising oneself and building a relationship. It also serves, I think, to overcome the wariness when meeting a stranger. One has to assuage the other's distrust, as well as one's own. Flirting and courting have to proceed carefully. This is a plausible interpretation of the looking-at/looking-away sequence. It occurs not merely in humans. Smuts (1985) observed it in baboons;[47] I think it also occurs in dogs. It can be understood as an expression of interest, but softened, toned down, to take away the threatening aspect that looking-at may have. Toning down expression of sexual interest during first encounters appears not to be a cultural creation but rather an aspect of the species-specific, individually varied courtship dance. Grammar and his collaborators[48] studied it in pairs at their first meeting. Expressing interest and availability was often subdued, because of the risks of too overt expression. Flirters have a number of concerns at stake, such as not to be taken advantage of, concerns for autonomy, worries about social and other repercussions. This context of wariness probably accounts for the fact that flirting includes so many behaviors borrowed from the hostility repertoire: teasing, pulling hair, or slapping shoulders.

BEING IN LOVE

Being-in-love is not a very transparent term. It is about love, and it is not love. English language has tried to improve by introducing *infatuation* (*foolishness* in origin), and *limerence*.[49] Other languages do have unambiguous terms: *estar enamorada* in Spanish, *être amoureux* in French, *verliefdheid* in Dutch, *Verliebtheit* in German. Hatfield and Rapson[50] use *passionate love*.

   Being in love and the other terms all refer to a distinct emotion, with a distinct appraisal and kind of action readiness. The appraisal goes further than being charmed. Someone is appraised as a unique person, possessing unique and wonderful qualities, and forming the focus of one's world. One is enraptured; he or she is the only important thing in life.[51] Never before has one met someone like this, and experienced something like this; and that each time one falls in love. It reorients life, for the moment. The love object has outstanding qualities, whether in physical attractiveness, in charm, in endearing handicaps, in innocence or sophistication—all qualities that may turn into aggravations after having fallen out of love. Love is blind for as long as it lasts, which is more than a year for a third of the male students, and for half of the female ones, in a Dutch study with first-year students on *verliefdheid*.[52]

   With this comes the action readiness, specified by Hatfield and Rapson[53] as a "state of intense longing for union with another." One seeks intimate proximity, and as fully as can be, bodily, mentally, and sexually. This is the common denominator for the actions that being in love impels. One of these actions is thinking about the other: in thought, the other is near. A near constant preoccupation with the other is perhaps the most striking characteristic of being in love. Thirty percent of the male students subjects in the self-report study on *verliefdheid* mentioned it, and 45% of the women. One subject expressed it thus: "I sometimes think that I want always to be with him".[54]

Seeking physical proximity and intimacy is a fuller expression, though. One achieves it by gazing, the successor to looking at/looking away. People in love make prolonged eye contact. They seek to sit and stand close to each other, lean toward each other, make their feet touch.[55] Many participants in the student study mentioned the desire to touch the other, the constant desire to make love, and almost constantly feeling sexually excited.[56]

Caring for the other is often a salient aspect of being-in-love, with actions coming from the very foundations of the caring-for repertoire: gently stroking, touching with one's fingertips, and feeding, taking the other out for dinner, giving her or him tidbits, feeding with a spoon. And giving presents: flowers, sweets, signs of attention. All that also points to something else: giving presents shows respect.[57] It not merely involves caring for the other: it has an undertone of humbly serving the love object. Being in love renders one dependent on another individual, and at risk of being left.

The desire for union extends to emotional intimacy, -toward mental fusion, mental intertwinement. One seeks shared identity, and to incorporate the other as part of oneself. Attention is absorbed by what the other feels, wants, intends, as well as whether the other reciprocates what one feels, want, and intends oneself. The aim toward fusion is in this sense real. His pain is my pain, her pleasure is my pleasure. "Merging and union are not just metaphors but deep insights into the nature of the self and the transformation of the self in love," writes Solomon,[58] and this also occurs in being in love. It becomes evident in concrete fashion. Lovers tend to adopt the partner's political, artistic, food and fashion preferences. They feel hurt when the other has different views or interests.

Emotional intimacy may, in fact, be the main or sole manifest aim in the desire for union. Bodily and sexual union may be secondary or absent in conscious experience. This occurs between adolescents, or did occur before sexual matters were matters of course, and it occurs in adolescents' crushes for teachers and public performers. It also occurs in the crushes in younger children, from 3 years onward, that may have all the signs of passionate love, but where the physical may be restricted to hugging and kissing,[59] and perhaps an occasional erection.

What makes one fall in love? Not uniqueness; that idea merely manifests having fallen in love. Attractiveness and charm certainly help, but when they do, they still need support from the individual's current state to elicit uniqueness appraisal and desire for union. One only falls in love when one is ready for it. Readiness may be hormonal, or have to do with social and emotional changes involved in adolescence and early adulthood. When

questioned, 59% of first-year students admitted to be in love at that moment, with all but 5% being in love now or having been in the recent past.[60]
But readiness also comes from quite different sources, such as dissatisfaction in a current relationship, loneliness, openness for novel experience.[61]
The full nature of this readiness for love is unclear, however. Under any of
those conditions, people may crave for falling in love without the lightning
hitting; or the lighting may strike from a limpid sky.

Physical attractiveness is not the only, or even the main, source of falling
in love. At least as important are emotional consonance, and intimacy itself.
They form the foretaste for union, so to speak; they evoke desire to complete that foretaste with the bodily and sexual. Emotional intimacy, intellectual interchange carrying mutual recognition and understanding,
emotional trust, all may come first and develop into falling in love. De
Botton[62] describes a rather common incident: a man and a woman finding
themselves in neighboring chairs on a 1-hour airplane flight. They enter
into what turns out a lively conversation, with sentences chasing each other
like playing kittens; at the baggage belt they have fallen in love. One of the
most gripping descriptions that I know is of the meeting, in 1945, of the
Russian-born English philosopher Isaiah Berlin and the Russian poetess
Anna Akhmatova. A one-night conversation (they did not touch each
other) led to both being shattered, him on coming back to his hotel room
muttering "I am in love, I am in love," and she writing five verses about it.
They never met again.[63]

But intimacy itself is not usually given in advance. It has to grow, and be
allowed to grow. At its base is a sense of affinity, of fitting together of one's
inclinations in interaction, and what the other offers in response. Falling in
love—or readiness to fall in love—often come from highly personal appeals
in how someone looks and reacts, intensifying the attractiveness of ways of
looking and responding that were mentioned under "being attracted." One
may fall in love because of the other's hesitancy, or because of his or her
fowardness, depending on what fits best. Lightning may strike, a foretaste
may make crazy for more, because of ways of looking, responding, and not
responding, and what they seem to promise for further interaction. And often, such small features of interaction, and of things said, may later appear
to have been indications of a common sensitivity or earlier fate, as experiences in marital therapy suggest.[64]

Intimacy breeds falling in love and sexual desire in many contexts, such
as those between teacher and pupil, leader and follower, therapist and patient, priest and member of his flock. All desires for mental and emotional
union readily take on the imagery of bodily fusion and of penetration. One
finds it in the images in mystic's poems on the love for God or Jesus. Sufi poems can be read as statements of mystic union, and as poems of love; so has
been done for the Song of Songs.

Interestingly, sexual intimacy is almost equally powerful as emotional intimacy in eliciting falling in love. Often, at least in Western culture, one first goes to bed together, and then, having fallen in love, decides to stay, and bring in books, toothbrush, and clothing. Among the students interviewed by Rombouts,[65] one fourth stated that they first made love, then fell in love. "And yes, we both thought, just like comrades make love and sleep together, and bang! like a dam that collapsed. Yes, something had happened to me".[66]

Desire for union is unleashed, it would appear, when events are appraised as containing promises for such union. Sexual attraction, sexual experience, and intimacy all may be appraised to contain it, either through arousal of one's sexual system or because of previous experience, or of expectations given by ideology, or because of what did happen in the interaction.

The latter appears vital for falling in love: receiving a moment of promise, a brief response from the object that suggests interest. It may be a confidence; it may be a single glance, such as a young girl may think she received from a pop-star. Then give him or her a brief lapse of time—anywhere between half an hour or half a day, the self-reports suggest—during which fantasies can develop. After that sequence no more than one single confirmation, real or imagined, is needed for "crystallization" to occur, and to precipitate having fallen in love.[67] "Unleashed" is a correct designation: many instances of falling in love are *coups de foudre*, lightning strokes. See the bang! in the above citation, and see Berlin's singsong on coming back to his hotel.

The falling-in-love metaphor, the frequent sudden emergence of being in love, suggests that something special is going on. Being in love often, or typically, is a frenzy. The elements of the experience given earlier also indicate that: one's love is the only important thing in life, it reorients life. Falling in love, crystallization, represents what dynamic system theorists call a state change, the flipover of one form of organization into another. The state flips from being interested, attracted, even charmed, into one that takes full control of attention, perceptual salience, and action. It brings out full passion, with the evaluative priorities and the love-is-blind bias. The usual background orientation to one's interests and autonomous position falls away, and is replaced by abandoning to the perspectives of someone else.

Being-in-love shares all this with other strong passions focused on a specific outcome: notably with those of addictions, the frenzy of the alcoholic when there is no drink in the house, or of the cocaine addict who cannot get his shot. The same mechanisms are involved, namely the massive investment of a particular end-state or object with incentive value, and the vigorous engagement of the desire system. With respect to being in love, such engagement has been demonstrated by functional magnetic resonance imaging (fMRI) recordings of participants while looking at photographs of the person they had said to be in love with.[68] As discussed in chapter 5, being-in-love poses the same problem as addiction and, probably, any other strong surface concern, such as Destroying the Enemy: Why, when, and how desire focuses so exclusively on a particular contingency—getting the drug or the drink that may not give any pleasure but only relieve desire, and obtaining proximity and acknowledgment of one's proximity in being in love. The problem with being in love is compounded by the fact that in-fatuation may occur and remain even when no true satisfaction—no sexual access, not even calm pleasure of togetherness—has ever occurred. It may merit to more closely examine instances of such unsatisfied infatuations, to pinpoint why and when they do not fade, as those of Stendhal with his Matilde, and Paul Ree with Lou Salomé, with whom he never had been al-lowed to make love: He jumped to his death when she finally left him.[69] Is it the partial encouragement stressed by Stendhal that does it?

This persistence even when (or perhaps in particular when) not satisfied may be specific or unique to being in love. It makes one wonder about the nature and function of falling and being in love. Perhaps it is functional in a specific fashion. Sexual approach to an unfamiliar individual, recall, is a risky business. Distrust is in order, specifically when called to an encounter leading to postures in which one's throat is easily bitten. The fates of Holophernes and Samson attest to the risks; they'd better been wary of the charms of Judith and Delilah. How this holds for animals as much as for hu-mans was evident in how hostile behaviors permeate courting.[70] That means: to achieve sexual interaction one has, for the moment, to put all shields and weapons down. One has to render oneself vulnerable, emotion-ally as well as physically. For a moment, one has to trust the other. For a mo-ment, love has to be blind. Indeed, that is probably one of the things that oxytocin (OT) and vasopressin (VP) do: blocking fear of novelty, that is, in-stilling trust when there is not yet enough familiarity to justify it.[71] OT, at least, is powerful in enhancing partner recognition, and directly impacts on the olfactory mechanisms, so essential for recognition in rodents. This places falling in love apart from the other addictive frenzies. In monoga-mous voles, bonding occurs after repeated intercourse because and when dopamine and OT or VP are released simultaneously; in related nonmonogamous species (mountain voles), this sensitivity (density of the relevant receptors) is considerably less.[72] In this dependence on dopa-mine–OT/VP linkage, the frenzy of being in love thereby differs from her-oin or alcohol deprivation frenzy.

All this matches the fact that falling in love occupies a particular place among the emotions. It is a two-person emotion. Its core aim is reciprocity, -reciprocity in the desire for union. One not only aims at union but at play-ing out that union in coregulation and synchrony, to use Fogel's (1993) terms.[73] Being motionless in each other's arms is not really the ultimate goal in falling or being in love. "To say I love you ... is essentially a plea, even a demand, for a response in kind".[74]

Falling in love has an other interesting feature. It resembles imprinting in newly hatched birds, in that it blocks bonding to subsequently appearing individuals. Having fallen in love renders one more or less solidly insensitive to other charms, at least for a while. There is evidence for mechanisms for such inhibition. In male prairie voles, activation of a particular dopamine receptor subtype (D1) in the nucleus accumbens blocks bonding, notably upon prolonged mating with a particular female.[75] This, too, may have a functional interpretation: It allows growth of a stable relationship and stable joint offspring care.

This is to say that being-in-love is incomplete and febrile as long as it is not solidly reciprocated. Anxiety and agitation reign. Armstrong[76] (2002) lists three components of being-in-love: longing, being enraptured, being tormented; the three belong together. Being-in-love is not a happy emotion, because risks of lack of reciprocity are readily felt, as do the risks of being dependent on someone else. It moves between Armstrong's three poles. One must perhaps add that the aims of being-in-love cannot be fulfilled, since when they are, when union is stable, being-in-love rapidly yields place to love. It readily loses the epithet "passionate." The desired union is itself also unstable because the union of discrete entities is the home for their discreteness. Perfect union is possible only when the uniqueness of one, or both, is destroyed. Well, perhaps there are exceptions, when there is extreme emotional endowment in simultaneously maintaining and fusion, and one's identity.

SEXUAL EXCITEMENT

Sexual excitement (sometimes referred to as *sexual arousal*) is not always a clear-cut emotion, in the same way that startle is not: Responses are stereotyped. They mostly form a standard pattern of physiological reactions—standard for any given species, that is. The pattern is specific. In mammals, sympathetic arousal is accompanied by increased genital bloodflow, itself a parasympathetic response. In males, this may become manifest in erection; in females, in genital lubrication. Both may in humans occur within seconds after seeing exciting pictures.[77] There also is activation of elements of the reflex motor system, such as the Achilles tendon reflex, perhaps to be interpreted as incipient forward locomotion.[78] There may be more: there often is this peculiar sense of trembling allover.

Ratings of slides of other-sex nudes and scenes of intercourse indicate that exciting stimuli are usually appraised as both pleasant and arousing.[79] However, exciting stimuli are not always appraised as pleasant. Excitement is distinct from sexual desire, and indeed not always correlated with desire. Discrepancy may also occur in sexual dysfunction: Sexual stimuli may cause erection without the subject feeling desire for sexual interaction.[80] Excitement may occur along with felt and verbally expressed disgust and gaze aversion.[81] There is no hypocrisy here: Sexual excitement and sexual desire just are different emotions.[82]

Excitement is triggered in first instance by simple stimuli, like smells, visual stimuli, and tactual genital stimulation. In human males, the major visual stimuli for excitement are elementary sex attributes: prominent female shapes, naked skin when that is not usual, views of the female genitals. Witnessing intercourse in others is exciting for both sexes.[83] There also is retroaction of ongoing sexual action on excitement: imagining engaging in sexual action enhances the excitement from viewing pictures of such action.[84] Common lore has it that scantily clad women provide special attraction to men, due to the suggestions for undressing them. Stimuli associated to primary stimuli, such as words or female underwear, may also cause sexual excitement. Even hearing the word "breast" may send thrills to the genitals of an adolescent boy.

Physical sexual excitement is automatic. It does not need conscious awareness. Sexual content of priming stimuli presented below awareness affects recognition times in subsequent lexical decision tasks[85] and can probably influence genital response.[86] Such responses habituate slowly upon repeated presentation, if at all, in contrast to liking ratings and, presumably, desire.[87]

Elementary appraisal processes are thus involved; the stimuli appear to impinge directly on relevant sensitivities, that are obviously different for men and women, and for the heterosexual and homosexual individuals among them. Excitability also depends on hormonal state; excitability in women probably shows cycle variations.[88] It also depends on priming, by previous or actual sexual excitement and by excitation transfer from other sorts of arousal.[89] But more complex appraisal processes are usually of major additional importance, as shown by the arousing effects of longer stimulus exposure and stimulus exploration, and of fantasy, as well as by the excitement due to stimulus novelty and to viewing body parts that one is not used to seeing.

Automatic appraisal may be disturbed, though, or perhaps not even occur in the first place. Awareness of stimulus meaning and prolonged stimulus exposure may weaken or annul automatic excitement. It may be due to cognitive distraction: facilitation found after subthreshold priming is not found after suprathreshold priming.[90] It may also be due to interference by anxiety and other attentional processes, that appear essential for sustaining and augmenting excitement, as detailed in the "cognitive" model of sexual excitement by Janssen and colleagues.[91] Feedback from, and elaboration of ongoing excitement appear essential for full excitement response. Variations at this point may also be decisive for the transition from excitement to desire.

SEXUAL DESIRE

Sexual desire has been defined as "the wish to obtain a sexual object that one does not now have or to engage in sexual activity in which one is not now engaging".[92] The term has two readings. In the first, *sexual desire* refers to undirected sensitivity for sexually relevant stimuli, and propensity for undirected sexual reactions. These are more or less direct results of high activity of the motivational system. Birds begin to sing when spring is there. Male cats and dogs plant their odor flags. Female cats and dogs in heat wail. All three attract the attention of receptive members of the species without, of course, intending to do so. Perception becomes sensitized and the range of relevant stimuli increased, so much so that cats in heat may rub a human's leg and adopt the receptive stance when touched lightly on the flanks. I suspect that there is increased restlessness, instigating in naive animals to undirected, aimless search. In naive humans, the same may be true; stories of children reared in isolation, such as Genie's story, suggest as much.[93]

In humans, undirected sexual desire is often called randiness or being horny. People, objects, or just words become charged with sexual meanings. Cues of sexuality—roundnesses, pairings of any sort—become painfully salient. The classic film *Extasy*, from 1933, tellingly represents this sensitivity. A young woman, unsatisfied by an inhibited husband, alone in her room, is obsessed by her eye being caught by a painting on the wall of two people holding hands, and by a statuette of two horses touching their necks.[94] The sensitization influences thought and fantasy. Forty-five percent of the adolescent boys in a study by Knoth, Boyd, and Singer[95] (1988) had sexual fantasies "many times a day"; and fantasies in young women appear to be only slightly less frequent.[96]

Sexual desire in this sense waxes and wanes over the life course; but it is unclear to what extent it does, since in research desire and excitement tend to be conflated. The latter may vary more than the former. Sexual desire is also held to differ between men and women, and that for biological or evolutionary reasons: indiscriminate for the former, highly selective for the latter.[97] I am not sure. Evidence for the role of economic or other dependence in women was cited in connection with being attracted. Further evidence may perhaps be found in psychopathology. In psychiatric literature in pre-psychopharmacologic times, stories abounded of demented women behaving in extreme provocative fashion; I do not know whether what I learned when a student still holds, but it suggests that, in those women, inhibitions were weakened, rather than drives enhanced.

In the second meaning, *sexual desire* refers to the articulate emotion of wanting to obtain sexual access to, and union with, a particular individual. The individual is appraised as a target for sexual interaction—as emanating calls for such interaction, as it were. Action tendency follows this call by seeking proximity and actual interaction in some way. "In some way" alludes to the fact that one—the person or animal—does not always know toward one is driven. Human adults often do know, of course, although what one is set to seek becomes clear only gradually, when it does. But more generally, sexual activity is guided by the sensitivities of the various competences, rather than by goals and foresights. Those competences include procedures for approach, seduction, warming up, positioning, maintaining position, excitement, and copulation. Advance potentiation of these competences probably accompanies desire and approach in most or all species and, presumably, is enhanced by available anticipations of stimuli and satisfactions to come.

Sexual desire thus is an emotion.[98] It is felt as "drive" and the behavior looks as driven, by its goal-directedness and control precedence. It is passionate; even everyday sexual desire is to some extent. Male rats cross electrified grids to approach females in heat; humans go to great length and cost to obtain access to their objects of desire and complete their actions. Desire motivates approach and interaction, sensitizes to cues for accessibility of, and actual access to the target, or for receiving and being entered. Males at least may spend considerable physical energy to do all this. Priorities shift to following up the actions and reactions; regrets emerge when action is interrupted or one has let an occasion pass. Obstacles render impatient, and may render further action disorderly.

Sexual desire, in individuals with a properly responsive motivational system, is triggered in principle by the same stimulus events, thoughts and fantasies as elicit being attracted, being charmed, being in love, and being excited. Sexual desire in many instances pursues the path that one of the other emotions laid out and pointed to. But there are additional conditions, or absence of conditions that shape the other ones. Desire would appear to require a sense that its object is attainable: within sight or within grasp, even if requiring great effort. True, effort may be too big, risks too large. Desire may drop or sink into mere longing, along the lines of Brehm's motivation model described in chapter 6:[99] It briskly drops when difficulty surpasses expected benefit, and only fantasy may remain.

Whether a sexual target appears attainable may depend on complex appraisals. Attainable appears what one is capable to attain, by strength or money. There is more that leads to this appraisal: what appears due to one, for reasons of social status or socio-sexual role; or to what one literally is able to command. Strength of sexual desire, it would seem, is partly an outcome of apparent availability

Factors thus can be suggested that may ensure the transition from excitement to desire. Inversely, the difference between the conditions for excitement and desire highlights that stern moral restraint, as advocated in some conservative Christianity and Islam, is not a psychological necessity to curb desire; nor a very successful procedure, for that matter. Curbing desire needs other measures, mostly, I think, of a true moral nature, such as instilling interpersonal respect and curbing arrogance.

Some sexual dysfunctions show that the emotion of sexual desire may not emerge, competent stimuli notwithstanding. One may remain unmoved, even if one would want this to be otherwise. Loss of "libido," lack of desire, is a common complaint in sexual dysfunction.[100] One may be aware of the discrepancy between cognitive assessment of how attractive a person is, how much one would like to desire sex, and how little the desire does actually arise. This represents one more instance of the discrepancies between knowledge and appraisal—appraisal that grips the body. Why and when loss of libido occurs, apart from physiological conditions and exhaustion, I do not know. Anxiety, depression, grief, and emotions of guilt do play a role, but probably not always and not only; but this is a domain I know little about.

LUST

Lust is the "animal desire for sexual indulgence," says the Concise Oxford Dictionary. The adjective "animal" may be taken to stress the nonvoluntary character of the desire and its often nonconscious arousal. The germs of lust can be evoked automatically by the relevant information, even if only glimpsed, on bodily attractions, prospects of lustful experiences or delightful intimacy, even before one has taken stock of any of those.[101]

Regan and Berscheid used the term lust for sexual desire.[102] I use it separately for the emotion that drives consummatory action, from caressing to intercourse. Lust is the appraisal of someone as my sexual target—as the participant in exploring and traveling through the field of aims of each of my sexual actions. Experience of lust thus is the appraisal of someone else as a sexualized person, caressable, embraceable, penetrable or to be penetrated by. But the appraisal includes appraisal of oneself as sexualized. Sartre spoke about le corps sexué. In lust, the body comes into awareness as a body-to-be-touched, an instrument of penetration or of receiving penetration. It hums of it and aches for it.[103] The sexualized body also is felt as the instrument for one's sexual actions. One's skin clamors for being stroked, one's hands clamor for stroking.

The action tendency of lust seeks to do all this, and to receive the action-confirming sensations. The striving for physical union contains reciprocity and synchronization of appraisal and action readiness: insistent striving for complementarity. I stroke, she feels; he strokes, I feel.

Lust is a passion, as much as sexual desire is. It is a felt "drive state" that pushes behavior forward; each moment of lust points to the next moment, until the bloom of enjoyment. Such sexual drive is not human privilege. It occurs over the entire animal kingdom. Bingham[104] described how two young chimpanzees interacted. How they were sitting high on a vertical grill; he had an erection, and she had grasped his penis. How they then descended from that grill, he with his arm around her, regardless of interruptions by other chimpanzees. How, on the floor, they sought a sitting embrace that continued into a belly-to-belly coital position, all this again resuming each time after interruptions. Such stubborn going-on can be found way down in the evolutionary chain. I once observed two dragonflies endeavoring to make love. She was seated on a bending blade of grass. He alighted on her, to which she responded by bending her hind part sideways (if I recall correctly), her wings trembling violently. Things did not proceed smoothly because the wind stirred the blade of grass. He fell off several times, but stubbornly flew up again and repositioned himself over her. Each time, she resumed her trembling. Then, when having been active over her for a brief period, both calmed down and he flew off; satisfied, I presume. The interaction took a long time; I did not clock it; it may have been 10 minutes.

The synchronization in lust involves finely attuned interaction. Male animals show actions of invitation that the female may (or may not) accept. A male stickleback performs a zigzagging dance in front of the female, which may make her follow him to a nest he has made, where she enters and lays her eggs, which he then fertilizes.[105] Other invitations consist of presenting one's sex organs for viewing, smelling or approaching; making seductive noises, such as lip-smacking; and handling or kissing the partner's sexual organs, which elephants and monkeys as well as humans do.[106] Inciting the chosen partner is general. A female porcupine, a sow, or a bitch may move herself backwards onto a male's erected penis.[107] A young male, when near a female in heat but with a dominant male present, may make a stealthy gesture of invitation—rapidly touching his own penis—and makes away; but when the older male has turned his back, he rapidly goes to her and is accepted.[108] A lioness may seek to arouse a dozing lion by repeatedly passing in front of him, swinging her tail into his face, upon which he finally and reluctantly raises himself and performs his obligations.[109] Humans tend to act in very similar fashions. They adopt provocative postures, utter seductive words in seductive tones of voice. In several cultures, a woman may express her desire by uncovering her genitals in front of the man of her choice.[110]

Lust thus, like being in love, develops into a two-person action readiness, with the synchronization of the sensitivities and actions of both partners. It is one of the marvels of nature that such synchronization can be observed even in the dragonflies: he comes flying in, and she trembles; he comes onto her, and she bends her hind-part aside. Much of that, or all of it, does not entirely consist of stereotyped behaviors. Actions are guided in some way by particulars of the situation. "Cows that are fully receptive follow the bull about continuously, and repeatedly place themselves directly in front of his head with their genitals close to his nose".[111]

In primates and humans, synchronization is expanded by the faculty of empathy. Partners notice what the other partner in the sex play feels, or, at least, what the domain of actions and potential actions is within which the sex play of the moment occurs. The partner is perceived as a person or a conspecific. Empathy appears to play a role in the sex play of gibbons and bonobos.[112] Tenderness before, during, and after sexual interaction is not rare. Stallions may touch the mare's neck after pairing; a female gibbon was observed during front-to-back coitus to reach backwards to touch the male with her hand.[113] In a marine zoo, I observed a sea lion just sweetly touching one of his females with his flipper when she passed by.

Lust thus is readily fleshed by affection and various other forms of emotional interaction. Modulating the relationship is often one of the objects of the interaction, at least in humans. He affirms his dominance, or she does; he affirms his subservience, or she does. Overpowering and being overpowered are exciting to men as well as women in sexual interaction and masturbation fantasies.[114] Sexual interactions explore how far relational roles can be stretched.

Among these, aggression and inflicting pain take an intriguing place. Possessiveness and inflicting pain, as well as seeking to be the target of either, are present in both sexes, in practice as well as in fantasy.[115] Scratching and biting during sex are cross-culturally common. They appear to enhance sexual excitement in women as well as men.[116] Violence during intercourse has also been observed in domestic chickens, rodents, macaques, and baboons. A rooster may pounce upon a hen such that the feathers fly all around, to which she submits while making protesting movements. "The normal mating pattern of the mink, marten, and sable begins when the male springs upon the female and seizes the skin of her neck in his mouth. His long, sharp, canine teeth pass completely through her pelt and his jaws may remain locked for most of the copulatory period".[117] Either sex may do it. "During copulation, the male elephant seal holds the female by biting her neck. Female sea lions grip the male's neck in their teeth before copulating".[118] The violence may occur in the same species that also manifest playful tenderness, such as minks and sables. The meaning of this mixture of sex and aggression is unclear. Zillmann, in an exhaustive study, proposed an excitation-transfer hypothesis,[119] but the animal phenomena may suggest also some more direct role in the affective interchange. It may play in retaining autonomy or wariness, simultaneously with the measure of trust that has to accompany lust. Remember Samson and Delilah again.

SEXUAL ENJOYMENT

Sexual enjoyment is a full-fledged emotion by itself. It includes the emotion during orgasm, may persist thereafter, and may occur without.[120] The emotion consists of pleasure, and events past and present appraised as pleasant, perhaps as fulfillments. It includes delighting in the other person, his or her body, in one's body sensations, in the interaction, and in the sense of union achieved. The emotion further consists of the action tendency of enjoying, with full deployment of acceptance wriggles. It aims at just being and remaining there, to do what one does, and to submit to the experience. It also aims at increasing the scope of pleasure, by enhancing sexual acceptance wriggles: opening up for experience, attending to it, letting it stream in, adopting or maintaining non-analytic attention, and doing whatever one can to deepen and prolong the experience. Many behaviors maximize experience: clasping with legs or arms, brushing with lips, and receptive stillness, abandoning to one's abandonment. Sexual enjoyment is one of the relatively rare states in which full immersed experience, as discussed in the preceding chapter, is possible, because the immersion can be shared instead of leaving the other alone. Relaxing after making love offers plenty opportunity for prolonging the sharing. There are the enjoyments of a gesture, of hearing or whispering her or his name, watching one's partner revealing him- or herself in the way of caressing. The emotion of sexual enjoyment may well be the decisive element that makes people fall in love after sex. In fact, intercourse and orgasm stimulate neuropeptide release that strengthens bonding. In men, it has been observed to be accompanied by vigorous activity in the Desire System (ventral tegmental area, striatum), at levels similar to that observed in heroin rushes.[121] I come back to this.

SEXUAL EMOTIONS AND THE ORGANIZATION
OF SEXUAL BEHAVIOR

The sexual emotions manifest two remarkable properties: their large degree of independence, and their large degree of interdependence.

The distinguished emotions represent independent processes. Each has its own elicitors, antecedent appraisal, and modes of action readiness. Stimuli for one of the sexual emotions may be irrelevant for the others. Witnessing sex scenes may arouse excitement but not desire or lust. Physical attractiveness is important for arousing interest, but much less so for being-in-love and for triggering lust.

Each of the sexual emotions may occur without any of the others. Being attracted is most of the time not followed up; you notice and go your way. Most instances of being charmed remain brief dreams. Being-in-love may fade before the day or night is over. Lust, of course, may be aroused by a glimpse of skin and a glimpse of opportunity, in men at least, even when one is all but charmed by the target. And after sexual enjoyment, many people hasten home.

Most importantly: each of the sexual emotions produces pleasures of its own. The fact has been alluded to in chapter 3. Each of the sexual emotions can be very satisfying, regardless of its having a sequel. Seeing someone attractive gives pleasure. Flirting is one of the joys of life. A brief mutual gaze may give great satisfaction and go straight to the heart. A friend told me the story of how, as a young man, he had been sitting in Italy in a train opposite a girl of 15 or so, herself seated between two boys who looked like her brothers. They went from Bologna to Brindisi, which is a very long stretch. All the time, she had her eyes slanted modestly downward; this was in the 1950s. After a 2-hour ride, just before the end of the journey, she lifted those eyes at him and looked into his, for a split second. Then, with infinite slowness, she let here lashes slide down again. He remembered the meeting and the emotion for the 50 years after.

Falling in love, too, is a thrilling experience, regardless of its pains and insecurities. So, too, for the smaller erotic satisfactions. A stolen kiss is a small treasure to be guarded, and makes one walk home with an elastic gait, smiling at all passers-by. Foreplay is part of the pleasure, and may sometimes be all of it. The deployment of lust is lustful, by itself: holding that body, skin to skin, being one flesh. Women in particular often say that it is almost as well when orgasm does not follow.[122] All sexual emotions are to some extent self-contained sequences of appraisal, impulse, action, and satisfaction. They can be goals in themselves, autonomous sources of satisfaction. On the city square of Verona, in front of what was the Capulet mansion with its famous balcony, stands a statue of Juliet. Her chest is bare. The public passes by on her right side. Her breast at that side is bright, shining bronze that contrasts with the green patina over all the rest of the statue.

At the same time, the sexual emotions are highly interdependent. They all derive from the sexual concern: the coherent sexual motivational system, with its neural and neurohumoral state of readiness. The system potentiates all its competences and sensitizes all its sensitivities, the dispositions for the sexual emotions. They, the sexual emotions, in a particular sexual encounter, all have bearing on a constant object, a particular person. The changes in action readiness, over these emotions, are modulations of the interpersonal relationship. Moreover, excitement by the stimulus events probably adds to the central neural and humoral potentiation of the system, in line with the dual potentiation model. Attractiveness does so; target availability and desire do so; actual sexual interaction does so. Each sexual emotion probably sensitizes the others and their sensitivities, in multiply reciprocal and circular causal fashions.

In a given encounter, the various emotions are not only jointly potentiated; they are intimately connected. One sexual emotion leads to action leads to interaction that creates a novel situation that elicits a further sexual emotion. One does not need to form goals on what to do next: the emotions show the way. Attractiveness makes you stop walking, which elicits a smile, or slowing down of the attractive person's pace. The slowing down facilitates interaction that helps throwing the charm. That in turn makes you show yourself under the most favorable light. Trust builds up that permits you to come closer, and allows the other to do so. Proximity favors the touching of hands and other parts of skin, that are among the proper triggers of desire and lust. And lust produces the material for the emotion of enjoyment.

Such interlocking is evident in the mentioned observations of flirtation in bars. Similar sequences are evident at more elementary levels. Male animals are attracted by the smell of receptive females. The smell brings them nearer, and induces close inspection of her genitalia, and so forth.[123] In animals, grooming goes from affection to sex.[124] A receptive female dove remains unmoved by a nearby male unless he performs the bow-and-coo display; upon that display, her estrogen level rises.[125]

The emotions thus constitute a sort of natural sequel. It can deploy itself in the absence of anticipation and forethought. A sexual sequence may well develop without a prewired species-specific program, in what the French call *de proche en proche*: one thing leading to the other, in the same way as do "ritualized" threat sequences in wolves, described earlier.[126] But, of course, even if *de proche en proche*, adult human sexual activity is usually also driven and guided by the anticipated pleasures of lust and sexual union.

A word more about the sexual motivational system. I referred to it as a competence, focusing on the relevant sensitivities and primary sexual action dispositions. But the scope of its operation is of course huge—much wider than primary sexual feeling, striving, and action. It not only potentiates the emotions as described but, in addition, the indefinitely large domain of "motivational vicissitudes,"[127] that extends to interests, preferences, envies, jealousies, and fantasies, and the cognitive processes linked to all those.

WHAT HAVE SEX AND LOVE TO DO WITH EACH OTHER?

No mention has been made, so far, of what may be considered an important emotion in relation to sex: love. Sex is so central in love, and love in sex, that in the English language (and some others), the same word is used for very different forms of affinity, or for very different desires for union and proximity. Other languages do distinguish, such as ancient Greek that separates *eros* and *agapè*.

Different types or dimensions of love have to be distinguished, and indeed have been. Sternberg distinguished three dimensions: passionate love, intimacy, and commitment, of which only passionate love refers to sexuality. Intimacy does not. Hatfield and Rapson as well as Solomon describe love as the desire for union, which can exist entirely in the form of desire for emotional intertwining and mutual responsiveness. Solomon also defines love as the fusion of identities, and redefinition of oneself in terms of the other. He or she is part of me, and I am part of him or her. Losing one's beloved is losing part of oneself. His pain is my pain, her welfare is my welfare.[128] Any of those, striving for intimacy, toward caring, and toward worth enhancement, can be focused when asking about the relationship between love and sex. All this is best summarized in Shaver's view: three behavioral systems come together in love: attachment, caregiving, and sex. *Love*, in the following, refers to only the first two of them.[129]

Obviously, sex and love, as conceptualized in this way, are separate, but frequently co-occur. That is what the concept of passionate love implies. But also, they frequently do not. There is much casual sex, and striving after lust or pleasure only, and use of sex for purposes of earning a living, obtaining favors, or exerting power and dominance. In very many human sexual interactions there is an impersonal element: one is a pleasure instrument. There also are the forms of love without a prominent sexual component: parental and filial love, many friendships, and the caring comradeship in long-standing marriages.

So what have sex and love to do with each other? There are several theories. One is that love and sex have become linked in evolution because an enduring relationship between parents promotes survival of the offspring and increases likelihood, for the men, that the offspring carries their genes.[130] From a functional viewpoint, the theory merely asserts that the two often go together because it happens to be so. Another, more subtle theory is that mutual affection represents the fair deal of protection and food-provision in exchange for sexual access, in groups with scramble competition (larger groups in which many males have to compete for many females without a single dominant male).[131] But this still does not explain why and how the linking occurs when it occurs.

Let us look more closely at the proximal processes. Sex and love do have to do with each other in several ways. Both grow out of contact, and they need contact for their realization. Love often grows from sexual interaction: one was together in a pleasant, satisfactory way; trust was sought and spent. As I mentioned, the sequence of sex to love is frequent. It probably has been a major pattern in the common classes in earlier periods of our culture, where one married when the girl became pregnant. Beginnings of a development toward pair-bonding are found in the consortships of chimpanzees: After the usual gratuitous sexual interactions, a male and female may set off together to a secluded place in the woods, together with her children if she has any, sleep together, and have sex even when she is not in heat.[132]

Inversely, love is one of the conditions conducive to sex. A close link from intimacy to sex is already manifest in some primates, notably the bonobos, between females as well as between females and males.[133] Sex is a way to affirm or establish a bond. In humans, any growing intimacy may end in falling in love, as in the De Botton and Berlin–Akhmatova stories given. Intimacy of any kind tends to evoke sexual desire. Traveling on a plane does. Being accepted in self-disclosure in psychotherapy may make the patient fall in love and then goes under the name of transference love; falling in love with the patient under that of countertransference.

Sex can evidently grow out of love, and vice versa. Sexual interaction is a relationship in which certain intimacies are necessarily involved, expected, and accepted if one is inclined to them. It makes other intimacies accepted and acceptable. Coming out of bed, walking around naked when making coffee is not offensive, and then has its own attractions. Inversely, deepening of the relationship in turn creates the desire for more intimacy, and the abandonment that is one of the attractions of sex. All this probably has clear neurophysiological underpinnings. Male-female bonding in a monogamous rodent species (prairie voles) results from repeated sexual intercourse, as a consequence of the neuropeptide (OT/VP) and dopamine release that follows. OT/VP enhance establishing partner identity (recognition of the partner's smell), and concurrent dopamine arousal probably helps fixing incentive value on that particular partner, thus forming a bond. VP, in males, activates various courtship behaviors, and the aggressive components of bonding, such as possessiveness. The incentive value has the nature of appraisal of affection: OP/VT activates the amygdala.[134] In humans, OT/VP releases have been observed to follow orgasm, as was mentioned when discussing the emotion of enjoyment.

Sex and bonding (and caring) may each result from distinct motivational systems, but these systems thus tend to interact closely. Their sensitivities overlap, and their motivational activators overlap. Trust is a condition for both, or for all three. The systems are activated concurrently (in certain species), not perhaps because evolution happened to arrange it so, but because in those species they dynamically tend to call each other.

There also are incompatibilities between the systems. Sex thrives on novelty, presumably because of the excitements of non-self-evident well-functioning. Bonding, by contrast, thrives on familiarity. There may well be more conditions under which the two systems clash. Prewired or acquired incest taboos may form one of them. OT/VP may attenuate distrust, but does not always neutralize it. The systems retain their relative independence.

The links between sex and love thus are both intimate and relatively loose. This, of course, fits the hypothesis that their causal relations are bidirectional, which in turn fits their loose links with sexual orientation, emphasized by Diamond.[135]

IMPLICATIONS

This chapter explored whether the psychology of emotion adds to understanding sex, and what sex has to do with emotions.

Emotion analysis does add to understanding sex. The driving force clearly is emotional. Sexual desire is an emotion. So are attraction, being charmed, being in love, lust and enjoyment. What is experienced as "sex drive" is the action readiness for whatever the final goal or the subgoal of a given step. *Sex drive* is a collection of emotions, or awareness of them (depending on the context in which *sex drive* is being used). Emotions form the essential mechanism of the sequence of steps that underlies sexual interaction. They form each step's starting signal, as well as the termination signal of the preceding step. Whatever is needed to explain the behavioral characteristics of sexual behavior—its goal directedness, its urgency, its control precedence, its seeking detours on the way to get hold of satisfactions—are likewise aspects of the motivational states that are equivalent to the feelings of being driven and of urge.

Does analysis of sex contribute to the theory of emotions? It indeed does so in an important way, even if not all we have encountered is specifically sexual. Major aspects of the sexual emotions bring to the fore major "basic emotions" not regularly found in lists of such emotions.

The first is sexual excitement. It is not just a variant of excitement in general, because of its obvious sexual specificity. It resembles a basic emotion in possessing all characteristics cited in that connection: serving a fundamental adaptational task, biological foundation, universality, emotion-specific behaviors, internal coherence of the various aspects.[136] Like startle, however, it lacks action readiness.

The second is sexual desire. Desire is occasionally included among the emotions, although rarely so in current emotion reviews.[137] But again it is basic: It is universal, it is commanded by a major neurohumoral system, it imposes control precedence. Pondering sex shows that excluding sexual desire the status of a basic emotion is silly.

The third is love: the emotion or emotion class centered around the action tendency toward union or fusion with a person. It is instantiated both by what completes sexual desire, and by love in the colloquial sense. It, too, is a basic emotion if ever there is any, according to the mentioned criteria.

A fourth emotion of interest is being-in-love,. It is not a cultural invention; empirical data do not support that hypothesis.[138] The phenomenological description reminds one of other emotional changes, that even may have related contents: addiction, religious conversions[139] and adoption of political fanaticism. The similarities are worth exploring. But interestingly, the desire for union in being in love may have a specific structure, namely being aroused by concurrent bonding and sexual activation. At least, bonding in voles depends on concurrent oxytocin or vasopressin *and* dopamine activity.[140]

Exploration of the sexual emotions has been instructive in another regard. The emotions are evidently rooted in a genetically prepared motivational system, and being-in-love even in two of them. They show very considerable phylogenetic continuity, even in specific action tendencies and actions like looking-at/looking-away, courting, tactile stimulation to incite excitement in the partner, aggressive admixtures, down to practices such as love-feeding and kissing, including deep kissing. Even bonobos may do the latter, to greet a human friend.[141] Interestingly, all those actions are in some way "natural." They are unlearned, but very likely not genetically preprogrammed. They appear to result from self-organizing of the desire for union, together with the means available for achieving close interaction: locomotion, eyes, feet, hands, mouth, and tongue.

At the same time, there is appreciable cross-cultural diversity at the levels of practice and practices. It is present in almost all domains. Even kissing among lovers is not completely universal. Cultures appear to exist (or to have existed), where lovers never kiss, such as the Thonga in South Africa and the Siriono in South America.[142]

And then, even biologically prepared actions require learning. Courting requires social skills that are borrowed from other types of social interaction. The skills are built in infancy; rhesus monkeys reared in the absence of peers fail in sexual interaction, and are terrified when being approached invitingly.[143]

NOTES

[1]Ekman, 1992; Tomkins, 1962; Izard, 1977; Oatley & Johnson, Laird. 1987.
[2]Bain, 1865.
[3]Everaerd, 1988.
[4]Hatfield & Rapson, 1993.
[5]Fisher, 2004.
[6]Regan & Berscheid, 1999.
[7]Aharon et al., 2001; Etcoff, 1999.
[8]Meyerson & Lindstrom, 1973.
[9]Aharon et al., 2001; Stark et al., 2005.
[10]Proust, 1988, p. 106.
[11]Regnault, 1990.

[12]Buss & Schmitt, 1993, Table 2 and p. 214.

[13]Buss, 1989; Hatfield & Rapson, 1993.

[14]Rombouts, 1992.

[15]Etcoff, 1999.

[16]Etcoff, 1999; Hatfield & Rapson, 1993; Hatfield & Sprecher, 1986.

[17]Aharon et al., 2001; Etcoff, 1999.

[18]Goldschmidt, 1996.

[19]Buss, 1994; Jones & Hill, 1993; Langlois & Roggeman, 1990; Perrett et al, 1999; Symons, 1995.

[20]Hatfield & Rapson, 1996, present an informative discussion; Ford and Beach, 1951, p. 88, give a systematic overview of cultural differences as inferred from cultural anthropology data.

[21]Buss et al., 1990; Buss & Schmitt, 1993.

[22]Van Hooff, personal communication, 2003.

[23]Hatfield & Rapson, 1996, p. 33.

[24]Grammer, Kruck, & Magnusson, 1998.

[25]Angier, 1999; Fisher, 2004.

[26]Malinowksi, 1929.

[27]Ford & Beach, 1951 p. 46ff.

[28]Young & Wang, 2004, p. 1052.

[29]Buss, 1994; Symonds, 1999.

[30]Buss & Schmitt, 1993, reports that women indeed tend to prefer younger men for a one-night stand.

[31]Giroud, 2002.

[32]Brantome, 1655.

[33]Hatfield & Rapson, 1993, p. 15.

[34]Buss & Schmitt, 1993.

[35]Rombouts, 1992.

[36]a.o. Hatfield & Rapson, 1993, p. 28/29.

[37]Mithen, 1996.

[38]This is an item in Buss and Schmitt's (1993) research. Many women value this feature in a man, in particular when he is a candidate for a brief sexual encounter.

[39]Valins, 1966.

[40]Barefoot & Straub, 1974.

[41]e.g., Ford & Beach, 1951.

[42]Hatfield & Rapson, 1993, quoting a listing by Christopher & Frandsen, 1990.

[43]Concise Oxford Dictionary.

[44]Draghi-Lorenz, 2001; Keltner & Buswell, 1997.

[45]Perper & Fox, 1980.

[46]Kellerman, Lewis, & Laird, 1989.

[47]Smuts, 1985.

[48]Grammer et al., 1998.

[49]Tennov, 1979.
[50]Hatfield & Rapson, 1993.
[51]Armstrong (2002) gives this as the appraisal aspect.
[52]Rombouts, 1992.
[53]Hatfield & Rapson, 1993, p. 5.
[54]Rombouts, 1992.
[55]Byrne, Ervin, & Lamberth, 1970; Kellermans et al. 1989.
[56]Rombouts, 1992.
[57]Mauss, 1914/1957.
[58]Solomon, 1988, p. 199.
[59]Hatfield & Rapson, 1993, p. 41f.
[60]Rombouts, 1992.
[61]Rombouts, 1992.
[62]Botton, 1994.
[63]Ignatieff, 1998, p. 161.
[64]I owe this suggestion, and relevant illustrations, to my friend Louis Tas, psychoanalyst.
[65]Rombouts, 1992.
[66]Rombouts, 1992, p. 60.
[67]Rombouts, 1992; Stendhal, 1820/1949.
[68]Fisher, 2004.
[69]Giroud, 2002.
[70]Ford & Beach, 1951.
[71]Kosfeld, Heinrichs, Zak, Fischbacher, & Fehr, 2005.
[72]Young & Wang, 2004.
[73]Fogel, 1993.
[74]Solomon, 1988, p. 37.
[75]Young & Wang, 2004, p. 1050.
[76]Armstrong, 2002.
[77]Geer & Janssen, 2000; Janssen, 1993; Laan & Everaerd, 1995a.
[78]Both, Everaerd, & Laan, 2003.
[79]Bradley et al., 2001.
[80]Barlow, 1986.
[81]Laan, Everaerd, Van Bellen, & Hanewald, 1994.
[82]Regan & Berscheid, 1999.
[83]Laan & Everaerd, 1995a; Janssen & Everaerd, 1993.
[84]Dekker & Everaerd, 1988.
[85]Janssen, Everaerd, Spiering, & Janssen, 2000; Spiering, Everaerd, & Janssen, 2003.
[86]Janssen et al., 2000. Sexual primes caused a significant decrease in penile circumference, which, however, may correspond with an increase in length.
[87]Laan & Everaerd, 1995b.

[88]Angier, 1999, chapter 11; Van Goozen, Wiegant, Endert, Helmond, & Van de Poll, 1997.

[89]Zillmann, 1983.

[90]Spiering et al.2003.

[91]Janssen, et al. 2000.

[92]Regan & Berscheid, 1999, p. 17.

[93]e.g., Genie's story, Curtiss, 1977.

[94]*"Extacy"*, directed by Machaty, starred principal actress Hedy Lamarr, who later in the film appears in the nude. The film was influential in the movement towards sexual emancipation.

[95]Knoth, Boyd, and Singer, 1988.

[96]Leitenberg & Henning, 1995.

[97]Buss, 1994.

[98]Everaerd, 1988; Singer & Toates, 1987.

[99]Brehm, 1966.

[100]Everaerd, 1988; Geer & Janssen, 2000.

[101]Reference is again to the studies of Dekker & Everaerd (1988) and Janssen et al. (2000).

[102]Regan & Berscheid, 1999.

[103]Hite, 1976.

[104]Bingham, 1928, quoted from Ford & Beach, 1951, p. 27/8.

[105]Tinbergen, 1951.

[106]Ford & Beach, 1951, Chapters 3 and 5.

[107]Ford & Beach, 1951, p. 95.

[108]Observation made by Van Hooff; personal communication.

[109]From a nature film I once saw on TV; probably on National Geographic.

[110]Ford & Beach, 1951, p. 93.

[111]Ford & Beach, 1951, p. 95.

[112]See Carpenter, 1940, for gibbons and De Waal and Lanting, 1997, for bonobos.

[113]Bingham, 1928.

[114]e.g. Friday, 1991; Leitenberg & Henning, 1995; Stoller, 1979.

[115]Friday, 1991; Leitenberg & Henning, 1995; Stoller, 1979.

[116]Ford & Beach, 1951.

[117]Ford & Beach, 1951, p. 59.

[118]Ford & Beach, 1951, p. 59.

[119]Zillmann, 1998.

[120]Friday, 1991; Hite, 1976.

[121]Holstege et al., 2003. Whether it does likewise in women is, so far, unknown.

[122]Hite, 1976.

[123]Ford & Beach, 1951, p. 53.

[124]Ford & Beach, 1951.

[125]Erickson & Lehrman, 1964.

[126]Fogel, 1993, p. 29–30.

[127]The term alludes to Freud's analysis of "drives and their vicissitudes," Triebe und Triebschicksale", Freud, 1946.

[128]Solomon, 1988.

[129]Notably, Hatfield and Rapson, 1993; Shaver, Hazan, and Bradshaw, 1988; Solomon, 1988; Stendhal ,1820/1949; Sternberg, 1986.

[130]Buss & Schmitt 1993.

[131]De Waal, 1989.

[132]Goodall, 1986.

[133]De Waal & Lanting, 1997.

[134]Keverne & Curley, 2004; Young & Wang, 2004.

[135]Diamond, 2003.

[136]Everaerd, 1988.

[137]Ortony & Turner, 1990.

[138]e.g., Averill, 1985; Jankowiak & Fischer, 1992.

[139]see James, 1902/1982.

[140]Young & Wang, 2004.

[141]De Waal & Lanting, 1997.

[142]Ford & Beach, 1951, p. 49.

[143]Harlow, 1969.

10

Revenge

DESIRE FOR VENGEANCE

Desire for vengeance certainly is one of the most potent of human passions. It has been one of the major preoccupations in the world literature. Witness Euripides' Medea, the Oresteia, Hamlet, or Tess, Cain's killing of Abel, God's expulsion of Adam and Eve from paradise, and his near-destruction of the human race with the Flood. It is also a major theme in history. Jews were massacred during the Crusades on the grounds of being blamed for what happened to Jesus. It is a dominant theme in recent and in current affairs. In World War II, Lidice in Czechoslovakia, Oradour in France, and Putten in the Netherlands were destroyed, and their male populations deported or killed because of attacks by resistance fighters on high-ranking German officers. Serbian violence in Croatia, in the 1990s, obtained added strength and motivation from fury about the collaboration of the Croatians with the German invaders, and atrocities committed, 50 years earlier. The major motivation for the September 11, 2001, terrorist attacks in the United states was taking revenge for offense against Islam and for American presence in Saudi Arabia. Vengeance made those attacks a source of joy to some Islamic groups elsewhere the world. American popular feeling desired vengeance after them.

Vengeance is not restricted to religious or political contexts. It occurs in personal relationships: unkindness is responded to by unkindness and sexual unfaithfulness by paying back in kind. Desires for vengeance are not confined to instigating physical violence. More frequent are actions that cause milder harm, such as destroying one's offender's cherished possessions, going to bed with her or his best friend, publicly making a fool of him or her. Still more frequent are vengeful thoughts that remain fantasies: imagining the offender's illness or misfortune. Everyday thoughts and acts are revenges for erotic unfaithfulness, indiscretions, having been slighted, having been cheated, having had one's bicycle stolen, unfriendly words, lacks of attention. The examples come from questionnaire studies with students. They show that desire for vengeance is not confined to the aberrant few. In one of our own studies, 46% of the respondents admitted to remembering at least one instance of a vengeful impulse. In another study, all participants recalled an instance of desire for revenge, and 45% rated the intensities of their emotion as strong or very strong (6 or 7 on the 7-point scale). In a larger study by Crombag and colleagues, 64% remembered an event from their recent past that had incited their "urge to get even"; 29% of these had actually taken some vengeful action.[1]

The power of desire for vengeance can be inferred from the very existence of the Law of Talion. An eye for an eye, a tooth for a tooth. The law of Talion is stated in the book of Exodus,[2] among a number of other prescriptions that God gave to Moses, to regulate interactions within the tribe. It in fact represented a major advance in lawfulness, because it served to hem in blind vengeance. For an eye, no more than an eye; for a tooth, no more than a tooth. That is the significance of the law of Talion.[3] Evidently, such regulation was needed. Desire for revenge itself appears to be immoderate.

Vengeance might thus be expected to form one of the major topics in the psychology of emotion. Again: not so. Few major psychological studies have appeared on the topic over the last 80 or so years. One is a excellent book by Susan Jacoby called *Wild Justice*. Another is Scheff's *Bloody Revenge*. In philosophy, revenge was recently treated by Solomon.[4]

The absence of extensive discussion of vengeance in the psychology of emotion might be explained by the fact that it is not an emotion. Indeed, it is not. But the desire for revenge, the urge to retaliate, most certainly is. The desire is an emotion. It has all the usual features of one. It is a state of impulse, of involuntary action readiness, generated by an appraisal, often accompanied by bodily excitement, and with every aspect of control precedence: preoccupation, single-minded goal pursuit, neglect of unwelcome information, and interference with other activities. It is a mere coincidence, I think, that no word for this emotion exists in current English. As a matter of fact, the English language has a word that is about right, but has gone out of usage: wrath. God, the main spender of wrath, is a vengeful

God. But some connotations of the word do not fit some of the contexts of vengeance. I therefore leave it at that: there is an emotion of appraised offense that instigates desire for vengeance.

THE PROBLEMS POSED BY VENGEANCE

There is good reason to examine that emotion. Desire for vengeance poses several major problems for the analysis of emotion. They are the apparent uselessness of revenge and its occasional self-destructiveness, its often extreme intensity, and its often extended duration. This chapter seeks to explore these problems, and to try to understand them.

The first problem, uselessness, is implicit in the very definition of vengeance. *Vengeance* has been defined as "an attempt, at some cost or risk to oneself, to impose suffering upon those who have made us suffer".[5] The primary aim of vengeance thus is to make the other party suffer. It comes after the fact of having suffered at someone's hands. It is not to prevent or stop that act. It concerns a separate attempt, that may come an hour, or a week, or years later. This aim and this delay set vengeance apart from anger, hostility, and aggression in general.

So what use has vengeance? It makes the offender suffer but cannot undo the deed. If someone was killed, it does not revive the dead one. If there was an insult, it does not take the blemish away. If one has been made a fool of in public, the foolish display remains. All that is odd.

It is odd in particular because of the functional perspective of current psychology of emotion. We suppose that emotions are in some sense functional. In principle at least, they are considered to be functionally appropriate in dealing with the emotion-arousing situation.[6] Every kind of emotion has some functional role, in seeking to establish or modify a person-environment relationship. Emotions thus are geared to some sort of gain. But what gain has vengeance? It is concerned with actions that do not aim at righting the suffered wrong, and it is incited by wrongs that cannot be undone.

Revenge may even be harmful to the individual, to the point of being self-destructive. The paradigm example again is literary: Euripides' Medea, who takes revenge on her partner Jason for intending to marry a Greek princess. Not only does she kill her rival, that princess, but also her own and Jason's children, to strike Jason the most devastating blow. She suffers herself, and puts her own life at risk. She would indeed have been killed, were it not that the Sun spirits her off to the abodes of the gods.

Real-life examples are close at hand, in the recent wave of vengeful suicide attacks that includes Mohammed Atta, who flew a jet airplane into the New York World Trade Center. The harm of revenge shows itself also at the domestic level. Quarrels in intimate relationships often go on interminably:

Neither party can leave the attacks of the other unanswered. The revenges bring harm to the offended party, here too, by spoiling an evening, souring a relationship, or costly legal consequences.

The second major problem that vengeance offers is the violence of vengeful violence. Many acts of vengeance are immoderate and cruel. Whereto this violence of violence? Revenge not only makes the object of vengeance suffer but tends to go to extremes. Medea again illustrates this. Jason's bride is made to die, cringing in a poisoned cloak. Jason's children are murdered in order "to break his heart," as Euripides has Medea say.[7] Such cruelty appears true to life. September 11, 2001, showed this clearly: the cool killing of the passengers of the airplanes and of the thousands in the New York World Trade Center. Civil wars and guerilla wars abound with instances of extreme cruelty; it seems plausible that this is because numerous accounts are to be settled. The Violencia in Colombia was a civil war that erupted at the level of villages and neighborhoods. Between 1948 and 1953, it took 150,000 lives. Its reports abound with the most horrifying examples of cruelty, from peasant to neighboring peasant: stabbing out eyes, cutting off genitals, cutting open pregnant women.[8] Personal revenges for suffered humiliations mingled in the authorities-ordered Tutsi-killings in Rwanda, and the Serbo-Croatian conflict that sported the same atrocities.[9] After the My Lai incident, in Vietnam, one of the soldiers involved, Private West, reported that "they had been in a mood for revenge" because some men of their platoon had been killed by the Vietcong the previous days.[10]

Or take marital violence: homicides of wife by husband and husband by wife. One may assume that vengeance plays the central role there, for unfaithfulness or years of frustration. The average number of knife stabbings and bullets fired in marital homicides is significantly higher than in murders in general.[11] Even simpler domestic revenges are often cruel, as in retaliatory unfaithfulness and verbal stabs coolly delivered.

The cruelty of revenge is often mixed with defamations. Take Saddam Hussein's revenge for Iraqi Shia's revolt. His Republican Guards destroyed the graveyards in the Shiites' holy cities of Kerbala and Nahaf. The same in the mutual revenges in the Lebanese civil war in the 1980s. The Christian Phalangists killed the Muslim population of the village of Karantina. Muslims then attacked the village of Damour. I quote the journalist Fisk: "The Christian militiamen were executed. The civilians were lined up against the walls of their homes and sprayed with machine-gun fire.... Many of the young women had been raped. Babies had been shot at close range in the back of the head.... And at some point they vented their wrath on the old Christian cemetery, digging up the coffins and tearing open the gates of vaults, hurling Damour's past generations across the graveyard".[12] Some years later, in 1982, the Christian Phalangist wrought horrors in the Sabra and Chatila Muslim refugee camps. Their commander was a certain Elie Hobeika, whose fiancee had been killed in Damour.[13]

The violence of revenge is not only physical. It is also emotional. The violence is carried by hatred, that is, the desire to harm the target's very existence. The targets are seen as outright evil, as people "to be smoked out of their holes." In the same vein is what a Bosnian rape victim told Mesquita.[14] Her rapist had said to her: "In this way, no Muslim man will ever want you."

As remarked before, only a small part of vengeful desires lead to violent acts. Much of it remains at the level of desire, and remain fantasies. However, vengeful fantasies, too, are often remarkably violent, even the everyday instances reported in the mentioned questionnaire studies. They often have a virulent quality: images of physical destruction of objects and of stabbing the offender, and wishes that he or she may be killed or fall seriously ill.

Persistence over time is the third remarkable feature of vengeful desire. It may stretch out over years. The thirst remains unquenched, or is evoked with ease, even decades after the events. Armenians have murdered Turkish diplomatic representatives, in retaliation for Turkish outrages against the Armenian people in 1915; such murders continue until the present day. Serbian violence toward Croatians in the 1990s was motivated in part by Croatian cruelties in the 1940s, when the Croats collaborated with the Germans; that collaboration was indeed constantly invoked by Serbian TV in the more recent conflict.[15]

The same temporal extension can be found at the individual level. Victims of rape, oppression, and humiliation suffer from the events for years afterwards, and many of them continue to fantasize about revenge, or dream about requiring satisfaction. Crimes are committed to obtain satisfaction for wrongs suffered years earlier, and kept as grudges over that time. The story of Ferdi E. serves as an illustration. Ferdi E. is a Dutch engineer who in 1975 with two colleagues founded an industrial development company. Some time after starting the company, his colleagues decided to drastically cut E.'s salary and to remove him from his responsible position in the company. He withdrew and continued to live quietly with his wife and children in an Amsterdam suburb. Meanwhile, he pondered revenge. Precisely what revenge he planned has remained unclear, but it included the need for a considerable sum of money. To obtain this, he decided to abduct a rich man for ransom. He selected Gerrit-Jan Heyn, the acting director of Holland's major supermarket chain. Carefully, over a period of weeks, he studied the man's habits. One day in September 1987—fifteen years after the insult—he accosted his victim when the man left his house for work in the morning, dragged him into his own car, and took him to a wood that he, E., knew well. There they chatted for awhile and had lunch with sandwiches that E. had prepared beforehand. Then E. murdered Heyn, cut off the man's thumb, and put it in a small tin he had brought for the purpose: It could later serve as proof of having him in his power. He buried the corpse, and set out to put in his claims for ransom: 1 million guilders, in uncut diamonds and bank notes. He managed to collect half the ransom; then silence reigned. Some 5 months later he was traced and caught, after having carelessly spent one of the (marked) ransom bills in a supermarket near his home. The story is remarkable for the psychology of revenge, because of the sequence of humiliation and vengeful planning, the amount of thought and preparation put into the execution, and the time span: years and years of emotion-fed work toward an emotion-fed goal.

In many of the mentioned incidents other emotions are involved than desire for revenge: jealousy, hatred, mere political motive, war, or instrumental purposes. Yet, they are appropriately given as illustrating revenge. Thoughts of revenge are documented in most of the examples—witness the words of Private West about My Lai, the explicit accusations in the Serbian press—and are almost inevitably aroused in fighting among people that are familiar to one another, as in marriages and civil wars.

In trying to find some tentative answers to the three problems of lack of gain, violence, and persistence, we may employ the clues provided by the present analysis of emotion. First, this analysis assumes that emotional feelings and impulses are determined by the individual's appraisal of events, including the fine grain of context and situation (chap. 4). Part of the explanation has to be found in such appraisal. Second, appraisal is assumed to result from the concerns that events touch upon (chap. 5); the strength of emotions is assumed to be determined by the number and strength of those concerns, and the event's appraised magnitude (chap. 6). The power of vengeance, and the violence of its violence can be expected to derive from the concerns at stake, and from how deeply the offenses threaten to damage them, and from the resulting control precedence (chap. 2). Third, duration of emotion is thought to depend on the persistence of events effects (chap. 7).

In seeking explanations the functional perspective serves as a heuristic. Emotional actions generally seek some gain. They are motives to improve one's situation: to promote satisfaction and decrease pain. What could be the gains of revenge, of which the desire is, by definition, evoked after one suffered harm that cannot be undone?

The answer is relatively straightforward. The gains of revenge are real enough. Even if harm cannot be undone, revenge may soften or undo some of its consequences. It may even reverse them. Desire for vengeance is as "rational" as any other emotion. This means that many instances of desires for vengeance will be nonrational, as there are many nonrational angers and fears. But, in principle, vengeance has its proper meaningful gains.

THE GAINS OF VENGEANCE

Deterrence: Protection of Interests

One of the possible gains of revenge is quite clear. Vengeance punishes and suppresses the punished behavior. It can deter the offender from repeating the offense. It thus protects the avenger's interests.

Taking revenge is rational when the costs it inflicts outweigh the benefits that offense can produce or, rather, when revenge implies threat of revenge with such costs in the future. A "tit for tat" strategy—immediately responding to offense by retaliation, and doing nothing harmful otherwise—is indeed effective in modifying behavior in a desired direction. This strategy is often followed in political and military interchanges. In the 1980s, the South Lebanese Hezbollah launched a rocket offensive, to which Israel retaliated by shelling Lebanon; Syria and Lebanon thereupon ordered Hezbollah to stop their offensive. In the trench warfare of World War I, a silent agreement developed in which German and British patrols from opposite trenches very much avoided each other, except for shooting fiercely when the others happened to begin; clashes were attenuated in self-regulatory fashion.[16] Threat of a lethal tit for tat exchange led to the mutual nuclear containment of the United States and the Soviet Union during the cold war. The effectiveness of this way of using revenge has been shown experimentally by Axelrod in an iterated prisoners dilemma game.[17] Two participants can each play two kinds of move. One kind allows him either to win much, and the other nothing, or both to win a little, depending on what the other player chooses. The other kind of move allows either the other player to win much and oneself nothing, or both a medium amount. When beginning with a cooperative move, and punishing the other with a hostile move if that other has made one, both players rapidly settle on a cooperative strategy that, over a number of games, offers optimal gain.

Deterrence thus is achieved by the threat of renewed revenge. The strategy ensures that the threat is credible: one's opponent can be pretty sure that a tit will follow his tat. In other than game situations, threats of revenge can be made credible without ever having been made true. Credibility can result from shows of force and insolence, or from indubitable possession of retaliatory potential, such as atomic stockpiles during the cold war. Credibility can also derive from reputation of being driven by vengeful emotions like hatred, indignation, or wrath. Emotions have control precedence. They tend to push for action, no matter what. Frank[18] has beautifully argued that such emotions are not at all irrational, though often considered so. They are functional because they ensure credibility of retaliatory threat. They offer the gain of deterrence.

Deterrence by threat of revenge not only occurs as cool strategy, but may flow from wrath. Think of outbursts of jealousy that make being unfaithful more unpleasant than staying true. Think of the jealous man who threw vitriol at his wife, thereby diminishing her appeal for others. Think of the drug dealer who better stays away from his competitor's clients.

However, the strategy offers serious risk. Revenge may make the conflict escalate instead of deterring the offender. It may initiate and maintain a destructive spiral of violence. Such spirals not only occur in tribal feuds or border wars. Marital quarrels may go on interminably, because each party cannot leave the other's attacks unanswered.[19] Under which conditions deterrence outweighs the incitement to spiraling is unclear,[20] nor what it is that prompts continuing vengeance despite lack of success in deterrence. Is it persistent hope for ultimate success in stopping the other's offenses? More likely, other expected or actual gains are involved.

Anyway, the gain of deterrence at best offers only a partial explanation of revenge. It does not explain its range of occurrence. It cannot explain desire for revenge for offenses that have no chance of being repeated, as when one's spouse has been killed, or when the offender now lives in a different part of the world. More importantly, even if the gain of deterrence may explain taking revenge, it does not explain the powerful desires for it. Most of all, it does not explain the focus of the desire, the aim that it seeks to achieve: to get even.

Restoring Equity in Suffering and Obligation

The focus of desire for revenge: it mostly is not to defend one's interests. It is to get even. "Getting even has always been one of the most basic metaphors of our moral vocabulary" writes Solomon.[21] But what does to get even mean? A clue is given by that further aspect of the aims of revenge: to make the offender suffer. Suffering is what vengeance seeks to produce.

But how does the offender's suffering make one get even. If he suffers, what do I gain? What is my profit? How could it possibly help?

An older psychology of vengeance sought the answer in an additive theory of affect. Steinmetz,[22] drawing from Hume, proposed that vengeance diminishes suffering because the pleasure of seeing the offender suffer annuls one's own suffering, or subtracts from it. Or, in a slightly different conception: because the mind has place for only one affect at a time, one's suffering is pushed aside by the pleasure of seeing the offender suffer. The idea is attractive in its neatness, but the affect mechanics do not satisfy our current view of emotions. It leaves out an essential aspect of revenge, which is that it is a social act. If the offender is struck by lightning, this may give joy but it may also rob me of my revenge. The presumed affect mechanics, moreover, may even be wrong, since bad moods are not necessarily improved by pleasurable events. They may even be exacerbated by them.[23]

Current views of emotions allow more satisfactory insight. As discussed in chapter 3, pleasures and pains do not simply add up or subtract. Each pleasure, each pain, has its own significance. Each results from patterns of appraisal that rest upon multiple event aspects and on relevance to multiple concerns. All these aspects compose the resulting affect. Indeed, being subjected to offense has a number implications that give that result its specificity. One is one's harm or loss. A second is that the harm or loss is caused by someone, the offender, and thus constitutes an interpersonal event telling on the relationship. He did it, or she did it, or they did it. A third is that the offender remains unscathed, and even may stand to profit by the event. A fourth is that offenders know what they have caused, and why, and enjoy it. One's suffering from offense includes all that. It includes his glory in having inflicted suffering upon me and, in the event, his glory in having gotten away with it. All that contrasts with my own situation. He walks in pleasure and I in suffering.

It is one of the most unbearable aspects of having suffered at the hands of someone else. This aspect of unavenged misery haunts victims of torture or persecution, or the kin of murder victims. Much of the upset of a crime victim precisely centers around the hallucinatory vision of the released criminal leading a quiet and happy life, while one's old suffering and one's irremediable loss remain. It has been observed in the close kin of murdered intimates.[24] It has been extensively reported as part of the experiences of the Mothers of the Plaza de Mayo in Argentina, during the dictatorial regime and after that, when general amnesty was declared. The torturers of their children were restored to freedom and civil liberty. Their own suffering and loss remained. And as to the impact of the ideas of the perpetrator's glories: many Western people have that scathing memory of viewing TV images of shouting and cheering Arab crowds after the September 11, 2001 attacks, or of the shown contentment of Osama bin Laden.

The victim's appraisal of offense, the suffering by the offense, thus includes the offender's gains. Vengeance does take these pains away. Medea says it quite precisely, at the end of the play, after Jason's ferocious reproaches for killing his children: "You were mistaken if you thought you could dishonor my bed and live a pleasant life and laugh at me," and "My pain's a fair price, to take away your smile".[25] Vengeance actually makes part of the suffering disappear. For certain, not all of it. The loss and the recollection of harm remain. But some of it, the poignancy of it, goes, the loneliness of it, the being-less-than-he or she, the sting of his or her gain.

These things also work the other way. After successful revenge there is glory. There is joy about the spoils that the revenge may have yielded; there is added joy because of Comparative Feeling when, now, he is down and I am up. Again hear Medea, when asking about the details of how her rival Glauke died, and Glauke's father who had expelled Medea from Corinth : "Tell me, how did they die? You'll give me double pleasure if their death was horrible."[26]

True enough, restoring balance of suffering did not show up much in the Crombag et al. study.[27] This may be due to the fact that it may not have played much of a role within the range of offenses of their student participants. But it may also be because balance of suffering cannot be the entire story. There is an aspect of revenge that it does not account for. "Getting even" is not the same as both getting the same. It is paying back and evening out. Revenge implies punishment. Offenders should not get their gain of offense for free. They should not get away with it with impunity. They should pay for what they got and caused me to suffer. That seems to say that there should be balance between acts and their consequences. In particular, there should be balance between what they obtain at my cost and what they pay for it at my hands.

This sounds like an elementary sense of justice, and it almost is. It reflects a sense of equity, that is, of balance between rewards and punishments, between rights and obligations, that should be similar for different people, except when recognized differences in social status offer counterbalance. Such sense of equity is widespread and varied in human interaction. It is basic in a large array of human emotions and forms of interaction. Children age three understand fairness and unfairness; they protest when another child gets a larger piece of cake. When free to divide a given sum of money between oneself and someone else, most people divide not too far off from fifty–fifty, as is shown by experiments with the ultimatum game, mentioned in chapter 5. Gratitude is an emotion that impels to repay services or gifts received, in something like equal measure.[28] Equity also plays in emotions of resentment, the feeling of being unfairly treated. And it plays in that of envy, with its urge to spoil the pleasure of those who have too much, and to hide one's pleasure when one has too much oneself. That latter, of course, unless one relishes inequity, and flaunts one's advantage in the others' face.

Rules of fairness and gratitude translate into feelings of decency. They were codified in many traditional societies, and play as rules of decency in current ones. But sense of equity does not need to operate at such a conceptual, ideological, or abstract level; neither is it fully a cultural acquisition. Disturbed sense of equity directly generates feelings of disturbance, from discomfort over resentment to anger to revenge.

About the origins of sense of equity one can make plausible guesses. Human behavior—even that of children—is rule based. Rules form the principles from which to act. If there are no rules, conduct finds no principles to go by. Our elementary sense of justice in vengefulness, fair sharing, and envy may well be based on the emotional gain of the rules of conduct that protect equity. It may come from finding that such rules facilitate social interaction. Sense of equity and its rules may come from the emotional gain of social order, and of knowing what to expect, very much along the lines suggested to explain that social values can form concerns in chapter 5. Inequity is emotionally upsetting because it upsets interpersonal order. Sense of justice and desire for revenge both may well come from the emotional turmoil caused by the upsetting of equity caused by unavenged wrongs. Justice lifts sense of equity to a conceptual plane. It indeed is likely to have emotional origins, among which the desire for revenge, as Solomon has suggested.[29]

Correcting Loss or Lack of Power

Willful offense not only upsets equity. It also causes imbalance of power. Willful offense proves the offender's power to do so, and the victim's lack of power to prevent, stop, or annul it. Unequal power changes are established, over and beyond the specific inflicted harm. The offender was able to do with you as he or she willed, handle you, walk over you, use you for his or her purposes. He or she was the actor, you were the object. All this has a time dimension. The unequal power change spells such inequality for the future. It goes beyond the moment.

Power imbalance is not confined to power for physical harm and social subjugation. It extends to power to inflict emotional offense. Such offense often cannot be countered. Unfaithfulness in love or being abandoned, by quitting or by dying, result from unilateral actions about which one's opinion was not asked. One had to suffer them. Interaction brims with power issues. In a simple domestic quarrel, a jibe that one cannot counter scores a point in the power contest that forms the backdrop of many marital relationships.

Sense of power lack or loss may not be due to actual offense. Feeling abandoned when one's partner dies is offense only when the dead one is blamed for it. In social encounters, one may feel slighted and neglected even when the other had no intent to slight or reject, but merely did not notice one's presumed worth or prominence. Resentful vengefulness may still result.

Revenge can effectively diminish or annul such power imbalances. Perpetrating vengeance renders one to be no longer the inferior one, the one to whom things can be done, or a superior one whose power can be contested. Through revenge, one gets even in power or corrects changes in power balance. Regained power, too, projects into the future. One proves oneself intolerant of insult and capable of doing things to others. One is able to stand up to defend one's rights. One demonstrates oneself as one that has to be reckoned with, in a way that is there for everyone to see. That is in fact the main theme of Euripides' Medea play. In her revenge, she usurps the right to not tolerate insult, and to respond to it with violence, which in the Athens of the day was reserved for men.

Desire for revenge indeed seeks to correct one's sense of power and the power relationship. In the mentioned study by Crombag and colleagues,

54% of the subjects who actually took revenge mentioned that as their reason to do so; it was in fact by far the most frequently checked response category.[30] Modification of the power relationship may occur in subtle shape. I remember someone who told about having experienced great triumph when, serving as a witness in the interrogation of a former German security police officer, this took place in the same room of the same prison where that officer had once interrogated and beaten him. Now he was sitting at the other side of the green cloth.

Modifying power relationships occurs among both the powerful and the powerless. It is perhaps most salient in revenge by the powerful. Revenge is an aspect of their arrogance. Baumeister has shown that violence tends to come from high self-esteem, rather than from compensation for low self-esteem, as has sometimes been supposed.[31] It plays in political contexts. "Who do those protesters, challengers, and deviates think they are?" was a common indignant comment by officials to political demonstrations in the second half of the last century. The powerful, of course, can commit revenge with impunity and little risk of re-retaliation. But revenge is also a tool of the weaker. September 11, 2001, is again a salient example. But so was the story of Medea—weak as a foreigner from Barbary, and as a weaker vessel.

Repairing power imbalance is more important to one individual than to another, and to one social group than to another. Cultures where social power is a central value are also those where revenge is prominent: in the "subcultures of violence," for instance, where each arrogance is immediately countered, in traditional Balkan societies and Sardinia, where revenge is institutionalized, and in Renaissance Italy, where the power-and-prestige symbolizing towers of San Geminiano were built over the recurrent revenges for slightings to honor of every kind; and in many Arab and Bedouin societies.[32]

Restoring Pride and Escaping Shame

Concern for power is not the only concern underlying desire for revenge. So is self-esteem. Revenge is a way to escape from shame and restore pride.

That offense to self-esteem awakens desire for revenge is fairly obvious. Self-esteem to a large extent hinges one's social position. That position rests on standing up to others in proving and maintaining it. It thus hinges on responding adequately to their slights. This holds for many societies. One pushes back when pushed away on entering the subway; one may behave rudely when meeting the pusher next time. It holds more prominently in honor societies. Revenge, in those cultures, is institutionalized response to insults to honor.

Revenge and shame are two tips of a seesaw.[33] This can be seen from the different ways in which loss of self esteem can be handled. In a culture that defines such loss as loss of face, shame is prominent; the major ways out are public self-debasement or suicide.

Self-esteem can be hurt in many ways and at many levels. In social-psychological experiments, threat to self-esteem is effectively used to instigate aggression. Retaliation for corrective punishments is more severe than without such threat.[34] Public insults are usually more serious. Rushdie, in describing Pakistani shame culture, tells the story of a man who, in his club, publicly courts a lady. His brother-in-law enters, cuts in, and departs with her. The man, with 10 brutes, then rides to the brother-in-law's country house, has them wreck the place, in the meanwhile shouting from his saddle to his sister, who sits knitting on the porch, that he couldn't have done otherwise since that fool had humiliated him in front of everyone.[35] An example of a different order is described by Mergaree.[36] A man buys a trifle at his front door from a 6-year-old girl. He finds only a dollar in his pocket, and she helpfully suggests that he go look for change. Humiliated by his clumsiness and the small girl's self-assuredness, he invited her in, raped, and strangled her.

Shame and desire for revenge also play at the political level. Sense of humiliation, dreams of retaliation and efforts to ready for revenge were manifest in France after its defeat in the 1870–1871 Franco-Prussian war, as they were in Germany after the 1919 Versailles treaty.[37] Hutu politics in Rwanda quite explicitly aimed to pay back what humiliations they suffered from the dominant Tutsis in the hundred years before 1965, having officially been labeled the inferior caste, both by the Tutsis and their German and Belgian protectors.[38] In the American press during the first war with Iraq, casting off the shame from the Vietnam defeat was an explicit theme. Felt humiliation is what fed the Palestinian intifadas, or at least part of it. Loss of pride, humiliation, and absence of respect for their cultural values were and are prominent themes in anger toward modernization and the West, by Muslim and other traditionalists.[39]

Humiliation: it is debasing people, putting them down through contemptuous treatment. Contempt may be expressed explicitly, or more subtly, by just not taking their human sensitivities and human rights into account. Humiliation takes many forms and degrees: insults in public, social rejection and expulsion, being the target of discrimination, enslavement, debasement by how one is treated or what one is being made to do, not being taken seriously, not being consulted in decisions that touch one's interest, and, most deeply and generally, being treated without the respect due to a human being. It can be directed at an individual as such, or as a member of a particular social group. Humiliation is perpetrated in individual relationships including intimate ones, in family relationships, in group interactions, in hierarchical relationships on the job, and in political interactions.

Not all sense of humiliation is caused by actual humiliation. Feeling humiliated may not come from contemptuous treatment but from resentment, inherent in one's comparing oneself with others and finding them to have superior power or capacities. Superiority of others is difficult to bear. One is stirred to deny it, to explain it as a result of malevolent action, or to blame it on lack of justice or of consideration in respecting honor. Desire to escape from shame may bias toward external attribution and revenge, even when no actual harm was done. Obviously, all shades exist between actual humiliation to efforts to guild the pill of one's incapacities or dependency. Gratitude is a general basis for resentment and for some slumbering readiness to take revenge. Gratitude is an ambivalent emotion. I forgot who said "Why does he hate me? I never did him a favor." And resentment can serve as an excuse for motives that in fact are entirely elsewhere, as in the case of political groups that seek to advance unanswerable claims such as, on occasion, did the Basque ETA and some Palestinian groups.

Offense to self-esteem can go deeper than shame. It can extend deeper than mere power inequality or what the term "loss of self-esteem" usually suggests. It can extend to loss of basic pride, the sense of self-worth and of identity. It occurs when being the object of protracted maltreatment, debasement, or insult, or having been: in child abuse or in a sick marriage, under years of political oppression, and under torture. All these can damage an individual's very sense of personal value. One has been treated as an object, as subhuman, as placed outside the human domain.[40] Miller labeled it *radical humiliation*. It is what cruelty is for, turning a human into a non-human, as that expert in cruelty, Stangl, the head of the Auschwitz and Sobibor extermination camps testified. As he said to Gitta Sereny: it allowed his SS men to accomplish their exacting tasks.[41] It presumably did so by taking away their sense of their victims being human. It threw those into the deepest possible humiliation, and destroyed their humanity at that very basic level of self-determination, of deciding about their movements and about which sensations to experience or avoid, upon which sense of worth and identity rest.

It is difficult to exaggerate the disruptive effects of having been subjected to radical humiliation, including having been called "insects" or "cockroaches," and having been treated as such. The effects appear irreversible. "Anyone who has been tortured, remains tortured…. Anyone who has suffered torture never again will be able to be at ease in the world, the abomination of the annihilation is never extinguished" is what Primo Levi[42] quotes from the Austrian philosopher Jean Améry who (like Levi) committed suicide. The same applies to other severe humiliations. Silver, Boon, and Stones[43] found that victims of sexual child abuse never find peace with what happened to them and often continue until old age to try to make sense of what befell them as children.

The relationships between offense to self-esteem, shame, and vengeance are clear. Both Scheff (1994) and Tajfel[44] have emphasized that offense to feelings of self-worth and self-esteem, in whatever form, leads to "humiliated rage." Why would that be so? Scheff describes the process in terms of unacknowledged shame. The rage comes from efforts to escape from awareness of shame. I think it is simpler and more straightforward than that. The attribution to others, responsible for the transformation, corresponds to what others actually do or did. It results from realistic appraisal of harm perpetrated on purpose. True, such appraisal vacillates when self-worth is struck. In much offense to self-esteem, shame is lurking around the corner.[45] It can hardly be otherwise when self-esteem is undermined.

Revenge can be truly instrumental in restoring self-respect and sense of identity. One is once again the cause of one's acts, one has regained the initiative, and this in the relationship with the person or persons who once took self-esteem away. Vengeance offers distinct proof of effectance, of being a cause of events, as any destructive activity does. That is why it is so important to have perpetrated the revenge oneself, and why destruction by others is not as satisfactory. The gains of revenge, here again, are tangible and real. They even are so deep, so vital, that they are worth serious loss in other respects. "My pain's a fair price." Loss of life may be among these losses, if only because life without self-esteem is loss of face, and thus hardly an option.

Involvement of damage to self-esteem and sensed identity explains a number of aspects of vengeance. It explains the very considerable importance of offenses to one's group in emergence of revenge. Self-esteem and identity are closely dependent on those of the group. One is an American, a Muslim, a Jew. It also explains the duration of vengeful desire. Damage to self-esteem is like the gown that Nessos threw over Hercules. It clings, it envelops, and does not go away. It does not diminish in time, because it colors one's dealings both with oneself and with one's environment. It is resuscitated by any dealing that recalls the humiliating events. Shame, too, is notorious for its incessant, burning duration, and its renewal with each new confrontation with memories of the original event. Successful revenge is perhaps the only way to achieve resolution.

Escape From Pain

The direct motor of vengeful desire is pain: the pain of insult, harm or loss, of having been slighted, of shame, of having been subjected to another person's power or whim, of humiliation. I use the word *pain* on purpose. Physical as well as mental pain, or *anguish*, possess that particular phenomenal quality of urge, physical quality, and the sense that here is no escaping from. Both mental and physical pain pervade the body and makes it cringe. They are probable related in their mechanisms, in that both activate the opiate system.[46]

All vengeful acts are attempts to escape pain. It is revenge's basic pushing power, and explains the persistence of the desire: it continues as long as the pain lasts. It also explains why revenge, if let loose, is immoderate. Its most proximal focus is to get rid of pain, and not to get even. The efforts are often in vain. Whatever the gains of revenge, they cannot undo the harm or truly wipe out the insult, the irreversible loss, or one's crushed sense of worth. The attempts are often as doomed as those of writhing and cringing in physical suffering.

When no meaningful way of escape from pain is in sight, less meaningful ones are sought. If there is offense but no offender, one constructs one. One smashes the kitchen shelf against which one had hit one's head, or the portrait of the one who deserted by dying; one bites the arrow that hit you. Revenge may be cooled upon innocent persons in scapegoating, lynchings of mere suspects, and further gratuitous violence. In the Middle Ages, Jews were massacred in revenge for supposedly having caused the Black Death.[48] Acts of rape have been understood as acts of "vengeance toward all women enacted upon the body of one".[49] The ubiquity of rape in civil wars, as in Colombia and on the Balkan, in Bangladesh and Rwanda, in the Lebanese civil war, illustrates this from another angle.

Or one goes to extremes. One seeks to remove every trace of his or her gains, every recollection of it, and everything that might remind one of the offense. One turns one's anger into hatred, seeking the object's total destruction, removing him or her from the records of history: "Domitian, Vespasian's son, whose monstrous behavior left such a mark upon the Romans that even when they had carved up his whole body they did not feel that they had exhausted their indignation against him: the Senate passed a decree that not even the name of this emperor should remain in inscriptions, nor any statue of portrait of him be preserved".[50]

This push of escape from pain toward extremes of action is evident in the tendency toward extreme violence and cruelty. Endeavor to escape pain may perhaps explain other instances of cruelty than those already mentioned. In cruelty, one fully controls the victim's most inner feelings. One can see each twitch of his or her feelings, and see them as contingent upon one's actions. This explanation of cruelty was proposed by Schopenhauer and by Bain.[51] The sense of power at issue here is of a different sort from the social power involved in power imbalance, mentioned earlier. It is the counterpoint to the power loss of being the victim of torture, and close to the sense of identity deriving from effectance, not implausible as an escape hole from excruciating pain.

WHERE DOES DESIRE FOR REVENGE COME FROM?

Desire for revenge is, I think, a universal emotion, even if certain cultures may condemn or suppress it. Is it also an innate emotion, a product of evolution? I do not think so. It is a cheap hypothesis. Revenge represents a solution to the particular problem of suffering offense at the hands of someone else, and the disturbance of equity. It fits this problem, and one's innate dispositions for anger, in such a manner that individuals may easily discover revenge for themselves, when they have an eye for it. It is thus easily constructed even without models from the outside, on the basis of the anger capacities that include capacity to hurt, threaten, and intimidate, and on the experience that threat is an effective deterrent. Extension of anger to revenge is possible by the cognitive capacities that carry remembering one's earlier suffering and who caused it, and the attribution of intent.

The universal background notwithstanding, desire for revenge and vengeful actions shows huge cultural variation, in its frequency, nature, the attitude taken toward it, and what elicits it. The source for those variations is obvious. Power, power imbalance, offense to self-esteem are not objective facts. Beyond a bottom layer of subjugation and humiliation they depend on cognitive appraisals, in terms of one's concerns, one's prior expectations, and the norms in the social environment. The frequency and nature of desires for revenge depend on the strength of the concerns for power and for self-esteem, and the ideology surrounding them. In some cultures, power status is at stake in every act and encounter; in other cultures, every event is measured in terms of its connotations for honor. Cultures also differ in other concerns that influence the meaning of hostility, such as concerns for group harmony and solidarity.

Finally, they differ in the ideology regarding revenge as such. In honor cultures, revenge upon offense is an obligation. Not taking revenge is deeply shameful, and is so treated by the environment.[52] Grasping opportunities for vengeance, by contrast, is positively honorific. There exist strong pressures toward revenge, and impulse toward taking it thereby gains considerable impetus. In Somalia, Greece, Albania and Corsica, women make up songs at funerals, and "with ferociously blood-thirsty sentiments" urge revenge."[53] This land was never one to reward virtue, but it was always strong in taking revenge and punishing evil. Revenge is its greatest delight and glory.... Revenge is an overpowering and consuming fire. It flares up and burns away every other thought and emotion.... Vengeance ... as the glow in our eyes, the flame in our cheeks, the pounding in our temples.... Vengeance is not hatred, but the wildest, sweetest kind of drunkenness, both for those who must wreak vengeance and for those who wish to be avenged".[54] And see the consequences for propensity for revenge. Black-Michaud[55] quotes a story of a feud in an Albanian mountain tribe in the 19th century. By accident a man killed his friend when he lost control of his axe while working. The victim's family, on the urging of the tribal elders, let itself be compensated by a payment of blood money. However, the victim's son, 6 years old at the time of the accident, revived the feud 20 years later, claiming that he was not bound by an agreement made without his involvement.

The important influence of culture, and culture's operation by way of ideologies and appraisals, mean that revenge, however much universal, is not a necessary or ubiquitous response to offense. Its universality does not imply that it is an automatic answer to offense. There exist alternative ways of responding—alternative solutions to the problem of having been subjected to offense. One may suffer in silence. One may abandon oneself to despair, or fully submit to the aggressor. One may appraise it as loss of face, and feel shame or guilt.[56] One may become angry, harbor a grudge, and leave it at that. Or one may seek recognition of one's suffering by the offender, of their having perpetrated it, and their recognizing their blameworthiness, as endeavored in the South African truth commissions. Blumenfeld (2002) gave a telling account how only such recognition finally satisfied her desire for revenge toward her father's murderer.[57]

Revenge is one solution among several. Additional conditions determine whether desire for revenge ensues, or one of the alternative solutions. Experimental research has explored several of them. One is weakness of factors that inhibit hostility, or strength of those that foster it; those factors include values such as friendship and economic dependence[58] and the likelihood of re-retaliation.[59] Revenge, as said earlier, is much easier for the powerful than for his victims. Conditions further include propensity for appraisals that favor occurrence of anger rather than fear, grief or mere distress, like propensity for attribution of evil intent, of felt unfairness, or of norm violation of the offense and, of course, the magnitude of the offense.[60] Propensities that attenuate vindictiveness presumably include values of forgiveness, nonviolence, and "civilization" in Norbert Elias's terms—civilized restraint of emotions.

LEVELS OF OFFENSE AND LEVELS OF GAIN

The chapter began by stating a puzzle. People seek revenge, whereas revenge does not yield the tangible gains of warding off harm of terminating offense. If my analysis is correct, the gains are there nonetheless. Revenge represents gain at five different levels. They correspond to five levels in the appraisal of offense. The uppermost level of gain is possible deterrence of future offense. The second is restoration of equity in suffering and obligations. The third level is that of restoring sense of power. The fourth level concerns escaping from shame and regaining basic pride. Fifth, there is relief from pain, in any possible way.

Five levels of gain. Not all revenge reaches all five levels. Cool political revenge includes only the first, although for most politicians, soldiers, and policemen, it readily involves the personal concern of putting down upstarts. The tone of former President Nixon, on tapes in which he discussed nuclear attack on North Vietnam with Henry Kissinger, attests to this. Gain in equality of suffering may be the main theme of everyday revenges in erotic jealousy; defending power dominance or restoring power balance may be the main thing in the petty revenges of domestic quarrels. The deeper layers of self-esteem—identity, self efficacy—are perhaps engaged mainly, or only, when offense is pervasive and cuts deeply, as in torture, enslavement, political oppression, or rape.

The gains of revenge are the aims of its action readiness: restoring disturbed balances between oneself and others, and between oneself and one's sense of oneself. Desire for revenge again points to the merit of emphasizing the relational nature of emotions and, in particular, its often interpersonal nature. It pertains to relationships with others, it pertains to aims to establish or modify these relationships, and it calls on representations of actions of, attitudes toward, and images of those others. Desire for revenge is interpersonal, as are the offenses that evoked it. It is not only *my* affair, it is also *his* or *her* affair. It holds him or her accountable. It takes away his or her glory. It annuls or covers *my* shame by *his* or *her* shame, and my pain by theirs. From those representations of the other desire for revenge draws its potency. And all this has major impact because it subsumes his or her acts and mine under a social order that includes us both.

Desire for vengeance aims at repairing various disturbances, and sometimes succeeds in doing so. It thus is "rational" in the sense of the rationality of emotions generally:[61] The desire is appropriate to its conditions. As I already said: Not every individual instance of desire for vengeance is rational; but as such, desire for vengeance is.

All this about the functionality of revenge is based on what people do, and what they say moves them to desire and take revenge. But does it actually help? Are the gains real? Does taking revenge indeed diminish one's pain?

The evidence is mixed and confusing. Only a few investigations have looked for differences in emotions after offense that was or was not followed by taking revenge. People that had taken revenge generally felt satisfied[62] or even triumphant[63] that they had done so. But in no instance did it diminish their pain or hostility toward the offenders, or shorten their emotional upset.[64] There are several possible explanations. One is that all studies, so far, came from students in Western cultures (the United States, the Netherlands) that do not tend to approve of revenge and, probably, did not report on (or ever experienced) truly serious offenses. It may be different among the today's Palestinians, and it may have been different in the United States after September 11, or after Hurricane Katrina in New Orleans. A second is that on the whole the gains remain hidden behind the core fact that the revenge did not annul the offenses. Third, it may be that the gains are short-lived, and that unavenged offenses lead to emotional adjustments that cover up the pains. Finally, functional theory may be wrong. All impression of gain is illusionary. Better let bygones be bygones, as Aristotle suggested.[65] A functional value of emotions like desire for revenge may have existed in the evolutionary past, but no more obtain in industrialized society. I don't believe it. Explorations should proceed and penetrate more deeply, given that vengeance is as much a live issue today as it was before. The issue is, perhaps, not so much how to deal with vengeance, but to recognize its hoped-for gains, and deal with what makes those gains desirable.

VENGEANCE IS MINE, SAITH THE LORD

The harm of vengeance is that revenge itself consists of an offense that calls for new vengeance, the escalatory spiral of violence.

Vengeance can cause more harm than setting off this spiral. It often conflicts with other values of the offended individual or of society. The Oresteia treats exactly that problem. Clytaimnestra killed her husband Agamemnon, among other reasons because he had sacrificed their daughter Iphigeneia. Agamemnon's son Orestes revenged his death on Apollo's orders, and killed his mother. Immediately, the vengeful furies set out to pursue him because of the sin of matricide. The furies acted not only on behalf of morality, but also on behalf of Orestes's own feelings of guilt in having killed his mother. Likewise, Medea hesitated at a vital moment in her revenge because of her love for her children. All this readily translates into contemporary contexts. Revenge conflicts with values of sympathy for the target or his or her kin. It also conflicts with the values of intra-group harmony and solidarity, with those of forgiveness and interpersonal understanding and of seeking civilized solutions. Similar the small scale revenges in personal relationships. Repaying your spouse for an unkindness may sour the current evening.

Revenge thus upsets harmony and the social order in other ways than unavenged evil does. Therefore, generally, desire for revenge is taken out of the hands of the individual or the subgroup. Vengeance is mine, saith the Lord, but since what the Lord saith is being disputed, vengeance is to the law, the state, or the United Nations.

Does this mean that the gains of revenge have to remain entirely out of reach? I do not think so. Not entirely; not in all regards.

Desiring revenge is not the same as taking it. Desiring revenge by itself harms nobody and does not upset society. That is to say: desire for revenge is respectable when an injustice has been done, or humiliation and abuse took place. Desire for revenge belongs to the full human response to offense and injustice. Who is not out for revenge has not been hit by the offense. The desire is not puny, or infantile, or primitive, or pathological, or immature. It is healthy, and the germ for coming to oneself again. Moreover, it is a sign of taking moral justice seriously.[66] This respectability should be recognized.

Surely revenge through the Law is the path of Right. It is wrong when a witness or victim is in court derided as "being out for revenge."[67] The juridical system may well recognize how justified is desire for revenge without seeking to satisfy that desire in meeting out punishment. Who has been offended should be recognized as having a claim to one's pound of flesh, even if the claim cannot be honored.

Of course, not all desire for revenge is respectable. Desire for revenge is as respectable as was the offended concern. Desire for revenge toward an oppressor is not only respectable: it is laudable, even when the vengeful actions were to be condemned.

A main point in the present analysis is that several different concerns underlie the desire for vengeance. I discussed defense of material interests, imbalance of suffering, desire for power and sense of power, concern for self esteem, and the concern to escape from pain. Offense to the different concerns can be kept separate. They should not be confused, both in seeking justification for the desire and in evaluating the vengeful acts. What may be appropriate to one concern may not be to another. Offenders may be physically attacked because of threats to safety that they are claimed to present, whereas the offense was actually to public regard or self esteem, or to one's image of power. A dramatic example was discussed by Scheff:[68] the outbreak of World War I. While that war was in progress, Bertrand Russell called it a "war of vanity": French, British, German and Austrian pride weighed more heavily in the escalation that led to that war than actual threat to national securities and international loyalties. It is of course this confusion of concerns that played in the discussion in the United States of whether Iraq possessed weapons of mass destruction or had close ties to Al Quaida.

NOTES

[1] Crombag, Rassin, & Horselenberg, 2003.
[2] Bible, Exodus 21:24.
[3] Hirzel, 1907-10; Jacoby, 1983
[4] Jacoby, 1983; Scheff, 1994; Solomon, 1989, 1994.
[5] Elster, 1990, p. 155.
[6] Frijda, 1986.
[7] Euripides, Medea, line 1398.
[8] Pearce, 1990.
[9] Rwanda: Braeckman, 1994, Croatia: Glenny, 1992.
[10] Tiede, 1971
[11] Wolfgang, 1958
[12] Fisk, 1991, p. 100
[13] Fisk, 1991, p. 387

[14]Mesquita, personal communication, 1995.
[15]Glenny, 1992.
[16]Quoted from Frank, 1988.
[17]Axelrod, 1984.
[18]Frank, 1988.
[19]Scheff, 1994.
[20]Elster, 1990.
[21]Solomon, 1994, p. 304.
[22]Steinmetz, 1928.
[23]For evidence, see Biglan and Craker, 1982.
[24]Sprang, McNeil, & Wright, 1989.
[25]Euripides, 1966, lines 1354-56, and line 1362.
[26]lines 1132-1133.
[27]Crombag et al., 2003.
[28]W.I. Miller, 1993.
[29]Solomon, 1994.
[30]Crombag et al., 2003.
[31]Baumeister, Smart, & Boden, 1996.
[32]Balkan: Black-Michaud, 1975, Sardinia: Marongiu and Newman, 1987, Italy: Burckhart, 1860/1935, Arab societies: Bourdieu, 1966.
[33]Scheff, 1994.
[34]Caprara, Bonanno, Carrabbia, & Mazzotti, 1988.
[35]Rushdie, 1983.
[36]Mergaree, 1966.
[37]Scheff, 1994.
[38]Braeckman, 1994.
[39]Buruma & Margalit, 2004, Stern 2003.
[40]Margalit, 1996; W. I. Miller, 1993.
[41]Sereny, 1974/1983.
[42]Levi, 1989, p.25.
[43]Silver, Boon, and Stones, 1983.
[44]Scheff, 1994; Tajfel & Turner, 1979.
[45]Scheff, 1994.
[46]Panksepp, 1998.
[47]The examples come from Hall, 1899, and from Steinmetz, 1928.
[48]Girard, 1982.
[49]Jacoby, 1983, p. 193.
[50]Procopius, 1981, p. 78.
[51]Bain, 1876; Schopenhauer, 1819.
[52]Elster, 1990; Miller, 1993.
[53]Black-Michaud, 1975; the songs are mentioned at p. 78.
[54]Djilas, 1958, quoted from Elster, 1990, p. 163/4.
[55]Black-Michaud, 1975.

[56]Mesquita & Markus, 2004.
[57]Blumenfeld, 2002.
[58]e.g., Kanekar, Bulsara, Duarte, & Kolsawalla, 1981.
[59]e.g., Bandura, 1983; Baron, 1977.
[60]Dyck & Rule, 1978; Johnson & Rule, 1986; Ohbuchi & Kambara, 1985; Ohbuchi & Megumi, 1986.
[61]De Sousa, 1988.
[62]Haidt & Sabini, 1999.
[63]Crombag et al., 2003.
[64]Atkinson & Polivy, 1976; Crombag et al., 2003; Haidt & Sabini, 1999.
[65]Elster, 1990.
[66]Solomon, 1994.
[67]Jacoby, 1983, mentions anecdotes of where this happens as, for instance, during a trial of a concentration camp hangman.
[68]Scheff, 1994.

11

Commemorating

People commemorate emotionally significant events from their public and personal past. In the Netherlands, for instance, several commemorations have marked the 1953 flood that took 1,400 lives, and a plane crash in Amsterdam that killed 500 people. The end of World War II is commemorated each year, on May 4, the day the German troops in my country surrendered. The 50th anniversary of the war's end was extensively celebrated in 1994 in France, and in 1995 in the Netherlands, in many towns and villages on the day the Allied troops entered there. Commemoration ceremonies were held in churches, at the foot of war monuments, at places were people had been shot or the executed buried. American and Canadian men of 70 years of age went to Europe and held reunions in the places where they had been as 20-year-old soldiers. Why commemorate?

Can the psychology of emotions contribute its understanding? I think it can; it is worthwhile to try.

Commemoration of public events like disasters and war are usually organized by governments, city councils, or citizen committees. Participation is often massive. Individuals also privately commemorate. They visit the grave of their relatives or friends, or pay homage by going to an other place of memory, such as the plaque on a street corner naming a person who had been shot there. They watch television programs that show the public ceremonies, the past events, or the life and person of commemorated people.

Such commemorations usually have large emotional impact. Television programs broadcast people's expressions of grief during the public ceremonies, visits to the graves of those who died, and visits to the places of disaster or one-time misery. A televised news program reported on the Paris World War II concentration camp Drancy, and showed an ex-prisoner returning for the first time after 50 years. He stepped down from the taxicab that brought him there, looked up at the camp's entrance, and let air escape from his pointed lips in the way you do upon sudden pain.[1]

The commemorations' emotional impact to a large extent rests on the emotions of those who partake and have suffered from the remembered events or lost friends or kin by them. Their emotions are alive, even when the events occurred 50 years ago. They may come to the fore without commemorations or visits to graves. They may come like thieves in the night, unexpectedly, because of some word or image associated to the events. I have friends who describe how they, till the present day, are suddenly brought off balance by seeing or reading something associated with the war. It may just be because of an indirect reference or an allusion to an event that befell him- or herself, or someone else. They describe the sudden and unexpected upsurge of diffuse emotion, a lump in the throat, a feeling of tears behind the eyes, that renders them unable to finish what they were saying or to continue their work. It happens before they even knowing why—what it was that caused it, finding only after the fact that it was an association to former serious and damaging events. Intrusive emotions like these are common among survivors of disasters and other traumas.[2] I knew a woman who a few years ago, then 87 years old, after having suffered a stroke, put a suitcase with a change of clothing in readiness "because at any moment they may come and haul us away." Many survivors, once every few months, wake up, wet with sweat, from a dream of persecution or interrogation. Some of these emotions never go away. "Saturated by numbers, too dry for anyone, also for the poet who feels his throat be throttled, till forty, fifty years after the facts."[3] Or. as Primo Levi wrote on February 4, 1984:

Since then, at an uncertain hour,
That agony returns:
And till my ghastly tale is told,
This heart within me burns.

Once more he sees his companions' faces
Livid in the first faint light

. . . .

'Stand back, leave me alone,
Go away. I haven't ... usurped anyone's bread.
No one died in my place. No one.
Go back into your mist.
It is not my fault if I live and breathe.
4

. . . .

Recollecting the traumatic events, or talking or writing about it, often does not seem to be of real help. Primo Levi, Bruno Bettelheim, Jean Améry all wrote extensively about their experiences of imprisonment and persecution, and all three committed suicide, 20 to 40 years after the events.

Persistence of emotions from events with massive personal impact is not exceptional. It led to proposing the law of conservation of emotional momentum, in chapter 1: the impact of major emotional events does not diminish with the course of time. Time does not heal wounds; it only softens scars. This appears to be the rule, and be in the nature of psychological trauma. Such persistent grief and emotional vulnerability are not illnesses needing cures. Some aspects of grief may require adjustment, as for instance inability to experience it, but persistence of grief as such, and of emotional vulnerability are normal and "healthy." They are not specific to the consequences of war, oppression or disaster. Wortman and Silver[5] described the "myths of coping with loss," that one should be able to get over loss of a child. However, the grief often emerges again and again, over a lifetime. The wounds of incest, too, never heal. Dissociative experiences remain frequent, and a woman to whom incest happened may continue to seek sense in it for the rest of her life.[6] The myth was also held about the consequences of experiences of war, imprisonment, and disaster, until recognition of the posttraumatic stress disorder after the Vietnam war. Before that, psychiatry held the dogma that psychological disturbance that outlasts war experience for more than a few weeks had to be due to prewar vulnerability. When developing the notion of "late injury" for emotional and relational disturbances in ex-concentration-camp inmates, Niederland encountered disbelief and strong opposition.[7]

Why do the emotions remain? Because they are avoided, or not adequately "worked through," in the subsequent years? I do not think so. This way of viewing them, although fairly current, is inadequate. Rather, it is because one has been confronted with events that one cannot assimilate and with consequences that cannot be undone. It is because the confrontations have created debilitating expectancies. Those who experienced them know what evil things humans can do to humans, and that such things did happen and can happen to ourselves and those we love. They not just know this, but the expectancies are in their nerves and muscles, so to speak. They are set to expect that certain things that have happened and been done can happen again and be done again. One moment you and they are there, and the next they have gone, wiped away, as dust.

Commemorations not only follow war and disaster, nor only the evil content of those. For some, the commemorations recall their finest hour. Hardships, danger, taking risks produced intensities of feeling rare in normal times. They required the investment of potentials that one had but that were not often called upon, and that one even may have been unaware of. They involved comradeship, personal closeness and instances of personal self-sacrifice that fill many survivors with lifelong nostalgic memory or shining examples of what humans are also capable. One also commemorates events that produced pride and joy: foundation of one's state, gaining independence, the birth and dead of great men or women who inspired the world, with the birthday of Jesus of Nazareth as a prime example. The celebrated events generate glory, pride, and happiness now. In this chapter I emphasize commemorations of tragedies or the end of tragedies, because they present the more complex questions; but these are celebrated in the wider context that includes commemorating good things.

WHY COMMEMORATE ON SPECIFIC DAYS?
WHY IN CEREMONIAL SHAPE?

The major features of commemorating: that attention is paid to an event or person, that public ceremonies are arranged to do so, and that these ceremonies are held at specific days of the year, and at specific intervals of 1 year, or 5, 10, or 100 years. Commemorations of serious events like war and disasters share this with less serious ones like Columbus's discovery (for Europe) of America, Christmas, and time-linked events like birthdays, wedding days, and New Year's Eve. Each of those involves paying attention to the particular person or event. By fixing occasions for doing so at different days, and with various regular intervals, brings order into the amorphous flow of time, structures it, and marks one's own location in that flow. People appear to wish to do so. It is not a very surprising wish. They have a strong need for orientation in space, just as animals do. It is emotionally important to know where you are, and what and where the objects around you are. Disruption of orientation is a general basis for anxiety, as much or more so than anticipation of particular threats.[8] Plausibly, when the sense of time has also emerged, a need for temporal orientation has emerged with it: a need to punctuate the course of time, to create demarcation points in the continuity, to know how one relates to past events and future options. There is, I think, a desire to own one's past and future that belongs to a general need for orientation.

This seems the core of the desire to commemorate: to define one's location in the continuity of time. That occurs at multiple levels, from placing oneself in the stream of events as such, to placing oneself in their causal and moral nexus. One seeks to define one's position with regard to the past from which one has sprung or has been part of. One then seeks to appropriate one's past, to grasp one's role in past events, or how one was affected by it. Much of that goes well beyond temporal orientation only. Obtaining orientation on one's place in the causal nexus is part of the effort to define oneself: what did one cause and what suffer, what does one blame on others, and what retain as elements of one's fate. This, too, belongs to what commemoration offers, by the images it provides and the values that it assigns: the options to neglect what one does not wish to appropriate, or that one cannot blame on others, for instance. Commemorations indeed are highly selective along those lines. They have blind spots for one's own war crimes, or for negligence that caused a disaster to have been as severe as it was. Atypically, discussions in the foreign press prior to the WWII commemoration did precipitate discussions in the Dutch press of the docile attitudes that made the toll among the Jews in the Netherlands to be the heaviest in western Europe.[9]

Appropriating one's past, placing oneself in the temporal nexus, thereby forms an element in constructing one's identity. It contributes in two ways: by shaping or affirming the identity of one's group, and by accepting or redefining one's membership of that group. It helps shape the sense that this is the group to which I belong, with those particular properties and this history. Individual identity strongly derives from group identity, in particular when one is approached by others as a member of one's group.[10] All this can be articulated by commemorations, or activated if it was already there.

Constructing one's identity as a member of a group also implies coherence with the other individuals that share that past. Shared identity may extend over a large group, or over the small group of the family. One feels a member of a nation, clan, or ethnic group, and at the same or other times a member of one's family, as part of one's identity: I am the daughter or son of such and such, and I carry the imprint of that belongingness. Loss of actual coherence with one's group, its habits and language, therefore is deeply disturbing, since it robs one's sense of self of much of its supporting facts in the environment. The loneliness and threat to conception of self are evident in the suffering caused by being a refugee or displaced person.[11] Coherence is strengthened by participation in joint ceremonies.

The joint activities of commemoration enhance coherence quite directly. They satisfy one's general need to belong. They give it substance in the joint call on memories and the group's myths, the joint emotions and jointly witnessing their public expression, and in freely manifesting one's own engagement in the issues at hand. Obviously, having and avowing a common past, participating in common traditions, jointly recognizing the truth of affirmations about history and value form a group's strongest glue. The bonding goes still further. It focuses bonding to the persons who are the objects of commemoration—the lost or regretted ones—to the people that belonged to the past—one's ancestors—and to those that shared the events in the past—one's fellow victims, fellow fighters, or fellow victors.

The mentioned orientation, identity affirmation, and coherence all are produced by the ceremonial events that characterizes commemorations: shared performance at prescribed moments of time, and socially shared, stylized and conventional activities.

Indeed, that is what commemorations consists of. One does something, something more than merely thinking of the event or person. One stops to reflect, often quite literally so. In commemoration of war and its termination, the street lights come on and the traffic stops, as it was before WWII in Britain on November 11 at 11:00 a.m. and still is in the Netherlands on May 4 at 8:00 p.m. One hoists flags at half-mast. One celebrates, organizes a meeting, reads some relevant text, or puts down flowers. One does this publicly, at the same time as others, and mostly together with others. Quite generally, people assemble in front of a statue or monument, listen to a speech by an official or a band playing the national hymn, watch a wreath being placed.

True enough, public and shared activities are not required for commemorating; nor even prescribed moments of time are. One can go to the cemetery at any day, and lay down flowers at one's own discretion. One can go and stand before one's ancestor shrine, or sit down, reread the letters or open the photograph album. But even private commemorations are mostly performed on selected days: remembering the day a close one died, remembering one's wedding day even after one's partner died, birthdays of lost ones, and putting flowers next to their portraits are examples. Advent of these days can stir and upset one's feelings, sometimes even before one has realized that it is the date's special meaning that does it. Even private commemorations have a conventional, stylized aspect. It is obvious, too, in private commemorations of public events for one's private share in them. One sits alone in one's room on May 4 at 8 p.m., but still looks out of the window to the traffic coming to a stop, or watches the ceremonies on television. Or, all alone, one may bring flowers to the place where one's dear one was killed, at that same communal moment. Even if private, their ceremonies, too, occur in a stylized and communal context. One does something of the kind that others do, and at a moment that others do it, and one knows it.

This means is that commemorations are rituals. Not only holding speeches, raising flags and singing national hymns constitute rituals, but commemorating as such is. A ritual is an occasion that is defined by the social community or by tradition to perform some action that is also defined by the community or tradition, that most often is performed publicly, and that is held to serve a moral or emotional purpose. Rituals in general serve to provide coherence, order, or stability. It often is their only function.[12] They exemplify orientation in time, by constructing a constant through time. They do so by the fixed, recurrent moment of execution and their prescribed or traditional form. In commemoration rituals, they also do this by creating temporal anchorage and reinforcing group identity.

Commemoration rituals provide order and coherence in a still further manner that is of deep emotional significance. Commemoration constitutes the commemorated event as an objective fact of the world. It testifies that it is a true historical event with a social significance and emotional implication of objectively large magnitude. It thereby transforms the recall of the event into something other than the memory of an individual or set of individuals, and lifts it out above the level of thoughts and feelings that only exist within an individual, above that of subjective reactions to an event that anyone can see in his or her own way. Rituals are actions that say things, said Leach.[13] What the ritual actions say—the laying of wreaths, the newspaper articles and TV shows, the speeches and ceremonies—is that the event was a true event, with a true impact and true importance. The person commemorated makes an objective claim on respect and love. Rituals are messages extended to the communal representation of reality. The communal representation, of course, adds to coherence. For a brief moment they dissolve the discontinuities between now and the past, between one individual and others, between those who are there and who are not there any more.

Continuity with the past is achieved by commemoration rituals tending to render the commemorated person or event present again. In this, they resemble funerals, in which the deceased is often addressed in the second person singular, as if he or she could hear it. One describes what kind of person he or she was, his or her qualities. One devotes loving attention, affirming the affection that one held and that continues to exist while, at the same time, affirming that he or she is gone forever. One takes one's leave with a formal last glance at the corpse, watches the interment or how the remains go up in flames. Those flames are sometimes arranged for precisely that purpose, months after the person actually died, as on Bali.

Funerals, by those features, mark the transition of the person's being with us toward his or her not being with us anymore. The deceased has not just departed for a voyage. His or her departure is final and irreversible, and the rituals provide an image to which memory can later return and upon which it can rest. Commemoration rituals show most of these same features. Like funerals, they are transition rituals. They enact the transition of the past into the present. In each public commemoration, one can recognize the three components that define transition rituals: separation, transformation, and aggregation.[14] The separation component enacts how the object of the commemoration was: his or her role, position or mode of life, that has changed. In commemorations, it is marked by presentations of life as it was before the event, the disaster, the termination of the war. In commemorations of the end of WWII, old and gray ex-soldiers parade in their old uniforms; paratroopers return to their drop zones and may get excited because the bridge that they fought for has recently been replaced (the incident occurred in Normandy and was widely reported in the newspapers). Stories told, shown and written revive the anxieties of the times, the misery and fear as well as the comradeships and the intimacy involved in sitting around a wood-shingle stove. The transformation is represented by the mourning, the band playing "The Last Post," the visits to the graves, and the images of liberation. The aggregation component consists of the festive holiday, the fairs, dancing on the city square as in France on July 14 and in Holland on May 5.

Presenting things as they were at the time, or the persons as we knew them, has a double role. On the one hand, it implies that it was so then, not now, the separation component. On the other hand, it provides access to experiencing the bonds that existed, and in some measure makes them come alive again, definitive absence of the persons notwithstanding. Commemorating contributes to the sense that the lost people are in some manner there, among us and with us, and that emotional bonds with them are still in force. Watching the presentations and performing the ritual acts contribute because in doing that, one participates in what happened then. It involves participation in the same sense in which, when extending good wishes for the coming year, on birthdays, one participates in building up that year, if only in the mind and in feeling. One partakes in the imagined future fate of the other. It involves participation in the same elementary sense in which the concept is used to understand religious rituals.[15] In commemoration, one imagines the fate and feelings of the lost persons, and what they had to go through, or the strengths of past heroes. It is a means both to integrate what has happened, and to decrease the distance to the lost individuals. One adds the events to one's store of experience, and also appropriates something that belonged to the past and the remembered person. The memories and the knowledge of the past become more one's possessions.

"Rituals are actions that say things; at the same time they are actions that do things" is the full quote from Leach.[16] Commemorative actions also do things. They profess one's bondedness and loyalty with the commemorated individuals, and one's respect for who they were and for what they may have done. They revive respectful relationships; I will return to what this means. They also enhance solidarity with others for whom the events or persons have similar meaning. Some of these gains of commemoration may strike as superstitious, or as aspects of magical thinking. Commemorating may be experienced as a way to pacify the dead, to prevent them from coming back and haunting us. To fail to commemorate, to forget putting the flowers or recalling the date often feels as if the dead are neglected and one thereby has hurt them. It may have nothing superstitious. Haunt they do, the dead, in emotions and in dreams, as illustrated by Primo Levi's poem.

UNFINISHED BUSINESS

The major motivation for commemoration of disasters and war, though, resides in the continuing emotional impact of the events on those who partook in and suffered from them, on their friends and kin, and on others to whom those events remained or became alive. Why? Because for many of those who lived them, the events represent unfinished business.

The emotions stemming from those past events are still alive and acute, however long the time that passed since. The emotions include panic, not just fearful memories. They include living grief, not just sad recollections. They include stupefaction, complete lack of grasp of what has happened and how it could have happened. There is a poem by a Dutch poet called Leo Vroman with these lines:

> Come tonight with further stories
> that the war's been passing by.
> And then tell them over'nd over,
> Over'nd over I will cry.[17]

And whenever I come across these lines, whenever they enter my thoughts, there is this brief urge to sit down, this brief feeling behind the eyes. In fact, it is not the emotions that have not passed but that the issues that precipitated the emotions are not over. They still are in operation, they still are current affairs.

What can that mean? Let us begin with stupefaction. Perhaps every survivor of mass destruction—of the persecution of the Jews, of the retaliatory killing of all inhabitants of Putten in Holland, Ouradour in France, Lidice in the Czech Republic, the Serbian massacres in Bosnia and the killing frenzies in Rwanda—has experienced this: the naive disbelief, the naive amazement on how it has been or is possible. The stupefied disbelief comes to the surface suddenly, when seeing a picture or reading an allusion. The question returns again and again: how on earth could it have happened. It just does not fit one's conceptions of life and the world.

The events not only do not fit those convictions: they run counter them. Recall what the horrors of war, mass destruction, and tyrannical oppression consisted of. They were of long duration: repeated bombardments, months of anxiety and uncertainty about one's fate and that of children and parents, loss of children and other kin, imprisonment under threat of life, torture, suffering the extremes of humiliation that formed part and parcel of many of the events concerned. They were events in which one had been victim of arbitrariness and the destruction of self-determination and self-identity; recall the quote from Améry given in the last chapter.

Such experiences, in those who suffered them, did shatter the basic convictions about life that enable an individual to live his or her life coherently, and without which this is difficult. Instead, they have created incorrigible expectancies. Those who experienced them know what things humans can do to humans, and that such things can happen to ourselves and those we love. So it has been, and so it can be again.

Research in psychotherapy has shown that emotional expectancies are not made or unmade by information but by living experience or by the living experience of others with whom we identify.[18] Such living experience creates emotional expectancies, and living experiences with having been subjected to major harm erode the central convictions that make life livable. It is the main and major effect of major trauma;[19] it amounts to destruction of the "symbolic universe".[20] The erosion makes the human vessel break, and a broken vessel never again gets whole. One of these convictions is a basic sense of being invulnerable, which makes it possible to face true dangers. It is that conviction that is destroyed when, in war or calamity, one sees one's kin and friends perish—the main cause of "battle fatigue" in war pilots after prolonged courses of duty.[21] Another such conviction is an implicit "belief in a just world",[22] a belief in equity and the belief that what one does, on the whole, meaningfully relates to its consequences. Those beliefs are fundamentally undermined in survivors of concentration camps and similar settings. Most likely, they are also weakened in their children, who may have grasped what evil humans can perpetrate. Of course, one needs no survivor parents to be faced with information on such evil. The media provide images virtually very day. But knowing that it faced your parents, and that it might have faced you, brings it closer home.

How deeply the losses of basic invulnerability and belief in a just world can cut can hardly be overestimated when gauging how much emotions underlying commemorations can be alive. There not only is no end to the devastatingly dolorous memories, there also is no end to the helpless and stupefied search for meaning: how the humiliations, the cruelties, the systematic destructions were ever possible. As already mentioned, continued persistent search for meaning has been found in victims of incest, it is found in survivors of WW-II and, probably, of in survivors of any other war that sported systematic destruction, in the Balkan, Rwanda, the Gulag. There is disbelief, each time that, at unexpected moments, thought happen to stumble upon those events.

And then there is grief. I mentioned what Wortman and Silver found. No death of a loved person ever fully becomes a settled fact. The tentacles of love continue to search for their object, the empty place remains, in bed, in feeling, in expectations, as in an ion split away from its molecule. Of course, this is proper to love and not unique for the aftermath of social events like disaster, war, and oppression. However, the scale of the unfinishedness may find no parallel outside such events. The expectations and sets toward one's social niche, in many cases one's whole social matrix, have been destroyed. The death were lost by other people's acts, by their using their destructive liberty.

The deaths represent unfinished business for additional and subtle reasons. The relationships to the lost ones were not completed. Conflicts with fathers, mothers and children have remained hanging, rendering the losses opaque and troubled; and thought cannot leave the broken-off relationships alone.[23] I had a good friend who, until 20 or 30 years after the war when he died, had a recurrent dream about his parents in Poland saying to one another: Why doesn't Henri write us? Thoughts and dreams continue also because there are interrupted expectations and fantasies on interactions, on the many friends that one could have had. There are forms of readiness closely bound up with personal identity. One feels that losing the emotions, and losing the longings for lost contact and lost lives would mean a last or ultimate surrender to the perpetrators of the evil.

Also, too often the business is unfinished because attachments that were cut off by the events had no natural termination point. Those left behind do not possess an image that can serve as such a termination point, to which the thoughts and feelings can return and find a moment of rest. It is as in mythologies that picture a wandering soul that only could find rest on its gravestone. Remember that the ritual function of funerals is to provide such a termination point. Many survivors from the wars, their children and kin did not bury their beloved. They do not know where these loved ones lie, and a large number of those latter does not lie at all, are dissolved in quicklime or blown away by the wind.

In the face of such events, the past is unfinished not only for those who suffered them, but also for many of their children and friends. For many of them, too, the stupefaction exists. For them, too, the gulf that separates them from their parents cannot be bridged. The unanswerable questions cannot even put: about how it was, about the tormenting uncertainty on how one themselves would have behaved under the circumstances, whether they would have belonged to the good or the wrong side, to the selfish or those who took risks by helping, whether one would have usurped someone's bread. The past wars, like World War II, Rwanda, the Balkans, and former oppression, represent unfinished business for whoever allows the reality and moral issues of those events to reach him or her and become something of a reality.

All this is of course has always been so. It is not unique for the events that we tend to commemorate. The past must have been as unfinished for the survivors of the massacres in France in the 14th century,[24] or of the Arabs by the hands of the Crusaders,[25] for the Aztecs after the *noche triste*, for the Armenians, the survivors of the Gulag, the American Indians, or you name it. In fact, the descendants of these groups may have commemorated and on occasion may still do.

Much of this also applies to the past that is glorified, and that is commemorated in glorification. Often, this, too, is in some sense unfinished, or is made to be so. One feels falling short of the heroes of yore: why are we not as glorious as those who discovered America in 1498, who sought to resist the Turks in 1389, or who made the Mexicans remember the Alamo? Unfinished business thus also is the potent source of vicious nationalism.

THE EMOTIONAL IMPACTS OF COMMEMORATING

One reason to want to commemorate is to make one's past one's own and form part of one's group. Another is to express sympathy with those who suffered, or with the cause that a commemoration may stand for, or to derive pride from former fate. Such motivations must be dominant in commemorations of events from long ago. In Amsterdam, each year, a strike is commemorated that was held during the occupation, in 1941, to protest against the beginning of persecution of the Jews. The number of people that attend has been increasing over the last 10 years, and its majority was not yet born when the war took place; not even their parents were.

But for many, commemorating is a strongly emotional occasion: those who lived the events, or whose parents, or other next of kin did. In commemorations of war and disaster, their emotions can be violent, and mostly involve grief, anger, distress from the recollections, or being moved by remembrances of heroism, friendship, and self-sacrifice. Participants may come to cry, even if they rarely did so during the years intervening between the event and the commemoration. They may be very happy to see old companions again and be among like-minded others.

The emotions that commemorations arouse are often sought and desired. One goes out to participate, to the public square or church to listen to speeches, goes on the street to take part in enjoyment, or watches television. But one often does not desire the emotions. Public ceremonies are confronted with distaste, one shuts off for the emotions, or withdraws into one's home. Usually, the emotions are mixed: they are both sought and disliked.

Dislike has a number of good reasons. One may stand exposed among strangers with one's emotion. Personal inclination to commemorate and public ceremonies may strongly clash. Ceremonial noise may not make recollection easier. More seriously, public ceremony can be felt to serve the glory of the officials or celebrants more than the remembered persons or issues. One may be hurt by vulgarity and pomp: there are things than can only be touched upon with reticence. Many a phrase is hollow when heroism is invoked that might not match what moved the fighters. I know at least of one resistance fighter in World War II who wrote in his farewell to his family, on the eve of his execution: "I have not fallen for a political ideal. I die and fought for myself." And even without all that: the emotions evoked by commemorations are often unbidden; so are the many of the recollections. The emotions may be difficult to manage, and in any case they hurt. Peace of mind is not to be gained, the misery cannot be undone, one does not get the lost ones back. Some things are better left alone.

But the emotional confrontations of commemoration are also avidly sought, and for equally good reasons. One wishes to become whole again and to obtain possession of one's experiences. Many emotional events have emotional significance that is hard to come by. Their emotional potential may merely lurk in the background, or that is signaled by stiffness of feeling, or emptiness of recollection. One would wish to vanquish incapacities of feeling and defensive withdrawals, to lose reticence. One would like to bring the unfinished business to an end, and to integrate the experiences into one's self-image and view of the world. More than anything else: one would like to escape from the solitude of recall. One would like to transmit one's experiences to one's children who, in turn, might then for the first time encounter one's true emotional history. These dilemmas are often described, by the parents, the partners, and the children. Rituals of commemoration may open up relationships and play a role in dealing with emotional events that one has not been able to assimilate.

"Unassimilated emotional events" is an unpleasant and, worse, inappropriate expression; so is "unassimilated emotions," which has often been used in this context. Both sound as if they refer to some sort of troubled digestion. But of course, many events one is simply unable to think of in a balanced manner. Thinking about them causes upset, or upset emerges even without thinking of them, when associations touch them, as in the case of a Jewish woman, survivor of an annihilation camp, who, emerging from surgical anesthesia after an operation, was seized by a panic attack upon seeing the chimney of the hospital's heating plant outside her window. Inversely, one may recall major events without a trace of feeling, which is eerie to the person as well as to those close to him or her.

What is the cause? Why is it that some emotions do not pass by, or do not turn into emotionally balanced memories? Well, I think the answer is simple. War, persecution, disaster, humiliation involve events that just cannot be assimilated or integrated. We, or most of us, have not been made that way, and that is all for the better. In many ways integration and resolving the unfinished business would represent betrayal of one's cause, one's family and friends, one's identity. One does, after all, not suffer from being hurt but from having been faced with immoral ignominy. One not only cannot resolve the business but, many feel, one should not.

Still, one would wish one could assimilate the unassimilable, integrate it, ignominy and all. That is, one would wish to regain being one's owner. One would wish to be capable of more fully confronting one's past, and appropriate it as what it is: having had to deal with evil. There remains unfinished business in that regard, and the yearning to finish it. One would like to insert what has happened and what has befallen us and others into our representation of the world and ourselves, and our place in the web of one's emotional ties and desires and moral perspectives. One would like to regain some trust, restore some measured measure of needed basic convictions, an adjusted symbolic universe.

Rituals of commemoration may offer at least some small possibility of doing so. They can do so because they provide an occasion for emergence and expression of feelings at a moment and in a context that it is safe and acceptable. Their nature as accepted rituals allows the link to the world and to others to be retained. Consonant responses by others facilitate expression and allow one to get around emotional defensiveness. One's emotions can merge into ritual manifestations and into the emotions of others. One stands out less and is less exposed, as wailing women allow during funerals. Ritual thus allows a person to experience emotions that are out of reach at other times. Rituals moreover present the proper context for using culturally presented models for emotional expression and thus save the individual efforts to find a form on his own. The models of stiffly swallowing one's tears, or standing silently for a minute or so, or of wailing loudly and passionately, being held by one's kin, or of throwing oneself upon the coffin, tearing one's clothes, strewing ashes upon one's head, wailing with outstretched arms all come from moulds that the culture offers, in which one can pour one's emotions.

The ritual supports coming to terms with one's emotions—insofar as they achieve that—also that in social context, when one pours out one's emotions, one is accepted in one's role as an emotionally affected person. This has an objectifying consequence. A commemoration ritual, as does any transition ritual, defines the person involved as someone with a particular social role: that of a bereaved person, as a hurt and damaged person, as an unjustly persecuted one, or as someone who has gone through much. The ritual lifts the individual out of his or her subjectivity, places him or her in a particular social role, and accepts him or her in that role, and lessens loneliness.

The ritual emphasizes the emotional significance of the commemorated event, and not so much the emotion. As I already noted, this invests that emotional significance with objectivity. It is about a sad or horrible state of the world, and not about an event causing sadness or horror. The commemoration is not about my feeling, my subjective state, because others, too, focus that event or those events. They, too, are concerned with something terrible that has happened. In commemorations of happy events, this works in similar fashion. They are about grandiose acts, or about a hero or genius, not about my joy or admiration.

By this emphasis, even emotions themselves are experienced in a more objective way. Ritual allows emotions with a certain distance.[26] The emotions become part of a story. They no longer result from pure confrontations with emotionally significant events, but obtain shape, like emotions expressed in the theater. It also feels that way. Rituals share experiencing emotions in that manner with witnessing emotions of other people, in reality or again in the theater. They also share it with telling about one's emotion in a more or less formal public context, outside an intimate relationship. It is not infrequent to hear someone reveal personal experiences during a public lecture that the speaker never told to spouse or children, much to the latter's dismay; telling about the experiences within the intimate relationship had impossible to do and manage. Commemorations indeed form a kind of emotion theater in which one is a player among other players. One slips into a role and in that way does not carry the full burden of going out of one's way to commemorate; and, as I said, one uses sanctioned forms.

One uses that theater for one's emotional ends. One can be a free rider on the emotions of others. It always has been so. "So she spoke, Briseis, weeping, and the other women wept with her, because of Patroclos, but beyond that each for her own miserable fate," wrote Homer.[27] This, too, not only occurs in connection with emotions that hurt. Ritual also allows to come closer to the great happy emotions, like those of sorrowful times: the joys of those times, the friendships, shared dangers, others' risk-taking at one's behalf, the profound joys of liberation and the return of friends believed dead. It is almost indecent to dwell on those joys when there is no public ritual context that legitimates them.

THE PRESENCE OF ABSENTS

Commemoration rituals can contribute in another, and perhaps more essential regard. They can do this through one of their central aspect: attesting affection and showing respect.

It is a remarkable aspect of commemorations. As in funerals, flowers and wreaths are given to the dead, warm words are spoken, signs of respect are made. Why? The dead cannot see or hear us and the flowers cannot give them pleasure; yet, the impulse to pay respect and bring flowers is strong and general. Does it flow from defensive denial? Does it manifest magical thinking? Has culture taught us arbitrary conventions? It is unlikely, because it also happens among those who know that the dead have gone forever. As to culture: loyalty and paying respect to the dead would seem to be a nearly universal phenomenon. Funerals belong to the first signs of homo sapiens.

Neither of these appear to touch the core of what motivates showing affection and respect, and of what one feels while doing so. Something appears involved that is more acute, psychologically more real, more producing a direct emotional yield. The yield, it would seem, is that showing affection and respect serve bonding. They maintain the emotional relationship with the lost persons.

Emotion psychology may be of help here, using the conceptions of action readiness detailed in chapter 2. Showing affection and respect are not merely ritual actions. They consist of actual gestures of actual respect and love and care. Their execution can actually achieve construction or reinstatement of a particular relationship. The nature and inherent aim of these gestures are independent of whether the person to whom they are addressed experiences them or not. Performing them makes actors construct or reenter an emotional relationship of respecting and caring, because they in fact enter a respectful or caring attitude. At least, they do if the actions are performed with conviction: directed at the target, in the body or in the mind, with the aim of care or respect. For respect this is perhaps clearest. Respect implies a relationship of submission; respectful behavior is submission behavior, one's head bent. By executing the behavior one recognizes and accepts the other in his or her respectable qualities and respect-demanding position toward oneself. Giving presents, giving flowers and wreaths fulfils a similar function. Presents and flowers are given, not so much to give pleasure to a person, as to affirm or confirm the other person's respectable position, and at the same time one's own as the bearer of respect and, in the event, of gratitude, of owing something to that person. That is the major meaning of giving presents in social interaction, as Marcel Mauss showed,[28] and recently was elaborated by Miller.[29] There is nothing magical in doing these things when the targets of respect or gratitude are absent. One moves into the respectful position and thereby one's aims and feelings put the targets in the corresponding position.

Showing affection operates in similar fashion. Its ritual demonstrations implement the fact that love has not ended. Love (some love) implies taking care, seeking to make the other be well, and one adopts the state of readiness to do this. Note that in dealing with the living, taking care does not depend on whether or not the target likes it. That is secondary. First, one takes care, period. So with the absent; so with the dead. There is a relationship, there is a streaming out to the object, in which one fulfils a particular relational role: that of parent, or child, or friend, and one need not reflect on the fact that the target is an idea rather than a physical presence. Also, neglect is

incommensurable with fulfilling that role and with those strivings and feelings, and one's being disturbed by one's neglect continues what the action
readiness of love impels one to feel with respect to the living. And there is
good reason not to adopt the critical stance that ask whether all this is useful, or whether the target likes it. Why deprive oneself of having, experiencing, and showing love and care, of reviving an element of the valued
relationship, particularly when ritual offers models for the movements?

In other words, in the behaviors of commemoration one calls up the state of
action readiness of which an emotional attitude consists. Calling it up adds to
integrating the other person into one's emotional repertoire. Having the corresponding emotion is essential for being able to do so: only through an emotion
can the action implement a state of action readiness, an inner attitude.

There are complements to entering such inner attitudes; they have already been hinted at. States of action readiness evoke the nature of their target, as the complement of what they are states of readiness for. States of
action readiness carry elements geared to the nature of their targets, and
implicitly or explicitly evoke expectancies and other representations of the
targets, linked to their role in one's relationships to them. Here, in this context, it concerns their role in the relationships of love or respect: as one's
friend, one's child or parent, one's teacher or pupil or colleague. Entering
such a state of action readiness has a double effect. One is to render the commemorated persons present, in some sense. Rituals engender such presence. The other is to evoke their nature as fulfilling their role in the
relationships—as one's friend, child or parent, teacher, pupil, or colleague.
That includes evoking or recreating images of their mode of being, their
way of behaving toward you, and their way of viewing the world.

And one assimilates one's recollections or recreations of the lost person's
mode of being and way of viewing things, and adds them to one's repertoire of modes of being and viewing things. It adds to, and may enrich,
one's fund of modes of experiencing. This is similar to—in fact, the same
as—the profit of asking advice to one's ancestors at one's ancestor shrine
or—what amounts to almost the same—as wondering how one's father,
teacher, spouse, child or friend, would have approached a given problem.

All this thus is not a matter of emotional denial, illusionary wish-fulfill-
ment, or willing suspense of disbelief. Such explanations do not touch the
core. One does expand; one does assimilate; one becomes enriched. In fact,
commemorations may contribute to acquisition of forms of seeing and experiencing over a broad spectrum. I mentioned the yearly commemoration
of the strike during the war in Amsterdam. Remember: that strike against
the occupation power was a highly risky manifestation of solidarity. In a recent one such commemoration, a young person walked with a banner saying: "For your example." Or, as another young person expressed it when
discussing his participation: "You make parents."

Commemorations satisfy bonding and the need to belong. They also do this by their very structure: public commemoration, of course, represents a very complete and explicit form of social sharing of emotions.[30] Emotions are shared mutually and collectively. Commemorations meet the major functions of emotion sharing: to come to grips with one's emotions, because it alleviates anxiety and insecurity[31] and because it may give some hold for restoring the shattered symbolic universe.[32] Perhaps this latter hope is the decisive factor distinguishing whether one seeks public commemorations or abhors them: Do they indeed provide supporting bondedness with others, or do they leave you alone with your shattered convictions?

Desire for bondedness also goes in a different direction: from those who were not witness to the remembered events to those who were. Our children, that is, the children of the participants in dramatic events, often long to approach their parents, and painfully regret when that appears not possible. It in fact is often is not possible, or at least extremely hard. It is a common complaint among the children of extermination camp survivors: The emotional life of their parents was and remains a closed book.[33] They, the children, remain outside a major period of their parents' life and, moreover, a period that colored the latter's relationship to them. The parents' emotions are inaccessible; the children often feel that their miseries do not count in the face of what their parents have gone through.

This silence and this separation can to some extent be alleviated in commemoration ritual. There is shared experience of emotional meanings that obtained objective form through objectifications, one does not have to look at each other when emotions emerge, and the parents may show some emotion in this objectified context.

COMMEMORATING THE PAST
AND LIVING THE PRESENT

The preceding suggests some background of the commemoration of public events. One wishes to be connected to one's history, one's group, and one's personal past. One wishes to be connected to lost individuals and to others around us who shared the history or with whom one would want to share it. One wishes to come to terms with emotional events that do not allow one's rest.

Is that the full story? It is not likely. Commemoration has its eyes on the past, whereas the present is filled with events that equal or surpass the ones that one commemorates. As I told, in 1995 we celebrated the end of WWII, but what was there to celebrate? Crimes to humanity have continued without interruption, and unrelentingly go on doing so.

Commemoration also flows from motivations that are relevant to the future, though. It becomes clear when realizing what is primarily involved in why the dramatic events so often represent unfinished business. The business touched upon by many commemorations is unfinished because even if it did not produced destruction of basic convictions that make life possible, it did undermine them. It turned them to wishes or obligations, rather than convictions. It left one with the stupefaction of how the events had come to pass, and that they can emerge again, at any moment. There are incessant extreme cruelty, destruction on grand scales, and generally on scales not proportionate to the issues that move the destructors. There is incessant fear, incessant uncertainty about those one loves. There is continuous perpetration of humiliation, and the destruction of the identity of individuals, by individuals and by collectives. There is persecution of defenders of freedom of thought and suppression of such freedom, there are the various forms of intolerance in fascism, racism, nationalism, and fundamentalism.

I several times mentioned the need to give meaning to experienced misery, and to one's past generally. That need usually does not lead to indeed finding such meaning. It may, however, lead to seeing implications of the past for the present and future. Commemorations urge to reflect upon those implications. The aggregation component of the transition ritual gives urgency to the desire to come to grips with the past, and to alert to what may be tried with desperation to ton down strivings for their repetition. This forms the sense of commemorations that go beyond orientation in time and in one's past, to strengthening group identity, and to come to terms with one's own past and present suffering.

In itself, there is nothing beautiful or recommendable in commemorating. There most certainly is in itself nothing attractive in finding a purport of the past for the future. In 1989 the Serbs commemorated their defeat at the hands of the Turks in the Battle of the Blackbird Field, in 1389, and it formed the starting point for the latest Balkan wars.[34] It formed the occasion for rousing Serbian nationalism, under the theme that glorious fighting for the honor of the Serbian people was as possible now as it was six hundred years ago. Flemish nationalists have yearly held the Yzer-pilgrimage, commemorating the 4-year defense of that region that cost thousands of lives, in World War I; it has turned to not much more than affirmations of nationalist animosity. For the Irish Protestants, the Battle of the Boyne, which ensured their domination for some 300 years, has primarily been a recurrent occasion for affirming that dominance. The death of Rudolf Hess was commemorated by extreme rightist groups, as is Hitler's birthday, glorifying Nazi ideology.

It is well to remember that commemoration rituals influence emotions and emotion processing by exactly the same mechanisms as those that lead to collective manifestations of hatred. Mass aggression and blind enthusiasm for a Leader are engendered by the arousal of group identity and collective focusing upon certain emotional issues that in turn lead to emergent group norms. These norms may include that it is acceptable to show grief and that violence is abhorrent, but also that one's group is superior and the others devoid of human dignity, or that violence toward those others is acceptable and even recommendable.[35] Many commemorations are drenched in desires for vengeance, glorification of one's group, and calling glory what were outrages.

It all depends upon the theme in the name of which a commemoration is held. In 1985, WWII was commemorated in (then) West Germany under the device formulated by its president: "It is not at issue to control the past. We know that that is impossible. The past cannot in retrospect be changed or undone. However, who closes the eyes for the past is blind for the future. Who does not want to be reminded of perpetrated inhumanity is vulnerable to its repetition".[36]

What determines the commemoration device? I do not know. Power politics, propaganda, and access to the media may play vital roles So may be the fact whether or not one's group is engaged in current controversy or oppression, real or imagined; so may be a group's morality, or that of its leaders and spokesmen, and the participating individuals. The main point here is that the functions of commemoration ritual at the level of the individuals' emotions and at that of the social reality are two very distinct issues.

NOTES

[1]Trombley, 1995.
[2]Horowitz, 1992.
[3]Frijda, M.H.,1995.
[4]from Levi, 1984 (1988, p. 64.) Part of the poem "The survivor". The first four lines given are from Coleridge's Rhyme of the Ancient Mariner; the remaining lines are from the poem's body.
[5]Wortman & Silver, 1989.
[6]Ensink, 1992; Silver, Boon & Stones, 1983.
[7]Niederland, 1980.
[8]e.g., Mandler, 1984
[9]Ephimenico, 1995; Hilbrink, 1995.
[10]Tajfel, 1981.
[11]Apfelbaum, 2000.
[12]Staal, 1990.
[13]Leach, 1971.
[14]Van Gennep, 1909.
[15]Éliade, 1957.
[16]Leach, 1971, p. 521.

[17]Vroman, 1957, p. 17. From the poem "Vrede" (Peace). Translation present author.
[18]e.g., Bandura 1969.
[19]Janoff-Bullman, 1992.
[20]Rimé, 2005.
[21]Grinker & Spiegel, 1945.
[22]Lerner, 1980.
[23]e.g., Bruggeman, 1994; Epstein, 1979.
[24]e.g., Tuchman, 1978.
[25]Maalouf, 1983.
[26]Scheff, 1977.
[27]Homer, (1950)19, 302.
[28]Mauss, 1914/1957.
[29]W. I. Miller, 1993.
[30]Rimé, 2005.
[31]Schachter, 1959.
[32]Rimé, 2005.
[33]H. Epstein, 1979.
[34]Glenny, 1992.
[35]Rabbie & Lodwijkx, 1987; Van Ginneken, 2003.
[36]Von Weizsäcker, 1985, p. 39.

References

Abu-Lughod, L. (1986). *Veiled sentiments*. Berkeley: University of California Press.

Adams, D. B. (1979). Brain mechanisms for offense, defense and submission. *Behavioral and Brain Sciences 2*, 201–241.

Aharon, I., Etcoff, N., Ariely, D., Chabris, D. F., O'Connor, E., & Breiter, H. C. (2001). Beautiful faces have different reward value: fMRI and behavioral evidence. *Neuron, 32,* 537–551.

Ahles, T. A., Blanchard, E. B., & Leventhal, H. (1983). Cognitive control of pain: Attention to the sensory aspects of the cold pressor stimulus. *Cognitive Therapy and Research, 7,* 159–177.

Ainslie, G. (2001). *Breakdown of will*. Cambridge, England: Cambridge University Press.

Allport, G. W. (1937). *Personality: A psychological interpretation*. New York: Holt.

Anderson, A. K., & Phelps, E. A. (2001). Lesions of the human amygdala impair enhanced perception of emotionally salient events. *Nature, 411,* 305–309.

Angier, N. (1999). *Woman: An intimate geography*. New York: Houghton Mifflin.

Apfelbaum, E. (2000). And now what, after such tribulations? Memory and dislocation in the era of uprooting. *American Psychologist, 55,* 1008–1013.

Aristotle. (1941). *Nicomachean ethics*. New York: Random House.

Armstrong, J. (2002). *Conditions of love: The philosophy of intimacy*. London: Penguin.

Arnold, M. B. (1960). *Emotion and personality* (Vol. 1). New York: Columbia University Press.

Arntz, A., Rauner, M., & Van den Hout, M. (1995). "If I feel anxious, there must be danger": *Ex consequentia* reasoning in inferring danger in anxiety disorders. *Behavioral Research and Therapy, 33*, 917–925.

Asch, S. E. (1952). *Social psychology.* New York: Prentice Hall.

Atkinson, C., & Polivy, J. (1976). Effects of delay, attack, and retaliation on state depression and hostility. *Journal of Abnormal Psychology, 85*, 570–576.

Averill, J. R. (1985). The social construction of emotion: With special reference to love. In G. J. Gergen & K. E. Davis (Eds.), *The social construction of the person* (pp. 89–109). New York: Springer-Verlag.

Axelrod, R. (1984). *The evolution of cooperation.* New York: Basic Books.

Baars, B. J. (1997). *In the theater of consciousness: The workspace of the mind.* New York: Oxford University Press.

Bain, A. (1865). *The emotions and the will.* New York: Appleton.

Bain, A. (1876). The gratification derived from the infliction of pain. *Mind, 1*, 429–431.

Balleine, B. W., & Dickinson, A. (1998). Consciousness—The interface between affect and cognition. In J. Cornwell (Ed.), *Consciousness and human identity* (pp. 57–85). Oxford: Oxford University Press.

Bancroft, J. (1995). Are the effects of androgens on male sexuality noradrenergically mediated? Some consideration of the human. *Neuroscience and Biobehavioral Reviews, 19*, 325–330.

Bandler, R., & Keay, K. A. (1996). Columnar organization in the midbrain periaqueductal gray and the integration of emotional expression. In G. Holstege, R. Bandler, & P. B. Saper (Eds.), The emotional motor system. *Progress in Brain Research*, Vol. 107, 285–300.

Bandura, A. (1969). *Principles of behavior modification.* New York: Holt, Rinehart & Winston.

Bandura, A. (1983). Psychological mechanisms of aggression. In R. G. Geen & E. I. Donnerstein (Eds.), *Aggression: Theoretical and empirical reviews* (Vol 1, pp. 1–40). New York: Academic Press

Banse, R., & Scherer, K. R. (1996). Acoustic profiles in vocal emotion expression. *Journal of Personality and Social Psychology, 70*, 614–636.

Bard, P. (1934). On emotional expression after decortication with some remarks on certain theoretical views. *Psychological Review, 38*, 309–329, 424–449.

Barefoot, J. C., & Straub, R. B. (1974). Opportunity for information search and the effect of false heart rate feedback. In H. London & R. E. Nisbett (Eds.), *Thought and feeling: Cognitive alteration of feeling states* (pp. 107–115). Chicago: Aldine.

Bargh, J. A. (1997). The automaticity of everyday life. In R. S. Wyer (Ed.), *Advances in social cognition* (Vol. 10, pp. 1–61). Mahwah, NJ: Lawrence Erlbaum Associates.

Barlow, D. H. (1986). The causes of sexual dysfunction: The role of anxiety and cognitive interference. *Journal of Consulting and Clinical Psychology, 54*, 140–148.

Baron, R. A. (1977). *Human aggression.* New York: Plenum.

Barrett, L. F. (2005). Feeling is perceiving: Core affect and conceptualization in the experience of emotion. In L. Barrett, P. M. Niedenthal,& P. Winkielman (Eds.), *Emotion: Conscious and unconscious* (pp. 255–286). New York: Guilford.

Barsalou, L. W. (1999). Perceptual symbol systems. *Behavioral and Brain Sciences, 22*, 577–660.

Barsalou, L. W. & Wiemer-Hastings, K. (2005). Situating abstract concepts. In D. Pecher & R. Zwaan (Eds.), *Grounding cognition: The role of perception and action in memory, language, and thought* (pp. 129–163). New York: Cambridge University Press.

Batson, C. D. (1991). *The altruism question. A scientific exploration of why we help one another.* Hillsdale, NJ: Lawrence Erlbaum Associates.

Baumeister, R. F. (1991). *Escaping the self: Alcoholism, spirituality, masochism, and other flights from the burden of selfhood.* New York: Basic Books.

Baumeister, R. F., & Leary, R. M. (1995). The need to belong: Desire for interpersonal attachment as a fundamental human motivation. *Psychological Bulletin, 117*, 497–529.

Baumeister, R. F., Smart, L., & Boden, J. M. (1996). Relation of threatened egotism to violence and aggression: The dark side of high self-esteem. *Psychological Review, 103*, 5–33.

Bayens, F., Eelen, P., & Van den Bergh, O. (1990). Contingency awareness in evaluative conditioning: A case for unaware affective-evaluative learning. *Cognition and Emotion, 4*, 3–18.

Beebe-Center, J. G. (1932). *The psychology of pleasantness and unpleasantness.* New York: Van Nostrand.

Bentham, J. (1823). *An introduction to the principles of morals and legislation* (repr. London: Methuen).

Ben-Ze'ev, A. (2000). *The subtlety of emotions.* Cambridge, MA: MIT/Bradford.

Berger, S. M., & Hadley, S. W. (1975). Some effects of a model's performance on an observer's electromyographic activity. *American Journal of Psychology, 88*, 263–276.

Berkowitz, L., & Harmon-Jones, E. (2004). Toward an understanding of the determinants of anger. *Emotion, 4*, 151–172.

Berlin, I. (1969). *Four essays on liberty.* Oxford, England: Oxford University Press.

Berlyne, D. E. (1960). *Conflict, arousal and curiosity.* New York: McGraw-Hill.

Berridge, K. C. (1999). Pleasure, pain, desire, & dread: Hidden core processes of emotion. In D. Kahneman, D. Diener, & N. Schwarz (Eds.), *Foundations of hedonic psychology: Scientific perspectives on enjoyment and suffering* (pp. 525–557). New York: Sage.

Berridge, K. C. (2003). Pleasures of the brain. *Brain and Cognition, 52*, 106–128.

Berridge, K. C. (2004a). Motivation concepts in behavioral neuroscience. *Physiology and Behavior, 81*, 179–209.

Berridge, K. C. (2004b). Unfelt affect and irrational desire: A view from the brain. In A. R. S. Manstead, N. H. Frijda, & A. Fischer (Eds.), *Feelings and emotions: The Amsterdam Symposium* (pp. 243–262). Cambridge, England: Cambridge University Press.

Berridge, K. C., & Winkielman, P. (2003). What is an unconscious emotion? (The case for unconscious "liking"). *Cognition and Emotion, 17*, 181–211.

Bertenthal, B. L., Campos, J. J., & Kermoian, R. (1994). An epignetic perspective on the development of self-produced locomotion and its consequences. *Current Directions in Psychological Science, 3*, 140–145.

Bhagavad Gita. (1962). (J. Mascaró, Trans.). Harmondsworth, England: Penguin Books.

Biglan, A., & Craker, D. (1982). Effects of pleasant activities manipulation on depression. *Journal of Consulting and Clinical Psychology, 50*, 436–438.

Bindra, D. (1961). Components of general activity and the analysis of behavior. *Psychological Review, 68*, 205–215.

Bindra, D. (1978). How adaptive behavior is produced: A perceptual–motivational alternative to response-reinforcement. *Behavioral and Brain Sciences, 1*, 41–91.

Bingham, H. C. (1928). Sex development in apes. *Comparative Psychology Monographs, 5*, 1–165.

Black-Michaud, J. (1975). *Feuding societies*. Oxford, England: Basil Blackwell.

Blass, E. M., & Shah, A. (1995). Pain reducing properties of sucrose in newborns. *Chemical Senses, 20*, 29–35.

Block, G., & Drucker, M. (1992). *Rescuers: Portraits of moral courage in the Holocaust*. New York: TV Books.

Blumenfeld, L. (2002). *Revenge: A story of hope*. New York: Simon & Schuster.

Bohus, B. (1993). Physiological functions of vasopressin in behavioural and autonomic responses to stress. In P. Burbach & D. de Wied (Eds.), *Brain functions of neuropeptides* (pp. 15–40). Carnforth, England: Parthenon.

Boiten, F. A. (1993a). Component analysis of task related respiratory patterns. *International Journal of Psychophysiology, 15*, 91–104.

Boiten, F. A. (1993b). *Emotional breathing patterns*. Unpublished doctoral dissertation, University of Amsterdam, Department of Psychology.

Boiten, F. A. (1996). Autonomic response patterns during voluntary facial action. *Psychophysiology, 33*, 123–131.

Boiten, F. A., Frijda, N. H., & Wientjes, C. J. E. (1994). Emotions and respiratory patterns: Review and critical analysis. *International Journal of Psychophysiology, 17*, 103–128.

Bolles, R. C. (1970). Species-specific defense reactions. *Psychological Review 77*, 32–48.

Bolles, R. C. (1975). *Theory of motivation* (2nd ed.). New York: Harper & Row.

Bolles, R. C., & Fanselow, M. S. (1980). A perceptual-defensive model of fear and pain. *Behavioral and Brain Sciences, 3*, 291–323.

Bonanno, G. A. (2001). Emotion self-regulation. In T. J. Mayne & G. A. Bonanno (Eds.), *Emotions: Current issues and future directions* (pp. 251–285). New York: Guilford.

Bornstein, R. F. (1989). Exposure and affect. Overview and meta-analysis of research, 1968–1987. *Psychological Bulletin, 106*, 265–289.

Both, S., Everaerd. W., & Laan, E. (2003). Modulation of spinal reflexes by aversive and sexually appetitive stimuli. *Psychophysiology, 40*, 174–183.

Botton, A. de (1994). *Essays in love*. New York: Picador.

Bourdieu, P. (1966). The sentiment of honour in Kabyle society. In J. G. Peristiany (Ed.), *Honour and shame: The values of Mediterranean society* (pp. 191–242). Chicago: University of Chicago Press.

Bouton, M. E. (2005). Behavior systems and the contextual control of anxiety, fear, and panic. In L. Barrett, P. M. Niedenthal, & P. Winkielman (Eds.), *Emotion: Conscious and unconscious* (pp. 205–230). New York: Guilford.

Bradley, M. M., Codispoti, M., Cuthbert, B. N., & Lang, P. J. (2001). Emotion and motivation: I. Defensive and appetitive reactions in picture processing. *Emotion, 1,* 276–298.

Braeckman, C. (1994). *Rwanda: Histoire d'un génocide* [Rwanda: History of a genocide]. Paris: Payard.

Brantôme. (1665). *Les dames galantes* [The gallant ladies]. Edité par Pascal Pia, Paris, Gallimard, 1981.

Brehm, J. W. (1966). *A theory of psychological reactance.* New York: Academic.

Brehm, J. W. (1999). The intensity of emotion. *Personality and Social Psychology Review, 3,* 2–22.

Brehm, J., Brummett, B. H., & Harvey, L. (1999). Paradoxical sadness. *Motivation and Emotion, 23,* 31–44.

Brehm, J., & Self, E. (1989). The intensity of motivation. *Annual Review of Psychology, 40.*

Breugelmans, S. (2004). *Cross-cultural (non)equivalence in emotions. Studies of shame and guilt.* Unpublished doctoral dissertation, University of Tilburg, Tilburg, The Netherlands.

Brickman, P., & Campbell, D. T. (1971). Hedonic relativism and planning the good society. In M. H. Apley (Ed.), *Adaptation-level theory: A symposium* (pp. 287–302). New York: Academic.

Brickman, P., Coates, D., & Janoff-Bulman, R. (1978). Lottery winners and accident victims: Is happiness relative? *Journal of Personality and Social Psychology, 37,* 917–927.

Bridger, W. H., & Mandel, J. J. (1964). A comparison of GSR fear responses produced by threat and electrical shock. *Journal of Psychiatric Research, 2,* 31–40.

Briggs, J. L. (1970). *Never in anger: Portrait of an Eskimo family.* Cambridge, MA: Harvard University Press.

Brooks, V., & Hochberg, J. (1960). A psychophysical study of "cuteness." *Perceptual & Motor Skills, 11,* 205.

Browning, C. R. (1993). *Ordinary men: Reserve Police Battalion 101 and the final solution in Poland.* New York: Harper Perennial.

Bruggeman, J. (1994). The significance of absent objects in the analysis of transgenerational conflicts. *Zeitschrift für psychoanalytische Theorie und Praxis, 9,* 1–11.

Buck, R. (1999). The biological affects: A typology. *Psychological Review, 106,* 301–336.

Bühler, C. (1931). *Kindheit und Jugend* [Childhood and youth]. Leipzig, Germany: Hirzel.

Bühler, K. (1908). Tatsachen und Probleme zu einer Psychologie der Denkvorgänge [Facts and problems for a psychology of thought processes]. *Archive für die gesamte Psychologie, 12,* 1–122.

Burckhart, J. (1860). *Die Kulturgeschichte der Renaissance in Italien* [The history of Renaissance culture in Italy]. Vienna: Phaidon, 1935.

Burke, E. (1757). *A philosophical enquiry into the origin of our ideas of the sublime and beautiful* Oxford, England: Oxford University Press, 1990.

Buruma, I., & Margalit, A. (2004). *Occidentalism.* London: Penguin.

Buss, D. M. (1989). Sex differences in human mate preferences: Evolutionary hypotheses tested in 37 cultures. *Behavioral and Brain Sciences, 12,* 1–49.

Buss, D. M. (1994). *The evolution of desire.* New York: Basic Books.

Buss, D. M., & Schmitt, D. P. (1993). Sexual strategies theory: An evolutionary perspective on human mating. *Psychological Review, 100,* 204–232.

Butler, R. A. (1957). The effect of deprivation of visual incentives on visual exploration motivation in monkeys. *Journal of Comparative and Physiological Psychology, 50,* 177–179.

Byrne, D., Ervin, C. R., & Lamberth, J. (1970). Continuity between the experimental study of attraction and "real life" computer dating. *Journal of Personality and Social Psychology, 16,* 157–165.

Cabanac, M. (1992). Pleasure: The common currency. *Journal of Theoretical Biology, 155,* 173–200.

Cacioppo, J. T., Larsen, J. T., Smith, N. K., & Berntson, G. G. (2004). The affect system: What lurks below the surface of feelings? In A. R. S. Manstead, N. H. Frijda, & A. H. Fischer (Eds.), *Feelings and emotions: The Amsterdam symposium* (pp. 223–242). Cambridge, England: Cambridge University Press.

Camras, L. A. (2000). Surprise! Facial expressions can be coordinative motor structures. In M. D. Lewis & I. Granic (Eds.), *Emotion, development, and self-organisation* (pp. 100–124). New York: Cambridge University Press.

Cantor, N., & Sanderson, C. A. (1999). Life task participation and well-being: The importance of taking part in daily life. In D. Kahneman, E. Diener, & N. Schwarz (Eds.), *Foundations of hedonic psychology: Scientific perspectives on enjoyment and suffering* (pp. 230–243). New York: Sage.

Cappon, D., & Banks, R. (1961). Orientation perception: A review and preliminary study of distortion in orientation perception. *Archives of General Psychiatry, 5,* 380–392.

Caprara, G. V., Bonanno, S., Carrabbia, D., & Mazzotti, E. (1988). Experiments on delayed aggression: A methodological contribution. *Archivo di Psicologia, Neurologia e Psichiatria, 49,* 28–37.

Carpenter, C. R. (1940). A field study in Siam of the behavior and social relations of the gibbon *(Hylobates Lar). Comparative Psychology Monographs, 16,* 1–212.

Carver, C. S., & Scheier, M. F. (1990). Origins and functions of positive and negative affect: A control-process view. *Psychological Bulletin, 97,* 19–35.

Christopher, F. S. & Frandsen, M. M. (1990). Strategies of influence in sex and dating. *Journal of Social and Personal Relationships, 7,* 89–105.

Chwelos, G., & Oatley, K. (1994). Appraisal, computational models, and Scherer's expert system. *Cognition and Emotion, 8,* 245–258.

Clore, G., & Gasper, K. (2000). Feeling is believing. In N. H. Frijda, A. S. Manstead, & S. Bem (Eds.), *Emotions and beliefs: The influence of thinking upon feeling* (pp. 10–44). Cambridge, England: Cambridge University Press.

Clore, G. J., & Ketelaar, T. (1997). Minding our emotions: On the role of automatic, unconscious affect. In R. S. Wyer (Ed.), *Advances in social cognition* (Vol. 10, pp.105–120). Mahwah, NJ: Lawrence Erlbaum Associates.

Clore, G. L. & Ortony, A. (2000). Cognition in emotion: Always, sometimes, or never? In R. D. Lane & L. Nadel (Eds.), *Cognitive neuroscience of emotion* (pp. 24–62b). New York: Oxford University Press.

Clore, G. L., Storbeck, J., Robinson, M. D., & Centerbar, D. (2005). The seven deadly sins of research on affect. In L. Barrett, P. M. Niedenthal,& P. Winkielman (Eds.), *Emotion: Conscious and unconscious* (pp. 348–408). New York: Guilford.

Clynes, M. (1977). *Sentics: The touch of the emotions.* New York: Anchor/Doubleday.

Concise Oxford Dictionary (7th ed.). (1982). Oxford, England: Clarendon Press.

Crombag, H., Rassin, E., & Horselenberg, R. (2003). On vengeance. *Psychology, Crime, and Law, 9,* 333–344.

Crombez, G., Eccleston, C., Boayens, F., & Eelen, P. (1998). Attentional disruption is enhanced by the threat of pain. *Behaviour Research and Therapy, 36,* 195–204.

Csikszentmihalyi, M. (1990). *Flow: The psychology of optimal experience.* New York: HarperCollins.

Csikszentmihalyi, M., & Csikszentmihalyi, I. S. (Eds.). (1988). *Optimal experience: Psychological studies of flow in consciousness.* Cambridge, England: Cambridge University Press.

Curtiss, S. (1977). *Genie: A psycholinguistic study of a modern-day "wild child."* New York: Academic.

Dalgleish, T., & Power, M. (Eds.). (1999). *The handbook of cognition and emotion.* Chichester, England: Wiley.

Damasio, A. (1994). *Descartes error: Emotion, reason, and the human brain.* New York: Putnam.

Damasio, A. (2000). *The feeling of what happens: Body, emotion, and consciousness.* London: Random House.

Damasio, A. (2003). *Looking for Spinoza: Joy, sorrow, and the feeling brain.* London: Heinemann.

Davey, G. C. L. (1995). Preparedness and phobias: Specific evolved associations or a generalized expectancy bias? *Behavioral and Brain Sciences, 18,* 289–325.

Davitz, J. R. (1969). *The language of emotion.* New York: Academic.

Davis, M., & Shi, C. (1999). The extended amygdala: Are the central nucleus of the amygdala and the bed nucleus of the stria terminalis differentially involved in fear versus anxiety? *Annals of the New York Academy of Sciences, 877,* 309–338.

Deci, E. L., & Ryan, R. M. (1985). *Intrinsic motivation and self-determination in human behavior.* New York: Plenum.

De Gelder, B. (2005). Nonconscious emotions: New findings and perspectives on nonconscious facial expression recognition and its voice and whole-body contexts. In L. Barrett, P. M. Niedenthal,& P. Winkielman (Eds.), *Emotion: Conscious and unconscious* (pp. 123–149). New York: Guilford.

De Gelder, B., Snyder, J., Greve, D., Gerard, G., & Hadjikhani, N. (2004). Fear fosters flight: A mechanism for fear contagion when perceiving emotion expressed by a whole body. *Proceedings of the National Academy of Sciences, 101,* 16701–16706.

De Gelder, B., Vroomen, J. H. M., & Pourtois, G. R. C. (2001). Covert affective cognition and affective blindsight. In: B. De Gelder, E. de Haan, & C. Heywood (Eds.), *Out of mind* (pp. 205–221). Oxford, England: Oxford University Press.

De Houwer, J., Baeyens, F., & Field, A. P. (Eds.). (2005). Associative learning of likes and dislikes [Special issue]. *Cognition and Emotion, 19.*

Dekker, J., & Everaerd, W. (1988). Attentional effects on sexual arousal. *Psychophysiology, 25,* 45–54.

De Meijer, M. (1991). *Emotional meaning in large body movements.* Tilburg, The Netherlands: Tilburg University Press.

Dennett, D. C. (1991). *Consciousness explained.* New York: Little, Brown.

Depue, R. A. & Collins, P. F. (1999). Neurobiology of the structure of personality: Dopamine, facilitation of incentive motivation, and extraversion. *Behavioral and Brain Sciences, 22,* 491–569.

Depue, R. A., & Morrone-Strupinsky, J. V. (2005). A neurobehavioral model of affiliative bonding: Implications for conceptualizing a human trait of affiliation. *Behavioral and Brain Science, 28,* 313–350.

Derryberry, D., & Tucker, D. M. (1994). Motivating the focus of attention. In P. M. Niedenthal & S. Kitayama (Eds), *The heart's eye. Emotional influences in perception and attention* (pp. 167–196). San Diego, CA: Academic.

De Sousa, R. (1987). *The rationality of emotions.* Cambridge, MA: MIT Press.

De Sousa, R. (1998). Desire and serendipity. *Midwestern Studies in Philosophy, 12,* 120–134.

De Waal, F. B. M. (1982). *Chimpanzee politics: Power and sex among apes.* London: Jonathan Cape.

De Waal, F. B. M. (1989). *Peacemaking among primates.* Cambridge, MA: Harvard University Press.

De Waal, F. B. M. (1996) *Good natured: The origins of right and wrong in humans and other animals.* Cambridge, MA: Harvard University Press.

De Waal, F. B. M. (2004). On the possibility of animal empathy. In A. S. R. Manstead, N. H. Frijda, & A. H. Fischer (Eds.), *Feelings and emotions: The Amsterdam Symposium* (pp. 381–401). Cambridge, Cambridge University Press.

De Waal, F. & Lanting, F. (1997). *Bonobo: The forgotten ape.* Berkeley: University of California Press.

Diamond, L. M. (2003). What does sexual orientation orient? A biobehavioral model distinguishing romantic love and sexual desire. *Psychological Review, 110,* 173–192.

Dickinson, A., & Balleine, B. (2002). The role of learning in the operation of motivational systems. In R. Gallistel & H. Pashler (Eds.), *Stevens' handbook of experimental psychology* (Vol. 3, pp. 497–562). New York: Wiley.

Diener, E., Diener, M., & Diener, C. (1995). Factors predicting the well-being of nations. *Journal of Personality and Social Behavior, 69,* 851–864.

Diener, E., & Suh, M. (1999). National differences in subjective well-being. In D. Kahneman, E. Diener, & N. Schwarz (Eds.), *Foundations of hedonic psychology: Scientific perspectives on enjoyment and suffering* (pp. 434–452). New York: Sage.

Dijksterhuis, A. (2004). Think different: The merits of unconscious thought in preference development and decision making. *Journal of Personality and Social Behavior, 87,* 586–598.

Dijksterhuis, A., & Aarts, H. (2003). On wildebeests and humans: The preferential detection of negative stimuli. *Psychological Science, 14,* 14–18.

Djilas, M. (1958). *Land without justice.* London: Methuen.

Draghi-Lorenz, R. (2001). *Young infants are capable of non-basic emotions.* Unpublished doctoral dissertation, University of Portsmouth.

Dumas, G. (1933). *Les émotions* [The emotions]. In: G. Dumas (Ed.), *Nouveau Traité de Psychologie. Tome 3,* Paris: Alcan,

Duncan, K. (2003, April 12). Interview in *NRC Handelsblad.*

Duncker, K. (1941). On pleasure, emotion and striving. *Philosophy and Phenomenological Research, 1,* 391–430.

Dyck, R. J. & Rule, B. G. (1978). Effect on retaliation of causal attributions concerning attack. *Journal of Personality and Social Psychology, 36*, 521–529.

Eccleston, C., & Crombez, G. (1999). Pain demands attention: A cognitive–affective model of the interruptive function of pain. *Psychological Bulletin, 125*, 356–366.

Efran, J. S., & Spangler, T. J. (1979). Why grown-ups cry: A two-factor theory and evidence from *The Miracle Worker. Motivation and Emotion, 3*, 63–72.

Eilan, N. (1992). The a priori and the empirical of emotion: Smedslund's "conceptual analysis" of emotion. *Cognition and Emotion, 6*, 457–466.

Ekman, P. (1984). Expression and the nature of emotion. In K. Scherer & P. Ekman (Eds.), *Approaches to emotion* (pp. 319–344). Hillsdale, NJ: Lawrence Erlbaum Associates.

Ekman, P. (1992). An argument for basic emotions. *Cognition and Emotion, 6*, 169–200.

Ekman, P., & Friesen, W. V. (1978). *The Facial Action Coding System.* Palo Alto, CA: Consulting Psychologists Press.

Ekman, P., & Friesen, W. V. (1982). Felt, false and miserable smiles. *Journal of Nonverbal Behavior, 6*, 238–252.

Ekman, P., Friesen, W. V., & Ancoli, S. (1980). Facial signs of emotional experience. *Journal of Personality and Social Psychology, 39*, 1125–1134.

Ekman, P., Friesen, W. V., & Ellsworth, P. (Eds.). (1982). *Emotion in the human face* (2nd ed.). New York: Cambridge University Press.

Ekman, P. E., Friesen, W. V. & Simons, R. C. (1985). Is the startle reaction an emotion? *Journal of Personality and Social Behavior, 49*, 1416–1426.

Éliade, M. (1957). *Le sacré et le profane* [The sacred and the profane]. Paris: Gallimard.

Elias, N. (1939). *Der Prozess der Zivilization* [The civilizing process]. New York: Urizen Books, 1969.

Ellsworth, P. C., Carlsmith, J. M., & Henson, A. (1972). The stare as a stimulus to flight in human subjects: A series of field experiments. *Journal of Personality and Social Psychology, 21*, 302–311.

Ellsworth, P. C., & Scherer, K. R. (2003). Appraisal processes in emotion. In R. Davidson, K. R. Scherer, & H. H. Goldsmith (Eds.), *Handbook of the affective sciences* (pp. 572–596). Mahwah, NJ: Lawrence Erlbaum Associates.

Elster, J. (1990). Norms of revenge. *Ethics, 100*, 155–178.

Elster, J. (1999a). *Alchemies of the mind.* Cambridge, England: Cambridge University Press.

Elster, J. (1999b). *Strong feelings: Emotion, addiction, and human behavior.* Cambridge, MA: MIT Press.

Ensink, B. (1992). *Confusing realities: A study on child sexual abuse and psychiatric symptoms.* Amsterdam: VU University Press.

Ephimenico, S. (1995, March 10). Le souvenir de l'Holocaust en Hollande. *Le Monde.*

Epstein, H. (1979). *Children of the Holocaust.* New York: Putnam.

Epstein, S. (1973). Expectancy and magnitude of reaction to a noxious UCS. *Psychophysiology, 10*, 100–107.

Erickson, C., & Lehrman, D. (1964). Effects of castration of male ring doves upon ovarian activity of females. *Journal of Comparative and Physiological Psychology, 58*, 164–166.

Erlhagen, W. & Schöner, G. (2002). Dynamic field theory of movement preparation. *Psychological Review, 109*, 545–572.

Ervin, F. R., & Sternbach, R. A. (1960). Hereditary insensitivity to pain. *Transactions of the American Neurological Association, 85,* 70–74.

Etcoff, N. (1999). *Survival of the prettiest.* London: Little, Brown.

Euripides. (1966). *Medea* (P. Vellacott, Trans.). Harmondsworth, Middlesex, England: Penguin Books.

Everaerd, W. (1988). Commentary on sex research: Sex as an emotion. *Journal of Psychology and Human Sexuality, 1,* 3–15.

Eysenck, M. W. (1997). *Anxiety and cognition: A unified theory.* London: Psychology Press.

Fanselow, M. S. (1994). Neural organization of the defensive behavior system responsible for fear. *Psychonomic Bulletin & Review, 1,* 429–438.

Farthing, G. W. (1992). *The psychology of consciousness.* Englewood Cliffs, NJ: Prentice Hall.

Fazio, R. H. (2001). On the automatic activation of associated evaluations: An overview. *Cognition and Emotion, 15,* 115–142.

Fest, J. C. (1973). *Hitler.* Berlin, Germany: Propyläen Verlag.

Fisher, H. E. (1992). *Anatomy of love.* New York: Random House.

Fisher, H. E. (2004). *Why we love: The nature and chemistry of romantic love.* New York: Holt.

Fischer, I. (1892). *Mathematical investigations in the theory of values and prices.* New Haven, CT: Yale University Press.

Fisk, R. (1991). *Pity the nation: Lebanon at war.* Oxford, England: Oxford University Press.

Fiske, S. T. (1982). Schema-triggered affect: Applications to social perception. In M. S. Clark & S. T. Fiske (Eds.), *Affect and cognition: The 17th Annual Carnegie Symposium on Cognition* (pp. 55–78). Hillsdale, NJ: Lawrence Erlbaum Associates.

Fiske, S. T. (1987). People's reactions to nuclear war: Implications for psychologists. *American Psychologist, 42,* 207–217.

Fiske, S. T., & Taylor, S. E. (1984). *Social cognition.* New York: Random House.

Flykt, A. (2006). Preparedness for action: Responding to the snake in the grass. *American Journal of Psychology, 119,* 29–43.

Fogel, A. (1993). *Developing through relationships.* New York: Harvester.

Fogel, A., Nwokah, E., Dedo, J. Y., Messinger, D., Dickson, L., & Holt, S. A. (1992). Social process theory of emotion: A dynamic systems approach. *Social Development, 1,* 122–150.

Ford, C. S. & Beach, F. A. (1951). *Patterns of sexual behavior.* New York: Harper.

Frank, R. H. (1988). *Passion within reason: The strategic role of the emotions.* New York: Norton.

Frederick, S., & Loewenstein, G. (1999). Hedonic adaptation. In D. Kahneman, E. Diener, & N. Schwarz (Eds.), *Foundations of hedonic psychology: Scientific perspectives on enjoyment and suffering* (pp. 302–329). New York: Sage.

Fredrickson, B. L. (2001). The role of positive emotions in positive psychology: The broaden-and-build theory of positive emotions. *American Psychologist, 56,* 218–226.

Fredrickson, B. L., & Branigan, C. (2005). Positive emotions broaden the scope of attention and thought-action repertoires. *Cognition and Emotion, 19,* 313–332.

Fredrickson, B. L., & Kahneman, D. (1993). Duration neglect in retrospective evaluations of affective episodes. *Journal of Personality and Social Psychology, 65,* 45–55.

Freeman, W. J. (1999). *How brains make up their minds*. London: Weidenfeld & Nicolson.

Freud, S. (1915). *Triebe und Triebschicksale*. Leipzig, Germany: Fischer Verlag.

Friday, N. (1991). *Women on top: How real life has changed women's sexual fantasies*. New York: Simon & Schuster.

Frijda, M. H. (1995). Unpublished poem.

Frijda, N. H. (1953). The understanding of facial expression of emotion. *Acta Psychologica, 9*, 294–362.

Frijda, N. H. (1956). *De betekenis van de gelaatsexpressie* [The meanings of facial expression]. Amsterdam: Van Oorschot.

Frijda, N. H. (1986). *The emotions*. Cambridge, England: Cambridge University Press.

Frijda, N. H. (1987). *De wetten van het gevoel* [The laws of emotion]. Deventer, The Netherlands: Van Loghum Slaterus.

Frijda, N. H. (1987). Emotion, cognitive structure and action tendency. *Cognition and Emotion, 1*, 115–144.

Frijda, N. H. (1988). The laws of emotion. *American Psychologist, 43*, 349–358.

Frijda, N. H. (1989). Aesthetic emotions and reality. *American Psychologist, 44*, 1546–1547.

Frijda, N. H. (1992). The empirical status of the laws of emotion. *Cognition and Emotion, 6*, 467–478.

Frijda, N. H. (1993). Moods, emotion episodes, and emotions. In M. Lewis & J. M. Haviland (Eds.), *Handbook of emotions* (pp. 381–403). New York: Guilford.

Frijda, N. H. (1993b). The place of appraisal in emotion. *Cognition and Emotion, 7*, 357–388.

Frijda, N. H. (2000). Spinoza and current emotion theory. In Y. Yovel (Ed.), *Desire and affect: Spinoza as psychologist* (pp. 235–264). New York: Little Room.

Frijda, N. H. (2001). Foreword. In A. J. J. M. Vingerhoets & R. R. Cornelius (Eds.), *Adult crying: A biopsychosocial approach* (pp. xiii–xviii). Hove, England: Brunner-Routledge.

Frijda, N. H. (2004). Emotion and action. In A. S. R. Manstead, N. H. Frijda, & A. H. Fischer (Eds.), *Feelings and emotions: The Amsterdam Symposium* (pp. 158–173). Cambridge, England: Cambridge University Press.

Frijda, N. H. (2005, July). *Refined emotions*. Paper presented at the International Society for Research on Emotion meeting, Bari, Italy.

Frijda, N. H., Kuipers, P., & Terschure, E. (1989). Relations between emotion, appraisal, and emotional action readiness. *Journal of Personality and Social Psychology, 57*, 212–228.

Frijda, N. H., Manstead, A. R. S., & Bem, S. (Eds.). (2000). *Emotions and beliefs: The influence of feeling upon thought*. Cambridge, England: Cambridge University Press.

Frijda, N. H., Markam, S., Sato, K., & Wiers, R. (1995). Emotion and emotion words. In J. A. Russell, J.-M. Fernández-Dols, A. S. R. Manstead, & J. Wellenkamp (Eds.), *Everyday conceptions of emotion* (pp. 121–144). Dordrecht, The Netherlands: Kluwer.

Frijda, N. H., Mesquita, B., Sonnemans, J., & van Goozen, S. (1991). The duration of affective phenomena, or emotions, sentiments and passions. In K. Strongman (Ed.), *International review of emotion and motivation* (pp. 187–225). New York: Wiley.

Frijda, N. H., Ortony, A., Sonnemans, J., & Clore, G. (1992). The complexity of intensity. In M. Clark (Ed.), *Review of personality and social psychology* (Vol. 13, pp. 60–89). Beverley Hills, CA: Sage.

Frijda, N. H., & Tcherkassof, A. (1997). Facial expression and modes of action readiness. In J. A. Russell & J. M. Fernández-Dols (Eds.), *The psychology of facial expression* (pp. 78–102). Cambridge, England: Cambridge University Press.

Frijda, N. H., & Zeelenberg, M. (2001). Appraisal: What is the dependent? In A. Schorr, K. R. Scherer, & T. Johnston (Eds.), *Appraisal processes in emotion: Theory, methods, research* (pp. 141–156). Oxford, England: Oxford University Press.

Gallese, V. (2005). Embodied simulation: From neurons to phenomenal experience. *Phenomenology and the Cognitive Sciences, 4*, 23–48.

Gallese, V., & Metzinger, T. (2003). Motor ontology: The representational reality of goals, actions, and selves. *Philosophical Psychology, 16*, 365–388.

Gallistel, C. R. (1980). *The organization of action: A new synthesis.* Hillsdale, NJ: Lawrence Erlbaum Associates.

Gaver, W. W., & Mandler, G. (1987). Play it again Sam: On liking music. *Cognition and Emotion, 1*, 259–282.

Geer, J. H. & Janssen, E. (2000). The sexual response system. In J. Cacioppo, L. Tassinary, & G. Berntson (Eds.), *Handbook of psychophysiology* (pp. 315–341). New York: Cambridge University Press.

Georgopoulos, A. P. (1995). Motor cortex and cognitive processing. In M. S. Gazzaniga (Ed.), *The cognitive neurosciences* (pp. 507–517). Cambridge, MA: MIT Press.

Gibson, J. J. (1979). *The ecological approach to visual perception.* Boston: Houghton Mifflin.

Girard, R. (1982). *Le bouc émissaire* [The scapegoat]. Paris: Grasset.

Gilboa, E., & Revelle, W. (1994). *Duration of emotions: Cognitive and self-report measures.* Unpublished manuscript.

Giroud, F. (2002). *Lou: Histoire d'une femme libre.* Paris: Fayard.

Glass, D. C., & Singer, J. E. (1972). *Urban stress: Experiments on noise and social stressors.* New York: Academic.

Glenny, M. (1992). *The fall of Yugoslavia: The third Balkan war.* Harmondsworth, Middlesex, England: Penguin.

Goffman, E. (1974). *Frame analysis.* New York: Harper & Row.

Goldschmidt, T. (1996). *Darwin's dreampond: Drama in Lake Victoria.* Cambridge, MA: MIT Press.

Goodall, J. (1972). *In the shadow of man.* New York: Dell.

Goodall, J. (1986). *The chimpanzees of Gombe: Patterns of behavior.* Cambridge, MA: Belknap.

Gottlieb, G. (2002). Developmental–behavioral initiation of evolutionary change. *Psychological Review, 109*, 211–218.

Gould, S. J. (1991). Exaptation: A crucial tool for evolutionary psychology. *Journal of Social Issues, 47*, 43–65.

Grammar, K., Flink, B., Oberzaucher, E., Atzmüller, M., Blantar, I., & Mitteroecker, P. (2004). The representation of self reported affect in body posture and body posture simulation. *Collegium Anthropologicum, 28. Suppl 2*, 159–173.

REFERENCES
317

Grammar, K., Kruck, K. B., & Magnusson, M. S. (1998). The courtship dance: Patterns of nonverbal synchronization in opposite-sex encounters. *Journal of Nonverbal Behavior, 22,* 3–29.

Gray, J. A. (1982). *The neuropsychology of anxiety: An enquiry into the functions of the septo-hippocampal system.* Oxford, England: Oxford University Press.

Gray, J. A. (1987). *The psychology of fear and stress* (2nd ed.). Cambridge, England: Cambridge University Press.

Gray, J. A. (1994). Framework for a taxonomy of psychiatric disorder. In S. van Goozen, N. E. van de Poll, & J. A. Sergeant (Eds.), *Essays on emotion theory* (pp. 29–60). Hillsdale, NJ: Lawrence Erlbaum Associates.

Gray, J. A. & McNaughton, N. (1996). The neuropsychology of anxiety: Reprise. In D. A. Hope (Ed.), *Nebraska Symposium on Motivation* (Vol. 43, pp. 61–134). Lincoln: University of Nebraska Press.

Greenberg, J., Solomon, S., & Pyszczynski, T. (1997). Terror management theory of self-esteem and cultural world-views: Empirical assessments and conceptual refinements. In M. P. Zanna (Ed.), *Advances in experimental social psychology* (Vol. 29, pp. 61–139). San Diego, CA: Academic.

Gross, J. J. (1999). Emotion regulation: Past, present, and future. *Cognition and Emotion, 13,* 551–574.

Groves, P. M., & Thompson, R. F. (1970). Habituation: A dual-process theory. *Psychological Review, 77,* 419–450.

Gurr, T. R. (1970). *Why men rebel.* Princeton, NJ: Princeton University Press.

Güth, W., Schmittberger, R., & Schwarze, B. (1982). An experimental analysis of ultimatum bargaining. *Journal of Economic Behavior and Organization, 3,* 367–388.

Haidt, J., & Sabini, J. (1999). *What exactly makes revenge sweet?* Unpublished manuscript.

Hall, G. S. (1899). A study of anger. *American Journal of Psychology, 10,* 516–591.

Hare, R. D. (1976). Psychopathy. In P. H. Venables & N. J. Christie (Eds.), *Research in psychophysiology* (pp. 325–348). London, Wiley.

Harlow, H. F. (1950). Learning and satiation of response in intrinsically motivated complex puzzle performance in monkeys. *Journal of Comparative and Physiological Psychology, 43,* 289–294.

Harlow, H. F. (1958). The nature of love. *American Psychologist, 13,* 673–685.

Harlow, H. F. (1960). The heterosexual affectional system in monkeys. *American Psychologist, 17,* 1–19.

Harlow, H. F. (1969). Age-mate or peer affectional systems. In D. S. Lehrman, R. A. Hinde, & E. Shaw (Eds.), *Advances in the study of behavior* (Vol. 2, pp. 334–384). New York: Academic.

Harmon-Jones, E., & Sigelman, J. (2001). State anger and prefrontal brain activity: Evidence that insult-related left–prefrontal activation is associated with experienced anger and aggression. *Journal of Personality and Social Psychology, 80,* 797–803.

Hatfield, E., & Rapson, L. L. (1993). *Love, sex, and intimacy: Their psychology, biology, and history.* New York: HarperCollins.

Hatfield, E., & Rapson, L. L. (1996). *Love and sex: Cross-cultural perspectives.* Boston: Allyn & Bacon.

Hatfield, E., & Sprecher, S. (1986). *Mirror, mirror: The importance of looks in everyday life*. Albany: State University of New York Press.

Hebb, D. O. (1946). On the nature of fear. *Psychological Review, 53*, 259–276.

Hebb, D. O. (1949). *The organization of behavior*. New York: Wiley.

Hebb, D. O. (1972). *Textbook of psychology* (3d. ed.). Philadelphia: Saunders.

Hermans, D., De Houwer, J., & Eelen, P. (1996). Evaluative decision latencies mediated by induced affective states. *Behaviour Research and Therapy, 34*, 483–488.

Hermans, D., De Houwer, J., & Eelen, P. (2001). A time course analysis of the affective priming effect. *Cognition and Emotion, 15*, 143–166.

Higgins, E. T. (1997). Beyond pleasure and pain. *American Psychologist, 52*, 1280–1300.

Hilbrink, C. (1995). *In het belang van het Nederlandse volk* [In the interest of the Dutch people]. Den Haag, The Netherlands: SDU University.

Hilgard, E. R. (1977). *Divided consciousness: Multiple controls in human thought and action*. New York: Wiley.

Hirzel, R. (1907–1910). Die Talion [The talion]. *Philologos, Zeitschrift für das classische Altertum, 9*(Suppl. 155), 407–482.

Hite, S. (1976). *The Hite report: A nationwide study of female sexuality*. New York: Dell.

Hoebel, B. G., Rada, P. V., Mark, G. P., & Nothos, E. N. (1999). Neural systems for reinforcement and inhibition of behavior: Relevance to eating, addiction, and depression. In D. Kahneman, E. Diener, & N Schwarz (Eds.), *Foundations of hedonic psychology: Scientific perspectives on enjoyment and suffering* (pp. 558–572). New York: Sage.

Höffding, H. (1893). Zur Theorie des Wiedererkennens [To the theory of recognition]. *Philosophische Studien, 8*, 86–96.

Hofstede, G. (1980). *Culture's consequences: International differences in work-related values*. Beverly Hills, CA: Sage.

Holland, P. C. (1992). Occasion setting in Pavlovian conditioning. In D. L. Medin (Ed.), *The psychology of learning and motivation* (Vol. 28, pp. 69–125). New York: Academic.

Holstege, G. (1997). The emotional motor system. *The encyclopedia of human biology* (2nd ed., Vol. 3, pp. 643–660). San Diego, CA: Academic.

Holstege, G., Georgiadis, J. R., Paans, A. M. J., Meiners, L. C., Graaf, F. H. C. E. van der, & Reinders, A. A. T. S. (2003). Brain activation during human male ejaculation. *Journal of Neuroscience, 23*, 9185–9193.

Homer. (1950). *Illiad*. Harmondsworth, Middlesex, England: Penguin Books.

Horowitz, M. J. (1992). Stress response syndromes (3d ed.). Northvale, NJ: Jason Aronson.

Horowitz, M. J. & Becker, S. S. (1973). Cognitive response to erotic and stressful films. *Archives of General Psychiatry, 29*, 81–84.

Hugdahl, K. & Öhman, A. (1977). Effects of instruction on acquisition and extinction of electrodermal responses to fear-relevant stimuli. *Journal of Experimental Psychology: Human Learning and Memory, 3*, 608–618.

Hume, D. (1739/1740). *A treatise of human nature*. Harmondsworth, England: Penguin.

Humphrey, N. (1993). *A history of the mind*. London: Vintage.

Hunt, H. F., & Brady, J. V. (1955). Some effects of punishment and intercurrent "anxiety" on a simple operant. *Journal of Comparative and Physiological Psychology, 48,* 305–310.

Hupka, R. B., Lenton, A. P., & Hutchison, K. A. (1999). Universal development of emotion categories in natural language. *Journal of Personality and Social Psychology, 77,* 247–278

Hutcheson, F. (1728). *An essay on the nature and conduct of the passions and affections.* Menston, England: Scolar, 1972.

Ignatieff, M. (1998). *Isaiah Berlin: A life.* London: Chatto & Windus.

Ikemoto, S., & Panksepp, J. (1999). The role of nucleus accumbens dopamine in motivated behavior: A unifying interpretation with special reference to reward-seeking. *Brain Research Reviews, 31,* 6–41.

Isen, A. M. (2004). Some perspectives on positive feelings and emotions: Positive affect facilitates thinking and problem solving. In A. R. S. Manstead, N. H. Frijda, & A. Fischer (Eds.), *Feelings and emotions: The Amsterdam Symposium* (pp. 263–281). Cambridge, England: Cambridge University Press.

Izard, C. E. (1977). *Human emotions.* New York: Plenum.

Jacobs, W. J., & Nadel, L. (1985). Stress-induced recovery of fears and phobias. *Psychological Review, 92,* 512–533.

Jacoby, S. (1983). *Wild justice.* New York: Harper & Row.

James, W. (1884). What is an emotion? *Mind, 9,* 188–205.

James, W. (1902). *The varieties of religious experience.* Harmondsworth, England: Penguin, 1982.

Jankowiak, W. R., & Fischer, E. E. (1992). A cross-cultural perspective on romantic love. *Ethnology, 31,* 149–155.

Janoff-Bulman, R. (1992). *Shattered assumptions: Towards a new psychology of trauma.* New York: Free Press.

Janssen, E., & Everaerd, W. (1993). Determinants of male sexual arousal. *Annual Review of Sex Research, 4,* 211–245.

Janssen, E., Everaerd, W., Spiering, M., & Janssen, J. (2000). Automatic cognitive processes and the appraisal of sexual stimuli: Towards an information processing model of sexual arousal. *Journal of Sex Research, 37,* 8–23.

Jeannerod, M. (1997). *The cognitive neuroscience of action.* Oxford, England: Blackwell.

Jennings, H. S. (1904). *Behavior of the lower organisms.* New York: Columbia University Press.

Johnson, T. E., & Rule, B. G. (1986). Mitigating circumstance information, censure, and aggression. *Journal of Personality and Social Psychology, 50,* 537–542.

Johnson-Laird, P. N., & Oatley, K. (1989). The language of emotions: An analysis of a semantic field. *Cognition and Emotion, 3,* 81–124.

Johnstone, T., & Scherer, K. R. (2000). Vocal communication of emotion. In M. Lewis & J. M. Haviland (Eds.), *Handbook of emotions* (2nd ed., pp. 220–235). New York: Guilford.

Jones, D. M., & Hill, K. (1993). Criteria of facial attractiveness in five populations. *Human Nature, 4,* 271–296.

Kagan, J. (1994). *Galen's prophecy: Temperament in human nature.* New York: Basic Books.

Kahneman, D. (1999). Objective happiness. In D. Kahneman, E. Diener,& N. Schwarz (Eds.), *Foundations of hedonic psychology: Scientific perspectives on enjoyment and suffering* (pp. 3–25). New York: Sage.

Kahneman, D., & Miller, D. T. (1986). Norm theory: Comparing reality to its alternatives. *Psychological Review, 93,* 136–153.

Kahneman, D., & Tversky, A. (1979). Prospect theory: An analysis of decisions under risk. *Econometrica, 47,* 313–327.

Kahneman, D., & Tversky, A. (1982). The simulation heuristic. In D. Kahneman, P. Slovic, & A. Tversky (Eds.), *Judgment under uncertainty: Heuristics and biases* (pp. 201–208). New York: Cambridge University Press.

Kahneman, D., & Tversky, A. (1984). Choices, values, and frames. *American Psychologist, 39,* 341–350.

Kaiser, S., & Wehrle, T. (2001). Facial expressions as indicators of appraisal processes. In K. R. Scherer, A. Schorr, & T. Johnston (Eds.), *Appraisal processes in emotion: Theory, methods, research* (pp. 285–300). Oxford, England: Oxford University Press.

Kanekar, S., Bulsara, R. M., Duarte, N. T., & Kolsawalla, M. B. (1981). Perception of an aggressor and his victim as a function of friendship and retaliation. *Journal of Social Psychology, 113,* 241–246.

Katz, D. (1944). *Gestaltpsychologie* [Gestalt psychology]. Basel, Switzerland: Schwabe.

Keele, S. W. (1982). Learning and control of coordinated motor patterns: The programming perspective. In J. A. S. Kelso (Ed.), *Human motor behavior: An introduction* (pp. 161–188). Hillsdale, NJ: Lawrence Erlbaum Associates.

Kellerman, J., Lewis, J., & Laird, J. D. (1989). Looking and loving: The effects of mutual gaze on feelings of romantic love. *Journal of Research in Personality, 23,* 145–161.

Keltner, D., & Buswell, B. N. (1997). Embarrassment: Its distinct form and appeasement functions. *Psychological Bulletin, 122,* 250–270.

Keltner, D., Ellsworth, P. C., & Edwards, K. (1993). Beyond simple pessimism: Effects of sadness and anger on social perception. *Journal of Personality and Social Psychology, 64,* 740–752.

Keltner, D., & Haidt, J. (2003). Approaching awe, a moral, spiritual, and aesthetic emotion. *Cognition and Emotion, 17,* 297–314.

Keverne, E. B., & Curley, J. P. (2004). Vasopression, oxytocin and social behaviour. *Current Opinion in Neurobiology, 14,* 777–783.

Kitayama, S., Markus, H. R., & Kurokawa, M. (2000). Culture, emotion, and well-being: Good feelings in Japan and the United States. *Cognition and Emotion, 14,* 93–124.

Kling, K. C., Shibly Hyde, J., Showers, C. J., & Buswell, B. N. (1999). Gender differences in self-esteem: A meta analysis. *Psychological Bulletin, 125,* 470–500.

Knoth, R., Boyd, K., & Singer, B. (1988). Empirical tests of sexual selection theory: Predictions of sex differences in onset, intensity, and time course of sexual arousal. *Journal of Sex research, 24,* 73–89.

Köhler, W. (1929). *Gestalt psychology.* New York: Liveright.

Köhler, W. (1948). *The place of value in a world of fact.* New York: Liveright.

Kortlandt, A. (1962). *Observational study of chimpanzees in the wild.* Motion picture.

Kosfeld, M., Heinrichs, M., Zak, P. J., Fischbacher, U., & Fehr, E. (2005). Oxytocin increases trust in humans. *Nature, 435,* 673–676.

Koster, E. H. W., Crombez, G., Van Damme, S., Verschuere, B., & De Houwer, J. (2004). Does imminent threat capture and hold attention? *Emotion, 4,* 312–317.

Krauss, R. (1930). Ueber graphischen Ausdruck [On graphic expression]. *Zeitschrift für Angewandte Psychologie, 14,* Issue 48.

Kreitler, H., & Kreitler, S. (1972). *Psychology of the arts.* Durham, NC: Duke University Press.

Kroon, R. (1988). *Aanleidingen en structuur van schuldgevoel* [Elicitors and structure of guilt feeling]. Master's thesis, Department of Psychology, University of Amsterdam.

Kruglanski, A. W., & Webster, D. M. (1996). Motivated closing of the mind: "Seizing" and "freezing." *Psychological Review, 103,* 263–283.

Krumhuber, E., Cosker, D., Manstead, A., Marshall, D., & Rosin, P. L. (2005, July). *Temporal dynamics of smiling: Human versus synthetic faces.* Poster presented at the 15th International Society for Research on Emotion meeting, Bari, Italy.

Krumhuber, A., & Kappas, A. (2005). Moving smiles: The role of dynamic components for the perception of the genuineness of smiles. *Journal of Nonverbal Behavior, 29,* 3–24.

Krumhuber, E., Manstead, A. S. R., & Kappas, A. (in press). Temporal aspects of facial displays in person and expression perception: The effects of smile dynamics, head-tilt, and gender. *Journal of Nonverbal Behavior.*

Kubovy, M. (1999). On the pleasures of the mind. In D. Kahneman, E. Diener,& N. Schwarz (Eds.), *Foundations of hedonic psychology: Scientific perspectives on enjoyment and suffering* (pp. 134–154). New York: Russell Sage.

Kuppens, P., Van Mechelen, I., Smits, D. J. M., & De Boeck, P. (2003). The appraisal basis of anger: Specificity, necessity, and sufficiency of components. *Emotion, 3,* 254–269.

Laan, E., & Everaerd, W. (1995a). Determinants of female sexual arousal: Psychophysiological theory and data. *Annual Review of Sex Research, 6,* 32–76.

Laan, E., & Everaerd, W. (1995b). Habituation of female sexual arousal to slides and film. *Archives of Sexual Behavior, 24,* 517–541.

Laan, E., Everaerd, W., Van Bellen, G., & Hanewald, G. (1994). Women's sexual and emotional responses to male- and female-produced erotica. *Archives of Sexual Behavior, 23,* 153–169.

Laborit, H. (1979). *L'inhibition de l'action: Biologie,physiologie, psychologie, sociologie* [From inhibition to action: Biology, psychology, sociology]. (Vol. 1). Paris: Masson.

Lagerspetz, K. (1961). Genetic and social causes of aggressive behavior in mice. *Scandinavian Journal of Psychology, 2,* 167–173.

Lambie, J., & Marcel, A. (2002). Consciousness and emotion experience: A theoretical framework. *Psychological Review, 109,* 219–259.

Lamme, V. A. F. (2003). Why visual attention and awareness are different. *Trends in Cognitive Science, 7,* 12–18.

Landis, C., & Hunt, W. A. (1939). *The startle pattern.* New York: Farrar and Rinehart.

Landman, J. (1993). *Regret: The persistence of the possible.* New York: Oxford University Press.

Lang, P. J. (1993). The three-system approach to emotion. In N. Birbaum & A. Öhman (Eds.), *The structure of emotion* (pp. 18–30). Bern, Switzerland: Hogrefe.

Lang, P. J. (1994). The motivational organization of emotion: Affect–reflex connections. In S. H. M. Van Goozen, N. E. Van de Poll, & J. A. Sergeant (Eds.), *Emotions: Essays on emotion theory* (pp. 61–96). Hillsdale, NJ: Lawrence Erlbaum Associates.

Lang, P. J., Bradley, M. M., & Cuthbert, B. N. (1990). Emotion, attention, and the startle reflex. *Psychological Review, 97,* 377–395.

Langhoff, W. (1935). *Die Moorsoldaten* [The marsh-soldiers]. Stuttgart, Germany: Verlag Neuer Weg.

Langlois, J. H., & Roggeman, L. A. (1990). Attractive faces are only average. *Psychological Science, 1,* 115–121.

Lanzetta, J. T., Cartwright-Smith, J., & Kleck, R. (1976). Effects of nonverbal dissimulation on emotional experience and autonomic arousal. *Journal of Personality and Social Psychology, 33,* 354–370.

Larsen, J. T., McGraw, P., & Cacioppo, J. T. (2001). Can people feel happy and sad at the same time? *Journal of Personality and Social Psychology, 81,* 684–696.

Larsen, R. J., & Diener, E. (1987). Affect intensity as an individual difference characteristic: A review. *Journal of Research in Personality 21,* 1–39.

Lazarus, R. S. (1966). *Psychological stress and the coping process.* New York: McGraw-Hill.

Lazarus, R. S. (1991). *Emotions and adaptation.* New York: Oxford University Press.

Lazarus, R. S., & Folkman, S. (1984). *Stress, appraisal and coping.* New York: Springer.

Leach, E. (1971). Ritual. In D. L. Sills (Ed.), *International encyclopedia of the social sciences* (Vol. 13, pp. 521–526). London: Macmillan.

Leary, M. R. (1999). Making sense of self-esteem. *Current Directions in Psychological Science, 8,* 32–35.

LeDoux, J. (1996). *The emotional brain.* New York: Simon & Schuster.

Lehman, D. R., Wortman, C. B., & Williams, A. F. (1987). Long-term effects of losing a spouse or child in a motor vehicle crash. *Journal of Personality and Social Behavior, 52,* 218–231.

Lehmann, A. (1914). *Die Hauptgesetze des menschlichen Gefühlslebens* [The main laws of human feelings]. Leipzig, Germany: Reisland.

Leitenberg, H., & Henning, K. (1995). Sexual fantasy. *Psychological Bulletin, 117,* 469–496.

Lerner, M. (1980). *Belief in a just world.* New York: Plenum.

Leventhal, L., & Scherer, K. (1987). The relationship of emotion to cognition: A functional approach to a semantic controversy. *Cognition and Emotion, 1,* 3–28.

Levey, A. B., & Martin, I. (1990). Evaluative conditioning: Overview and further options. *Cognition and Emotion, 4,* 31–37.

Levi, P. (1984). *Ad ora incerta.* [The survivor]. In P. Levi, *Collected poems* (R. Feldman & B. Swann, Trans.). London: Faber and Faber, 1988.

Levi, P. (1989). *The drowned and the saved* (R. Rosenthal, Trans.). New York: Vintage.

Levy, R. I. (1973). *Tahitians: Mind and experience in the Society Islands.* Chicago: University of Chicago Press.

Lewin, K. (1937). *Towards a dynamic theory of personality.* New York: McGraw-Hill.

Lewis, M. (1992). *Shame: The exposed self.* New York: Free Press.

Lewis, M. D. (1996). Self-organising cognitive appraisals. *Cognition and Emotion, 10,* 1–26.

Lewis, M. D. (2005). Bridging emotion theory and neurobiology through dynamic system modeling. *Behavioral and Brain Sciences, 28,* 105–131.

Lipps, T. (1907). Zur Einfühlung [On empathy]. *Psychologische Untersuchungen, Vol. II,* 73–102.

Loewenstein, G. (1994). The psychology of curiosity: A review and reinterpretation. *Psychological Bulletin, 116,* 75–98.

Lorenz, K. (1937). Über die Bildung des Instinkbegriffs [On the concept of instinct]. *Die Naturwissenschaften, 25,* 289–300.

Lorenz, K. (1952). *King Solomon's ring.* New York: Cromwell.

Lorenz, K., & Tinbergen, N. (1938). Taxis und Instinkthandlung in der Eirollbewegung der Graugans [Taxes and instinctual action in egg-roll-movements of gray geese]. *Zeitschrift für Tierpsychologie, 2,* 1–29.

Lutz, C. (1988). Ethnographic perspectives on the emotion lexicon. In V. Hamilton, G. H. Bower, & N. H. Frijda (Eds.), *Cognitive perspectives on emotion and motivation* (pp. 399–419). Dordrecht, The Netherlands: Kluwer.

Lykken, D. T. (1999). *Happiness: The nature and nurture of joy and contentment.* New York: St. Martin's Griffin.

Maalouf, A. (1983). *Les croisades vues par les Arabes* [The Crusades as seen by the Arabs]. Paris: Éditions J'ai lu.

MacLean, P. (1990). *The triune brain in evolution: Role in palaeocerebral functions.* New York: Plenum.

Malinowski, B. (1929). *The sexual life of savages in North-Western Melanesia.* London: Kegan Paul.

Mandler, G. (1984). *Mind and body: The psychology of emotion and stress.* New York: Norton.

Mandler, G., & Shebo, B. (1983). Knowing and liking. *Motivation and Emotion, 7,* 125–144.

Marcel, A. (1983). Conscious and unconscious perception: An approach to the relations between phenomenal experience and perceptual processes. *Cognitive Psychology, 15,* 238–300.

Marcel, A. (1988). Phenomenal experience and functionalism. In A. Marcel & E. Bisiach (Eds.), *Consciousness in contemporary science* (pp. 121–158). Oxford, England: Oxford University Press.

Margalit, A. (1996). *The decent society.* Cambridge, MA: Harvard University Press.

Margalit, A. (2003). *The ethics of memory.* Cambridge, MA: Harvard University Press.

Mark, V. H., & Ervin, F. R. (1970). *Violence and the brain.* New York: Harper & Row.

Markus, H. R., & Kitayama, S. (1991). Culture and the self: Implications for cognition, emotion, and motivation. *Psychological Review, 98,* 224–253.

Marongiu, P., & Newman, G. (1987). *Vengeance.* Toronga, NJ: Rowman & Littlefield.

Marris, P. (1974). *Loss and change.* New York: Pantheon.

Mascolo, M. F., & Griffin, S. (Eds.). (1998). *What develops in emotional development?* New York: Plenum.

Mauro, R., Sato, K., & Tucker, J. (1992). The role of appraisal in human emotions: A cross-cultural study. *Journal of Personality and Social Psychology, 62,* 301–317.

Mauss, M. (1957). *Essai sur le don* [The gift]. London: Routledge & Kegan Paul. (Original work published 1914)

McGraw, K. M. (1987). Guilt following transgression: An attribution of responsibility approach. *Journal of Personality and Social Behavior, 53,* 247–256.

McDougall, W. (1908). *An introduction to social psychology.* London: Methuen.

McSweeney, F. K., & Swindell, S. (1999). General-process theories of motivation revisited: The role of habituation. *Psychological Bulletin, 125,* 437–457.

Mehrabian, A. (1968). Relationship of attitude to seated posture, orientation, and distance. *Journal of Personality and Social Psychology, 10,* 26–30.

Meinhardt, J., & Pekrun, R. (2003). Attentional resource allocation to emotional events: An ERP study. *Cognition and Emotion, 17,* 477–500.

Meltzoff, A. N. (2002). Elements of a developmental theory of imitation. In A. N. Meltzoff & W. Prinz (Eds.), *The imitative mind: Development, evolution, and brain bases* (pp. 19–41). Cambridge, England: Cambridge University Press.

Meltzoff, A. N., & Moore, M. K. (1989). Imitation in newborn infants: Exploring the range of gestures imitated and the underlying mechanisms. *Developmental Psychology, 25,* 954–962.

Mergaree, E. I. (1966). Undercontrolled and overcontrolled personality types in extreme antisocial aggression. *Psychological Monographs, 80* (Whole No. 613).

Merkelbach, H. L. G. J., de Jong, P. J., Muris, P., & van den Hout, M. A. (1996). The etiology of specific phobias: A review. *Clinical Psychology Review, 16,* 336–361.

Merleau-Ponty, M. (1945). *Phénoménologie de la perception* [Phenomenology of perception]. Paris: Presses Universitaires de France.

Mesquita, B. (1993). *Cultural variations in emotions: A comparative study of Dutch, Surinamese and Turkish people in the Netherlands.* Unpublished doctoral dissertation, University of Amsterdam.

Mesquita, B. (2001a). Emotions as cultural phenomena. In R. J. Davidson, H. Goldsmith, & P. Rozin (Eds.), *Handbook of the affective sciences* (pp. 871–890). Oxford, England: Oxford University Press.

Mesquita, B. (2001b). Emotions in collectivist and individualist contexts. *Journal of Personality and Social Psychology, 80,* 68–74.

Mesquita, B. (2003). Emotions as dynamic cultural phenomena. In R. J. Davidson, K. R. Scherer, & H. H. Goldsmith (Eds.), *Handbook of affective sciences* (pp. 871–890).

Mesquita, B., & Ellsworth, P. C. (2001). The role of culture in appraisal. In K. R. Scherer, A. Schorr, & T. Johnstone (Eds.), *Appraisal processes in emotion: Theory, methods, research* (pp. 233–248). New York: Oxford University Press.

Mesquita, B., & Markus, H. R. (2004). Culture and emotion: Models of agency as sources of cultural variation in emotion. In A. R. S. Manstead, N. H. Frijda, & A. Fischer (Eds.), *Feelings and emotions: The Amsterdam Symposium* (pp. 341–358). Cambridge, England: Cambridge University Press.

Meyer, L. B. (1956). *Emotion and meaning in music.* Chicago: University of Chicago Press.

Meyer, W. U., Reisenzein, R., & Schützwohl, A. (1997). Towards a process analysis of emotions: The case of surprise. *Cognition and Emotion, 21,* 251–274.

Michotte, A. E. (1946). *La perception de la causalité*. [The perception of causality]. New York: Basic Books, 1954.

Milikowski, M., & Elshout, J. J. (1995). What makes a number easy to remember? *British Journal of Psychology, 86,* 537–547.

Miller, D. T. (1999). The norm of self-interest. *American Psychologist, 54,* 1053–1060.

Miller, W. I. (1993). *Humiliation*. Ithaca: Cornell University Press.

Mineka, S., Cook, M., & Miller, S. (1984). Fear conditioning with escapable and inescapable shock: Effects of a feedback stimulus. *Journal of Experimental Psychology: Animal Behavior Processes, 10,* 307–323.

Mineka, S., & Hendersen, R. W. (1985). Controllability and predictability in acquired motivation. *Annual Review of Psychology, 36,* 495–529.

Mineka, S., & Zimbarg, R. (1966). Conditioning and ethological models of anxiety disorders: Stress-in-dynamic-contexts anxiety models. In D. A. Hope (Ed.), *Nebraska Symposium on Motivation, Vol. 43. Perspectives on anxiety, panic, and fear* (pp. 135–210). Lincoln: University of Nebraska Press.

Mithen, S. (1996). *The prehistory of mind: The cognitive origins of art and science*. London: Thames & Hudson.

Montaigne, M. de. (1580). *Essais I* [Essays I]. Paris: Gallimard, Ed.Folio, 1965.

Montgomery, K. C. (1952). Exploratory behavior and its relation to spontaneous alternation in a series of maze exposures. *Journal of Comparative and Physiological Psychology, 45,* 50–57.

Mook, D. G. (1996). *Motivation: The organization of action* (2nd ed.). New York: Norton.

Moors, A., De Houwer, J. (2005). Automatic processing of dominance and submissiveness. *Experimental Psychology, 52,* 296–302.

Moors, A., De Houwer, J., & Eelen, P. (2004). Automatic stimulus–goal comparisons: Support from motivational affective priming studies. *Cognition and Emotion, 18,* 29–54.

Morgan, C. T. (1943). *Physiological psychology*. New York: McGraw-Hill.

Morris, J. S., Öhman, A., & Dolan, R. J. (1998). Modulation of human amygdala activity by emotional learning and conscious awareness. *Nature, 393,* 467–470.

Morris, W. N. (1999). The mood system. In D. Kahneman, E. Diener, & N. Schwarz (Eds.), *Foundations of hedonic psychology: Scientific perspectives on enjoyment and suffering* (pp. 169–189). New York: Sage.

Muchembled, R. (1989). *La violence au village* [Violence in the village]. Brussels: Brepols.

Murphy, F. C., Nimmo-Smith, I., & Lawrence, A. D. (2003). Functional neuroanatomy of emotion: A meta-analysis. *Cognitive, Affective, and Behavioral Neuroscience, 3,* 207–233.

Murphy, S. T. (2000). Feeling without thinking: Affective primacy and the nonconscious processing of emotion. In J. A. Bargh & D. K. Apsley (Eds.), *Unraveling the complexities of social life: A festschrift in honor of Robert B. Zajonc* (pp. 39–54). Washington, DC: American Psychological Association.

Murphy, S. T., & Zajonc, R. B. (1993). Affect, cognition, and awareness: Affective priming with optimal and suboptimal stimulus exposures. *Journal of Personality and Social Psychology, 64,* 723–739.

Murray, H. A. (1938). *Explorations in personality*. New York: Oxford University Press.

Nafe, J. P. (1924). An experimental study of the affective qualities. *American Journal of Psychology, 35,* 507–544.

Narmour, E. (1990). *The analysis and cognition of basic melodic structures: The implication–realization model.* Chicago: University of Chicago Press.

Niedenthal, P. M., Barsalou, L. W., Ric, F., & Krauth-Gruber, S. (2005). Embodiment in the acquisition and use of emotion knowledge. In L. Barrett, P. M. Niedenthal, & P. Winkielman (Eds.), *Emotion: Conscious and unconscious* (pp. 21–50). New York: Guilford.

Niedenthal, P. M., Halberstadt, J. B. & Setterlund, M. B. (1997). Being happy and seeing "happy": Emotional state facilitates visual encoding. *Cognition and Emotion, 11,* 403–432.

Niedenthal, P. M., & Kitayama, S. (Eds.). (1994). *The heart's eye: Emotional influences in perception and attention.* San Diego, CA: Academic.

Niederland, G. W. (1980). *Folgen der Verfolgung. Das Überlebenssyndrom. Seelenmord.* Frankfurt, Germany: Suhrkamp.

Nietzsche, F. (1901). *Der Wille zur Macht* [The will to power]. (W. Kaufman & R. J. Hollingdale, Trans.). New York: Vintage Books, 1968.

Nieuwenhuys, R. (1996). The greater limbic system, the emotional motor system, and the brain. In G. Holstege, R. Bandler, & P. B. Saper (Eds.), The emotional motor system. *Progress in Brain Research, 107,* 551–581.

Nisbett, R. E., & Wilson, T. D. (1977). Telling more than we can know: Verbal reports on mental processes. *Psychological Review, 84,* 231–259.

Numenmaa, T. (1997). *Divine motions and human emotions: Plato's theory of psychic powers.* University of Tampere, Tampere, Finland.

Nussbaum, M. C. (2001). *Upheavals of thought: The intelligence of emotions.* New York: Cambridge University Press.

Oatley, K. (1992). *Best laid schemes: The psychology of emotions.* Cambridge, England: Cambridge University Press.

Oatley, K., & Duncan, E. (1992). Incidents of emotion in daily life. In K. Strongman (Ed.), *International review of studies of emotion* (Vol. 2, pp. 249–294). Chichester, England: Wiley.

Oatley, K., & Jenkins, J. (1996). *Understanding emotions.* Oxford, England: Blackwell.

Oatley, K., & Johnson-Laird, P. (1987). Towards a cognitive theory of emotion. *Cognition and Emotion, 1,* 51–58

Obrist, P. A. (1981). *Cardiovascular psychophysiology: A perspective.* New York: Plenum.

Ohbuchi, K., & Kambara, T. (1985). Attacker's intent and awareness of outcome, impression management, and retaliation. *Journal of Experimental Social Psychology, 21,* 321–330.

Ohbuchi, K., & Megumi, S. (1986). Power imbalance, its legitimacy, and aggression. *Aggressive Behavior, 12,* 33–40.

Öhman, A., Flykt, A., & Esteves, F. (2001). Emotion drives attention: Detecting the snake in the grass. *Journal of Experimental Psychology: General, 130,* 466–478.

Öhman, A., Lundqvist, D., & Esteves, F. (2001). The face in the crowd revisited: A threat advantage with schematic stimuli. *Journal of Personality and Social Psychology, 80,* 381–396.

Öhman, A., & Mineka, S. (2001). Fears, phobias, and preparedness: Toward an evolved module of fear and fear learning. *Psychological Review, 108,* 483–522.

Öhman, A., & Wiens, S. (2004). The concept of an evolved fear module and cognitive theories of anxiety. In A. R. S. Manstead, N. H. Frijda, & A. Fischer (Eds.), *Feelings and emotions: The Amsterdam symposium* (pp. 58–80). Cambridge, England: Cambridge University Press.

Ortony, A., Clore, G., & Collins, A. (1988). *The cognitive structure of emotions.* Cambridge, England: Cambridge University Press.

Ortony, A., & Turner, T. (1990). What's basic about basic emotions? *Psychological Review, 97,* 315–331.

Osgood, C. E., Suci, G. J., & Tannenbaum, P. H. (1957). *The measurement of meaning.* Urbana: University of Illinois Press.

Owren, M. J., & Bachorowski, J.-A. (2000). The evolution of emotional expression: A "selfish-gene" account of smiling and laughter in early hominids and humans. In T. J. Mayne & G. A. Bonanno (Eds.), *Emotions: Current issues and future directions* (pp. 152–191). New York: Guilford.

Owren, M. J., & Rendall, D. (2001). Sound on the rebound: Bringing form and function back to the forefront in understanding nonhuman primate vocal signalling. *Evolutionary Anthropology, 10,* 58–71.

Panksepp, J. (1998). *Affective neuroscience: The foundations of human and animal emotions.* Oxford, England: Oxford University Press.

Panksepp, J., Nelson, E., & Bekkedal, M. (1997). Brain systems for the mediation of social separation-distress and social-reward. *Annals of the New York Academy of Sciences, 87,* 78–100.

Panksepp, J., & Watt, D. (2003). "The ego is first and foremost a body ego": A critical review of Damasio's (2003) *Looking for Spinoza: Joy, Sorrow, and the Feeling Brain. Neuro-Psychoanalysis, 5,* 201–215.

Parducci, A. (1995). *Happiness, pleasure, and judgment.* Mahwah, NJ: Lawrence Erlbaum Associates.

Parkes, C. M. (1972). *Bereavement: A study of grief in adult life.* New York: International Universities Press.

Parkinson, B. (1995). *Ideas and realities of emotion.* London: Routledge.

Parkinson, B. (1999). Relations and dissociations between appraisal and emotion ratings of reasonable and unreasonable anger and guilt. *Cognition and Emotion, 13,* 347–386.

Parkinson, B. (2001). Putting appraisal in context. In K. R. Scherer, A. Schorr, & T. Johnston (Eds.), *Appraisal processes in emotion: Theory, methods, research* (pp. 173–186). Oxford, England: Oxford University Press.

Parkinson, B., Fischer, A., & Manstead, A. R. S. (2005). *Emotion in social relations: Cultural, group, and interpersonal processes.* Hove, England: Psychology Press.

Pearce, J. (1990). *Colombia: Inside the labyrinth.* London: Latin American Bureau.

Pecchinenda, A. (2001). The psychophysiology of appraisals. In K. R. Scherer, A. Schorr, & T. Johnston (Eds.), *Appraisal processes in emotion: Theory, methods, research* (pp. 301–317). Oxford, England: Oxford University Press.

Perper, T., & Fox, V. S. (1980, April). *Flirtation and pick-up patterns in bars.* Paper presented at the meeting of the Eastern Conference of Reproductive Behavior, New York.

Perrett, D. I., Burt, M. D., Penton-Voak, I. S., Lee, K. J., Rowland, D. A., & Edwards, R.(1999). Symmetry and human facial attractiveness. *Evolution and Human Behavior, 20,* 295–307.

Pfaffman, C. (1960). The pleasures of sensation. *Psychological Review , 67,* 253–268.

Phan, K. L., Wager, T. D., Taylor, S. F., & Liberzon, I. (2002). Functional neuroanatomy of emotion: A meta-analysis of emotion activation studies in PET and fMRI. *Neuroimage, 16,* 331–348.

Phelps, E. A. (2005). The interaction of emotion and cognition: Insights from the study of the human amygdala. In L. Barrett, P. M. Niedenthal,& P. Winkielman (Eds.), *Emotion: Conscious and unconscious* (pp. 51–66). New York: Guilford.

Piaget, J. (1936). *La naissance de l'intelligence chez l'enfant* [The birth of intelligence in the child]. Neuchatel: Delachaux & Niestlé.

Piaget, J. (1976). *Le comportement moteur de l'évolution* [Behavior and evolution]. New York: Random House.

Piët, S. (1987). What motivates stuntmen? *Motivation and Emotion, 11,* 195–213.

Planalp, S. (1999). *Communicating emotion: Social, moral, and cultural processes.* Cambridge, England: Cambridge University Press.

Plato. *The collected dialogues of Plato.* (E. Hamilton & H. Cairns, Eds.). Princeton, NJ: Princeton University Press, 1994.

Plutchik, R. (1980). *Emotion: A psychoevolutionary synthesis.* New York: Harper & Row.

Plutchik, R. (2002). *Emotions and life.* Washington, DC: American Psychological Association.

Poffenberger, A. T., & Barrows, B. E. (1924). The feeling value of lines. *Journal of Applied Psychology, 8,* 192.

Pope, L. K., & Smith, C. A. (1994). On the distinct meanings of smile and frowns. *Cognition and Emotion, 8,* 65–72.

Power, M., & Dalgleish, T. (1997). *Cognition and emotion: From order to disorder.* Mahwah, NJ: Lawrence Erlbaum Associates.

Premack, D. (1962). Reversibility of the reinforcement relation, *Science, 136,* 235–237.

Premack, D. (1965). Reinforcement theory. In M. R. Jones (Ed.), *Nebraska Symposium on Motivation* (pp. 123–180). Lincoln: University of Nebraska Press.

Pribram, K. H. (1970). Feelings as monitors. In M. B. Arnold (Ed.), *Feelings and emotions: The Loyola Symposium* (pp. 39–54). New York: Academic.

Prinz, J. J. (2004). *Gut reactions: A perceptual theory of emotion.* New York: Oxford University Press.

Procopius. (1981). *The secret history* (G. A. Williamson, Trans.). Harmondsworth, Middlesex, England: Penguin Books.

Proust, M. (1988). *A la recherche du temps perdu: Sodome et Gomorrhe II* [In search of lost time: Sodom and Gomorrah II]. Paris: Pleiade.

Rabbie, J. M., & Lodewijkx, H. (1987). Individual and group aggression. *Current Research on Peace and Violence, 10,* 91–101.

Reber, R., Winkielman, P., & Schwarz, N. (1998). Effects of perceptual fluency on affective judgments. *Psychological Science, 9,* 45–48.

Reddy, V. (2000). Coyness in early infancy. *Developmental Science, 3,* 186–192.

Regan, P. C. & Berscheid, E. (1999). *Lust: What we know about human sexual desire.* Thousand Oaks, CA: Sage.

Regnault, L. (1990). *La vie quotidienne des pères du désert en Égypte au I'VE sciècle.* Paris: Hachette.

Reisenzein, R. (1994). Pleasure–arousal theory and the intensity of emotions. *Journal of Personality and Social Psychology, 67*, 525–539.

Reisenzein, R. (1995). On Oatley and Johnson-Laird's theory of emotion and hierarchical structures in the affective lexicon. *Cognition and Emotion, 9*, 383–416.

Reisenzein, R. (1996). Emotional action generation. In W. Battmann & S. Dutke (Eds.), *Processes of the molar regulation of behavior* (pp. 151–165). Lengerich: Pabst Science.

Reisenzein, R. (2000). Exploring the strength of association between the components of emotion syndromes: The case of surprise. *Cognition and Emotion, 14*, 1–38.

Reisenzein, R. (2001). Die Allgemeine Hedonistische Motivationstheorie der Sozialpsychologie [The general hedonistic motivation theory of social psychology]. In R. K. Silbereisen & M. Reitzle (Eds.), *Bericht über den 42. Kongress der DGPs in Jena 2000* (pp. 649–661). Lengerich: Pabst Science.

Reisenzein, R., Bördgen, S., & Holtbernd, T. (in press). Evidence for strong dissociation between emotion and facial displays: The case of surprise. *Journal of Personality and Social Psychology,*

Richter, C. P. (1927). Animal behavior and internal drives. *Quarterly Review of Biology, 2*, 307–343.

Rimé, B. (2005). *Emotion et expression* [Emotion and expression]. Paris: Presses Universitaires de France.

Rimé, B., Delfosse, C., & Corsini, S. (2005). Emotional fascination: Responses to viewing pictures of September 11 attacks. *Cognition and Emotion, 19*, 923–932.

Rimé, B., Phillipot, P., Boca, S., & Mesquita, B. (1992). Long-lasting cognitive and social consequences of emotion: Social sharing and rumination. *European Review of Social Psychology, 3*, 225–258.

Rizzolatti, G., Fadiga, L., Fogassi, L., & Gallese, V. (1999). Resonance behaviors and mirror neurons. *Archives Italiennes de Biologie, 137*, 85–100.

Robinson, M. D. (1998). Running from William James' bear: A review of preattentive mechanisms and their contributions to emotional experience. *Cognition and Emotion, 12*, 667–696.

Robinson, M. D., & Clore, G. L. (2002). Belief and feeling: Evidence for an accessibility model of emotional self-report. *Psychological Bulletin, 128*, 934–960.

Rolls, E. T. (1999). *The brain and emotion.* Oxford, England: Oxford University Press.

Rombouts, H. (1992). *Echt verliefd* [Truly in love]. Amsterdam: Boom.

Roseman, I. J. (1984). Cognitive determinants of emotion: A structural theory. In P. Shaver (Ed.), *Review of personality and social psychology: Vol. 5. Emotions, relationships, and health* (pp. 11–36). Beverley Hills, CA: Sage.

Roseman, I. J. (1991). Appraisal determinants of discrete emotions. *Cognition and Emotion, 5*, 161–200.

Roseman, I. J. (2001). A model of appraisal in the emotion system: Integrating theory, research, and applications. In K. R. Scherer, A. Schorr, & T. Johnstone (Eds.),

Appraisal processes in emotion: Theory, methods, research (pp. 68–91). New York: Oxford University Press.

Roseman, I, J., Dhawan, N., Rettek, S. I., Naidu, R. K., & Thapa, K. (1995). Cultural differences and cross-cultural similarities in appraisals and emotional responses. *Journal of Cross-Cultural Psychology, 26,* 23–48.

Roseman, I. J., & Smith, C. A. (2001). Appraisal theory: Overview, assumptions, varieties, controversies. In K. R. Scherer, A. Schorr, & T. Johnstone (Eds.), *Appraisal processes in emotion: Theory, methods, research* (pp. 3–19). New York: Oxford University Press.

Roseman, I. J., Wiest, C., & Swartz, T. S. (1994). Phenomenology, behaviors, and goals differentiate discrete emotions. *Journal of Personality and Social Psychology, 67,* 206–221

Rosen, J. B., & Schulkin, J. (1998). From normal fear to pathological anxiety. *Psychological Review, 105,* 325–350.

Rosenberg, E. L., & Ekman, P. (1994). Coherence between expressive and experiential systems in emotion. *Cognition and Emotion, 8,* 201–229.

Rossiaud, J. (1988). *La prostitution médiévale* (Prostitution in the Middle Ages]. Paris: Flammarion.

Rothbart, M. K. (1973). Laughter in young children. *Psychological Bulletin, 80,* 247–256.

Rothbaum, F., Weisz, J. R., & Snyder, S. S. (1982). Changing the world and changing the self: A two-process model of perceived control. *Journal of Personality and Social Psychology, 42,* 5–37.

Rotteveel, M. (2003). *Affect and action: Contrasting conscious and nonconscious processes.* Academisch proefschrift, Universiteit van Amsterdam.

Rotteveel, M., de Groot, P., Geutskens, A., & Phaf, R. H. (2001). Stronger suboptimal than optimal affective priming? *Emotion, 1,* 348–364.

Rozin, P. (1999). Preadaptation and the puzzles and properties of pleasure. In D. Kahneman, E. Dienper, & N. Schwarz (Eds.), *Well-being: The foundations of hedonic psychology: Scientific perspectives on enjoyment and suffering* (pp. 109–133). New York: Russell Sage.

Rozin, P., Haidt, J., & McCauley, C. R. (2000). Disgust. In M. Lewis & J. M. Haviland (Eds.), *Handbook of emotions* (2nd ed., pp. 637–653). New York: Guilford.

Ruch, W. (1993). Exhilaration and humor. In M. Lewis & J. M. Haviland (Eds.), *Handbook of emotions* (pp. 605–616). New York: Guilford.

Ruch, W. (1995). Will the real relationship between facial expression and affective experience please stand up: The case of exhilaration. *Cognition and Emotion, 9,* 33–58.

Ruckmick, C. A. (1925). The psychology of pleasantness. *Psychological Review, 32,* 30–35.

Rushdie, S. (1983). *Shame.* New York: Knopf.

Russell, B. (1968). *The autobiography of Bertrand Russell* (Vol. 2). London: George Allen and Unwin.

Russell, J. A. (1991). Culture and the categorization of emotions. *Psychological Bulletin, 110,* 426–450.

Russell, J. A. (2003). Core affect and the psychological construction of emotion. *Psychological Review, 110,* 145–172.

Sartre, J. P. (1939). *Esquisse d'une théorie phénomenologique des émotions* [The emotions]. New York: Philosophical Library, 1948.

Schachter, S. (1959). *The psychology of affiliation.* Stanford. CA: Stanford University Press.

Scheff, T. (1977). The distancing of emotion in ritual. *Current Anthropology, 18,* 483–505.

Scheff, T. J. (1994). *Bloody revenge: Emotions, nationalism, and war.* Boulder, CO: Westview.

Scherer, K. R. (1984). On the nature and function of emotion: A component process approach. In K. R. Scherer & P. Ekman (Eds.), *Approaches to emotion* (pp. 293–317). Hillsdale, NJ: Lawrence Erlbaum Associates.

Scherer, K. R. (1992). What does facial expression express? In K. T. Strongman (Ed.), *International review of studies of emotion* (Vol. 2, pp. 139–165). New York: Wiley.

Scherer, K. R. (1993). Studying the emotion-antecedent appraisal process: An expert system approach. *Cognition and Emotion, 7,* 325–356.

Scherer, K. R. (1994a). Affect bursts. In S. H. M. Van Goozen, N. E. Van de Poll, & J. A. Sergeant (Eds.), *Emotions: Essays on emotion theory* (pp. 161–196). Hillsdale, NJ: Lawrence Erlbaum Associates.

Scherer, K. R. (1994b). Toward a concept of "modal emotions." In P. Ekman & R. J. Davidson (Eds.), *The nature of emotion: Fundamental questions* (pp. 25–31). New York: Oxford University Press.

Scherer, K. R. (1997). The role of culture in emotion-antecedent appraisal. *Journal of Personality and Social Behavior, 73,* 902–922.

Scherer, K. R. (2000). Emotions as episodes of subsystem synchronization driven by nonlinear appraisal processes. In M. Lewis & I. Granic (Eds.), *Emotion, development, and self-organization* (pp. 70–99). Cambridge, England: Cambridge University Press.

Scherer, K. R. (2001). Appraisal considered as a process of multilevel sequential checking. In K. R. Scherer, A. Schorr, & T. Johnstone (Eds), *Appraisal processes in emotion: Theory, methods, research* (pp. 92–120). New York: Oxford University Press.

Scherer, K. R. (2004). Feelings integrate the central representation of appraisal-driven response organization in emotion. In K. S. Manstead, N. H. Frijda, & A. Fischer (Eds.), *Feelings and emotions: The Amsterdam Symposium* (pp. 136–157). New York: Cambridge University Press.

Scherer, K. R., Schorr, A., & Johnstone, T. (Eds.). (2001). *Appraisal processes in emotion: Theory, methods, research.* New York: Oxford University Press.

Scherer, K. R., & Walbott, H. G. (1994). Evidence for universality and cultural variation of differential emotional response patterning. *Journal of Personality and Social Psychology, 66,* 310–328.

Scherer, K. R., Walbott, H. G., & Summerfield, A. B. (1986). *Experiencing emotions: A cross-cultural study.* Cambridge, England: Cambridge University Press.

Schimmack, U. (2001). Pleasure, displeasure, and mixed feelings. *Cognition and Emotion, 125,* 81–98.

Schopenhauer, M. (1819). *Die Welt als Wille und Vorstellung* [The world as will and mental representation]. Leipzig, Germany: Reclam.

Schroeder, T. (2004). *Three faces of desire.* Oxford, England: Oxford University Press.

Schwartz, S. H. (1992). Universals in the content and structure of values: Theoretical advances and empirical tests in 20 countries. *Advances in Experimental Social Psychology, 25,* 1–65.

Schwarz, N., & Bless, H. (1991). Happy and mindless, but sad and smart? The impact of affective states on analytic reasoning. In J. P. Forgas (Ed.), *Emotion and social judgment* (pp. 55–71). Oxford, England: Pergamon.

Schwarz, N., & Clore, G. L. (1988). How do I feel about it? Informative functions of affective states. In K. Fiedler & J. Forgas (Eds.), *Affect, cognition, and social behavior* (pp. 44–62). Toronto, Ontario, Canada: Hogrefe.

Scitovsky, T. (1976). *The joyless economy: The psychology of human satisfaction.* New York: Oxford University Press.

Searle, J. R. (1983). *Intentionality: An essay in the philosophy of mind.* Cambridge, England: Cambridge University Press.

Sereny, G. (1983). *Into that darkness.* New York: Vintage Books. (Original work published 1974)

Shand, A. F. (1914). *The foundations of character: Being a study of the tendencies of the emotions and sentiments.* London: Macmillan.

Shaver, P., Hazan, C., & Bradshaw, D. (1988). Love as attachment: The integration of three behavioral systems. In R. J. Sternberg & M. L. Barnes (Eds.), *The psychology of love* (pp. 69–99). New Haven, CT: Yale University Press.

Shaver, P., & Rubinstein, C. (1980). Childhood attachment and adult loneliness. *Review of Personality and Social Psychology, 1,* 42–37.

Shizgal, P. (1999). On the neural computation of utility: Implications from studies of brain stimulus reward. In D. Kahneman, E. Diener, & N. Schwarz (Eds.), *Foundations of hedonic psychology: Scientific perspectives on enjoyment and suffering* (pp. 500–524). New York: Russell Sage.

Shweder, R. A. (1991). *Thinking through cultures.* Cambridge, MA: Harvard University Press.

Shweder, R. A., & Haidt, J. (2000). The cultural psychology of the emotions: Ancient and new. In M. Lewis & J. M. Haviland (Eds.), *Handbook of emotions* (2nd ed., pp. 397–416). New York: Guilford.

Silver, R. L., Boon, C., & Stones, M. H. (1983). Searching for meaning in misfortune: Making sense in incest. *Journal of Social Issues, 39,* 81–102.

Simon, H. A. (1973). *The sciences of the artificial.* Cambridge, MA: MIT Press.

Singer, B., & Toates, F. (1987). Sexual motivation. *Journal of Sex Research, 23,* 481–501.

Sloman, A. (1987). Motives, mechanisms and emotions. *Cognition and Emotion, 1,* 217–234.

Sloman, A. (1999). *Why can't a goldfish long for its mother? Architectural prerequisites for various types of emotions.* British HCI Group one-day meeting on the role of emotion in HCI.

Smedslund, J. (1992). Are Frijda's "Laws of Emotion" empirical? *Cognition and Emotion, 6,* 435–456.

Smith, C. A., & Ellsworth, P. C. (1985). Patterns of cognitive appraisal in emotion. *Journal of Personality and Social Psychology, 48,* 813–838.

Smith, C. A., & Ellsworth, P. C. (1987). Patterns of appraisal and emotion related to taking an exam. *Journal of Personality and Social Psychology, 52,* 475–488.

Smith, C. A., & Kirby, L. D. (2000). Consequences require antecedents: Toward a process model of emotion elicitation. In J. Forgas (Ed.), *Feeling and thinking: The role of affect in social cognition* (pp. 83–106). Cambridge, England: Cambridge University Press.

Smith, C. A., & Pope, L. K. (1992). Appraisal and emotion: The interactional contributions of dispositional and situational factors. In M. S. Clark (Ed.), *Review of personality and social psychology* (Vol. 14, pp. 32–62). Newbury Park, CA: Sage.

Smith, N. K., Larsen, J. T., Chartrand, T. L., Cacioppo, J. T., Savage, H. A., Katafiasz, H. H., & Moran, K. E. (2006). Being bad isn't always good: Affective context moderates the attention bias toward negative information. *Journal of Personality and Social Psychology, 90,* 210–220.

Smuts, B. B. (1985). *Sex and friendship in baboons.* New York: Aldine.

Sokolov, J. N. (1963). *Perception and the conditioned reflex.* Oxford, England: Pergamon.

Solomon, R. L. (1980). The opponent-process theory of acquired motivation. *American Psychologist, 5,* 691–712.

Solomon, R. C. (1988). *About love: Reinventing romance for our times.* New York: Simon & Schuster.

Solomon, R. C. (1989). *A passion for justice.* Reading, MA: Addison-Wesley.

Solomon, R. C. (1993). *The passions* (2nd ed.). Indianapolis, IN: Hackett.

Solomon, R. C. (1994). Sympathy and vengeance: The role of emotions in justice. In S. H. M. van Goozen, N. E. van de Poll, & J. A. Sergeant (Eds.), *Emotions: Essays in emotion theory* (pp. 291–311). Hillsdale, NJ: Lawrence Erlbaum Associates.

Solomon, R. C. (2003). *Living with Nietzsche.* New York: Oxford University Press.

Solomon, R. C. (2004a). Emotions, thoughts, and feelings: Emotions as engagements with the world. In R. C. Solomon (Ed.), *Thinking about feeling: Contemporary philosophers on emotions* (pp. 76–90). New York: Oxford University Press.

Solomon, R. C. (2004b). *Not passion's slave.* Oxford, England: Oxford University Press.

Solomon, R. C. & Stone, L. D. (2002). On "positive" and "negative" emotions. *Journal for the Theory of Social Behavior, 32,* 417–436.

Solomon, R. L. & Wynne, L. C. (1953). Traumatic avoidance learning: Acquisition in normal dogs. *Psychological Monographs, 67*(No. 354).

Sonnemans, J. (1991). *Structure and determinants of emotional intensity.* Unpublished doctoral dissertation, University of Amsterdam.

Sonnemans, J., & Frijda, N. H. (1994). The structure of subjective emotional intensity. *Cognition and Emotion, 8,* 329–350.

Sonnemans, J., & Frijda, N. H. (1995). The determinants of subjective emotional intensity. *Cognition and Emotion, 9,* 483–507.

Spelke, E. S., Philips, A., & Woodword, A. L. (1995). Infants' knowledge of object motion and human action. In D. Sperber, D. Premack, & A. J. Premack (Eds.), *Causal cognition* (pp. 44–78). Oxford, England: Clarendon Press.

Spielberger, C. D., Jacobs, G., Russell, S., & Crane, R. S. (1983). Assessment of anger: The State Trait Anger Scale. In J. N. Butcher & C. D. Spielberger (Eds.), *Advances in personality assessment* (Vol. 2, pp. 159–187). Hillsdale, NJ: Lawrence Erlbaum Associates.

Spiering, M., Everaerd, W., & Janssen, E. (2003). Priming the sexual system: Implicit versus explicit activation. *Journal of Sex Research, 40*, 134–145.

Spinoza, B. (1677). *Ethica* (G. H. R. Parkinson, Trans.). London: Everyman's Library, 1989.

Sprang, M. V., McNeil, J. S., & Wright, R. (1989). Psychological changes after the murder of a significant other. *Social Casework, 70*, 159–164.

Sroufe, L. A., & Waters, E. (1976). The ontogenesis of smiling and laughter: A perspective on the organization of development in infancy. *Psychological Review, 83*, 173–189.

Staal, F. (1990). *Rules without meaning: Ritual, mantras and the human sciences.* New York: Lang.

Stapel, D. A., & Koomen, W. (2000). How far do we go beyond the information given? The impact of knowledge activation on interpretation and inference. *Journal of Personality and Social Psychology, 78*, 19–37

Stapel, D. A., Koomen, W., & Ruys, K. I. (2002). The effects of diffuse and distinct affect. *Journal of Personality and Social Psychology, 83*, 60–74.

Stark, R., Schienle, A, Girod, C., Walter, B., Kirsch, P, Blecker, C., et al.. (2005). Erotic and disgust-inducing pictures—Differences in the hemodynamic responses in the brain. *Biological Psychology, 70*, 19–29.

Stein, N., & Trabasso, T. (1992). The organization of emotional experience: Creating links between emotion, thinking, and intentional action. *Cognition and Emotion, 6*, 225–244.

Steiner, J. E., Glaser, D., Hawilo, M. E., & Berridge, K. C. (2001). Comparative expression of hedonic impact: Affective reactions to taste by human infants and other primates. *Neuroscience and Biobehavioral Reviews, 25*, 53–74.

Steinmetz, S. R. (1928). *Ethnologische Studien zur ersten Entwicklung der Strafe, nebst einer psychologischen Abhandlung über Grausamkeit und Rachsücht* [Ethnological studies on the first development of punishment, next to a psychological treatise on cruelty and desire for vengeance] (Vol. 1, 2nd ed.). Groningen, The Netherlands: Noordhoff.

Stellar, E. (1977). Homeostasis, discrepancy, dissonance: A theory of motives and motivation. *Motivation and Emotion, 1*, 103–138.

Stendhal, H. (1820). *De l'amour* [On love]. Paris: Verda, 1949.

Stern, J. (2003). *Terror in the name of God: Why religious militants kill.* New York: HarperCollins.

Sternberg, R. J. (1986). A triangular theory of love. *Psychological Review, 93*, 119–135.

Stevens, S. S. (1971). Mathematics, measurement, and psychophysics. In S. S. Stevens (Ed.), *Handbook of experimental psychology* (pp. 1–49). New York: Wiley.

Stoller, R. J. (1979). *Sexual excitement: Dynamics of erotic life.* New York: Pantheon.

Stone, A. A., Shiffman, S. S., & DeVries, M. W. (1999). Ecological momentary assessment. In D. Kahneman, E. Diener, & N. Schwarz (Eds.), *Foundations of hedonic psychology: Scientific perspectives on enjoyment and suffering* (pp. 26–29). New York: Sage.

Storbeck, J., & Robinson, M. (2004). When preferences need inferences: A direct comparison of the automaticity of cognitive versus affective priming. *Personality and Social Psychology Bulletin, 30*, 81–93.

Storbeck, J., Robinson, M. D., & McCourt, M. E. (2006). Semantic processing precedes affect retrieval: The neurological case for cognitive primacy in visual processing. *Review of General Psychology, 10*, 41–55.

Stuss, D. T., Van Reekum, R., & Murphy, K. J. (2000). Differentiation of states and causes of apathy. In J. C. Borod (Ed.), *The neuropsychology of emotion* (pp. 340–366). New York: Oxford University Press.

Sundararajan, L. (2005, July). Harmony: A Confucian model of emotional refinement. Paper presented at the International Society for Research on Emotion meeting, Bari, Italy.

Suomi, S. J., & Harlow, H. F. (1976). The facts and functions of fear. In M. Zuckermann & C. D. Spielberger (Eds), *Emotions and anxiety* (pp. 3–34). Hillsdale, NJ: Lawrence Erlbaum Associates.

Symons, D. (1995). Beauty is in the adaptation of the beholder: The evolutionary psychology of human female sexual attractiveness. In P. R. Abramson & S. D. Pinkerton (Eds.), *Sexual nature, sexual culture* (pp. 80–118). Chicago: University of Chicago Press.

Tajfel, H. (1981). *Human groups and social categories.* Cambridge, England: Cambridge University Press.

Tan, E. S. H. (1996). *Emotion and the narrative film: Film as an emotion machine.* Mahwah, NJ: Lawrence Erlbaum Associates.

Tan, E. S. H. (2000). Emotion, art and the humanities. In M. Lewis & S. Havilland (Eds.), *Handbook of emotion* (2nd ed., pp. 116–134). New York: Guilford.

Tan, E. S. H., & Frijda, N. H. (1999). Sentiment in film viewing. In C. Plantinga & G. Smith (Eds.), *Passionate views: Film, cognition, and emotion* (pp. 48–64). Baltimore: Johns Hopkins University Press.

Taylor, S. E. (1991). Asymmetrical effects of positive and negative events: The mobilization–minimization hypothesis. *Psychological Bulletin, 110,* 67–85.

Taylor, S. E., & Lobel, M. (1989). Social comparison activity under threat: Downward evaluation and upward contacts. *Psychological Review, 96,* 569–575.

Teasdale, J. D. & Barnard, P. (1993). *Affect, cognition, and change.* Hillsdale, NJ: Lawrence Erlbaum Associates.

Teitelbaum, P. (1971). The encephalization of hunger. *Progress in Physiological Psychology, 4,* 319–350.

Tellegen, A., & Waller, N. G. (1997). Exploring personality through test construction: Development of the multidimensional personality questionnaire. In S. Briggs & J. Cheek (Eds.), *Personality measures: Development and evaluation.* (Vol 1, pp. 000–000). JAI.

Tennov, D. (1979). *Love and limerence: The experience of being in love.* New York: Stein & Day.

Tesser, A. (1988). Toward a self-evaluation maintenance model of social behavior. In L. Berkowitz (Ed.), *Advances in experimental social psychology* (Vol. 21, pp. 181–227). New York: Academic.

Thelen, E. (1995). Motor development: A new synthesis. *American Psychologist, 50,* 79–95.

Tiede, T. (1971). *Calley: Soldier or killer?* New York: Pinnacle.

Tiger, L. (1992). *The pursuit of pleasure.* Boston: Little, Brown.

Timberlake, W. (2001). Motivational modes in behavior systems. In R. R. Mowrer & S. B. Klein (Eds.), *Handbook of contemporary learning theories* (pp. 155–120). Mahwah, NJ: Lawrence Erlbaum Associates.

Tinbergen, N. (1951). *The study of instinct*. London: Oxford University Press.

Titchener, E. B. (1908). *Lectures on the elementary psychology of feeling and attention*. New York, Macmillan.

Toates, F. M. (1986). *Motivational systems*. Cambridge, England: Cambridge University Press.

Tomasello, M., Carpenter, M., Call, J., Behne, T., & Moll, H. (2006). Understanding and sharing intentions: The origins of cultural cognition. *Behavioral and Brain Sciences,*

Tomkins, S. S. (1962). *Affect: Imagery and consciousness* (Vol. 1). New York: Springer.

Trombley, S. (1995). *A concentration camp in Paris*. TV-film.

Tuchman, B. W. (1978). *A distant mirror: The calamitous 14th century*. Harmondsworth, England: Penguin.

Tucker, D. M., Deryberry, D., & Luu, P. (2000). Anatomy and physiology of human emotions: Vertical integration of brain stem, limbic, and cortical systems. In J. C. Borod (Ed.), *The neuropsychology of emotion* (pp. 56–79). New York: Oxford University Press.

Valins, S. (1966). Cognitive effects of false heart-rate feedback. *Journal of Personality and Social Psychology, 4,* 400–408.

Van Bezooyen, R. A. M. C. (1984). *Characteristics and recognizability of vocal expressions of emotion*. Dordrecht, The Netherlands: Foris.

Van Dijk, W. W. (1999). *Dashed hopes and shattered dreams: On the psychology of disappointment*. Unpublished doctoral dissertation, University of Amsterdam.

Van Dijk, W. W., Ouwerkerk, J. W., Goslinga, S., & Nieweg, M. (2005). Deservingness and *Schadenfreude. Cognition and Emotion, 19,* 933–940.

Van Gennep, A. (1909). *Les rites de passage* [The rites of passage]. Paris: Émile Nourry.

Van Ginneken, J. (2003). *Collective behavior and public opinion*. Mahwah, NJ: Lawrence Erlbaum Associates.

Van Goozen, S., Frijda, N. H., & Van de Poll, N. E. (1992). Anger manifestations in an experimental paradigm: Studies in women. In F. Farabollini & S. Parmigiani (Eds.), *From conflict to cooperation: Multidisciplinary studies on aggression in animals and humans* (p. 39).

Van Goozen, S. H. M., Wiegant, V. M., Endert, E., Helmond, F. A., & Van de Poll, N. E. (1997). Psychoendocrinological assessment of the menstrual cycle: The relationship between hormones, sexuality and moods. *Archives of Sexual Behavior, 26,* 359–383.

Varela, F. J., Thompson, E., & Rosch, E. (1991). *The embodied mind*. Cambridge, MA: MIT Press.

Vingerhoets, A. T. J. M, Cornelius, R. R., van Heck, G. L., & Becht, M. C. (2000). Adult crying: A model and review of the literature. *Review of General Psychology, 4,* 354–377.

Von Holst, E., & Mittelstaedt, H. (1950). Der Reafferenzprinzip. Wechselwirkung zwischen Zentralnervensystem und Peripherie [The reafference principle: Interactions between central nervous system and periphery]. *Naturwissenschaften, 37,* 464–475.

Von Holst, E., & von St. Paul, U. (1963). On the functional organisation of drives. *Animal Behaviour, 11,* 1–20.

Von Weizsäcker, R. (1985). Die Deutschen und ihre Identität [The Germans and their identity]. In *Von Deutschland aus. Reden des Bundespräsidenten* (pp. 39–60). Berlin, Germany: Corso bei Siedler.

Vroman, L. (1957). *Slaapwandelen.* [Sleepwalking]. Amsterdam: Querido.

Watson, D. (2000). *Mood and temperament.* New York: Guilford.

Watson D., & Tellegen, A. (1999). Issues in the dimensional structure of affect: Effects of descriptors, measurement error, and response formats. Comments on Russell and Carroll (1999). *Psychological Bulletin, 125,* 601–610.

Watson, D., Wiese, D., Vaidya, J., & Tellegen, A. (1999). The two general activation systems of affect: Structural findings, evolutionary considerations, and psychobiological evidence. *Journal of Personality and Social Psychology, 76,* 820–838.

Watson, J. B. (1929). *Psychology from the standpoint of a behaviorist* (3rd ed.). Philadelphia: Lippincott.

Wehrle, T., Kaiser, L., Schmidt, S., & Scherer, K. R. (2000). Studying the dynamics of emotional expression using synthesized facial muscle movements. *Journal of Personality and Social Behavior, 78,* 105–119.

Weiskrantz, L. (1997). *Consciousness lost and found: A neuropsychological exploration.* Oxford, England: Oxford University Press.

Weisman, A. D. (1972). *On dying and denying.* New York: Behavior.

Weiss, J. M. (1971). Effects of punishing a coping response (conflict) on stress pathology in rats. *Journal of Comparative and Physiological Psychology, 77,* 14–21.

Wertham, F. (1978). The catathymic crisis. In I. L. Kutash, S. B. Kutash, L. B. Schlesinger (Eds.), *Violence: Perspectives on murder and aggression* (pp. 165–170). San Francisco: Jossey-Bass.

White, R. W. (1959). Motivation reconsidered: The concept of competence. *Psychological Review, 66,* 297–333.

Wiepkema, P. (1990). Stress: Ethological implications. In S. Puglesi-Allegro & A. Polivera (Eds.), *Psychobiology of stress* (pp. 1–13). Dordrecht, The Netherlands: Kluwer.

Williams, M. G., Watts, F. N., MacLeod, C., & Mathews, A. (1997). *Cognitive psychology and emotional disorders* (2nd ed.). Chichester, England: Wiley.

Winkielman, P., & Cacioppo, J. T. (2001). Mind at ease puts a smile on the face: Psychophysiological evidence that processing facilitation elicits positive affect. *Journal of Personality and Social Psychology, 81,* 989–1000.

Wolfgang, M. E. (1958). *Patterns of criminal homicide.* Philadelphia: University of Pennsylvania Press.

Wortman, C. B., & Brehm, J. W. (1975). Responses to uncontrollable outcomes: An integration of reactance theory and the learned helplessness model. In L. Berkowitz (Ed.), *Advances in experimental social psychology* (Vol. 8, pp. 277–336). New York: Academic.

Wortman, C. B., & Silver, R. C. (1989). The myths of coping with loss. *Journal of Consulting and Clinical Psychology, 57,* 349–357.

Wright, R. A. (1996). Brehm's theory of motivation as a model of effort and cardiovascular response. In P. M. Gollwitzer & J. A. S. Bargh (Eds.), *The psychology of action: Linking cognition an motivation to behavior* (pp.424–453). New York: Guilford.

Wundt, W. (1902). *Grundzüge der pysiologischen Psychologie* [Fundamentals of physiological psychology] (Vol. 3). Leipzig, Germany: Engelmann, 5th. Ausgabe.

Young, L. J., & Wang, Z. (2004). The neurobiology of pair bonding. *Nature Neuroscience, 7,* 1048–1054.

Young, P. T. (1927). Studies in affective psychology. *American Journal of Psychology, 38,* 157–193.

Zaalberg, R. (2005). *The expression of emotions in social situations.* Unpublished doctoral dissertation, University of Amsterdam.

Zajonc, R. B. (1968). The attitudinal effects of mere exposure. *Journal of Personality and Social Psychology Monograph, 9*(2, Part 2).

Zajonc, R. B. (1980). Thinking and feeling: Preferences need no inferences. *American Psychologist, 35,* 151–175.

Zajonc, R. B. (2004). Exposure effects: An unmediated phenomenon. In A. R. S. Manstead, N. H. Frijda, & A. Fischer (Eds.), *Feelings and emotions: The Amsterdam Symposium.* Cambridge, England: Cambridge University Press.

Zeelenberg, M., van Dijk, W. W., Manstead, A. S. R., & van der Pligt, J. (1998). The experience of regret and disappointment. *Cognition and Emotion, 12,* 221–230.

Zeeman, E. C. (1976). Catastrophe theory. *Scientific American, 234,* 65–83.

Zelazo, P. D. (1996). Towards a characterization of minimal consciousness. *New Ideas in Psychology, 14,* 63–80.

Zillmann, D. (1983). Transfer of excitation in emotional behavior. In J. T. Cacioppo & R. E. Petty (Eds.), *Social psychophysiology: A sourcebook* (pp. 215–240). New York: Guilford.

Zillmann, D. (1998). *Connections between sexuality and aggression.* Mahwah, NJ: Lawrence Erlbaum Associates.

Author Index

Subject Index

A

Acceptance wriggles, 68, 69-70, 72, 85, 134, 177, 247
Action readiness, 3, 4, 6, 25-46, 48, 53-55, 102, 126, 184, 187, 204-208, 213, 299
arousal of, 112-115
modes of, 33-36, 185, 228, 235, 252
processes of, 46-50
variants of, 36-38, 215-217
Action tendencies, 25-28, 30, 32, 36, 39, 215
Action, 43, 48-50, 56
Activity pleasures, 27-28
Aesthetic emotions, 38, 80, 84
Affect, 14, 31, 48, 65, 87, 99-103, 113, 126, 144-146, 188, 200, 212, 220
Affect bursts, 42, 185
Affect schema, 112, 137
Affiliation, 132-133
Affordances, 44, 108, 134, 204, 211
Aims, of action readiness, action tendency, 27-33, 37, 46-49, 55
Alliesthesia, 76, 82, 83, 84, 136
Analytic attention, 201, 208-209
Anger, 28, 34, 36, 57, 105, 216-217

Apparent reality, 8-10, 50, 106, 110, 163
Appraisal, 93-116
components, 53, 94-95, 102, 104-105
dimensions: see appraisal components
elementary, 98-101
as an antecedent of emotions
as a component of emotions
as a consequence of emotions
patterns, 101-103
processes, 98-113
theory, 6, 98-106
Attention
in appraisal, 98, 101, 108, 113-114
and emotion experience, 201-203, 205, 208-209, 212, 220
modes of, 208, 229
Attraction, sexual, 228-233

B

Backward masking, 72, 99, 100, 101, 103, 114, 218
Basic emotions, 35, 52-56, 227, 252
Being moved, 38
Being-in-love, 139, 228, 235-240, 252
Bewusstheiten, 211